In Pursuit
of Excellence

In Pursuit of Excellence

Fifth Edition

Terry Orlick, PhD

Human Kinetics

Library of Congress Cataloging-in-Publication Data

Orlick, Terry.
 In pursuit of excellence / Terry Orlick, PhD. -- Fifth Edition.
     pages cm
 Revised edition of the author's In pursuit of excellence, 2008.
 Includes bibliographical references and index.
 1. Sports--Psychological aspects. I. Title.
 GV706.4.O73 2015
 796.01'9--dc23
                             2015020534

ISBN: 978-1-4504-9650-6 (print)

The web addresses cited in this text were current as of June 2015, unless otherwise noted.

Acquisitions Editor: Justin Klug; **Senior Managing Editor:** Amy Stahl; **Copyeditor:** Mark Bast; **Indexer:** Michael Ferreira; **Graphic Designers:** Denise Lowry and Tara Welsch; **Cover Designer:** Keith Blomberg; **Photograph (cover):** © Medals/Aflo Foto Agency/age fotostock; **Photo Asset Manager:** Laura Fitch; **Photo Production Manager:** Jason Allen; **Art Manager:** Kelly Hendren; **Associate Art Manager:** Alan L. Wilborn; **Illustrations:** © Human Kinetics; **Printer:** Sheridan Books

Human Kinetics books are available at special discounts for bulk purchase. Special editions or book excerpts can also be created to specification. For details, contact the Special Sales Manager at Human Kinetics.

Printed in the United States of America   10   9   8   7   6   5   4   3   2   1

The paper in this book is certified under a sustainable forestry program.

Human Kinetics
Website: www.HumanKinetics.com

United States: Human Kinetics
P.O. Box 5076
Champaign, IL 61825-5076
800-747-4457
e-mail: humank@hkusa.com

Canada: Human Kinetics
475 Devonshire Road Unit 100
Windsor, ON N8Y 2L5
800-465-7301 (in Canada only)
e-mail: info@hkcanada.com

Europe: Human Kinetics
107 Bradford Road
Stanningley
Leeds LS28 6AT, United Kingdom
+44 (0) 113 255 5665
e-mail: hk@hkeurope.com

Australia: Human Kinetics
57A Price Avenue
Lower Mitcham, South Australia 5062
08 8372 0999
e-mail: info@hkaustralia.com

New Zealand: Human Kinetics
P.O. Box 80
Mitcham Shopping Centre, South Australia 5062
0800 222 062
e-mail: info@hknewzealand.com

E6311

This fifth edition of *In Pursuit of Excellence* is dedicated to every athlete, every student, every coach, every parent, every teacher, and every performer for choosing to become the best you can possibly be and for helping others to be the best they can be.

CONTENTS

Preface ix
Acknowledgments x

Part I Discovering Excellence 1

Chapter 1   Choice of Excellence 3
Chapter 2   Wheel of Excellence. 11
Chapter 3   Focus for Excellence. 29
Chapter 4   Journey to Excellence. 47

Part II Focusing for Excellence 61

Chapter 5   Self-Examination 63
Chapter 6   Intensity, Relaxation, and Recovery. . .73
Chapter 7   Distraction Control. 97
Chapter 8   Positive Images 111
Chapter 9   Simulation. 129
Chapter 10   Zen Experiences 143

Part III Creating Excellence 155

Chapter 11   Perspectives. 157
Chapter 12   Goals 171
Chapter 13   Commitments 183

Chapter 14   Connections 201

Chapter 15   Challenges. 215

Chapter 16   Actions 225

Part IV Living Excellence 235

Chapter 17   Confident and Composed 237

Chapter 18   Balanced 249

Chapter 19   Consistent 261

Chapter 20   Coachable 275

Chapter 21   Team-Oriented 291

Chapter 22   Self-Directed 307

Chapter 23   Adaptable 315

Chapter 24   Positive Transitions 329

Appendix: Planning Forms for Positive
Performance Enhancement. 349
Bibliography 359
Additional Resources 361
Index 365
About the Author. 373

PREFACE

This book tells you in simple and practical ways how you can excel in your life and live your dreams. You can turn challenges into opportunities in every part of your life so that you can succeed in your sport, school, profession, and relationships. You can make your focus work for you to raise the level and consistency of your performance. Perhaps most importantly, this book will help you see that you control your own destiny through your decisions and your focused actions. You are the only one who can take full control of you and your own focus—this alone puts you in a position to direct the course of your own life.

The strategies presented in this book work because they are derived from the hard-learned experiences of real people who have excelled in sport and many other high-performance domains. You can apply and adapt these lessons to surmount every conceivable challenge in your life. The recurring theme in their experiences is that focus is incredibly powerful. The focus you adopt in your life leads your performance and your reality in positive or negative ways. You decide.

As you read, keep in mind that different strategies work for different people, in different contexts, at different points in their lives. Clear your mind of clutter. Open your mind to possibilities and read with full focus and full intent to act on what is most relevant to you right now. I wish you the best in this quest.

Simple joys,
Terry Orlick

ACKNOWLEDGMENTS

Although I am the sole author of this book, there are many people who have guided my path and my life in positive and life enhancing ways. I would like to thank all the amazing athletes, coaches, teachers, students, family members, and other positive and caring human beings, who perhaps without realizing it, supported me in my ongoing journey to personal and performance excellence.

I have been inspired by many of the people I have taught, coached, and worked with over many years. My three insightful daughters Jewelia, Skye, and Anouk and my running partner (my dog Zen) have been ongoing reminders for me to continue to embrace the magical moments in every day and to continue to fully embrace my life by making a positive difference in the lives of others while I am on this beautiful planet.

Thank you to the following people, who agreed to share their stories with you the readers of this book: Dan Nadeau, Elizabeth Manley, Adam Kreek, Jordan Hanssen, Patrick Fleming, Markus Pukonen, Beckie Scott, Kerrin Lee-Gartner, Sue Holloway, Thomas Grandi, Sylvie Bernier, Silken Laumann, Lori Fung, Laurie Graham, Alex Baumann, Brian Orser, Eric Heiden, Gaetan Boucher, Juan Belmonte, Kim Alletson, Chris McCormack, Chris Hadfield, Laura Christian, Pat Messner, Sandy the gymnast, Karin the gymnast, Theresa Jenn Lopetrone, Noella Klawitter, Bruce Malmberg, and the high-performance military pilots featured in chapter 19.

Thank you to the readers of this fifth edition of *In Pursuit of Excellence* for choosing to read this book and for choosing to continue to pursue your own goals and dreams. Choose to be the master of your own destiny. Choose to follow your own best path; choose to fully live your life with no regrets.

Thanks are also extended to all the good people at Human Kinetics who have supported me in helping others to live their dreams by publishing new and revised editions of *In Pursuit of Excellence*. Thank you to Justin Klug and Amy Stahl from Human Kinetics for helping me turn my fifth edition of *In Pursuit of Excellence* dream into a positive reality.

PART I
Discovering Excellence

Docisions and Choices

Virtually everything you do or do not do in your life is ruled by the choices you make and act on or fail to act on every day. You can choose to excel or choose not to excel. You can choose to bring a positive and fully connected focus into what you do or choose not to. You can choose to be negative or stressed out about things beyond your control or choose not to. You can choose to let other people's comments, actions, or inactions upset you or choose not to. You can choose to approach obstacles or challenges in positive ways or in negative ways. You can choose to dwell on the negatives, which drag you down, or focus on the positives, which can lift your spirits and give you positive energy. You can choose to embrace your dreams and pursue them with full focus or let them drift away without really trying. These are *your choices*, and your choices direct the quality and consistency of your performance and the joyfulness of your life. You docide for better or worse.

I have never met an Olympic champion, world champion, or world leader in any high-performance field who did not decide that he or she was going to go after his or her goals with full intensity and absolute focus. If you want to perform and live to your true personal potential, at some point you have to docide to pursue it with a persistent, positive, and fully connected focus. Once you docide to pursue your dream or follow a path with full focus and total commitment, the next challenge often becomes staying on that path when it becomes bumpy. The first big step is choosing to excel or dociding to be the best you can possibly be. The next major step, which is sometimes even more challenging, is deciding to persist through the obstacles regardless of what they may be. No one reaches his or her true personal potential without facing and overcoming numerous obstacles, setbacks, and challenges along the way. Overcoming adversity is a normal part of the journey to excellence for almost everyone in every field.

People who are successful at persisting through obstacles, challenges, setbacks, bad patches, uncertainties, doubts, and sometimes fear find a way to keep a sense of purpose, passion, or perspective in their pursuit. They draw strength from having meaningful reasons for doing what they are doing and are able to retain or sustain those positive reasons for continuing to pursue their dreams. What are your personal reasons for doing what you are doing? Why are you pursuing what you are pursuing? Why are you continuing to do it? What are you hoping your pursuit of personal excellence will give you in the short run and in the long run? What do you like or love about doing what you are doing? What do you hope continuing with your pursuit will give you, your family, coaches, friends, or loved ones who have supported you over the years?

If you can sustain your passion for pursuing your dream and retain positive reasons for doing it every day, pure excellence will become a realistic goal. If you lose your passion for doing what you are doing and are not able to find meaningful reasons for continuing to do it, pure excellence in this specific domain will become an elusive goal. Retention of passion, retention of purpose, retention of love or joy for the pursuit, retention of choice, and retention of a positive and fully connected focus are all essential for living your dreams of personal and performance excellence.

The Choice of Focus

A positive and fully connected focus drives consistent high-level performance in every pursuit. The requirements for high-quality focus are simple—stay focused on the positives and stay fully connected with what you are experiencing or pursuing. To accomplish this goal, you have to decide to focus fully, find good reasons for focusing fully, and commit yourself to work on improving your positive and fully connected focus so that it works for you and not against you—every day, every assignment, every practice, every training session, every preparation session, every simulation, every meet, every race, every game, every interaction, every presentation, every shift in focus, and every part of every performance—from the first second to the last second.

You can choose to bring a high-quality fully connected focus into all your pursuits and interactions, or you can choose to just go through the motions, to slop through whatever you are doing, or to be there physically but not mentally. The best choice for ongoing performance enhancement is to focus fully on performing with quality, to the best of your ability all the time.

You can choose to listen with full focus or choose to nod your head as if you are listening and not listen at all. You can choose to be fully wherever you are—fully focused with every fiber of your being—or choose to be only partially there or not there at all mentally.

You can choose to focus on the positives or focus on the negatives. You can choose to focus on the lessons learned or not learned every day in every context. That is your choice, and you make these choices every day.

When I am working with athletes, students, or other performers, I often ask, "If you are there physically (at practice, training, in class, at work, with another person, or performing), why not be fully there?" What is the point of being there physically but not mentally? If you are there, why not be there fully—fully focused, fully connected, fully positive, fully open to ongoing learning, fully open to connecting and being your best? I challenge you to see how long you can maintain or sustain a positive fully connected focus in a class, conversation, practice, training session, or performance. I challenge you to see how quickly you can regain a positive and fully connected focus if your focus drifts away. I challenge you to find something positive in every situation you enter—to see every context as an opportunity to test yourself, learn something, and improve something and to grow your positive and fully connected focus.

As soon as you begin to get your thoughts and focus working for you and not against you, you immediately begin to take control of your destiny in positive ways. This simple shift in focus from negative to positive and from disconnected to fully connected can immediately turn poor performances into good performances, good performances into great performances, and great performances into consistently great performances.

Perspective Is Everything

A powerful example of choosing to find a positive perspective in an extremely difficult circumstance came to me from Dan Nadeau, an officer and highly regarded instructor in the Royal Canadian Mounted Police (RCMP), a championship shooter, and father of three wonderful children. After reading a previous edition of this book, Dan wrote to me to share his story about how he got through what is every parent's worst nightmare.*

> I have read several of your books, and the one that has affected me the most was *In Pursuit of Excellence*. In your book you speak of athletes you have worked with and how they have enhanced their performance and reached their goals. I also have a success story that I will share with you, as your insight and knowledge has been a major contribution in my being able to live life and not simply exist in it.
>
> I have suffered the loss of my three children, Angela, Kurtis, and Christan. They were all born with cystic fibrosis. Angela passed away in 1979 while I was doing my RCMP training in Regina. Kurtis passed away in January 1995, and my oldest son, Chris, passed away 13 months later. As the children were growing up, it was a very painful and extremely stressful task to keep the boys positive toward life, despite their knowledge that if a cure was not found, their life expectancy was short.
>
> In the early part of 1990, I was introduced to your work by my assistant coach. We were coaching a local high school volleyball team. Between the two of us we gathered as much material as we could find on the subject of focus, imagery, and visualization. It was at this time that my life as I knew it began to change. Through the acquired learning of the various life skills you detailed in your books and articles, I felt a surge of newfound inspiration. I brought this sense home with me. I would often find myself and my boys engaged in discussion on how powerful our minds are and how we can control our thoughts and feelings. This opened a door of communication between my children and me that completely changed how we perceived our situation. We were able to deal with the loss of Angela and finally able to discuss openly what each of us was feeling. The few years that followed provided us with many fun and exciting events. My boys have redefined the definition of courage. They were both visualizers and used it daily in keeping themselves positive. The last afternoon I spent with my son Christan, he said to me, "Dad,

*Excerpts from Dan Nadeau's letters courtesy of Dan Nadeau.

I can still see my dream. I'm just too tired to get there right now." He passed away that night.

Since then I have had some really trying times. When I lose sight of my focus, I bring myself back to those final few years I had with Chris and Kurtis. I can't begin to tell you how grateful I am for those years, how grateful I am to have been inspired by you and your knowledge.

I am presently instructing at the RCMP Academy in Regina and continuously pass on what I have learnt and continue to learn from you to the next generation of RCMP officers. I may not have a gold medal around my neck, but I have a comfort zone and thank you for that.

I wrote back to Dan, sincerely thanked him for sharing his story, and requested more details on how he used my material to get through the huge challenges he was living. This was his response:

At the time I was introduced to your book my life was a living hell. On the outside I was a vibrant individual, police officer, volleyball coach—a community icon, as someone put it. Inside I was an angry, confused, and worn-out man. No one had any idea how afraid and depressed I was. I had never gotten over the guilt of not being there for my daughter when she passed away, and the outlook for my two sons was not good. They were getting older, and unless a cure was found, they would not be with me much longer. There was so much stress in my work and in my personal life that it just became a way of life—don't think, don't deal with it, just keep myself busy.

While reading your book the first time, in all honesty I got angry and frustrated. I was reading about athletes training mentally and physically to win, to stay focused, and to be positive. That's a great thing. As a coach that is what you want to see in all your players. But as a father of two young boys who were fully aware of their impending outcome, it was difficult to keep my perspective on life. My oldest son wanted to play slow-pitch ball, and the doctor advised that it would not be good for him. I decided it would and let him play. I was sitting in the bleachers watching my son play ball, and the tears were running down my face. He was having the time of his life. His first at-bat, he got a hit right between first and second, all the way to the fence. He ran the bases and collapsed at third base, completely out of breath. That didn't matter to him—he hit a triple.

I continued reading your book, and upon finishing it, I found myself thinking more and more about the stress that I was feeling, all the hours I spent worrying, how I had no harmony in my life. The positive self-direction chapter was the catalyst, in a metaphoric sense, not in the perspective of an athlete, but rather a personal challenge for me in my life. The biggest revelation for me was the fact that I was coaching young athletes on how to play their sports well and how to make the connection to other productive aspects of their lives. My children needed coaching as well, and I wasn't coaching them.

As you put it, think of the process, not the outcome. All I thought about was the outcome. Quiet reflection—this is where the transformation took place. I started thinking a little more rationally. I felt I was slowly coming to terms with my situation. I was engaging in conversations with my sons more and more. We established a form of communication that allowed all of us to speak openly about our fears. What a gut-wrenching initiation. Many tears, many hugs, many "I love you guys."

I read your book a second time, and this time I shared with the boys my thoughts on how so many things in the book could be applied to life itself. Many good days followed that transformation. My sons have since passed on, but what fond memories I have to reflect on. The second reading was done in a totally different mind-set, which allowed me to heal, to learn, and to become aware of a man who wrote of simple joys. He showed me where to look. Because of your ability to express life in a pure, honest, and rational way, I have been able to celebrate my life every day and make a difference in many people's lives. When a loved one leaves you behind there is no filling the void, but you can make a conscious choice to continue living your life in honor of theirs.

A little over a year after I received Dan's first e-mail, he wrote to me to share how he had directed his focus and perspective (chapters 3 and 11) and imagery (chapter 8) toward a best-ever shooting performance and a major competition victory.

I simply wanted to share with you my experience in competing for the Connaught Cup. This cup is awarded to the best shooter in the RCMP. Each province is represented by their best shooter. I was representing our training academy. The event was held today, and I won the cup. As you know, you have been my mentor for many years. I can't begin to tell you how much you have contributed to the quality of life that I share every day with hundreds of cadets and coworkers.

In the days leading up to the competition, I prepared myself using your Focusing for Excellence CDs. Wow—what a tremendous help. Last night I listened to CD 4, *Performing in the Zone*, after which I sat down and did some focused imagery, seeing myself perform my best ever. Today I not only won the Connaught Cup but shot my all-time best. I'm still in a state of amazement in what one can achieve when inspired through the wisdom of a mentor such as you. On a final note, today my son Kurtis would have celebrated his 23rd birthday. He was a part of me today on the range, and I felt his spirit. Hard to explain. All I can say is that it felt good.

Over the many years since he first contacted me, Dan continued to update me about his success in applying the practical lessons from *In Pursuit of Excellence* to his work. We have also done and continue to do presentations and applied workshops together on performance excellence, focusing through adversity, and enhanced quality of living in different parts of the world.

Until recently, Dan was still doing firearms instruction for the RCMP and teaching essential focusing skills to all the cadets. He continues to use the wheel of excellence and wheel of focus (presented in this book) as the basis of his instruction in the mental-training side of police work. As a result, more than 6,000 cadets have a better mind-set at the start of, during, and after every shift.

In Dan's own words,

> I personally make it a part of my cadets' training, and the senior officers are starting to take notice of the benefits. Since I have been instructing here I have not had one of my cadets fail firearms yet—knock on wood. I have been involved in coaching for over 25 years. I know I have a natural ability to motivate and inspire people and over the years have gained a lot of experience. I have all this knowledge, I want to continue working in this area of expertise, and I know my potential—unlimited. I must say, Terry, you have been an unbelievable source of information and inspiration to many of us Mounties.

I have maintained contact with Dan Nadeau over the years since he first sent me this e-mail, and we have become close friends and done some super presentations together in various parts of the world. Dan is a very wise and inspiring human being who has touched the lives of many people in very meaningful ways. I am thankful that through my writing I was able to reach out to Dan and that he found true value in what he read in this book at a difficult time in his life when he really needed something that could help him find a way through very challenging times. So thank you, Dan, for making contact and for all the great things you have done for your RCMP cadets and many others whom you have touched in positive ways throughout your life journey.

Pursuing your dreams by learning from every experience, every training session, every performance, and every challenge you face in your life is a choice. You can choose to continue to learn and apply the lessons you learn from many life experiences inside and outside your sport or performance contexts. Every day you can learn something of value about your best and less than best focus in the different contexts of your life, including your next practice, experience, performance, interaction, mission, or life journey. When you choose to act on the lessons you learn every day, you free yourself to become a better learner, better performer, better person, and happier human being over the course of your life. By doing this you separate yourself from those who never come close to living or contributing to their true potential.

+ Choose to focus on the positives rather than the negatives.
+ Choose to focus on the opportunities rather than the obstacles.
+ Choose to bring a positive and fully connected focus to your practices, training, performances, education, and daily human interactions.
+ Choose to focus fully on the step in front of you rather than on distractions outside of your control.
+ Choose to live, love, and perform closer to your true potential.

The control you have over your choices, your focus, and your destiny is real and powerful. It is the key to unlocking the door to your true potential. Choose to live your dreams.

CHAPTER 2
Wheel of Excellence

The wheel of excellence can free you to access incredible inner strength by directing the full power of your focus in positive and fully connected ways. When you strengthen the quality and consistency of your best focus, you immediately begin to add more quality and consistency to your performances and to your life.

The wheel of excellence was created over many years of ongoing focused consulting, interviewing, learning, and interacting with some of the world's best athletes and best performers, including astronauts, surgeons, fighter pilots, top classical musicians, corporate leaders, coaches, and educators in different parts of the world, who excelled in other challenging high-performance pursuits.

Seven critical elements guide the pursuit of personal and performance excellence in all positive human endeavors. The center or core of the wheel of excellence is a positive and fully connected focus. It is this focused center of the wheel of excellence that radiates the positive energy that drives the six other essential spokes of human excellence: commitment, mental readiness, positive images, confidence, distraction control, and ongoing learning. These seven essential elements of excellence combine together in positive and life-enhancing ways to create the wheel of human excellence (see figure 2.1). This integrated wheel of essential interconnected skills or parts guides or drives the highest levels of excellence in every sport and every other important human performance pursuit.

You can be or become your absolute best and give yourself the best possible chance of living your dreams by "dociding" to embrace and improve all parts of the wheel of excellence. You can improve the ongoing quality and consistency of your best focus and best performances by choosing to focus on improving any part of the wheel that you believe will benefit you and your performance. You are fully capable of strengthening any part of the wheel of excellence at any time, at any age or stage of your development.

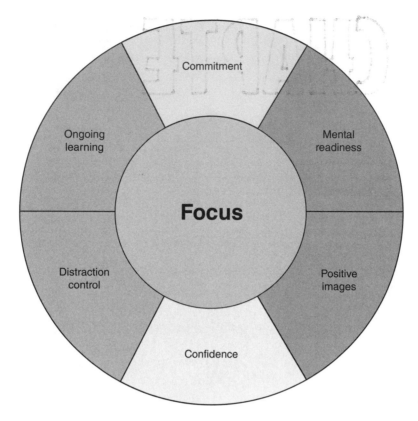

Figure 2.1   The wheel of human excellence.

You simply have to **do**cide to do it.

+ Choose to focus on doing what works best for you.
+ Choose to focus on practicing the focus that works best for you.
+ Choose to focus on making small positive refinements or improvements in your focus and your performance every day.

When you choose to make the wheel of excellence a natural part of who you are and what you do, and it begins to work well for you, all you have to do is free yourself to connect fully and focus fully on doing what you are capable of doing in any context, whether it is a performance, training setting, practice session, game, race, or competition. Just connect fully and free yourself to perform, nothing more and nothing less. Then after each performance or practice session, take a few quiet moments to reflect on when your performance was best and less than best and remember the lessons learned:

+ What went well, and where was your focus when things went well or best (in this practice or performance context)?
+ What didn't go so well, and where was your focus when things didn't go as well as you had hoped (in this practice or performance context)?

+ Make a commitment to yourself to continue to bring your best focus into your training, practice, and performances and continue to draw out the positive focus lessons from your best and less than best experiences or performances.

+ Act on the lessons you are learning every day to free yourself to focus in ways that will empower you to perform your best more consistently.

+ Remember that negativity toward yourself (and toward others) can be a huge energy drain, so do your absolute best to stay positive with yourself and as much as possible stay away from negative people, especially before important events.

Focus

A positive and fully connected focus is the most important element of excellence. That is why it is the center of the wheel of excellence. Your focus is your core or foundation for excellence, the center of the circle, the hub of your wheel of excellence.

People who perform their best, or excel at the highest levels consistently, have learned how to focus in positive and fully connected ways. To perform your best consistently, you need to find and respect a focus that frees you to be the way you want to be within your performance context and within your life outside of your performance. Excellence begins to blossom when you begin to trust yourself to focus fully in positive ways that connect you completely and absolutely with each step in the moment-by-moment process of your performance pursuit. A positive and fully connected focus frees you to raise the quality, level, and consistency of your best performances.

When you choose to raise the quality, consistency, and connectedness of your focus, you free yourself to continue to learn, experiment, grow, create, enjoy, and perform closer to your capacity. Your consistency in your performance excellence will begin to flow naturally when you develop confidence in your focus and know in your heart and soul that your fully connected focus will take you where you want to go. Consistent high-level performance depends on consistent high-quality focus. When you develop, direct, fully connect, and sustain your best focus for the duration of your performance, you strengthen all elements of excellence that add quality and consistency to your performance and joyfulness to your life.

All elements of excellence (positive and fully connected focus, commitment, mental readiness, positive images, confidence, distraction control, and ongoing learning) grow from your focus, are directed by your focus, connect you and reconnect you with your positive mission, and make personal excellence possible. When acted on, the seven essential elements in the wheel of excellence empower you to become the person and performer you have the potential to be. All you have to do is act on each of these elements of excellence—all of which are within your personal control.

Commitment

The heart of human excellence often begins to beat when you discover a pursuit, activity, mission, possibility, or opportunity that absorbs you, frees you, challenges you, or gives you a sense of meaning, purpose, joy, or passion. When you find something within a pursuit, or within yourself, that makes you feel more fully alive, that you are truly committed to developing, everything else can grow.

Do you have a vision of what you would like to pursue, where you want to go, what you want to accomplish, or what you would like to do with this part of your life? If yes, then have the courage to follow your convictions. Choose to do what you really want to do. Make it clear in your mind. Think about it often. Find a way to follow the path you would like to pursue—a path with heart! If you do not have a vision of something specific you would like to pursue, think about the direction you might want to go, about what you might like to accomplish and how you might make it happen. Even if you don't start with a big commitment to a specific goal, simply getting fully focused on doing good things you want to do will take you in positive directions, and good things will begin to happen. If you are on a path you like, your commitment, joy, focus, and performance will grow.

Commitment is an essential ingredient, guiding the pursuit of excellence. With focused commitment, you can achieve almost anything; without it, high-level goals within your grasp become virtually impossible to attain.

Commitment to excellence requires a specific focus. Your commitment will grow when your focus is centered on

- continuing to learn and grow;
- pursuing your dreams and making a meaningful contribution;
- becoming the best that you can be;
- developing your mental, physical, and technical links to excellence;
- setting clear personal goals and relentlessly pursuing them;
- persisting through obstacles, even when they appear insurmountable or impossible;
- continuing to learn how to enhance the quality and consistency of your best focus and best performance and acting on the lessons learned; and
- keeping the joy and passion in your pursuit.

The roots of excellence are nurtured by engaging yourself in doing something you want and like to do. High levels of excellence are inspired by having a positive vision of where you want to go—in your sport, performance, relationships, or life. To excel in any challenging pursuit, you must either have, or develop, a passionate or life-enhancing reason for doing it. You need a good reason that is powerful enough to keep you pursuing your goals though the ups and downs of the journey. High levels of personal commitment grow naturally out of love for and joy in what you are doing, combined with positive visions of where you want to go and what you are willing to do to get there. Commitment continues to grow from embracing the special moments, absorbing yourself in your mission, overcoming obstacles, and loving the experience of ongoing personal growth. Many personal reasons, or sources of commitment, can drive excellence:

+ Pure enjoyment, passion, or love for the activity or pursuit
+ The excitement of the pursuit and the feeling of being fully alive every day
+ The feeling of being accepted, competent, needed, valued, important, successful, or special
+ The feeling of pursuing a dream, living your potential, or becoming what you are capable of being
+ The feeling of making a meaningful contribution or making a difference
+ Pride in your performance, creation, or contribution
+ The feeling of overcoming challenges, stretching limits, or proving something to yourself or others about who you are and what you are capable of doing
+ The feeling of giving something back to people who have supported you or giving something forward to people who will follow you
+ The joy or love of ongoing learning and loving what you are doing
+ The good feeling that comes with having the courage to follow your own convictions and live your dreams to do what you really want to do!

If you enjoy what you are doing (at least parts of it) and are able to remain focused and committed to it, you will become competent at it—which is a worthy and beneficial goal. If you want to become truly great at something, and to continue to perform at high levels over extended periods, you usually have to love it or at least love parts of it. Most performers who excel at the highest levels say that the pursuit itself becomes their passion and drives their lives in positive ways for extended periods. They are passionate about their pursuits, love the joyful parts, and are willing to put up with or focus through the tough parts to get to where they want to go. They draw positive energy from the parts they like and learn lessons from the parts that are not joyful. High-level performers are able to achieve most of their goals and grow from their journey by focusing on something positive every day and staying committed to their goals through the negatives or obstacles.

On the path to excellence, some obstacles may initially seem insurmountable. Every performer experiences this feeling, even the greatest performers in the world. If you believe that the obstacles are too great to overcome, you will probably prove yourself right even when you are wrong. Most seemingly impossible obstacles can be overcome by seeing possibilities, focusing on what is within your control, taking the first step, and then focusing on the next step and the step after that. If your commitment wavers, remember your dream goal or mission goal and why it is important to you, find simple joys in your daily pursuits, rejoice in the little victories or small steps forward, and embrace the process of ongoing learning. With a positive perspective and persistence, you will get through, focus through, or find a way through all the obstacles.

The commitment you make to yourself to go after your goals and persist through adversity is a huge part of reaching high-level goals. Equally important is your commitment to take time for mental, physical, and emotional recovery. Relaxation and regeneration are critical parts of consistent high-level performance, especially over the long term.

Sometimes the best way to enhance your performance and your life is to listen to your body, listen to your heart, and respect your basic needs for relaxation, rest, personal space, good nutrition, and joyful moments away from your performance domain. Failure to respect your needs for finding some balance between quality training and exertion and high-quality rest, between stress and relaxation, will eventually affect your performance, your life, and your love for what you are doing. Commit to focus on doing things that will be most beneficial for you and your ultimate goals over the short term and the long term. Respect your need for rest and recovery and for embracing simple joys away from your training or performance sites.

Mental Readiness

There is a big difference between talking about what you want to do and being mentally ready to actually do it. Mental readiness has everything to do with being positive, focused, persistent, and fully committed to acting on your positive intentions. Excellence requires that you choose to get yourself mentally ready for focused, decisive action. Acting decisively in positive and fully focused ways every day is essential in training, work, and performance contexts because only positive action counts. Only fully focused actions will take you to your goals. Focused excellence blossoms when you want to be at training or performance sites rather than when you feel that you have to be there. Choosing to want to be there will take you to your dreams.

Mental readiness for training and performances requires a specific focus. Your mental readiness will grow when your focus is centered on

- preparing, practicing, training, working, performing, and competing with full focus and your ideal level of intensity;
- bringing a positive focus into training, work, and performances;
- shifting back to a positive focus if you start to become negative;
- focusing in ways that free you to perform your best;

+ creating positive learning opportunities;

+ taking advantage of every training and performance opportunity;

+ refining essential mental, physical, technical, and tactical skills necessary to excel in your pursuit;

+ evaluating the effectiveness of your focus in practice and after every performance and acting on the lessons learned at your next opportunity;

+ continuing to find simple joys both within your performance pursuit and outside it; and

+ relaxing, resting, recovering, and staying positive with yourself and others through the ups and downs of the challenging journey to personal excellence.

To excel in any pursuit, you need to be mentally ready to think, focus, and act in positive ways. When you are mentally ready, you will find it much easier to learn essential performance skills, practice those skills to perfection, and perform those skills effectively under demanding conditions. The ultimate benefit of mental readiness is that you will be focused on getting the best out of what you have right now—at this point in your training, performance, season, career, or life.

You must also be mentally ready to draw lessons from each of your experiences and act on them. Great performers have effective action plans or focusing routines that prepare them mentally to accomplish whatever they want to accomplish each day and each performance, and they act on the lessons learned. To perform your best more consistently, challenge yourself to find effective ways to get mentally ready and fully focused on achieving your goals. The following strategies can help you focus in positive ways:

+ Think about some of the good things you have already accomplished.

+ Think about some things you still want to learn, improve on, or accomplish.

+ Think about specific goals you want to achieve and write them down.

+ Think about what your goals are for today.

+ Run through some of your goals in your mind and imagine yourself accomplishing them.

+ Before going to practices or performances, think about what you are going to focus on to achieve your goals.

+ Every day ask yourself, *What am I going to do today that will take me one step closer to my dreams? What am I going to focus on so that I can accomplish my goals today?*

+ Continue to look for simple and effective ways to get yourself mentally ready to focus on achieving your goals.

+ For specific exercises to improve mental readiness and focusing for excellence, refer to my Focusing for Excellence CDs, specifically

Practicing in the Zone and *Performing in the Zone* (see the Additional Resources section in the back of this book; *note*: these Zone of Excellence CDs by Terry Orlick are also available on iTunes).

Positive Visions and Images

Many great accomplishments, new discoveries, and seemingly impossible feats begin with a single positive vision. Positive visions of what you want to accomplish and smaller visions of the steps you are going to take to get there can drive the pursuit of excellence. Visions, big or small, live in your mind before they become positive realities. Part of the ongoing challenge of pursuing excellence is sustaining positive visions and a positive perspective through the various stages of your journey.

Your visions or images depend on what you focus on. Your positive visions will grow when you focus on positive thoughts, positive imagery, positive visualization, or *feelization* to

- imagine where you want to go with your performance (or your life) and what you have the potential to be;
- speed up the learning and integration of technical skills, tactical skills, mental skills, physical skills, race plans, game plans, focusing plans, and refocusing plans;
- create positive images of the steps you need to take to get where you want to go;
- inspire you to continue to pursue your goals and go after your dreams;
- learn from your best performances and best parts of performances;
- identify clear and specific daily goals for ongoing improvement;
- mentally prepare yourself to follow your game plan or race plan and focus in ways that will free you to perform to your capacity;
- act and react in positive and decisive ways;
- strengthen your confidence; and
- improve the execution of your performance skills.

One of the main benefits of having a big positive vision and smaller step-by-step visions is to keep you focused on the positives and the possibilities (why you can do it, why you want to do it, and how you will do it) as opposed to focusing on the negatives (why you can't do it). Your chances of achieving high-level goals and living joyfully are greatly enhanced when you focus on positive thoughts, positive images, positive visions, and positive lessons that you continue to act on in positive ways.

Great performers do not begin their lives or pursuits as great performers. They work at getting into a habit of seeing things in positive ways and imagining themselves performing and executing technical skills in the ways they would like to perform them. In fact, most of the best performers in the world have highly developed imagery skills because they use these skills daily to create a positive focus for excellence. They draw on positive memories, recall the focus and feelings of previous best performances, and create positive visions of the future. They use their positive thoughts and positive imagery to prepare themselves mentally for quality practice, quality performances, and joyful life experiences.

To improve future performances, they carefully revisit positive parts of their current or past performances (so they know what is working) and assess parts of their performances that can be improved so they can make necessary adjustments. They think, see, feel, or imagine themselves making the improvement and being competent, confident, successful, and in control, which sets the stage for higher-quality performances. When learning new skills, procedures, routines, or tactics or when making refinements, they often run the desired actions through their minds many times, with quality and feel, to speed up the learning process. Some of them also use positive imagery to relax themselves or regain control when distracted.

Ella Ling/BPI/Icon Sportswire

Great performers like Novak Djokovic learn to draw on previous best performances and to envision future successes.

You, too, can experience the benefits of positive visions. Performing at a high level in your mind (and feeling it in your body) allows you to create the conditions for success without having actually executed those performances in the real world. This focusing process can enhance your confidence and performance, leaving you with good feelings about yourself, your readiness, and your capacity to do the things you want to do. With practice, you can preexperience and reexperience many desired actions, feelings, sensations, and skills that are important for the successful execution of your best possible performance.

Positive thoughts combined with positive images and positive feelings help create the mind-set and focus required for high-quality performance. What do you want to achieve or accomplish in your performance domain or in your life? Can you imagine or envision yourself accomplishing those goals or living your dreams? What positive steps can you take today to move forward toward your ultimate performance goals? Think about how you want to perform in your next competition, challenge, or performance. Make it clear in your mind. Imagine it, see it, and feel yourself doing it. Let your positive visions lead your actions and your reality in positive ways.

Confidence

Confidence is an essential ingredient, guiding the pursuit of excellence. Confidence opens doors that an absence of confidence has previously slammed shut. Performance confidence rises or falls based on the quality of your preparation, the quality of your focus, and the extent to which you believe in your capacity. Confidence comes from committing yourself to do the preparation or quality work, talking to yourself in positive ways about what you have done and what you can do, drawing lessons from your experiences and acting on them, and remaining positive with yourself through the many challenges along the way. Confidence blossoms when you discover what focus works best for you, respect the power of that focus, and regularly call on it.

Your confidence requires a specific positive and fully connected focus. Your confidence will grow when your focus is centered on trusting or believing in

- your own potential,
- your capacity to overcome obstacles and achieve your goals,
- your preparation or mental readiness,
- your best focus,
- your choices,
- the meaningfulness of your mission or pursuit, and
- those with whom you work or play.

We rarely begin performance pursuits with total confidence in our capacity to achieve our goals or execute certain tasks with quality and precision.

We grow confidence by rejoicing in the things we do well, acknowledging our improvements, learning from our successes and failures, absorbing the wisdom of others, and discovering that our best focus frees us to perform our best.

When you have unwavering belief in your capacity to carry out a mission and absolute focus on your performance, doors are opened to the highest levels of excellence. When distractions or negative thoughts interfere with your confidence, your performance wavers—not because you are any less capable but because you let those doubts interfere with your best focus. Pure confidence comes from feeling grounded in who you are and knowing in your heart and soul that you are capable of doing what you want to do. In the presence of pure confidence, you trust your focus and your performance soars. In the absence of confidence, you rarely touch your full potential.

The best way to increase your confidence is to strengthen your focus on the right things. Each element on the wheel of excellence can help you improve the quality of your focus, which in turn strengthens your confidence. Confidence in your focus is like a master key: it opens the door to higher levels of excellence, and higher levels of excellence open the door to greater confidence. The following strategies can help you strengthen your confidence:

+ Remember that someone believes in you.
+ Think in positive ways about your capacity.
+ Think about why you can achieve your goals.
+ Write down a list of reasons you can achieve your goals or reasons to believe you can achieve your goals.
+ Act as if you can do it. Think, talk, and walk as if you know you can do it! Think about your successes or best performances in training, simulations, and previous performances.
+ Think about how you will achieve your goals. Remind yourself of what you will focus on.
+ Continually draw out the focus lessons to improve the quality and consistency of your performances. Act on those ongoing lessons learned!

Although you may perform well without feeling fully confident, you are much more likely to perform to your potential on a consistent basis if your confidence and focus are working together for you and not against you. This comes from respecting yourself, respecting your best focus, and freeing your body and mind to perform without interference. Give yourself this gift. You are worthy of it.

Distraction Control

Distraction control frees you to focus through distractions or not let distractions interfere with the quality of your performance or the success of your mission. Some distractions are external, arising from other people (competitors, fans, or media) and their expectations, and other distractions come from specific circumstances in your environment. Some distractions are internal, arising from your own thinking, doubts, worries, fears, or expectations. Regardless of what kind of distractions you may face, maintaining a positive and fully connected focus before, during, and after performances is very important. Distraction control is especially important when you feel stressed, crowded, pressured, uncertain, or unappreciated or when you are performing in demanding or highly stressful circumstances.

Your ability to control distractions depends largely on what you choose to focus on or not focus on. Your ability to control distractions will be greatly enhanced when your focus is centered on

- you, your preparation, your warm-up, and doing what you want to do;
- relaxing and relaxed breathing;
- maintaining a positive focus in the lead-up time to your performance;
- practicing regaining a positive and effective focus when distracted before, during, or after a practice, event, or performance;
- refocusing or reconnecting quickly with your preperformance or performance focus plan;
- remembering your best performances and your best performance focus;
- staying focused on executing your preperformance and within-performance game plan;
- getting adequate rest before the performance; and
- reminding yourself to stay on your own best focus path for personal excellence.

Great performers have learned to activate positive shifts in focus by using simple reminders, images, or focus points that reconnect them with something positive within their immediate control. This process takes them back where they want to be—to a positive mind-set and a fully focused connection within the present performance moment. By strengthening your ability to refocus quickly, you will experience less stress and achieve greater consistency in your best performances and experience more enjoyment in your life.

Effective refocusing grows most readily from developing a simple refocusing plan and acting on that plan. When you become distracted by negative thoughts, lapses in concentration, setbacks, or dips in confidence—before, during, or after a performance—the goal is to regain a positive perspective quickly and reconnect instantly to your best focus. You can learn to reconnect more quickly and effectively by reflecting on what works best for you to get you back on track quickly. Plan some reminders that you can use to regain control, to refocus on what you control, and to focus on what works best for you. Plan your best focus path and practice using your refocusing reminders whenever the opportunity arises.

Ongoing Learning

Consistent high-level performers follow their own best paths. They are superb self-directed learners. They may not start that way, but they end up that way. The pursuit of excellence is a process of self-discovery and stretching personal limits and continuing to act on discoveries that lead you to your best focus and best performances. As you discover what works and feels best for you, remember to follow that path, especially in the face of obstacles.

Ongoing learning requires a specific performance-enhancing focus. Your skills for ongoing learning and improvement will continue to grow when you focus on

- keeping the joy in the pursuit;
- finding joy in what you do well and appreciating the small steps forward;
- drawing out relevant lessons from each experience, race, game, or performance;
- reflecting on what you did well and what focus freed you to do it;
- reflecting on what you can improve and how you can make those refinements;
- reflecting on how your focus affected your performance and how you can continue to respect your best focus;
- targeting relevant focus areas for improvement; and
- acting on the lessons you learn on an ongoing basis.

Ongoing personal excellence results from living the lessons you gain from your experiences. Great performers attain high levels of excellence because they are committed to ongoing learning. They prepare well, focus well, deal well with distractions, do thorough postperformance evaluations, and act on the lessons drawn from their ongoing experiences. Great performers see their own good qualities, look for positive parts of their performances, and target relevant areas for improvement. They gain inspiration, confidence, and inner strength by finding simple joys within their pursuits, looking for and remembering personal highlights, and continuing to reflect on what frees them to live fully and perform their best. They also grow from setbacks by channeling their lessons learned and energy toward their ongoing improvement.

To live your true potential, continue to reflect on the focus you carry into your most joyful experiences and best performances. Continue to extract the focus lessons from your best and less than best experiences and performances. Continue to refine your focus until it is consistently where you want it to be. Your rate of learning, the level and consistency of your performance, and the quality of your life are directly affected by the extent to which you engage in ongoing, constructive, personal performance evaluation, followed by positive action. Don't waste hard-learned lessons. Embrace them, remember them, and act on them.

Personal Excellence

Personal excellence is a lifelong journey that brings focus, challenge, meaning, joy, frustration, and perspective to life. As good or great as you are or become, you can always be a little bit better—a little more focused, confident, consistent, positive, or better equipped to deal with distractions.

The wheel of excellence can serve as a personal guide for improving anything important in your life. Decide what is most important for you right now. Then look at the wheel while keeping that goal in mind. Assess where you think your focusing skills are strongest and where they need strengthening. Target a specific area for improvement that seems most relevant for you right now. Write down a personal plan for making meaningful improvements in this area and focus on implementing it. Decide to do it and then *do* it! When you revisit the wheel later, select another target area that could help you improve. The following questions may help you clarify your personal direction for improvement.

Focus

+ Do you know what kind of focus helps you perform best?
+ Do you know what kind of focus helps you learn best?
+ Do you have a plan that will consistently get you into your best, fully focused state?
+ Are you working at improving the quality and consistency of your focus? Every day?
+ Are you focusing on doing the little things that work best for you? Every day?
+ Are you working at sustaining your best focus for the duration of each class, practice, work session, personal interaction, or performance? Can you do better? How?

Commitment

+ Are your goals clear, challenging, and targeted at being your best?
+ Are you doing something every day that takes you one step closer to your goals? What did you do today to take yourself one step closer to your goal?
+ Are you working at improving something every day and in every performance?
+ Is your commitment to positive and fully connected quality focus in training, learning, practicing, and performing strong enough to take you to your goals? Could your commitment be better, or could you act on it in a more consistent or focused way?
+ Are you keeping an element of joyfulness in your pursuit and in your life?

✦ Is your commitment to respect your personal needs for rest and recovery strong enough to sustain you through this challenging journey?

Mental Readiness

✦ Are you carrying a positive and fully connected mind-set into your work, education, interactions, practices, and performances? Can you do better? How?

✦ Are you looking for opportunities to embrace in everything you do?

✦ Are you carrying a positive perspective that centers on ongoing positive learning and growing?

✦ Are you mentally preparing yourself to focus fully on performing your best every day—in school, work, practices, relationships, and performances? Can you do better? How?

✦ Arc you dwelling on the positives and letting go of the negatives?

✦ Are you remaining open to new and ongoing performance and life-enhancing possibilities?

Positive Images

✦ Do you have a big vision of where you would like to go with your performance, your education, your profession, or your life?

✦ Do you keep that vision clearly in your mind? Do you visit it regularly?

✦ Can you imagine yourself performing exactly the way you would like to perform, accomplishing the things you want to accomplish, and being the way you would prefer to be?

✦ Do you imagine yourself focusing the way you would prefer to focus and achieving the goals you would like to achieve? Often?

✦ Do you imagine yourself doing the little things, taking the small daily steps that will take you to your goals? Every day?

✦ Are you embracing your positive images or positive visions by acting on them in positive ways in the real world every day?

✦ Are your positive visions providing you with inspiration and motivation to continue to pursue your goals and dreams?

Confidence

✦ Do you believe that you can live your dreams or attain your goals?

✦ Are you looking for good reasons to believe and focusing on why and how you can achieve your goals?

✦ Are you talking to yourself in ways that make you feel positive and confident?

✦ Are you choosing to be confident? Are you focusing on why you can achieve your goals and how you will achieve them?

+ Are you putting yourself in situations that will give you the best chance of believing in yourself and achieving your goals?

+ Are you looking for the good things in every practice, every training session, every performance, and every part of your life? Every day? Even if some parts didn't go well?

+ Are you acknowledging your progress, your simple accomplishments, and your simple daily joys and rejoicing in them?

+ Are you trusting yourself, your preparation, and your focus?

+ Are you acting as if you can do or accomplish whatever you want to do *every day*?

Distraction Control

+ Are you carrying a perspective that allows you to avoid or minimize the stress and unnecessary distractions in your life?

+ Can you maintain your best focus even when you face setbacks, major challenges, or distractions?

+ Can you refocus quickly and regain your best focus control when you encounter performance errors or setbacks? Can you do it consistently?

+ Are you good at turning negatives into positives? Could you be better or faster?

+ Do you have an effective plan for dealing with distractions? Are you using it effectively?

+ Are you acting on that plan at every opportunity?

+ Are you working on improving your skills at focusing through distractions and focusing through adversity?

Ongoing Learning

+ Are you committed to ongoing learning, to learning something from every performance and experience and using it to get better?

+ Are you looking for the positives in yourself, others, and your performances? Every day?

+ Are you drawing out relevant lessons from every performance and every important experience, both when things go well and when they do not go well?

+ Are you acting on those lessons every day or at every opportunity, before your next performance, training session, interaction, or event?

+ Are you reflecting on the role your focus plays in each performance and each important interaction?

+ Do you act on those reflections consistently? If not, why not?

To make meaningful improvements in the quality and consistency of your performance (and your life), you do not have to reinvent the wheel. You just have to target relevant areas for improvement and act on them. In my extensive consulting work with high-level performers (and those striving to be high-level performers), we almost always target two critical areas for improvement—fully connected focusing and distraction control. These two elements have an extremely powerful effect on the consistency of high-level performance in every performance domain.

When you look at the different success elements on the wheel of excellence and think about your performance and your life, you may immediately know where you are strongest and where you need the most work. Start with respecting your strengths and improving your weaknesses. And remember that these seven elements of excellence apply not only in sport but also in every other performance domain and every life pursuit, including life-enhancing relationships. Improving each of these elements of excellence will add quality and joy to your performance, work, relationships, and life. When implemented these seven elements of excellence free you to attain whatever is important to you in all parts of your life.

Whether your goals are big and bold or more modest, the success elements that make up the wheel of excellence will take you on an exciting journey toward your true potential in performance pursuits and in all other areas of your life. Each of these mental links to excellence has the potential to strengthen your focus, take you closer to your capacity, and add ongoing joy and meaning to your life.

CHAPTER 3
Focus for Excellence

Completing any challenging mission successfully requires that you find a way to focus on the positive in yourself and others and support yourself and others through the daily ups and downs and ongoing challenges of the journey.

What can you do today and every day to bring yourself one step, one stride, or one stroke closer to accomplishing your goals? What can you do to fully embrace your journey, focus through adversity, and live your dreams? In real-world high-performance contexts, thinking is not enough, deciding is not enough. Only positive focused action counts!

You can do this by respecting the 10 Oar Northwest Focusing Commandments. I initially wrote these 10 Focusing Commandments for a crew of four rowers (Adam Kreek, Jordan Hanssen, Patrick Fleming, and Markus Pukonen) who "**do**cided" to row across the Atlantic Ocean from South Africa to Miami, Florida, in the United States, unassisted in the summer of 2013. *Unassisted* means they had to carry everything they needed for survival with them, and there were no boats anywhere near them for the duration of their 73-day voyage. They heightened their challenge by choosing a very difficult route across the Atlantic Ocean that had never been attempted before and by having no support anywhere near them to rescue them in case of an emergency.

Adam Kreek, a gold medalist for the Canadian men's eight rowing crew at the Olympic Games in Beijing, China, contacted me and asked if I would be willing to help him and his crew on this very challenging superendurance journey. I immediately told him I would be happy to help him in any way I could. It was a great learning experience for me and for all four members of this Oar Northwest transatlantic crew.

I communicated with the crew before they left on their voyage, spoke with them when they were still on the ground in South Africa (their departure point), and had telephone contact with each of them when they were on the boat rowing across the Atlantic Ocean.

They had a very challenging start to their journey. There were extremely strong winds and currents and bad weather pushing them back toward South

Africa while they continued to row 24 hours a day toward North America. Two athletes rowed together (for 1-, 2-, 3-, or 4-hour shifts) while the other two athletes rested or slept. This continued for 24 hours per day for the duration of their voyage.

During the first few weeks rowing across the ocean, even though they were rowing 24 hours a day, sometimes they were still not moving forward at all due to the current and winds pushing them back toward Africa. Also, a couple of big storms hit them hard, damaging some of their equipment on board and snapping their spare oar in half like a toothpick.

At one point I received a message from Adam—who is one of the most positive people I have ever met or worked with—and he basically said, "What the heck am I doing out here in the middle of the ocean rowing my butt off—oar in, pull, oar out, oar in, pull, oar out, all day and all night—when my wife is at home pregnant without my support?"

After receiving that message from Adam, I immediately wrote the 10 Focusing Commandments and e-mailed them to Adam on their boat. I asked him to pin them up somewhere on the boat where each of the crew members could see them every day.

Here are the 10 Focusing Commandments I sent them to guide their challenging journey across the ocean and in their overall pursuit of excellence in sport and life:

1. Focus on what you can control.
2. Let go of what you cannot control.
3. Focus on the next positive step (or positive stroke) that is within your control.
4. Focus on the next stroke, the next stride, the next goal, or the next positive move.
5. Be kind to yourself and others; focus on supporting yourself and each other every day through the ongoing challenges of the journey.
6. Look for the positives in every day.
7. Look at how far you have come (from where you started).
8. Look at how much you have already accomplished.
9. Focus on why you can complete your mission successfully.
10. Focus on how you will complete your mission successfully.

Adam quickly memorized the 10 Focusing Commandments probably because they were important reminders for him at that time and maybe also because there is not much else to do when you are in an enclosed area on a 27-foot boat with three other people and not much personal space for 24 hours a day.

These 10 Focusing Commandments served as a great reminder for the crew and seemed to have a very positive effect on them for the remainder of their voyage. The other request I made of this crew was to record their highlights and share the challenges they were facing every day. Almost every day each crew member spoke into a camera and did this. I called them highlights and challenges, and they called them roses and thorns. Roses were the highlights, and thorns were the challenges. Sharing their highlights or roses with each other and sharing or reflecting on their challenges or thorns at the end of each day seemed to have a very powerful effect on keeping everyone focused on the positives, on what was important to them, and on what was within their control.

To give you some idea of the physical intensity of this rowing expedition across the Atlantic, the average weight loss for each of these very fit athletes during their 73-day mission was 50 pounds. They were literally rowing in pairs 24 hours a day (2 of them rowing and 2 of them resting for 4-hour shifts). They could not eat enough to maintain their weight because of the large number of calories they were burning off each day.

The pursuit of personal excellence in any challenging field—or pushing forward human barriers—is not easy. If it was easy, everyone would be great at everything. However, personal excellence is possible for you and virtually all other people, but only if you are willing to *do* what it takes to excel and become your best at whatever you are pursuing. Only if you focus fully on doing what is required to consistently perform close to your true potential will your positive goals and dreams become a positive reality.

Living your dreams or completing your mission to excellence successfully requires you to

+ act on your positive intentions every day;
+ focus and refocus on being positive every day;
+ focus and refocus on being fully connected every day;
+ focus and refocus on doing the right things at the right time;
+ focus on learning something or doing something of value every day;
+ focus or refocus through ongoing challenges or adversity every day;
+ support yourself and your teammates through the ups and downs of the journey; and
+ create and embrace some life-enhancing time for relaxation, recovery, and simple joys every day.

Focus-Centered Performance Enhancement

Fully connected focusing and refocusing skills are essential for ongoing positive learning, performing your best consistently, living your dreams, and achieving your highest levels of excellence. You cannot perform or live consistently close to your potential without positive and fully connected focusing skills. So it is essential that you find and respect your best performance focus, which includes positive and effective refocusing skills.

Nurturing positive and effective focusing and refocusing skills is the key target area for most of my consulting work with high-performance athletes, coaches, musicians, military pilots, race car drivers, surgeons, astronauts, adventure racers, business executives, teachers, students, parents, and performers in all disciplines—precisely because high-quality fully connected focusing and refocusing skills are essential for consistency in all high-performance disciplines.

All people at all ages in all contexts can gain from improving the quality and consistency of their focus. Positive and fully connected focusing skills enhance high-quality learning and best performances in all situations. High-quality positive and fully connected focusing skills also enhance consistency in all performance contexts and the quality of relationships at home, work, and play.

The quality and consistency of your focus rules your training, your performance, your relationships, your day, your life, and your world—for better or worse. As shown in figure 3.1, your focus is like your inner guide or the sun that radiates energy, power, positivity, meaningful direction, and pure

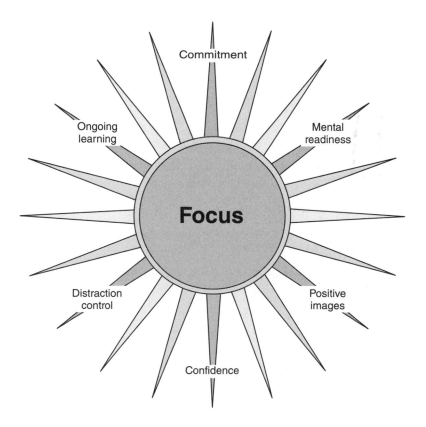

Figure 3.1 Focus radiates outward, illuminating every aspect of life.

connection to all the elements of the wheel of excellence. Your focus affects everything you do, see, feel, experience, and accomplish every day in every part of life. When you direct your focus in positive ways, it helps you live and grow to your full potential. This is why a positive and fully connected focus is so important.

The single most important goal in any performance context is to keep your focus centered on what connects you fully to your performance and frees you to perform your best. In the world of high-level performance, focus rules—for better or worse.

Your performance, good or bad, is grounded in your focus. Is your focus usually positive and fully connected? Is your focus positive and fully connected during your training and your performances? Is your focus positive and fully connected during your interactions with other people? Are you focusing in ways that are helping you to stay positive and fully connected so you can achieve your goals every day?

When your focus is positive and fully connected or exactly where you want it to be, how did you get it there? How do you keep it there? When your focus is not positive or fully connected or not where you want it to be, how do you change focus channels to get it back on track?

To enhance the quality and consistency of your best performances, you need to discover, understand, and respect your best focus. What focus frees you to feel your best and perform your best? What focus interferes with a free flowing best performance? Make it your goal to understand and respect the focus that works best for you. Make it your goal to understand and avoid focusing in ways that interfere with your best performances. Make a personal commitment to work on improving the quality and consistency of your best focus every day.

Take a time-out to think about one of your best-ever performances, when you performed to your potential in a context that was important to you. The goal of this exercise is to help you reflect on your best performance focus and to then make that best focus more consistent in your real-world performance arena. The following questions will help you identify your best and most fully connected focus and your less than best focus. In your best-ever performance or one of your best-ever performances

+ What were you focused on (or thinking about) going into this performance?
+ What were you focused on seconds before you started to perform, compete, or play?
+ How would you describe your focus or feelings of connectedness during this performance?
+ How fully connected did you feel during this performance?
+ Did you ever lose your fully focused connection during this performance?

+ If you lost your fully focused connection, did you try to do something to get back on track? If yes, what did you try to do?

+ If you never lost your fully focused connection, what kept you fully connected for the duration of this performance?

Think about one of your less than best performances, when you did not perform to your potential in a performance, race, or game that was important to you.

Focus exercise

+ What were you focused on (or thinking about) going into this performance?

+ What were you focused on seconds before you started to perform, compete, or play?

+ How would you describe your focus or feelings of connectedness during this performance?

+ What were you focused on during most of this performance?

+ Did you ever feel a fully focused, high-quality connection during this performance?

+ If you felt fully connected, even for a short time, how did you make that happen?

+ If you never experienced or regained a fully focused connection, what do you think kept you disconnected for the duration of this performance?

Take some time to think about your best focus or your most fully focused connection when you have performed your best (in parts of performances or in complete performances). Compare that best-connected performance focus with your focus when you have not performed your best. What do you think you have to focus on to give yourself the best chance of performing to your potential on a consistent basis? How are you going to make this happen in your next performance, presentation, game, race, event, or competition?

Focus in Practice

You can make a personal commitment to yourself to bring a positive, high-quality, fully connected focus into your practices or training sessions. This will help you to perform better in both practices and competitions or performance settings. The focusing goal in practice or training is to stay fully focused, positive, and fully connected with what helps you perform your best every day. This focus will help you continue to improve in small ways every day and ensure that you will not waste your time while you are there. "**Do**cide" that you are going to bring a positive and fully connected focus into your practice or training sessions every day. Commit yourself to respect your best focus for the duration of each practice or training session. Decide to focus fully on being your best and making good things happen.

Remind yourself of the following facts to get the best out of each practice or training session:

+ Quality practice and quality preparation enhance quality performance.
+ Quality practice and quality preparation depend on a positive and fully connected focus.
+ Quality focus depends on respecting the focus that brings out your best and works best for you.
+ Quality practice requires that you stay fully connected with your performance and quickly regain a positive and fully connected focus if your best-connected focus drifts away.
+ Quality focus in each practice or training session includes focusing on quality execution, listening intently and learning from positive feedback, refocusing on making little improvements or corrections, and staying fully connected within the drill, activity, piece, program, routine, set, or simulation you are doing.
+ Quality focus in practice or training often means that you focus fully on doing what is required to perform your best in competitions or performances. It also means that you learn to respect your best focus and extract the focusing lessons from each practice, simulation, or training session to continue to enhance the quality and duration of your best focus for ongoing learning and performance improvement.

Focus in Performances

The goal in performances, games, and competitions is to stay focused, stay positive, and stay fully connected with the right things at the right time so you can perform to your capacity and not waste an opportunity. Decide to bring your best focus into this performance, game, competition, or event. Commit fully to respect your best focus for the duration of the performance. This is the best way to make good or great things happen consistently.

Remind yourself of the following facts to bring out your best in each performance:

+ Quality performance—in games, competitions, and situations that count in your life—depends on you respecting your best focus.
+ Quality performance depends on you respecting a positive and fully connected focus that brings out your best and works best for you.
+ Quality performance requires you to stay positive and fully connected within your performance and regain a positive and fully connected focus quickly if it drifts away.
+ Quality focus in performances and competitions begins with you deciding what you want to do in the performance, game, or competition and deciding what focus you are going to carry into the performance.

+ Quality focus in performances and competitions requires that you respect your best focus, focus fully on connecting within the performance, and follow your game plan or focus plan.

+ Quality focus in performances and competitions also requires that you commit yourself to maintain your best focus in the face of distractions, focus through distractions, and refocus quickly to get back on track within the performance whenever necessary.

In challenging, high-stress situations and critical parts of demanding performances, success is almost completely dependent on your focusing and refocusing skills. As an athlete or high-level performer, you already know how to execute the physical and technical skills; you have done them thousands of times. You just have to trust yourself and free yourself mentally to connect fully with the doing and let everything else go. This is what will give you your best chance of performing your best in potentially high-stress contexts. If you or your teammates lose it mentally—if you lose focus, lose connection, abandon hope, or are overcome with doubts or fear—and you do not have a preplanned refocusing plan, you will probably crash and burn. The loss of a positive and fully connected focus at critical moments within a performance will often negatively affect individual and team performance. This is why you need to have and to practice using effective focusing and refocusing plans.

At critical moments in high-stress contexts, performance can become 100 percent mental, both in sport and other high-performance or high-risk pursuits such as brain surgery, heart and lung transplant operations, rescue missions in military combat zones, police work, hostage negotiations, emergency response teams, and even doing a presentation in front of a large group of people or taking final exams that determine whether you pass or fail your course.

Nurturing Excellence

I have had the opportunity to learn from and work with many performers who have excelled in different disciplines. This group has included many Olympic and world champions in sport, high-performance coaches, astronauts, elite fighter pilots, helicopter rescue pilots, firefighters, exceptional cardiothoracic surgeons and brain surgeons, top classical musicians, dancers, actors, leading business executives, and other people who excel at embracing their lives. The most striking revelation about these exceptional performers from all over the world is how similar they are in their level of commitment, highly developed focusing and refocusing skills, positive performance perspectives, and highly developed wheels of excellence.

In some ways people who excel at the highest levels are more like you than you might expect. They get nervous and sometimes fearful before they compete or perform in big events. They experience ups and downs in their confidence and sometimes have doubts about their ability to perform to their potential or repeat their best performances. They also like to have fun with what they are doing. Almost all great performers, from professional team-sport athletes to top classical musicians, speak of the important role that fun, joy, passion, or love for the pursuit (or parts of the pursuit) plays in freeing themselves to excel. Their joy of the pursuit and their ongoing commitment to their mission helps them remain positive and fully focused through the ups and downs of their journey.

The reason why some high-level performers are able to continue to perform well consistently is that they have developed highly effective ways to put away distractions, doubts, and fears and focus exclusively on doing their jobs or executing their game plan when they get to the line and it is time to perform. What separates these performers is the quality of their focused

Miami Herald/Zumapress/Icon Sportswire

LeBron James and other exceptional performers have learned to center their focus exclusively on the task at hand.

connection in their performances and their focus on fully developing themselves in this one area of their life. They are willing to do whatever is required to make their journey successful. In other parts of their lives they often view themselves as normal or average.

All people have the capacity to excel, or become the best they can be, at something. To turn your capacity into a living reality, you have to make the decision to focus fully on doing everything possible to turn your dream into a positive living reality. You have to choose to pour your heart and soul into it. It is that simple. And it is totally within your control. When you docide to do something with full commitment and high quality, anything is possible. How far your journey takes you depends on the depth of your commitment and the direction of your focus.

Falling short of your potential in sport, performance, school, work, relationships, health, or life is usually a result of not focusing fully on being where you are or not focusing fully on doing what you really want to do. Focusing in positive and fully connected ways will always help you achieve your goals and live your dreams. Make sure you bring your positive and most fully connected focus into all your learning and performance contexts. This will raise the level and consistency of your performance and the quality of your life. Docide to act on your positive intentions—every day. This will free you to pursue your goals with a positive and fully connected focus, and a thousand other positive little decisions will naturally fall into place every day.

Personal excellence is a choice. Choose to do everything in your power to fulfill your goals and live your dreams, to improve your focus, to raise the level and consistency of your performance, to experience a greater sense of enjoyment and personal satisfaction in your pursuits, and to enhance the overall quality of your life. Decide to do it! A performance goal (or relationship goal) does not have to become the only thing in your life in order for you to attain it, but it must become the only thing in your life while you are engaged in the process of doing it, experiencing it, or performing within it.

Everyone begins at a different departure point with respect to personal strengths and assets. When you develop and stretch those assets, even for short periods, you become a better performer and person, and you feel more fully alive—you touch the essence of personal excellence. By improving your focus, you greatly increase your chances of journeying in positive directions and reaching your potential in different parts of your life. You can choose to go down this path of joy and excellence or choose not to. It's your decision.

The Power of Focusing
Beckie Scott

Beckie Scott was the first North American ever to win an Olympic gold medal in cross-country skiing. I started working with Beckie in the year leading into the Salt Lake City Olympics. In her previous Olympic experience, her best result was 45th. At the 2002 Salt Lake City Winter Olympics, she won an Olympic gold medal. In 2005–2006, her final race season, she started the season by winning back-to-back World Cup races, was on the podium in 10 World Cup races, and won a silver medal at the 2006 Torino Olympic Games.

When we began working together, Beckie was already highly committed to her training and competitions. To take the mental step up so that she could stand on the podium (and reach the top of the podium), Beckie had to fine-tune her race focus plan, decide to give everything she had in each race, race smart, and race to win.

She became a consistent winner by going into each race with a specific race focus plan, deciding to execute her race plan, being diligent in evaluating her race focus (in writing) after every race, drawing out the lessons (what went well and what could have been better), and planning to act on those focus lessons in the next race. By continually implementing and improving her race focus plans, she developed confidence in her focus and abilities, especially when she was challenged in a race or experienced severe discomfort (or lots of pain), which is part of endurance events.

Another important skill that helped Beckie become a better and more consistent high-level performer, and a better human being, was our work on dealing with distractions. Many distractions can affect high-performance athletes (and other high-performance people) over the course of their careers—poor results, setbacks, injuries, sickness, teammates, workmates, coaches, bosses, doubts, time away from home and family, and, in her case, new and higher expectations from others and increased time demands from outside sources that came with becoming an Olympic champion.

There are distractions you can plan for and distractions you can never plan for. During Beckie's preparation phase for the 2006 Olympic year, I was at a training camp in Chile with the Canadian alpine ski team when I received an e-mail from Beckie. Her husband and training partner, Justin, had just broken his neck in a bad mountain bike crash in the Rocky Mountains. Fortunately, Justin's spinal cord was not severed. He recovered fully and was with Beckie at the Torino Olympics and then became a coach with the Canadian National Cross Country Ski Team.

Distractions, large and small, are part of life. No one is immune to them. So the better your skills are for coping with them, dealing with them, focusing through them, and learning from them, the better you and everyone around you is likely to be. In the interview that follows, Beckie shares key components of her personal journey to excellence in the demanding sport of cross-country skiing.

Terry: What did we do together that helped you most in terms of pursuing and achieving your goals?

Beckie: I think initially it was the very thorough and detailed process of planning, executing, and evaluating that laid the groundwork for me and became the base for getting the best out of myself mentally in training, racing, and, ultimately, life. It was a step-by-step, day-by-day process that was in motion year-round. The process was always dedicated to improvement, the highest quality, and getting to where I wanted to go. It began with really detailed worksheets and a lot of careful thought and later evolved to a process that would become second nature.

I asked myself almost every day, *What am I going to do today to get closer to my goals? How am I going to do it?* And at the end of the day I asked myself, *What went well, and what could I have done better?* In the final year of my career, which I consider my most successful, I almost didn't have to ask the questions anymore. I knew exactly what I needed to do to reach my goals, how I was going to do it, and where to turn for a little help and support when I needed it. I was confident that when it was all over I could look back and say that I did everything I possibly could to get the best out of myself.

Developing and implementing a detailed race plan was another one of the crucial elements of my success. In the year before the Salt Lake City 2002 Olympics, we had the opportunity to race World Cup races on the same courses that we would be racing at the Olympics. I learned a tremendous amount during those World Cups about how the courses raced, and I felt very confident that given the opportunity, I could capitalize on this education.

During the year leading up to the 2002 Olympic Games, I also spent a great deal of time at the venue either by myself or with the team. I had decided to make a special effort to train on those courses as much as I could. When the Olympics rolled around, I had developed not only a tremendous level of comfort and familiarity with the environment and surroundings but also a specific race plan for the pursuit race. I was confident that if I could handle the physical aspect of the race, I had the best strategy going.

On race day, the pursuit race was two 5K races separated by about an hour and a half. I had followed my first 5K classic race plan to the letter and was sitting in a perfect position for the second 5K. A few seconds separated a group of about six women. I knew every uphill, corner, downhill, and flat on that course, and when the time came to make a move, I did. I didn't know how the other racers would react, of course, but I was even prepared for a sprint to the finish if it should happen—knowing I would swing wide out of the final corner and take the outermost lane if it came down to it. At the end of the day, I won that 10K Olympic race (the two 5K races combined) by one-tenth of a second. I know that all the homework I did beforehand and executing my race plan and strategy with full focus and precision had everything to do with it.

Terry: After you won the Olympic gold medal, there were lots of people wanting your time. How did you try to respect your own needs even though you had lots of people tugging at you?

Beckie: In the months that followed the Salt Lake City Games, there was an extreme level of attention and demand that came my way. Even though I felt completely ill-equipped to manage it initially, I resolved to enjoy as much of it as I could. Whenever it started to become stressful or unenjoyable, I just stepped away until I felt I could manage it again. I also really made an effort to strengthen and maintain my close friendships and relationships in this time because I recognized that these were the people who really cared and would always be there—Olympic champion or not.

Terry: Part of our plan for ongoing learning was ongoing evaluation and acting on the lessons learned—to pull out positive things from every performance, to assess your focus, and to learn from every experience. Can you comment on how you did that during the years we worked together?

Beckie: For five years (since we began working together), I sat down after nearly every single race, even time trials, and wrote out an evaluation that basically described what went well, what didn't go well, and what I needed to do to be better next time. This was an absolutely critical process for me in ensuring that no experience, good or bad, was ever wasted and that I continued to grow both as an athlete and as a person from each time I stepped to the starting line—whether it was a roller-ski time trial by myself with only my husband timing or an Olympic medal–winning race. On many occasions, through taking the time to go back and sift through what had happened, I picked up things that hadn't been obvious before. Every race was a learning opportunity.

Terry: What does being focused mean to you? Can you describe what it is, what it feels like, or how it unfolds for you?

Beckie: I think the best way I can describe being totally focused is through a description of a feeling. There aren't really any emotions attached to it or specific thought patterns. It's almost like wearing special glasses where everything inside you is crystal clear. Your thoughts, feelings, physical sensations, and everything outside you that doesn't matter, or won't get in your way, is irrelevant and fuzzy and blurry. You are entirely present, in the absolute moment, and able to react, respond, and perform as you need to, in the way that you need to. You're just "there," and it is a good feeling.

Terry: Can you describe a specific race day when you had one of your best performances—from a focus perspective?

Beckie: On race days, your focus has to be able to move around a little as you change gears from task to task, such as warming up, testing skis, racing, and coping with the discomfort of racing. When you are in a good, clear frame of mind and the focus is right on, you are able to shift from each of these points easily and capably. For example, for me, parts of the race preparation morning have to be really relaxed and totally focused on conserving energy and making the right decision about skis. Then, 45 minutes later, I'm completely focused on squeezing the very last ounce of effort out of myself while sustaining the absolute physical limit of pain threshold and keeping my technique smooth and efficient.

One of my best performances this last season was a 15K mass-start race in which I led from start to finish over an extremely demanding course in very cold conditions. I had decided beforehand that I liked cold weather (I actually don't), that I wasn't tired (I was), and that I could win if I skied a perfect race. I went into that race morning with my focus being positive, calm, and relaxed but also absolutely 100 percent determined that I would have a great race, and I proceeded with the prerace morning routine in that frame of mind. Everything flowed out from there, and even if there were some snags, or inconsistencies, or things that didn't go quite right, I coped and dealt with them easily.

When we started to race, my focus shifted into competition mode, and I just became completely "in" the race. With mass-start races, you begin a race surrounded by upward of 60 women, and you have to be able not only to ski your own race but also to react and respond to the race that is going on around you. We began racing, and even though I was aware of the competition behind and beside me, I stayed completely focused on the task in front of me, which was to get around the course as fast as humanly possible. This kind of complete focus (on the task and leaving the awareness door open) allows for self-talk during moments of pushing through extreme pain, allows for boosts and adrenaline rushes from the cheering crowds, allows for split-second decisions, and allows for adjustments and refinements when information comes in from coaches around the course.

The feeling when I crossed the finish line first, after 45 minutes of enduring some of the hardest, most physically demanding racing I had ever done, was not only sheer joy in the accomplishment but also tremendous pride in the fact that I had won this race more on pure mental determination and staying completely focused on doing what needed to be done to win than anything else.

Terry: Can you comment on the role of refocusing to get back on a positive track when a doubt or worry enters your mind and give a couple of specific examples that you have used?

Beckie: I think the most stressful moments of doubt and worry for me came in the form of illness and injury. When your body is your livelihood and you need to train as hard and as prolonged as we do to race successfully, being downed by illness or an injury has the potential to be tremendously upsetting.

I recognized this and was usually able to refocus, keep things in perspective, and keep myself on track with a couple of tactics. For illness, I would just tell myself that this was my body's turn, my body's way of saying, "Enough, I need to rest now." Often I would turn those days of hanging out on the couch or in bed into something constructive—trying to plan how I was going to come back after this bout with the flu or a cold better than ever. I used all that down time to my advantage and would be telling myself not only that was I going to come out of this well rested and motivated but also that my training was going to benefit from the time off and that this little break was exactly what my body and my mind needed to get better.

With injury it was a little different. The summer before the 2006 Olympics I suffered an injury to my shoulder, my rotator cuff, so that for a month I couldn't use my left arm. I not only had to stay positive and believe that I would heal but also had to fight hard to overcome feelings of despair and frustration with being in that position in the year of the Olympics.

Finally, I realized that I had to make a choice, and I decided again to let this work to my advantage. Because I couldn't use my arms, I started training exclusively with legs-only technique. I decided that I was going to perfect my skiing technique from the waist down. When it came time to use my arms again, I just flew, because I had been doing legs-only intervals and legs-only strength work in addition to the regular distance workouts. In the end, I think that because I decided that the injury was going to work to my advantage and I was going to come out of it better than before, I did.

Terry: How did you get yourself to race smart and give everything through the really tough times, like the last two races of your career following the 2006 Olympics when you were sick and feeling exhausted?

Beckie: In the last season of my career, I was fighting for the overall World Cup title with a great Norwegian champion. We were separated by only a few points. The overall title was basically going to be determined in the last two races, and these races were coming on the heels of a killer race and travel schedule following the Olympics.

On the morning of the second-to-last World Cup race, I woke up with a raging sore throat, aching body, and headache. I also had terrible jet lag and was very depressed by the surroundings. We were in one of the worst, most industrial, polluted places I had ever seen in my life. The air was brown, you couldn't see the horizon or drink the water, and it was just such a downer.

I knew, though, that this was one of my last two chances left to claim the overall title and that somehow I had to overcome the physical aspect to compete. I had to convince myself that I could do this and decided to tell myself I was just having a severe allergic reaction to the pollution (even though I've never had an allergic reaction to anything in my life). I decided it wouldn't affect my capacity or performance.

I also went back to something you had said before, which was "the body is dumb, meaning your body will follow your focus . . . you can convince it of anything," so I set about convincing myself that I felt great and was going to race just fine. I had to race smarter than anyone, I had to race great, and I had to draw on everything I had to at least secure my position as second overall and close the gap on first. I had to ignore completely what my body was feeling and telling me and make it do what I needed it to do.

So, we began racing the heats, and I just self-talked myself through the entire day, racing very tactically, aggressively, decisively, and, thankfully, fast enough to keep advancing. I had really bad chills between rounds and had to wear every item of clothing I had brought, but I just told myself it was the humidity and kept moving around and trying to stay warm. I ended up second that night, and it blew me away. I look back on that now and think that of all my racing experiences, that day, for me, defines mental toughness.

After that race, we traveled from China on to Japan, and I basically spent the next three days in bed trying to recuperate and gather any strength I could for the final push to the World Cup overall title. In spite of being sick, I was completely relaxed during this time, knowing at that stage that I had nothing to lose, that everyone was getting tired, that the pursuit was my best event, and that regardless of what happened in the upcoming race, I had already had an amazing season.

I went to the start of that race having only seen the course in my warm-up that morning. When we were all lined up and ready to begin the race, the commentator announced, "This is Beckie Scott's last race today," and everyone in the starting area clapped and cheered. It was such a great feeling to know that I would be leaving this sport successfully and with so many good friends that I decided right there at the start line that if I could almost win in China feeling like I had, I could definitely win here in Japan with three good days of rest behind me. I focused with every fiber of my being, and I raced as smart, determined, and tactically as well as I possibly could. I took the opportunity when it arose to win and gave everything I had to win the race. And I did. I won the last race of my career.

Terry: That was a great win! Over the course of your racing career you had a high commitment to ski racing, but you also seemed to maintain a commitment in your relationships with your family. How did you try to balance that?

Beckie: I have a very close extended family. To spend so much time apart from them and then stay focused on training and recovery in the brief periods that I was able to spend with them was really hard. But I just viewed it as part of my commitment to be the best racer I could be, and ultimately I saw the little time that I did have with them as critical to my overall happiness, balance, and enjoyment of life. Being with my family put things in perspective more often than not and probably kept me sane.

I also had an extremely supportive partner in Justin because he had been a cross-country ski racer and knew exactly everything I was going through. In the final years of my career, he became more and more of a training partner. Even when he wasn't able to take part in the actual training sessions, he would still be there. I'd be roller-skiing home as it was getting dark, hear the car pull up beside me, and look over to see our grinning golden retriever, Henna, sitting in the passenger seat. No matter how irritated I was from fatigue or the loneliness of training, I was uplifted and had to smile, because there they were, my unique little team, always ready to guide me home.

Terry: What do you think was the most important lesson that you learned from me?

Beckie: If I work backward from the present, more specifically this past season, I think the most important lesson I learned was the powerful nature of the deciding process and how things can be changed or affected just by deciding to do something. Even though that seemed to be one of the final chapters we worked on, I realize now it was present from the beginning, whether that was deciding to make every single day of training the highest quality possible with careful planning and evaluating, or deciding that adrenaline and nervous energy were a good thing and would help me ski faster instead of impeding me, or deciding that I was confident and fully prepared (even if preparations hadn't necessarily been ideal), or deciding to turn negative and potentially adverse situations into positive ones that could be beneficial or learned from. I think that virtually everything I was able to accomplish can be traced back to beholding the responsibility of decision making and the power that you have in just deciding something for yourself.

Terry: I am really interested in how your confidence in your capacity and your confidence in your focus changed over the years that we worked together. I know that this year you really knew that you could win or be on the podium consistently. How would you describe the strengthening of your belief or confidence in yourself and your focus?

Beckie: I remember asking a teammate at one of my first World Cup races in Europe when she thought Elena Valbe (a famous Russian skier who dominated women's skiing for years) would retire. I was 20 years old and had placed about 58th in that race, so there should have been a few more women I was thinking of other than just Valbe. But even way back then, and really with no signs of any great talent or ability on my part, I was determined I wasn't going to stay 58th my entire career and that someday I'd be good enough to challenge for World Cup wins. I was just unsure if I would be able to beat Valbe.

I think that every time I experienced success, or some measure of it, my confidence improved a little. With each new experience and training and all the little things, I was slowly piecing together a way to ensure success every time I stepped to the line. This evolved to the point where I had enough to start believing it was possible to win.

The final year of my career, I really felt that I knew exactly what I had to do to win or be on the podium consistently in all domains. Training, recovery, nutrition, psychology, everything—there wasn't one element from my overall approach to ski racing that I had overlooked or felt was lacking. Just having done this and trained and prepared for the season in this manner gave me a lot of confidence. I knew that when I went to the start line I was going in prepared as well as, if not better than, anyone there.

Terry: Any last comments, Beckie?

Beckle: I have to tell you that it is really a full-circle experience for me to think about being featured in your book. I remember getting my first copy of *In Pursuit of Excellence* when I was 18 years old from my coach Les Parsons in Vermilion, after having missed an entire season because of mononucleosis. He thought that reading your book would be a great way to start another training season, and from that point on, I basically carried the book

Beckie Scott *(continued)*

with me everywhere. Later on, the year before the Salt Lake City Olympics, I received a revised copy, which is where I found your website in the back pages. I contacted you, and the rest is history! I could never have imagined at age 18 when reading your book that I would someday come to be one of the featured athletes in it. What an incredible journey it has been.

CHAPTER 4
Journey to Excellence

The journey to personal excellence in sport and other high-performance pursuits can teach you important lessons about how to live your life fully and joyfully. Pursuing and achieving meaningful goals requires a high level of commitment and a persistent positive and fully connected focus. Although you might not fully realize it now, your positive and fully focused experiences as an athlete or performer in any other challenging pursuit can teach you many important lessons about how to excel in all areas of your life.

The Quest

The quest to become your personal best—to attain the highest standards of excellence, to live your life fully and joyfully, to make meaningful contributions to others, to become a positive inspiration to yourself and others—is a worthy human pursuit that can lead to ongoing personal growth, meaningful contributions to others, and a more joyful life for you and those with whom you live, work, or play.

If you don't care about the quality of your preparation, training, learning, contributions, performances, work, teaching, coaching, creations, products, services, relationships, joyfulness, or positive interactions with others, everything takes a marked turn for the worse. The pursuit of mediocrity or doing as little as possible in whatever you are doing will never take you to where you are capable of going.

Pursuing and attaining your highest levels of personal and performance excellence does not come easily, but it is certainly worthy of a determined and fully focused effort. To excel at anything, there are numerous obstacles and barriers to negotiate or push aside along the way. If you are passionate about becoming the best performer you can possibly be or you want to contribute something of real value in any field—sport, the arts, education, medicine, science, research, business, politics, technology, the military, police or rescue services, writing, teaching, coaching, filmmaking, acting,

Jeff Crow/Sport the Library/Icon Sportswire

Athletes like Serena Williams inspire us to change our ideas about the limits of what's possible.

consulting, counseling, or parenting—make a personal choice to do it! Choose to excel in the pursuits that are most important to you and act on your positive intentions in meaningful ways every day.

If you really want to excel or become the best you can possibly be in any part of your life, choose the following:

✦ To excel
✦ To commit fully to your goal
✦ To act on your positive intentions every day
✦ To continue to believe in yourself and your capacity
✦ To continue to nurture your best positive and fully connected focus
✦ To continue to believe in yourself and your capacity to do what you really want to do for the duration of your life journey
✦ To believe in the good people around you who can help you live your dreams and whom you can help to live their dreams

Barriers to Excellence

The greatest barriers in the pursuit of personal and performance excellence are psychological ones we impose on ourselves or others impose on us often without us even realizing it. Too often people think they can't do it—even when they can do it—so the result is they don't do it. They don't even really try to do it because they already know they can't do it—even when they actually can do it. All they need to do is change channels from why they can't to why they can.

At one time breaking the barrier of running a sub-4-minute mile was viewed as impossible, until one runner did it—and then almost immediately a host of others also did it because now they knew it was possible. The physical and technical skills of these runners did not change; what changed was their belief in what was possible. At one time cars were impossible, planes were impossible, space travel was impossible, and hundreds of other things were impossible until someone "**do**cided" to make them possible. As our beliefs about our limits and our unlimited possibilities change, the limits themselves change in all parts of our society and all parts of our life.

The world's best performers in all disciplines are made of the same flesh and blood as you and I, but their belief is different, their focus is different, their commitment is different, their passion is different, their persistence is different. That is what gives them their strength. Whenever you focus fully on positive possibilities, almost anything is possible. Your positive focus, your positive commitment, and your positive belief in your capacity will give birth to new and better realities. Give it a try and see what happens!

Have you ever done anything that you initially thought was impossible to do? Have you ever thought, *I am never going to be able to do this, I am not going to be successful with this, I am never going to finish this, there is no way this is going to work, there is no way I can win this, there is no way we can win this*—and yet you and your partner or team were successful? You, or you and your partner, or you and your team, accomplished a goal that initially seemed impossible. Most people have thought, at least momentarily, that they can't do something but then managed to do it because they were able to shift focus away from their doubts to connecting fully with doing what they wanted to do and were capable of doing.

Can you recall a personal experience when this happened to you? If you can, think about how you (or your team) managed to achieve your goal when you initially thought you could not. What did you focus or refocus on to make it happen? It is important to take time to reflect on your best focus and your less than best focus and to remember what you and your teammates did to turn negatives into positives or impossible into possible.

Every year there are teams or individual athletes who are not supposed to win—who outperform opponents highly favored to win. How do you think they do this? They usually win or raise the level of their performance because their individual or collective focus is centered on the right things at the right time. On that day they come in positive, focused, and mentally ready to play and give everything they have. When you make a commitment to focus fully on achieving your mission and attaining your goals, step by step, shift by shift, stride by stride, gate by gate, play by play, movement by movement, and moment by moment, from start to finish—good things happen. Athletes and others performing at their absolute best are almost always so fully focused on doing what they are capable of doing and freeing themselves to do it that there is no room for doubts or distracting thoughts to get in their way of achieving their positive mission.

Keep the Joy in the Pursuit

Sport and physical activity are not only about performing your best. They are also about feeling your best, embracing magic moments, and enjoying your life pursuits. It has been a long time since I have competed in anything, but I continue to have an abundance of joyful experiences when engaged in a variety of physical activities, mostly outdoors. I still run the trails through the woods next to my house every day for about an hour. I am not setting any world records, but I am fully embracing my life in small and joyful ways every day. I love flatwater kayaking, canoeing, paddleboarding, and swimming in the lake where I live, and I love cross-country skiing along the same trails that I run on in the summer. I never formally trained or competed in any of these activities, yet they offer many meaningful challenges and are a source of ongoing joy. I love to run on long stretches of sandy beach, especially at sunrise or sunset with the surf rolling in, to run along narrow trails in the woods or in the mountains, or to paddle my flatwater kayak on a perfectly calm lake or into a strong headwind.

Most of my everyday highlights include some kind of physical activity, probably because these activities make me feel free and most fully alive. They free me from all other concerns in my life and absorb me completely—physically, mentally, and emotionally. Here is a specific example of feeling free and completely engaged in the moment. One clear, crisp winter night, under a full moon, I set out with some friends and neighbors to cross-country ski up a mountain trail to a small log chalet nestled deep in the woods. On this majestic evening, the snow sparkled like dancing crystals under the moonlight. At the chalet we made a fire, had a sip of wine or water, shared a bit of stew, and joked a little; then we headed back down the mountain. As I skied down that curving trail under the light of the moon, I felt so fully connected to that mountain, not knowing where it ended and where I started.

I continued to embrace that fully connected feeling as I flowed freely along that path and passed the thousands of trees along that narrow snow-packed trail. I continued to move in and out of shadows as the moonlight darted through the trees. I was totally absorbed in the experience. It was novel, challenging, sensual, fun, exciting, physically demanding, and a meaningful encounter with nature—a pure highlight experience, the kind that makes you feel great and grateful for the gift of life and being fully alive. There are very few contexts where we can have such close, meaningful, and memorable contact with the essence of ourselves, the essence of others, and the magic of nature as when we are fully engaged in nature, sport, or physical activity. It can be an ongoing highlight over the course of your life.

Sport, physical activity, and nature provide abundant opportunities to free ourselves for short periods to enjoy special moments not readily available elsewhere in our lives. We can live out our quest for excitement, pure connection, joy, love, personal control, or risk by deliberately accepting positive challenges that we pursue with passion. Fully connected experiences like this can free us to feel more fully alive, more joyful, and more capable of directing our own destiny in positive ways. Highlights and personal satisfaction come from embracing positive experiences, choosing to become competent at doing something important to us, feeling joyful, feeling fully connected, and embracing positive opportunities within our control. The continual process of seeking out meaningful challenges within our stretched human capacity and embracing them ensures that we continue to fully live, love, learn, enjoy, and grow in positive and life-enhancing ways.

I have had the opportunity to paddle down some major white-water rivers, including the Nahanni River and the Coppermine River, in remote areas of northern Canada. I discovered that the challenge of running an untamed river is not a conflict between human and nature but rather a melding of the two. You do not conquer a river—you experience it, you work with it to find the best path. The calculated risk, the momentary sense of meaning, and the intensity of the experience let you emerge feeling exhilarated and somehow better or more complete because of that experience. For me, these experiences are always a quest for pure connection and self-fulfillment rather than for victory over others or the river. Fully embracing each day and each experience in positive and life-enhancing ways was and still is my primary goal. Each experience has the potential to lead you to some kind of personal growth, improved performance, self-discovery, and greater or clearer awareness of whatever you are seeking in your sport, relationships, or life. Positive and fully connected experiences in whatever you are choosing to do can bring ongoing joy and meaning to your life and the lives of your loved ones.

Finding a sense of meaning, joyfulness, purpose, or passion in whatever you are doing, experiencing, going through, or pursuing can make the difference between ongoing personal joy and excellence and just getting through another day. Personal meaning for each of us is unique and changes over the course of our lifetime. However, joyfulness in any part of our life flows most readily when we are fully connected to doing something of real value to us or others or when we are striving toward some goal we find worthy and feel is worthy of us.

You can experience joy and meaning by committing yourself to certain goals, ideals, or values; by embracing simple joys every day; by experiencing or appreciating someone or something of value to you; by being creative; by honoring others or choosing to do something of value for others; or by doing something with others or by yourself that you deem worthwhile.

Sport and other meaningful high-performance pursuits are wonderful mediums for providing a sense of purpose and continuous challenge, as well as a range of intensity and emotion that is difficult to experience elsewhere.

These positive pursuits can be rich and rewarding if you choose to pursue them on your own terms, with a positive life-enhancing perspective. They offer numerous opportunities for personal growth and stretching the limits of your human potential—physically, mentally, emotionally, and spiritually.

Personal excellence is a contest with yourself to bring out the best in yourself and others, to focus on the positives, and to nurture the pure potential that lives within you, your friends, and loved ones. Excellence is a pursuit in which you must support yourself to draw out the natural reserves within your mind and body to develop and stretch your human capabilities to the fullest. Each of us begins our life journey at a different starting point—mentally, physically, socially, emotionally—and with varying levels of support and guidance from others. Look for the opportunities and the positives within yourself, others, and each situation and context you enter. Develop your own strengths and potential to your full capacity. Make the most of what you have, wherever you are and whatever you have the potential to be. The true joy and challenge in the pursuit of personal excellence lies in joyfully pursuing your potential and fully living the various textures and contexts of your life.

Path to Personal Excellence
Kerrin Lee-Gartner's Journey

I began working with Kerrin Lee-Gartner when she was a 16-year-old on the Canadian women's alpine ski team, and I continued to work with her throughout her racing career. After eight years on the national team, Kerrin won the gold medal at the 1992 Winter Olympics in Mirabel, France, in women's downhill on what at that time was considered to be the fastest, most difficult women's racecourse ever. I conducted the following interview with Kerrin shortly after her Olympic victory. Our discussion focused on her path to personal excellence. I did a short follow-up interview with her in 2006. Her experiences demonstrate how you can act on the components of the wheel of excellence in the real world of high-level performance in sport and in your life after transitioning out of high-performance sport. Perhaps her experiences can serve as an inspiration or guide in your continued pursuit of personal and performance excellence.

Focus

Terry: When you talk about being focused in training, focused in races, can you describe what that is?

Kerrin: My very best focus is when everything happens naturally. I don't even think about it. A lot of people want to know exactly what I am thinking in certain parts of the course, or what I'm thinking in the start gate, or when I go through the finish. It's almost a feeling. The focus is so clear that you shut your thoughts off and you trust yourself and believe in yourself. You've already prepared for years. All you do is go; it's very natural. The focus is so crisp. You're so connected. That happened to me at the Olympics.

There are so many words to describe it—there's *autopilot, connection, tunnel vision,* or just being 100 percent focused. It's all more of a feeling. It turns from thoughts into feelings and natural motions on skis. You don't really have any distinct thoughts when you're going down. You don't see the people on the side of the hill. You don't see anything. You're just naturally doing what you do.

Commitment

Terry: You have achieved the highest goal in downhill skiing, and you were able to do it in a very stressful situation. How would you describe your commitment to go after that goal?

Kerrin: The commitment is more than 100 percent. It's committed through the ups and downs. Committed through the good results and the bad results. Committed when you're coming in 50th. and it looks like there's never an end to the bad results. You still have to be committed and still focused and still trying to win every race. I think the day that you let your commitment go is the day you don't have a chance to win.

Terry: How long did it take you to get ready for this one little run (the 1992 Olympic downhill)?

Kerrin: A lot of people assume it's an overnight success story. It's taken me nine years of hard work in international competition and many years before that. I think that all of your work with me during this time shows how long it has taken me.

Terry: Over the last eight or nine years you've had lots of setbacks, lots of challenges to overcome, lots of injuries, and maybe some people not believing in you as much as you believed in yourself. How did you get yourself to keep going after your goals through some of those struggles?

Kerrin: The obvious struggles were my knee injuries, and each one took six months to about a year and a half to really recover from. It wasn't just the physical recovery. The mental recovery was the hardest part. There are always waves in life, and when you're down in ski racing, with a physical disability like my knees were, it was always important to keep my goals set, to always believe in myself, and to look at the reasons why I was going through these struggles, to look at the end result really. I made little tiny goals for myself—little tiny steps, focused on little things. I stayed focused through every single bad thing, stayed focused, stayed focused, stayed focused. I think that's the only way through it, to go gradually and continue believing in yourself the whole way. That's the key to everything when you're down.

Mental Readiness

Terry: When you talk about mental readiness, what does that mean to you?

Kerrin: It means years of mental preparation. My first meeting with you was when I was 16 years old. I remember it clearly. I was not very good at imagining myself skiing. I didn't understand why I even had to do it. Now it's come to a point where it's a part of my everyday life. If I'm hanging a picture in the living room, first I imagine where I want it. Then I imagine how high I want it and how far away from the wall. I can see it all clearly. Then I hang the picture, and it's in the right spot. That's a simple example of what I can do when I ski, but when I ski I'm doing something dangerous. I'm doing something that I want to do very well. It's not worth making a mistake, so I have to use my imagination and my imagery constantly throughout the whole year.

Terry: How did you approach your training runs for the Olympic downhill?

Kerrin: I just tried to stay very relaxed, work on certain parts of the course all week long, and keep my goals small. I worked on a 30-second section instead of the whole thing. That way I kept the pressure off myself as well. I didn't feel the need to win every single training run. I just felt the need to ski certain parts of the course well, and I think that was the key to a lot of it. It allowed me to stay relaxed. It kept the press away a little bit. The press didn't think I was a key person, even though I thought I was.

Terry: You skied each section well, but you picked different sections to go after on different training runs.

Kerrin: Yes. We only got to ski the top 30 seconds of the course twice, and that was where I had trouble at the beginning of the week. The last training run, I concentrated solely on the first 30 or 40 seconds and then relaxed and basically just skied the rest. I still had a very good run, so I knew I was ready to do well.

Terry: What were your reminders going into the race?

Kerrin: Actually, I kept it pretty simple. I just had the reminder to just go for it, take the advantage, and I knew I had the chance to make it my day. I was very relaxed, which was obviously a key to it all.

Positive Images

Terry: Did you do much imagery in preparing for your Olympic race?

Kerrin: I've been doing imagery of the Olympics for about four years, but I started this course last February and have run it hundreds of times in my mind. So by the time I actually had the race-day run, I had done it many times before. I just hadn't won it in reality yet!

Terry: What do you experience in your imagery of the race run?

Kerrin: I think a lot of people assume that imagery is pictures in your mind, and actually when I was 16, when we first started working together, it was very much like watching a videotape. I could watch anybody with my eyes closed and picture anybody skiing in a certain part of the course. It's advanced itself to the special state where now it's more of a feeling. I can feel the feelings of skiing and feel the motions. My thoughts almost turn into feeling. I think it is important for athletes to do that in any sport.

Terry: What about imagery for getting through your injuries and back on track? Did you do anything there?

Kerrin: The first injury I had, I remember talking to you, and you said, "Remember to ski in your mind." I thought, *The last thing I want to do now is ski, because I'm injured.* But I remember it didn't take me very long to get back on my skis in my mind. I skied in my mind basically every single day through my injury and through the recovery. It helped me keep my focus on what I was going through it for, and it made the pain and struggle a lot easier to take because I was still doing something enjoyable in my head. Even if I was on crutches, in a cast, it made it a lot easier.

Terry: How did your first run go after those injuries?

Kerrin: I think by keeping my imagery there, it made it much simpler to get out on the downhill skis. In a real course, it made the speed adjustment much quicker. With the second injury, it just happened naturally. I had already succeeded in being able to imagine myself skiing perfectly, and I did it throughout the six months of recuperation. When I put my skis on, it was like I wasn't even off them.

Confidence

Terry: I am interested in how your confidence in your capacity has changed over the years. I know this year you really knew you could do it. How would you describe the strengthening of your belief?

Kerrin: Actually, it's amazing because people naturally assume you always believe in yourself from day one. When your results aren't there, the first thing that shatters is your belief and confidence. That's a key to success, and over the years I've developed belief in myself. I knew I could be on the podium, and I knew I would be a winner, but as much as I know and as much as I can believe, until it happens, 100 percent belief isn't there. I really talked myself into it this year. I knew I was skiing as well as anybody on the World Cup circuit. I've had top-five results consistently in the last two years, and I really, really believed, with 110 percent of myself, that if there was a course that I had a chance to win on, it was the Olympic course. Just by believing in myself, and always talking to myself positively, and putting positive thoughts in my mind, it only encouraged the belief I already had.

Terry: So how would you talk to yourself positively?

Kerrin: I would turn anything negative into a positive. If I had a bad run, I would take a positive out of it anyway. If I had a run where I was only good on half of it, I would take a positive and build on it. That made me believe in myself more each time I ran the course. Each time I did anything, I could build positive emotions on it. On race day at the Olympics, it was very flat light, very foggy, which is not pleasant in downhill. The first positive thing I did was say to myself, *You're good in flat light; you're one of the best skiers in flat light. This is your opportunity right now; go for it!* I really am one of the better skiers in flat light. Although I don't like it any more than anyone else, I can still be aggressive and I can still ski like I want to ski.

Distraction Control

Terry: The Olympic Games are a huge distraction for most athletes. How were you able to come through with a great run under the most distracting circumstances?

Kerrin: I've taken lessons from a lot of different races. One of the races I took a valuable lesson from was the 1988 Olympics. I was very distracted in 1988. I wanted to win badly. In preparing for 1992, what I did was take everything I learned, which included putting myself first, putting what I need first, and concentrating on what I needed to concentrate on in everyday races. I was relaxed. I knew what my job was. All I had to do was go out and do it. Once I was on the chairlift in the morning, everything was fine. I took an hour or two to deal with all the distractions in a one-block period. I left the rest of the time to myself. I think it's important to make sure that you're relaxed and ready to go. If you get too distracted, then you can't focus anyway, and you don't have a chance to win.

Terry: So you dealt with some of the people and media things and then had a time that you just clicked off to get away from it all?

Kerrin: Yes. Once I left the hill and the race site, which is where most of the stress and distractions are, I was on my own. It was like my normal everyday life—playing card games, reading books, and just staying relaxed. I remember in Calgary, all I did was think about the race all day long. In Mirabel I couldn't have been more relaxed.

Terry: What about on-site? What perspective allowed you to focus on your performance instead of the outcome?

Kerrin: I had a good teacher, Terry! I think I've learned, definitely, not to focus on the outcome of any event. Although you dream about it, and I dreamed about the gold medal for many years, I think the best thing for me is that I've learned to concentrate on what I need to concentrate on. I needed to concentrate on having a good warm-up in the morning, concentrate on being very smooth, very quick, looking for speed in the course. It carried right through to my race. I went to the start, and I wasn't concentrating on the final result; I was concentrating on what I needed to do to ski my best. It just became natural for me. I went through the same motions as I go through every race. It just happened naturally.

Terry: Were there any points where you had to refocus to get back on track within the race?

Kerrin: There was one, actually. It didn't show up too well on TV, but there was one spot where I caught my ski and it went out from underneath me. It really caught me off balance, and I remember my mind slipping away a bit there. It didn't take long to get it back. I just said, *Come on,* to myself. I got it right back together, and the bottom half of the course was exceptionally good.

Terry: A lot of athletes who win gold medals really struggle in their next races because of the expectations placed on them and the expectations they place on themselves. You had great races in your subsequent World Cups. How was your focus in those races?

Kerrin: Actually, I was tired going into the first World Cup race after my Olympic win. I wasn't expecting much of myself. I went out in the morning, and my warm-up didn't go as planned. I didn't ski as well as I had hoped. I had been thinking a lot about the outcome. I realized it right away, and I changed my thought pattern by admitting it and by getting the focus into my mind that I really needed to focus on. I changed into the mode that works for me. I thought of going for it, being aggressive, and of all my key thoughts. When I was standing in the start gate I knew that I had an opportunity to win the race. I pushed out of the gate and went into my automatic pilot without thinking about anything other than my key thoughts. I just kept my focus. I was second by three one-hundredths, and that's pretty close to winning. I was happy with that result after everything that had happened.

Terry: If a negative thought slips into your mind, what do you find is best for getting back on track?

Kerrin: When I notice myself thinking thoughts that I don't want to be thinking and don't work for me, or when I start thinking about the outcome or final result, I try to notice it first and rectify it by thinking of things that work for me.

Terry: Has it taken a while to be able to get your thoughts working for you like that?

Kerrin: It's taken a long time. I remember races in the past where I wouldn't even realize why I had blown it in that race until a year later. Last year at a downhill in Lake Louise I had been doing very well, winning training runs. On race day, I came in fifth, and I realized after the race that my approach was wrong. I was thinking the wrong things. Now I've started to realize when I'm thinking the wrong things before I even race. This gives me a chance to have a good race before racing.

Terry: So you change your thinking, or your focus, before the race begins, to have a better chance at performing well?

Kerrin: Exactly. If I wake up and I realize my head is there, in the right place, I let my thought patterns work naturally and I have a good race. If it's not there or something distracts me in the start or warm-up in the morning, then I know my refocusing thoughts. I know what brings me back to my good results and good focus.

Ongoing Learning

Terry: Part of your ongoing evaluation plan is to pull out positive things from every performance to enhance your confidence or feel good, as well as to learn from the experience. Can you comment on that?

Kerrin: It's taken me many years to pull something out of each run. If I'm last in a race I've learned to still pull something out of it. Most times I give 110 percent effort, and that's enough for me. If you try as hard as you can try and you give the effort you can give, you have to be satisfied with the result because you really couldn't have done more anyway. The lessons that I pulled out of the Olympics and applied to other World Cups afterward were to stay relaxed and to concentrate on what I know works. There are certain key thoughts that work for me on race day, and most of it is just relaxing and going for it, counting on my natural instincts to take over. When that happens, I have my best races.

Terry: I've noticed over the past couple of years that you are more willing to follow your own path, to do things that you know help you, even when some people may not agree. How has that unfolded?

Kerrin: I'm in an individual sport that is run in a team manner, so sometimes it's hard to do things like an individual and to follow my own path. I've come to realize that I must trust myself 100 percent and believe in myself. When I need something a little bit different from what the rest of the girls need, I am willing to take a risk and go for that to get the win.

Terry: So now that you know what you need to focus on to perform your best, you are able to respect those patterns and gain from them.

Kerrin: Exactly. You learn about yourself throughout your career. I've been out there for eight years, and I've learned a lot. I've taken lessons from many different things. Now I can apply those lessons. At the Olympics, I knew I had to be away from the team and had to be on my own and away from the distractions of the village. I did that, and it paid off.

Terry: Now that you have won the gold medal, lots of people are wanting your time. How are you planning to respect your needs for personal space even though you have people tugging at you?

Kerrin: At first it was difficult because it was hard for me to say no. I wasn't used to being an Olympic champion or having that much attention. I've realized I really have to listen to my insides. I have to listen to what I feel, and when I'm run-down and tired, I have to say no. I have to say, "I'm sorry, I can't do it tonight, or next week, or the week after; I need a couple of weeks off." I've realized it's OK to say no and to look after myself first, because my career is not finished. I know I can still win out there.

Terry: It's better to listen to yourself and to your body and do something positive about it before you are totally exhausted, rather than after.

Kerrin: Exactly. I think you have to learn to do that as an athlete. You really have to learn to respect your body. Often you realize a week before it happens that you are getting close to being too tired, and you have to take a week off. It's important to be able to listen to yourself and follow your feelings as well. If I think I need time off, I take it off instead of listening to other people. Because if I don't believe I'm on the right program, then I won't win a race. I really have to believe in what I'm doing 100 percent. The program has to be right for me.

Terry: You had a high commitment to ski racing, but you also seemed to maintain a commitment in your relationships with your family. How did you try to balance that?

Kerrin: I am from a large family of five children, and we were very close throughout my childhood. I think with the support that they gave me, it was natural for me to put them number one. Although my career was ski racing, and that was important to me, I think it's also important to keep my private life alive and separate. A lot of people were worried that when I got married my focus would be gone and I wouldn't be able to concentrate on winning a race. Surprisingly, it's done wonders for my skiing. It's made me relax, try hard, but know that it's not the end of the world if I don't win the race.

Terry: What are the most important lessons that you learned from me?

Kerrin: Hmm! The most important lesson is probably always to learn something from everything that happens and apply it to the next event. To stay relaxed. I've taken a lot of lessons from every race I've had. I've learned a lot about myself, and now I can be a lot more relaxed. My imagery is as clear as I could ever want it. I know exactly how to focus, and I just know how to apply everything that I know how to do. I know how to apply it on race day.

Terry: What advice might you have for other people who are in pursuit of excellence?

Kerrin: From everything I've learned through ski racing, the first and foremost thing is you have to believe in yourself and what you've chosen to do. No matter what profession you're in, I think if you try 100 percent to be as good as you can be, it doesn't matter how good you are as long as you believe within yourself that you've tried as hard as you can.

Terry: Are you applying the mental skills that you've been developing through your skiing to other areas of your life?

Kerrin: The mental skills I learned through ski racing come into play every single day, all the time. Learning to deal with distractions comes into play now with the press, or if you have an argument or a setback, it's learning to get through that. I have to deal with that and still get on with my life . . . staying relaxed, taking the good points out, always taking something positive and still feeling good about yourself and about the situation. I think everything that I do in sport relates to real life. It relates to everybody's career. It really relates to everything. I think that's the key to it all. Once you're relaxed and confident upstairs in your mind, then everything else will follow. Being completely focused is the only way you can achieve your goal.

A Look Back at the Journey

I conducted this short follow-up interview with Kerrin in the latter part of 2006, almost 15 years after our initial interview. At the time of this interview Kerrin was married and had two lovely daughters, ages 10 and 11. She had been working as a TV commentator for alpine skiing for the previous three Winter Olympic Games and many World Cup seasons. She had also been active in raising money for children in orphanages as well as other meaningful projects. I included her responses here to illustrate how you can continue to act on the wheel of excellence in your life after sport.

Terry: What did you learn from ski racing and the work we did together on strengthening your focusing skills that you are still using in your work and daily life?

Kerrin: All my mental training for ski racing has helped me in all avenues of my life. I think the reason that the transfer of skills was so easy and works so well is that you need many of those same skills to be successful in anything.

Since retiring from ski racing, I have worked at three Winter Olympics for CBC-TV as an analyst for alpine skiing. We call the races live, as they happen. Every now and then, I will make the mistake of mixing up my stats or saying something completely different than what I intended to say. Once this verbal mistake pops out on live television I don't really have time to dwell on it. So I just focus on the next step that is within my control. This is a simple example of how my training at focusing and refocusing has come in handy many times on occasions as simple as this. As a former Olympic champion, I have also been asked to speak at all kinds of functions. The simple message woven through each presentation remains the same:

✦ Decide what it is you want to do. Dream!

✦ Make the plan, do some goal setting, and adjust the goals as needed along the way.

✦ Prepare, work hard, analyze, learn, and work some more.

✦ Believe in your dream, your goals, your plan, and your preparation. Believe in yourself.

✦ Be determined, be focused, and be persistent.

✦ And always remember to try to enjoy the challenges and have fun!

Terry: Nice reminders! What has been the most important mental skill or perspective that you learned in your sport that you have carried into your life after high-performance sport?

Kerrin: The toughest lesson for me to start believing in as a racer happens to be the one thing that has changed me most as a person. As a racer, it was difficult for me ever to believe that I was good enough. I always saw my mistakes, dwelled on them, and compared myself to others, which only made me doubt myself and my abilities. The end result was often one of me trying too hard in all the wrong ways and ultimately not being at my best. As an athlete, it took a couple of years for me to believe in the benefit of learning from my mistakes and acting on them. It took a while to really understand that more can be learned from an oops that you act on than from a random success.

The process of trying, analyzing, learning, and trying again—with the benefit of that lesson—became one that I continue to use today in work, play, and parenting. This process creates belief, confidence, and ongoing improvement in whatever I am attempting to do.

Are there times when I still have doubts? Of course, but I have come to believe, as I did in skiing, that my best is good enough. And yes, some days my best just isn't quite what it was the day before. That is fine, too, because I will learn a lesson from it.

Chapter 24 includes an update on Kerrin Lee-Gartner's ongoing life journey to personal and performance excellence.

PART II
Focusing for Excellence

CHAPTER 5
Self-Examination

Your personal level of excellence will begin to flourish when you take the time to understand your best and less than best focus and make a personal commitment to respect your best focus more consistently. You can do this by simply becoming more aware of your focusing capabilities, both strengths and areas that need improvement. It is important to become fully aware of what *you* really want to do with your focus, your performance, and your life, as opposed to what others might want you to do. When you clearly understand what *you* really want to do, you can establish your priorities and thereby pursue the things most important to you and avoid those you don't want to pursue. Ultimately, to excel at anything, you have to choose to break through the negative or disconnected focus barriers of your own making. These are the self-inflicted barriers that prevent you from doing what you really want to do or getting to where you really want to go.

Positive performance contexts in which you are fully engaged provide wonderful opportunities for knowing yourself better and ongoing personal growth. Listen to yourself, respect your body, and guide your focus and your feelings in positive ways. Talk to yourself and your body and adjust your focus so that your mind and body do what you want them to do. Continue to discover and respect what focus works best for you, what focus works against you, and what focus empowers you to turn things from negative to positive or disconnected to fully connected. Continue to nurture your best possible focus and make it more consistent so you continue to embrace your ongoing positive journey and exciting new challenges. Take time to discover, refine, and respect your own best focus. Know that it will serve you well and take you where you want to go now and in the future.

To achieve your goals and live your dreams you have to continue to respect your best focus. If you perform at less than your best, you are probably not respecting your best fully connected focus. Think about your focus when you are performing your absolute best and your focus when you are performing far below your best. What is the difference?

Do you reflect on your best focus before, during, or after your games, races, competitions, or performances to help yourself fully understand and respect your best focus? Do you free or trust your body and mind to perform to your full capacity on autopilot? Where is your focus in your best performances? Where is your focus during your less than best performances? Find a way to respect your best performance focus consistently regardless of the context in which you are playing, performing, or competing. This is a critical step that will lead you to ongoing improvement and consistent high-level performance.

Focus Control and Commitment

Even the best performers in the world can continue to improve the quality and connectedness of their focus to ensure that it is consistently where they want it to be. Think about what you can do to improve the quality and consistency of your focus. Begin by reflecting closely on where your focus is in your best and less than best performances and learning experiences. Then choose focusing strategies that have worked for you or focusing reminders from this book that will help you to improve the quality and consistency of your best performance focus. Write down a focusing plan that you feel can help you to improve the quality and consistency of your focus—in training, practices, preparation, study sessions, conversations, and competitions. Practice focusing in positive and fully connected ways every day, in every opportunity, both inside and outside your performance context.

In addition to improving the level and consistency of your best focus, it is also critical that you maintain a highly focused commitment to your overall goals and dreams. What can you do today to improve the level of your commitment? Take an honest look at your commitment to act on what you need to do to get to where you want to go. Given your current performance level, is your commitment strong enough to take you to your goals? If yes—great! If not, you have two choices:

1. You can raise your level of commitment to bring it in line with your goals.
2. You can adjust or lower your performance goals so that they are more realistic based on your current level of commitment.

If your level of commitment to achieve your goals is not aligned with what is required to accomplish those goals, you may experience continued frustration.

The self-assessment scales in figures 5.1 and 5.2 are based on qualities that leading performers and coaches around the world use to describe the kind of commitment and focus required to become a great performer in a variety of high-performance domains. A rating of 10 means that the statement is completely true for you, a rating of 1 means that it is completely false for you, and a rating of 5 means that it is midway between being true and false for you.

Figure 5.1   Focus Control Rating Scale

Rate yourself on each item. Then go back and identify your strengths and the areas that might require improvement if excellence or being your absolute best is to become a realistic goal.

1. I am so focused during my performances (or in my work, school, or personal interactions) that everything else disappears. I get so absorbed in what I am doing or pursuing that nothing else in the world exists for me during that time.

   never   1 2 3 4 5 6 7 8 9 10   always

2. I focus on keeping my performance focus totally in the present, in the here and now (for example, one shot, one step, one move, one moment at a time).

   never   1 2 3 4 5 6 7 8 9 10   always

3. I refocus quickly, back into my completely absorbing, best focus, even if I become momentarily distracted or nervous or make a mistake in performance situations.

   never   1 2 3 4 5 6 7 8 9 10   always

4. I maintain a high-quality, fully connected focus in practice or preparation sessions.

   never   1 2 3 4 5 6 7 8 9 10   always

5. I quickly regain a high-quality, fully connected focus when distracted in practice or preparation sessions.

   never   1 2 3 4 5 6 7 8 9 10   always

6. Before I perform, I focus on things that make me feel confident and ready.

   never   1 2 3 4 5 6 7 8 9 10   always

7. Before I perform, I decide to bring my best focus into this performance.

   never   1 2 3 4 5 6 7 8 9 10   always

8. I have a strong inner confidence that I can do anything I set my mind to do, if I focus fully on doing it.

   never   1 2 3 4 5 6 7 8 9 10   always

9. I focus through errors, bad calls, or situations that go against me within a performance; I focus right back on the step in front of me.

   never   1 2 3 4 5 6 7 8 9 10   always

10. I stay motivated and completely focused even when behind, when facing obstacles or setbacks, or when down in points.

    never   1 2 3 4 5 6 7 8 9 10   always

11. I focus on learning from setbacks, criticism, or errors and turn them into positive opportunities to improve.

    never   1 2 3 4 5 6 7 8 9 10   always

12. After a performance I focus on what I did well and how I can be better in my next performance, and I act on those lessons.

    never   1 2 3 4 5 6 7 8 9 10   always

From T. Orlick, 2015, *In pursuit of excellence*, 5th ed. (Champaign, IL: Human Kinetics).

Figure 5.2 Commitment Rating Scale

Rate yourself on each item. Then go back and identify your strengths, as well as those areas that may require reassessment or realignment if excellence is to become a realistic goal.

1. I am willing to put aside other things to excel in my sport or other chosen pursuit.

    never 1 2 3 4 5 6 7 8 9 10 always

2. I really want to become an excellent performer in my sport or other chosen pursuit.

    never 1 2 3 4 5 6 7 8 9 10 always

3. I prepare myself mentally for each practice or learning opportunity so that I can continue to improve and get the best out of myself.

    never 1 2 3 4 5 6 7 8 9 10 always

4. I prepare myself mentally for each performance so that I can continue to improve and get the best out of myself.

    never 1 2 3 4 5 6 7 8 9 10 always

5. I am determined never to let up or give up (for example, I remain committed to achieving my goals, making the move, or completing the mission), even in the face of difficult challenges or obstacles.

    never 1 2 3 4 5 6 7 8 9 10 always

6. I take personal responsibility for my mistakes and work hard to correct them.

    never 1 2 3 4 5 6 7 8 9 10 always

7. I give 100 percent focus and effort in practices or preparation sessions, whether it's going well or not.

    never 1 2 3 4 5 6 7 8 9 10 always

8. I give 100 percent focus and effort in performances or competitions, whether it's going well or not.

    never 1 2 3 4 5 6 7 8 9 10 always

9. I give everything I can, even when the challenge seems insurmountable or beyond reach.

    never 1 2 3 4 5 6 7 8 9 10 always

10. I feel more committed to improvement in my performance domain (or other chosen pursuit) than to anything else.

    never 1 2 3 4 5 6 7 8 9 10 always

11. I am totally committed to making my focus as good as it can possibly be.

    never 1 2 3 4 5 6 7 8 9 10 always

12. I find great joy and personal satisfaction in my performance domain (or other chosen pursuit).

    never 1 2 3 4 5 6 7 8 9 10 always

From T. Orlick, 2015, *In pursuit of excellence*, 5th ed. (Champaign, IL: Human Kinetics).

Performers who excel at the highest levels rate themselves very high on both commitment and focus control—much higher than less-accomplished performers do. Top performers tend to have average scores from 9 to 10 for all items on the commitment and focus control scales. The higher the quality of your focus and the higher your commitment, the more likely you are to achieve your highest level of excellence.

Mission to Excellence Process

When I coach people on how to enhance their performance in any field, I usually begin by asking a series of performance-related questions to which they respond in writing. Together we discuss options for self-growth or living their dreams, some of which they implement. With some basic guidelines to follow, most students, athletes, and performers who really want to improve are fully capable of asking themselves these same questions and can successfully implement their own performance-enhancement strategies.

The following six-step process is designed to help you explore and act in positive ways to achieve your personal goals:

1. Select a target area for improvement within your sport, performance domain, or life. Select a situation in which you would like to have greater personal control. Choose some essential mental skills from the wheel of excellence that you would like to strengthen. Your specific target may be anything that you feel will increase the level or consistency of your performance or bring you closer to reaching your potential or living your dreams. Make sure that you choose a meaningful target area on which to set your sights for positive and meaningful change.

2. Complete the mission to excellence self-assessment later in this chapter, keeping your target area in mind. This self-assessment will help you pinpoint the circumstances within your situation or chosen target area that are related to your best performances and greatest control and your less than best performances or least control. Reflect closely on what you may have already tried that worked well for you or on what focus has worked best for you in some situations.

3. Review some of the strategies for excellence provided in this book. Choose the ones you believe will be most relevant to make the improvements you are seeking. Draw on anything you think might be useful in helping you accomplish your mission to excellence. If you want additional practical examples of how students, developing athletes, top athletes, and many other great performers in a variety of domains have strengthened their focus and mental game, see the additional resources from the *Journal of Excellence* and other resources listed at the end of this book.

4. After you have selected a target area for improvement, completed your mission to excellence self-assessment, and chosen some relevant

strategies to guide your improvement, write down your plan of action for enhancing your performance or personal growth in the target area you have chosen. More specifically, write down what you are going to do to initiate the positive changes you are seeking, when you are going to do it, how often you are going to do it, and in what circumstances you are going to do it or practice doing it.

5. Experiment with your plan by practicing and applying the various strategies you selected in different situations so that you can move closer to your goals. After implementing a strategy in a practice or performance situation, take a few minutes to think about what worked well, what didn't work, and what you need to continue to refine or change to improve your plan and performance. To continue to move closer to your goals, assess and refine your plan by drawing out and acting on the lessons learned from your ongoing experiences. Make a personal commitment to ongoing learning and improvement. "**Do**cide" to make it happen.

6. Where feasible, get together with other people who are pursuing personal growth or excellence (classmates, teammates, colleagues, coaches, athletes, performers, partners, friends, or family members). Share your experiences and the challenges you are facing and what is helping you get through those challenges successfully. Share views on effective ways to pursue your goals, maintain a positive and fully connected focus, and focus better through distractions.

This mission to excellence project is a great opportunity for you to apply relevant focusing and refocusing skills to something extremely important in your life. If you approach this six-step process with focus and commitment to make a real-world positive change, it will be an extremely valuable learning experience, and the chances of accomplishing your mission, or actually making the positive changes you are seeking, are very high. You can follow this same self-improvement process to bring about positive improvements in any part of your life.

Mission to Excellence Self-Assessment

The purpose of this self-assessment is to clarify your desired areas of improvement and target specific ways to make those improvements. Your mission to excellence can focus on something you would like to do or something you would like to stop doing. Or you can focus on improving your quality of living; performing better or more consistently in school, work, sport, music, or dance; or simply living more joyfully. Analyze in detail the precise circumstances and focus that surround your best and less than best experiences in your targeted area. You need to discover what you already do that allows you to perform well in some situations and what you do that interferes with your good or great performances or parts of performances. Use a performance notebook or diary to record your reflections on how your focus has been affected and is now affecting your performance or experiences positively or negatively. This approach can help you understand more fully the kind of focus that works for you and against you.

Specific events within your environment and within your thinking or focus lead to good or bad experiences and consistent or inconsistent performances. Usually it is only at certain moments that focus or a loss of focus becomes a problem. For one Olympic figure skater, this loss of focus happened only at important competitions, "when I see the judges peering over me as I begin and I start to think about being judged instead of focusing on the movement." For a world champion water-skier, it was "when I approach the first buoy on my slalom run and I think, *Uh-oh, I'm probably going to blow this.*" For a national team basketball player, it was "when the coach yells at me during the game and I start to worry about him instead of concentrating on playing ball."

You should reflect on precisely when a focusing problem arises and become aware of what you are thinking or, more important, what you are focused on at that moment. You should also become aware of what you focus on when the situation or your performance improves.

The following self-directed questions are designed to help you assess your focus and find your best possible focus for best performances and positive change. These questions have been used effectively as a guide to strengthen focus and enhance performance in sport, the performing arts, school, health, business leadership, military missions, relationships, and other challenging areas of life. Ask yourself the following questions and write down your responses:

+ What is it that you want to improve most at this time (for this mission to excellence)?

+ What are you doing that you don't want to do? Or failing to do that you would like to do more often? Specifically, what would you like to change, do, improve, or act on more consistently?

+ When, where, and under what circumstances is the greatest need for change or improvement? In what situations does this challenge or problem usually come up? What kinds of demands or expectations are being placed on you at that time? What are you usually thinking, feeling, or focusing on at that time?

+ How important is it for you to improve your focus, positive connection, reaction, or performance in this target area? Why is it important to you to improve in this area?

+ Think about the times when you have been in this given situation and your focus, connection, response, interaction, or performance has been at its best. What was going on then? What were you doing or saying to yourself? What were you focused on?

✦ Think about the times when you have been in this situation and your focus, connection, response, interaction, or performance seemed to be at its worst. What was going on then? What were you doing or saying or thinking to yourself? What were you focused on?

✦ What seems to be the major difference in your focus when you compare your best and less than best performances, actions, interactions, responses, or experiences in this situation?

✦ What do you think you can do to improve this situation, your response to it, or your focus and performance within it? What would be your ideal or best focus within this situation?

✦ Do you think you can improve your focus in this situation if you
  ✦ focus on bringing a more positive and more fully connected focus into this situation or performance?
  ✦ focus more fully on what is within your control within this situation or performance?
  ✦ focus less on what is going on around you, or what others around you are doing or not doing, and focus more on yourself, your best focus, and your own best performance?
  ✦ focus on taking better care of your needs for rest, relaxation, recovery, nutrition, personal space, or simple joys outside this situation or performance context?

✦ How strong is your commitment to make a positive change in this target area? Are you committed enough to practice and work regularly at improving your best focus, your most positive connection, your best response to distractions, and your overall performance in this area? If yes, great! If no, can you docide to make a full commitment to do what is required to make the positive changes you would like to make right now?

Selecting Improvement Strategies

After you have completed your mission to excellence self-assessment, you face the delightful challenge of selecting and implementing effective strategies for making the positive changes you are seeking. "How do I choose the best ones to start with?" you're asking, right?

After completing the mission to excellence self-assessment, you might already know what will work best for you or what you need to focus on to make the positive changes you are seeking. If not, before choosing a strategy for improvement, read through the various focus and performance enhancement options in the remainder of this book, along with the examples that show how athletes or performers have used them. Some approaches will be immediately more attractive to you than others, and some may seem particularly suitable for your situation. Try any strategy that makes intuitive sense to you. If just reading about it feels right, try it.

Through my ongoing consultation and interactions with tens of thousands of athletes and other high-level performers, what has come through loud and clear is the importance of unique and meaningful mental preparation, focus and refocusing plans, motivation, and effective ways of dealing with distractions and coping with or managing other issues. An approach that may work beautifully for you may not have the same effect on someone else. For example, in the same precompetition situation, one athlete may prepare best by thinking about something relaxing, another athlete may prefer to focus on reviewing the task at hand, and a third performer may choose to embrace the excitement and willfully channel it into executing his or her best performance.

Your belief or gut feeling about the potential effectiveness of a particular focusing strategy influences your commitment to work on it and, consequently, how well it will work for you. You are unlikely to have gone through life without knowing something about how you function. So your beliefs about what will or will not work for you often rest on a sound foundation. Your personal wisdom is based on the number of years you have lived and the extent to which you have experimented with and reflected on what focus works best for you in different contexts, performances, and experiences in your life. Read through the various focusing options for attaining the highest levels of excellence with an open mind and open heart, follow your gut feelings on strategy selection, and make refinements as needed along the way.

Select the self-improvement approaches or focusing or refocusing strategies that you feel are most appropriate for you in your particular situation. Then experiment with them and continue to refine them until they work best for you. You may choose a single approach, a combination of several interrelated approaches, or a personal strategy you come up with on your own. Keep in mind that a potentially valuable focusing or refocusing strategy that has not yet worked for you may at some point work beautifully for you if you just keep working on it. Often all you need is more persistence in practicing, refining, and focusing on the strategies that have already been somewhat successful in your past. When you find something that feels right and really works for you, continue to use it and fine-tune it. It will enhance your journey and take you where you want to go, and that's the main goal.

CHAPTER 6
Intensity, Relaxation, and Recovery

Intensity and relaxation are not polar opposites. They often work together in complementary ways to bring out the best in you and your performances. An optimal amount of intensity—not too much and not too little—is required to perform your best. The sweet spot for best performances often comes from a balance between focused intensity and focused relaxation. Best performances unfold naturally in sport, dance, music, the performing arts, and other meaningful performance pursuits by freeing yourself to perform in positive and free-flowing ways. Trust yourself to do what you know in your heart and soul you can do. Free your best performances to emerge naturally by connecting fully with what you are doing. Embrace the feeling of fully focused relaxed intensity and trust yourself to do what you know in your heart and soul you can do.

Discover and respect the focus that works best for you in the different parts of your life. Whenever you free yourself and your focus to connect fully to live, love, learn, grow, and perform consistently closer to your true potential, everything in your life will improve.

+ Choose to be the person you would love to be.
+ Choose to live your life in the ways you would love to live it.
+ Choose to perform the way you would love to perform.
+ Choose to lead your life with a positive and fully connected focus.
+ Choose to embrace simple joys and positive feelings of pure relaxation.
+ Choose to believe in yourself and your potential.
+ Choose to free yourself to live and perform in positive, powerful, and free-flowing ways.

You are the leader of your own destiny. You are the only one who can free you to live, love, focus, and perform in positive and fully connected ways. You are the only one who can choose to embrace the positives in your life—every day. No one else can do this for you!

"**Do**cide" to bring your most positive and fully connected focus into your daily training, performances, relationships, interactions, important life pursuits, moments of pure relaxation, and moments of meaningful personal reflection.

Every day you have opportunities to find simple joys, become better in some way, embrace your positive and fully connected focus, respect your preferred levels of intensity and relaxation, and free yourself to be more fully connected and relaxed wherever you are and whatever you are doing. Choose to learn, train, and perform with dedication, intensity, and passion. Choose to create a sense of balance in your life when you are away from your training and performance contexts. Choose to act in ways that will free you to live fully and recover fully—physically, mentally, and emotionally—every day so you can stay on a positive and life-enhancing path.

The sooner you discover and respect your own best focus, the sooner you will be empowered to live, love, learn, interact, and perform the way you would like to. Choosing a positive and fully connected focus empowers you, gives you more control over your life, and frees you to perform better and to feel more fully alive every day. Your focus leads your reality in all parts of your life—for better or worse.

Choose to embrace and nurture fully focused connections, positive intensity, and focused relaxation every day. These pure and simple connections will open doors to an abundance of simple joys and super joys every day. Choose to act on your positive intentions in positive and fully connected ways today and every day and see where it takes you.

Relaxed Intensity

By discovering and respecting your intensity relaxation sweet spot (not too high and not too low), you can make huge differences in the quality and consistency of your best practices and best performances. I have watched videos of cheetahs running freely on the African plains. If you watch cheetahs run, you will quickly see why they are the fastest land animal on our planet. If you watch closely, you will see that their speed and power are driven by relaxed intensity. Each stride combines explosive power and relaxed recovery. You can learn from the cheetah by bringing this image or feeling of focused intensity and relaxed recovery into your performances to free yourself to perform naturally and consistently at your highest levels.

When you enter your training context or performance arena, it is important to do the following:

+ Trust that you can actually do what you want to do today.
+ Believe that you are fully capable of accomplishing your goals.
+ Remember your good reasons for believing in yourself and your capacity.

+ Focus fully on doing whatever you want to do or accomplish today.
+ Connect fully with your mission or performance in a powerful and relaxed way.

To perform your best in your performance arena, it is important to enter your performance arena believing that you can actually do what you want to do and focused fully on accomplishing your personal goals. Going back to my cheetah example, I am pretty sure that if I could interview a cheetah, this athletic animal would tell me that he or she goes out on every hunt with the intention of being successful. The cheetah does not enter a challenging performance arena focused on these negative thoughts: *I don't think I am going to be successful today. I don't think I am going to be able to run fast enough today. I probably won't perform well today. I won't catch anything to eat today. I won't reach my personal goals today because I didn't get a good night's sleep, or because it's too early, or too late, or too hot, or too cold, or too windy, or not windy enough, or because there won't be enough animals out there, or my coach didn't tell me the game plan, or I am not sure what to focus on.* Remember that you, like the cheetah, need to enter your performance arena in the morning, afternoon, and evening focused fully on executing your task or mission knowing that you can be successful.

If you want to perform your best or achieve your personal goals in any high-performance context, your chances of being successful are greatly enhanced if you go in believing that you can do what you want to do and knowing what you need to focus on to make that happen. Even if you are not completely sure you can achieve your goal, your best option is to act like you can do it! Then focus fully on doing it for the duration of your event and see where that takes you!

If you do feel stressed in important performance contexts, it often helps to slow down or relax your breathing before you begin your performance. Breathe in slowly . . . breathe out slowly . . . breathe in slowly . . . breathe out slowly. Then focus fully on doing what you want to do to have your best performance in that context. Relax your breathing, relax your body, and free yourself to connect fully with whatever it is you want to accomplish in that performance context.

Focus on Doing What You Want to Do and Stay Totally Connected to the Doing

Focus on being fully connected with a feeling of relaxed intensity. Nothing else matters. This pure connection will free you to execute your performance to the best of your ability.

If in some situations you are feeling stressed or your intensity level feels too high, you can free yourself to perform in a powerful and fluid way by focusing on turning down your intensity a little. This will free you to perform in a more relaxed, flowing, and fully connected way. Ultimately you want to focus on doing whatever frees you to fully engage yourself in the process of performing your best from start to finish. When you focus on doing what works best for you in different contexts, you will be more in control and more successful at embracing your true potential in all parts of your performance and life.

In some situations, you may need to increase your intensity to reach your goal; for example, toward the end of a long hard race, adventure, shift, game, or performance when you are feeling really exhausted. Choosing to turn up your intensity level at the right time can free you to accomplish goals you would otherwise never be able to accomplish. Relaxed intensity can make you more powerful and determined and help you to flow to where you want to go, especially when your body is screaming at you to stop. Sometimes you can regain positive energy or raise your intensity level by just thinking about your ultimate goal and why you have been pouring thousands of hours into your pursuit. If you have come this far, you might as well "suck it up" and finish strong. Even if you fall across the finish line, finish with no regrets!

If you practice training and performing with a feeling of relaxed intensity, it will help you find that sweet spot where you are most powerful, most flowing, and most fully connected in ways that will enhance your performance. Your ongoing challenge as a high-performance athlete or high-level performer in any other pursuit is to continue to find positive ways to respect your best and most fully focused connection. Embracing and respecting this pure and positive connection will free you to perform your best consistently.

Guiding Focused Intensity

A leading Chinese coach once said to me, "You can jump over a very high fence when a big bull is chasing you." I have not yet had an opportunity to experience a big bull chasing me down, but I am pretty sure that if his big sharp horns were about to pierce through my backside, I would be able to pick up my pace. Being pumped up or energized in the right place at the right time can help you achieve greater heights, as long as you channel that energy in a positive and meaningful direction. However, in your haste to avoid being pierced by the horns of the big bull chasing you, you don't want to lose focus or trip and fall before you reach the finish line or crash into the fence rather than go up and over it. The lesson from the bull is that increased intensity at certain times in some contexts can help you reach greater heights and in other contexts may make you run into a wall or fall flat on your face. Your performance results depend on how much intensity and how much relaxation you bring into your event, the extent to which your focus is guiding your intensity in the right direction, and whether you are focusing on the right things at the right time.

Most athletes and performers in other disciplines are already activated, or excited, before important games, competitions, or performances, so they usually do not require additional stimulation to heighten their preperformance intensity. If athletes do need an intensity lift, it will most likely be when fatigue starts to set in toward the latter part of their race, game, or performance—when every stroke, every stride, every rush, every movement, every gate, every inch counts. At moments like that, the image of the charging bull with horns aimed at your back, or you "**do**ciding" to give everything you can possibly give, will likely be most helpful for you in achieving your ultimate goal.

Respect your personal best level of intensity and focus on sustaining a positive and fully connected focus for the duration of your game, race, dance, performance, match, competition, mission, or event. This will lead you to your best possible performances in the same way that it leads many of the world's best athletes and other great performers to their best performances. Choose to act on the focusing goals that work best for you in positive ways every day. This will free you to become the best performer you can be. When you and your teammates are able to sustain an ideal level of intensity and a fully connected focus for the duration of your playing time or game, you will perform your best and your team will win more consistently. Your individual best focus and collective team focus separate athletes and teams who perform their best and win consistently from athletes and teams who do not perform their best and do not win consistently—even when both teams have the physical and technical skills required to perform at a very high level.

Your ongoing challenge as a developing athlete or highly seasoned performer in any high-performance domain is to continue to discover and respect how you can attain and sustain your best possible focus and your preferred level of intensity. You need to be able to continue to focus in positive and fully connected ways that will help you excel and be your best not only for the duration of one practice, training session, performance, race, shift, period, game, competition, or tournament but every day over the course of your season, career, and life. Your best focus has to become a comfortable and natural part of who you are and what you do—today and every day.

+ What can you focus on to feel your best, perform your best, and be your best today?
+ What can you focus on to improve your performance in training?
+ What can you focus on to improve your performance in your competition or performance arena?
+ What can you focus on on-site to improve the quality and consistency of your best performances?
+ What can you focus on on-site to relax before your games, competitions, or performances?

+ What can you do or focus on off-site—away from your competition venue or performance arena—to relax completely, reenergize your mind and body, and embrace the simple joys of living your life fully and joyfully?

The heart of human excellence is really quite basic. Decide to go out there and play or perform with a fully connected focus and a feeling of relaxed intensity. Before every competition or performance, make a commitment to yourself to go out there and free yourself to be your best. After every competition, game, or performance, take time to reflect on what went well and why it went well so you can continue to enhance the quality and consistency of your best performances. There are many ways to bring an ideal level of positive and focused intensity to your high-performance pursuits. Focus on respecting what works best for you and recognize that what works best for you may change over time.

Finding the right level of focused intensity and focused relaxation is something we have to discover for ourselves. We are all capable of bringing an optimal level of focused intensity and focused relaxation to our pursuits. We are all capable of relaxing inside and outside of our performance arena. Performers who are consistent with their best performances know how to relax through the intensity at the competition site. They also make a personal commitment to themselves to get adequate rest and recovery away from their performance site so that when they return to their performance arena, they have the positive energy required to play, perform, and focus in positive and fully connected ways from the first to the last second.

The quality and consistency of your performance depends on seeing the situation or context you are entering in a positive way and making sure you connect your focus in positive and fully connected ways during that performance.

To perform your best in situations or contexts that previously created feelings of fear, uncertainty, or stress, shift your focus and regain control in the following ways:

+ Clear your mind of all thoughts of outcomes.
+ Slow everything down.
+ Breathe easily and slowly.
+ Focus completely on following your preferred precompetition warm-up plan.
+ When your game, race, or performance begins, focus fully on doing what frees you to perform your best. Let your body and focus lead you freely and easily. Let everything else go.
+ The quality of your performance (beginning, middle, and end) is dependent on you connecting fully with your performance and freeing yourself to perform. Nothing else matters!

Continue to focus on positive possibilities, personal bests, highlights, positive opportunities, taking a step up, reasons to believe in yourself and your mission, and how you can make a positive difference in your life and your performance every day. Continue to find effective ways to keep the passion, pride, joy, excitement, positive possibilities, and your best fully connected focus in your daily pursuits.

If you practice bringing a high level of positive and fully connected focus to your everyday practices and pursuits, you will learn how to consistently maintain a positive and fully connected focus for the duration of your performances or games. Train with a positive and fully connected focus to establish positive focusing patterns that you can carry with you into your games, races, or important performances. Athletes, performers, and teams who make a personal commitment to maintain an optimal level of focused intensity throughout their practices or training sessions place themselves in a solid position to perform their best in games and performances that really count.

If you don't train with a sustained positive focus and optimal intensity, somebody else will—and that will give your competitors an advantage. Try setting specific focusing goals for each of your practices or training sessions. Think about what you need to focus on to achieve your goals. Do this at home or before you get to practice. Create personal challenges for yourself in practice to raise the level of focus and intensity. Challenge yourself to meet personal performance goals in your practices or training sessions. Use your training sessions as an opportunity to practice your best focus so that you are more fully prepared and more fully focused for your important competitive events.

Practices and performances provide great opportunities for you to discover your preferred level of intensity and best focus for performing to your capacity in your sport or performance domain. Make a commitment to yourself to practice getting into your best performance focus zone and maintaining it, so it becomes your natural way of being and performing. Once you know how to focus in ways that free you to perform your best, your goal becomes maintaining that focus whenever you want to perform well. Decide to do it, plan to do it, practice doing it, and focus on doing it consistently.

Continue to reflect on how you can improve your focus and how you can relax through intensity to perform your best more consistently. Decide to focus on doing what works best for you right now—today, this practice, this training session, this race, this game, this performance, this run, this opportunity, this season, this life. The better you become at focusing and relaxing in the right ways at the right time, the better your performance will be and the happier your life will become. Choose to make positive and fully connected performance-enhancing focusing and beneficial life-enhancing relaxation away from your performance site your personal mission over the next weeks, months, and years or your life. This will lead you to where you have the capacity to go.

Respecting Performance and Life-Enhancing Relaxation

Relaxation and recovery are essential for maintaining high-quality performance, personal health, and overall high-quality living. As a high-performance person or highly committed athlete, it is very important that you respect your body's need for adequate rest and recovery.

On some occasions, relaxing is more productive than being physically intense, especially when you are recovering from an injury or illness or are just extremely fatigued (when, for example, you are in the middle of a long, hard training or competitive season that has included extensive travel). When your body or mind is feeling completely exhausted, it is usually best to take some time off to recover, heal completely, regain your positive energy, and feel more fully alive mentally and physically. Take some time off to just rest and relax and then do light, low-intensity training. When you are feeling fatigued or on the edge of getting sick, you will benefit more from rest and relaxation than from hard exertion. Listen to your body and respect your needs for life-enhancing relaxation. This will serve you, your performance, your team, and your life best in the long run.

You can reduce the stress in your life by making positive life-enhancing choices, listening to your body, and reducing the unnecessary stress in your life. People have different bodily responses to the onset of stress. Some people feel tension in their neck, back, or shoulders. Others experience shaky legs, queasiness in the stomach, a rapid increase in heart rate, sweaty palms, hot flashes, pounding in the head, dizziness, feelings of being helpless or out of control, or a loss of positive focus.

When you feel stressed in any part of your life, or stressed before or after a performance, what do you feel? Stop for a few minutes to think about it. Where does your focus go? Does your focus help you or hurt you? This is a first step in gaining an effective refocusing strategy for relaxing under pressure or in uncomfortable or unfamiliar contexts. When you become more aware of your early signals of negative stress, you can use these signals or feelings as reminders to relax and shift your focus back to something positive or something that you can control. Your goal is to become aware of your usual response patterns to potential stressors and begin to identify, manage, or change your responses in positive and performance-enhancing ways. This usually includes a plan for refocusing on something positive that you control—something you can do quickly before you become too uncomfortable, stressed, or uptight or lose control. For example, you could immediately shift focus away from unproductive stress to your relaxed breathing or to focusing on doing something positive you have done or like doing that puts you back in control.

To shift focus and relax quickly, many people focus on relaxing their breathing by

✦ breathing in and out slowly and easily while focusing on relaxing fully with each exhalation,

✦ focusing on different muscle groups (for example, in the legs, shoulders, arms, or neck),

✦ imagining themselves in a familiar, relaxed, calm, positive, supportive setting or context, and

✦ imagining themselves in a beautiful, quiet nature setting such as on the beach as waves wash gently onto the shore or by listening to a relaxation track from one of my CDs for athletes and other high-level performers.

You may also find that getting away from your performance site or sharing time alone or with a close friend in a quiet, relaxing place with no distractions will help with overall relaxation. Talking with someone who is positive and who places no demands on you, going for a walk, listening to music, having a hot shower or massage, going to a beautiful outdoor setting, or doing something positive you love to do can also help you to change mental channels, relax, rejuvenate, and get back onto a positive and relaxed path. There is no right way to relax. Whatever makes you feel more relaxed, less stressed, more joyful, more peaceful, happier, calmer, or more in control of you and your life is right for you.

AP Photo/Gregory Bull

Felix Hernandez uses his time between innings to relax in the dugout to maintain focus and controlled movements in his pitching.

Make a list of various possibilities or opportunities for relaxing and reenergizing in different contexts. Simple positive reminders such as *relax, breathe, calm,* or *be here* can also help you relax or shift focus quickly, especially if you practice the techniques and call on them before, or as soon as, you start to feel tense, negative, or stressed. Self-initiated relaxation, as well as relaxing by engaging in activities within your environment—a long easy run, a warm bath, a facial, a massage, or time with a loved one—can be helpful in reducing stress, easing tension, and adding simple joys to your day and life.

Two things happen to initiate effective relaxation. The first is psychological. Your focus shifts away from what caused the increased stress or tension—such as thoughts about how you are scared, how you are going to perform poorly, or how you feel like a failure—to a full focus on your relaxed breathing or executing your task, connecting fully to the step in front of you, and taking the next step forward. In short, your focus shifts from outcomes, fear of failure, or rejection to a positive, constructive, more relaxed, and absorbing focus. The shift away from negative self-evaluation and worry alone renders you less anxious and puts you more in control of you and what you are doing. The second part of effective relaxation is physiological. Your heart rate slows down, your breathing slows and becomes more regular, your muscles become less tense, and you begin to feel a sense of calmness or control flowing within your body and mind.

I remember one athlete saying to me while going through a relaxation exercise, "I don't need to relax in here; it's out there that I need it." It is out there, when the stress begins to rise, that we all need it. But if relaxation or a positive refocusing strategy is to be effective in high-stress contexts, you must be able to activate that response in the space of one long, slow, deep breath. To do this successfully, you usually have to practice—first under low-stress, then under medium-stress, and finally under high-stress conditions (out there in the real performance world). To ready yourself for the performance arena, take advantage of all the stressful situations you face in your daily life so that you'll be practiced at responding effectively by changing mental channels. Then you will be ready—out there—in real-world performance contexts when you need to be.

If you take time to learn and practice effective relaxation, you will become more aware of your body's internal environment and better able to adapt to your external environment. You will become more in control of your stress and relaxation experiences in potentially stressful situations that count.

Practicing Relaxation

Most people, especially those involved in demanding challenges or high-performance pursuits, enjoy and benefit greatly from practicing or engaging themselves in some kind of relaxation every day—between practices or work sessions, at the end of the day, or before going to sleep at night. If one of your goals is to develop your ability to call on a relaxation response quickly in a stressful setting, then conclude some of your relaxation sessions by repeating to yourself a reminder, such as *relax, breathe, calm,* or *focus,* every time you exhale. You can also imagine yourself being in a stressful context and remind yourself to relax and focus on what is within your control. This will strengthen the association between your positive reminder and total relaxation or fully connected focus. Practice using your positive reminder to relax and focus in a variety of settings.

The process for practicing effective relaxation goes something like this. Think to yourself *breathe, relax, calm, let go, loose, focus, connect.* Let that calm, relaxed sensation spread throughout your mind and body. Then scan your body for any areas of tension. You may find it helpful to imagine a beam of light scanning through your body. The light beam is charged with relaxation, so if any area of tension exists in your body (like your neck or shoulders), you can simply zap those areas with a light beam of relaxation.

Experiment with this process first in a quiet setting and then start to do it in less quiet settings. In the beginning, you may need a few minutes to get yourself feeling completely relaxed. Your goal is to be able to bring on a relaxation response with one long, slow, deep breath or within a few seconds. Try using your relaxation and focus reminders to relax yourself while sitting, reading, listening to music, standing, walking, running, talking, listening to another person, or driving; at school, work, or meetings; during workouts; on the beach; in bed; and so on. Simply decide to relax and focus wherever you want to feel more relaxed and in control!

You can try some of these techniques right now. Breathe in slowly, breathe out slowly, and then say to yourself, *Re-lax . . . re-lax . . . re-lax.* Now scan your body for any areas of tension. Are your shoulders relaxed? Relax your shoulders. Are your hands relaxed? Relax your hands and arms. Are your legs, ankles, and feet relaxed? Relax your legs, ankles, and feet. Is your jaw relaxed? Relax your jaw. These are good checkpoints. Zap any area of tension that you find in your body with a warm beam of relaxation. Set a goal to relax on the spot in different contexts four times today. You've already done it once—three more to go.

Next, practice your relaxation response in any potentially stress-provoking situation. If previous performance settings have resulted in unwanted stress or tension, begin to simulate performance conditions in practice and practice using your personal reminders to relax and focus. Move from using your relaxation reminders in simulated conditions in practice to performance or competition conditions and then from less important competitions to more important ones. This focus control practice will allow you to respect your preferred on-site relaxation level and free you to perform your best when you need it most.

Taking an exam, participating in a tryout, speaking in front of a class or large group of people, going to the dentist, having an argument, responding to a customs official, or getting a speeding or parking ticket all provide valuable opportunities to practice staying in control. When you detect any personal signals of tension, take a deep breath, exhale slowly, and think to yourself, *Re-lax, calm, focus*. With practice, this process itself can bring on a positive relaxation response. Relaxation alone is not likely to eliminate all stress in a highly stressful situation, but it will help you reduce your stress to a manageable level and get you focused on what will allow you or free you to achieve your goal.

In my consulting work, many athletes and performers engaged in other challenging pursuits have expressed a desire to be able to clear their minds and relax more completely, primarily for the following purposes:

+ To experience a deep and restful sleep, especially before and sometimes after an important performance, game, mission, or competition
+ To remain calm and conserve energy during the final hours leading up to an important performance, game, mission, or competition
+ To relax and revitalize the mind and body between demands, shifts, runs, races, periods, quarters, missions, competitions, or events
+ To rest and recover physically and mentally while traveling from one game, performance, competition, presentation, mission, or meeting to the next
+ To hasten recovery from fatigue, illness, injury, loss, or personal setbacks
+ To focus more completely for the duration of what they are engaged in
+ To experience more simple joys every day in all parts of their life

In response to requests by many athletes, and with their guidance and feedback, I developed a number of relaxation and focusing CDs (see Additional Resources in the back of this book; all eight CDs are now available on iTunes). One of my relaxation scripts is reproduced in figure 6.1. You can read the script yourself, have someone read it to you, listen to my voice on CD with relaxing music playing in the background, or create your own system. Whatever your method, try to get totally absorbed in the feeling of relaxation and focusing so that you can fully benefit from it and recall that feeling in the future.

If you want to use the exercise to relax and go to sleep, just lie down, play the CD, and listen. Chances are good that you will relax completely and drift off into a deep, restful sleep. The three-part relaxation exercise is designed to free you to enter a state of complete relaxation through muscle relaxation, relaxed breathing, and imagery related to a relaxing place.

To use the exercise as a lead-in to performance imagery, remind yourself before you begin listening to that CD track that at the conclusion of the exercise, while you are still in a deeply relaxed state, you will imagine and feel preselected performance skills flowing perfectly in your mind and body. If you want to use the exercise to calm yourself before an important competition, select an appropriate time to listen—a time when you want to be more relaxed and when you do not yet need to be highly activated for competing.

Figure 6.1 Relaxation Script

Get yourself into a comfortable position. Let yourself relax. Feel the relaxation spread through your body. Breathe easily and slowly. Become aware of your feet. Move your toes slightly. Let them relax. Now think into your lower legs. Let your calf muscles totally relax. Think into your upper legs. Let them totally relax. Feel your legs sink into a completely relaxed state. Relax your behind.

[Pause.]

Focus on the muscles in your lower back. Think relaxation into those muscles. Feel that relaxation spread into your upper back. Feel your whole body sink into a deep state of relaxation. Now focus on your fingers. Feel them tingle slightly. Think warmth into your fingers. Let them totally relax. Relax your forearms, your upper arms, and your shoulders. Totally relax. Relax your neck [pause] and your jaw. Feel your head sink into a totally relaxed and comfortable position.

Scan your body for possible areas of tightness and relax those areas. Feel your entire body encircled with soothing warmth and relaxation. Enjoy this wonderful state of complete relaxation.

[Pause for one minute.]

Now focus on your breathing. Breathe easily and slowly.

[Pause.]

As you breathe in, allow your stomach to rise and extend. As you breathe out, let your whole body relax. Breathe in—feel your stomach rise. Breathe out—relax. Breathe in—feel your stomach rise. Breathe out—relax. [Do this three times.] For the next 10 breaths, each time you breathe in, feel your stomach rise. Each time you breathe out, think to yourself, *Relax . . . relax . . . relax.*

[Pause for 10 breaths.]

Feel yourself sink deeper and deeper into a calm and wonderful state of complete relaxation.

Now in your mind you are going to a very special place. You can go here whenever you want to find peace and tranquility. In your special place the sun is shining. The sky is blue. You are totally relaxed, enjoying the warmth and tranquility.

[Pause.]

Feel the warmth. Enjoy the beauty.

[Pause.]

You can be here alone or you can share this place with a special friend. It is your place. You decide.

In your special place, it is so relaxing. You are calm, relaxed, confident, and happy to be alive. You are in control. You feel great.

Feel the calmness spread through your entire body and mind as you rest gently, enjoying the peace and tranquility of your special place. You are feeling so good and so relaxed. You are comfortable; you are warm; you are safe. You are in control of your body and mind. Enjoy this wonderful, restful state.

Available on the CD *Relaxation and Stress Control Activities* (see Additional Resources section at the back of this book).

From T. Orlick, 2015, *In pursuit of excellence*, 5th ed. (Champaign, IL: Human Kinetics).

To use the exercise as a lead-in to strengthening your confidence, remind yourself before you listen that at the conclusion of the exercise you will repeat to yourself your many assets; your strengths; and your many reasons to be positive and confident in yourself, your focus, and your capacity. In this case, you might want to write down some positive statements to think about before you begin the relaxation exercise. If your objective is to heal your body from an injury or speed your recovery from a strenuous or stressful day, then prepare yourself to send healing thoughts and revitalizing images to various parts of your body, both during and after the relaxation exercise.

Relaxing Through Exertion

When Florence Griffith-Joyner broke the women's 100-meter world record in 10.48 seconds, she commented, "The 10.60 [run in the first round of the competition] made me realize if I continued to focus on what I'm doing and stayed relaxed, my times would continue to drop." And they did!

Sue Holloway, following her Olympic silver medal performance in flatwater kayaking in pairs, spoke of the importance of relaxing through the exertion within her performance:

> Almost every three seconds or so toward the end of my race, I'd say, *Relax*, and I'd let my shoulders and my head relax, and I'd think about putting on the power, and then I'd feel the tension creeping up again, so I'd think about relaxing again, then power, relax. . . . I knew that in order to have that power I had to be relaxed. You can be powerful but tense, and the boat won't go. You windmill, and you stay on the spot and dig yourself into a hole. I wanted to feel the power, the boat coming up, lifting and going. Crossing the line, the thing I remember was just letting the emotion go and being able to say, *That's it, it's over!* I just knew that we'd gone our very hardest.

At first glance, exertion and relaxation may seem to be a contradiction in terms. But most of the best performances in sport occur when athletes feel loose and relaxed in the process of extending themselves. When Larry Cain paddled at a blistering pace to win Olympic gold, a definite sequence of reach–power–relax occurred with each stroke. He pushed his limits, but he also paddled relaxed. With top runners you see a similar sequence of stretch–power–relax accompanying each stride. Champion runners often speak of running relaxed after shattering world records.

To develop the skills that allow you to relax during exertion, set a goal to focus on doing this during training sessions and then remind yourself to relax while you are going hard in training. Think of on-site reminders that might help you enter a relaxed but highly focused powerful channel (for example, *loose–powerful, power–relax, reach–pull–relax, stretch–grab–relax, relax shoulders, relax ankles, relax your breathing*). Experiment with using reminders you think will work for you at appropriate times before and during practices, simulated competitions, and progressively more important performances, races, games, or competitions. In activities that involve repetitive sequences, reminders can be timed to go with the rhythmical flow of the activity.

Marathon runners would not continue to break personal barriers, running 26.2 miles, unless they were stretching, pushing, reaching, and relaxing through their limits. The best distance runners run relaxed, breathe steadily and consistently, relax muscles with periodic exhalation, scan muscles for tension, and focus on localized relaxation of tense areas. They use only those muscles required, relax nonessential muscles (including jaw and shoulder muscles), and relax working muscles in the recovery stage to conserve energy and run more efficiently. You can learn to relax your nonworking muscles while other muscles are working hard and learn to relax your working muscles in the recovery phase of sequential movements—if you focus on doing it in training. You know where all those muscles are; you simply have to practice tuning in to them and telling them what to do at critical moments.

By relaxing and focusing on specific things you want to happen within your body, you can effect physiological changes in your muscle tension, heart rate, blood pressure, respiratory rate, blood flow, and body temperature. You can even influence your rate of recovery from injury. When attempting to direct such changes, clearly visualize or think into the part of the body you want to influence. Then imagine and feel the desired change taking place (see chapter 9 and "Additional Resources" at the end of this book for more about this technique).

Applying Intensity and Relaxation

Think of your own performances. Did you ever fall short of your goals because you were too tight, rigid, anxious, tense, or stressed? Did you ever fail to achieve your best performance because you were too complacent or not really going after your goals? If the answer to these questions is yes, the way to resolve the problem is to "flip your switch" or "change channels" so that you bring your best focus into each of your performances and remain fully connected to what works best for you throughout your performance. Personal best performances occur when mind and muscle combine through focus and execution in a free-flowing way.

Reaching High-Level Goals
Thomas Grandi's Story

The story of Thomas Grandi, a world-class skier and person, demonstrates the critical role of focus and combining intensity and relaxation to reach high-level goals. I met Thomas Grandi at a dryland training camp in Alberta, Canada, and worked collaboratively with him for the remainder of his athletic career. When we met he had been racing against the best skiers in the world on the World Cup circuit for more than 12 years. He was 32 years old and still dreamed of winning a World Cup race.

Thomas's skiing events (giant slalom and slalom) require putting together two great runs on the same day because the times for two separate runs are combined for the final result. On some occasions Thomas had a great first run but a disappointing second run, and on other occasions he had a disappointing first run and a great second run. He had never been able to put together great back-to-back runs to win a World Cup race.

Thomas had the potential to win. He had been right up there with the best in the world on one run. Athletes do not lose their technical or physical skills from one run to the next, so it was clear to me that his success was related to his race focus and bringing the right level of relaxed intensity into each race run.

In our first meeting we talked a lot about focus and intensity, consistency of best performances, and his dream goals and reasons for wanting to achieve those goals. His reasons for still competing on the World Cup circuit were to live his dream of winning a World Cup race, to be the first male skier from his country ever to win a World Cup race in his disciplines, to give something back to the people who had supported him over the years, and to inspire younger ski racers who looked up to him and who would follow in his footsteps or ski tracks.

I asked Thomas what he focused on in his best-ever race run. He said that he mentally prepared himself for that run and that at the top of the hill about a minute before the start, he decided to really go for it—to attack from top to bottom. When he had a poor second run following a great first run, it was usually because he didn't want to blow it, or ski out of the course, because then he would have no result at all. When he had a great second run after a poor or mediocre first run, he really attacked the second run to make up for the poor showing on the first run and thought that he had nothing to lose.

So I said to Thomas, "Why don't you just decide to do it, to really go after it, before every race. Prepare well for the specific race, and a minute or two before that race run, just decide to do it—first run and second run! Attack from top to bottom and everywhere in between. What are you waiting for?"

He laughed and I laughed, but the question was a serious one that had serious consequences for his goals and his career in ski racing. At 32 or 33 years old, most athletes feel some urgency to do what they really want to do while still fully capable of doing it. Thomas was already starting to have recurring back problems and later some knee issues. We spoke about the urgency of deciding to do something now—this year, this season—while he was still capable and motivated to do it.

Within the first few races of the new season he put together great back-to-back race runs and won his first-ever World Cup race. The following week at the next World Cup race, he did the same thing and won again. Back-to-back World Cup wins against the best ski racers in the world—finally, he was living his dream. He had the best season of his life and followed that up the next year with an even better overall season.

Shortly before the beginning of that World Cup race season, I asked Thomas if we could do a short interview together so that I could share some of his journey with the readers of *In Pursuit of Excellence*. He said that he would be honored to do it. Here is a portion of that interview.*

*Excerpts from Thomas Grandi's e-mail interview courtesy of Thomas Grandi.

Terry: What did we do together that you feel helped you most in terms of pursuing and achieving your goals?

Thomas: I think that by talking about certain aspects of ski racing, I learned more about myself and the areas that I needed to improve. I can remember sitting down with you and talking about what I thought I needed to break through the last mental barrier. We talked about creating a sense of urgency that would make me ski the way I wanted to ski, taking risks, skiing every run like it was my last, and really taking advantage of every race. I created my sense of urgency by telling myself I was getting older, that each race was an opportunity I could never have back, and that I needed to seize every opportunity like it was my last. We also talked about creating a greater purpose, which would help me on those days when I didn't feel like pushing the limits and taking risks. My greater purpose was to put ski racing and specifically my events, GS and SL [giant slalom and slalom], on the front page. These two elements enabled me and pushed me to get out of my comfort zone and discover what was possible.

Terry: What are the most important lessons that you learned from me?

Thomas: One of the best lessons I learned from you was to analyze my race right after it, look at the good and bad, make notes of both and how I could be better in the next race, and move on. I used to have trouble dealing with both good and bad races. When I had a good race I would relive it too often and forget to prepare for the upcoming race. When I had a bad race I would also relive it and punish myself for my poor performance, beating myself up mentally. By writing race debriefs I learned to take the good and the bad, figure out how I could be better, and move on. I think this process really freed me to perform well consistently.

Terry: What does being focused in training and focused in races mean to you? Can you describe what it is, what it feels like, or how it unfolds for you?

Thomas: I would say that my focusing ability has evolved since I started working with you. I think a lot of athletes, including me, are constantly looking to get into the elusive "zone." You taught me that it doesn't have to be elusive, that I can actually control and enter the zone when I want to, by focusing to my fullest. In my two victories I can remember being fully focused. In Flachau, for example, after my first win, I was so relaxed that I knew exactly when to flip the switch. Ten minutes before my run I put my music on, cut out all the distractions in the start area, and enter my own world. I have done my warm-up by this point, so now I am actually calming myself down. My breathing becomes very steady, and I am not concerned about what anyone else is doing. It's all about me.

If I look at someone I look right through them. If I see people talking or laughing, their words don't register. I become fully grounded and present in the moment. When I enter the start, I tell myself, *This race is now, and I can never have it back. I need to ski with aggression and no regrets.* Occasionally I'll have one technical cue that I focus on. But in Flachau I was confident that everything was in me, so I didn't need to think at all. As long as I was present, I could react to anything and everything. I skied as though time were standing still. Although I was skiing the fastest I had ever skied and skiing a very aggressive direct line, I felt as if I had all the time in the world. I was truly enjoying my performance. I was in complete control. I could change the radius of the turn if I chose to.

On the second run the course started in complete sunshine, but halfway down it plunged into dark shadows that made it extremely difficult to see. I can remember saying to myself, *Holy shit, I can't see a thing.* For a split second I hesitated until I told myself my refocusing cue, which at the time was *Go now!* Those words clicked, and I charged through the flat light carving the last turns to the finish. In the finish when I saw my time I started to laugh, because I had taken the lead by over a second. I was living my dream and enjoying it to the fullest. I just let it come pouring out of me, and it was one of the best moments of my life.

Terry: That was a great example of refocusing instantly within the heat of the race when you moved into shadows and couldn't see. Can you comment on the value of refocusing to get back on a positive track in your sport?

Thomas: An alpine skier rarely has a mistake-free run. It happens occasionally, but typically you make one or two mistakes coming down the course. The ability to refocus quickly is critical. When a mistake happens there is no time to think about why it happened—it is a time to start racing again as quickly as possible. I have some key words to refocus, and it's as simple as *Come on!* I have learned to refocus and recover quickly and get back up to speed as quickly as possible.

Terry: How did you get yourself to continue to go after your dreams when things weren't going well?

Thomas: It sometimes surprises me that I did make it through the rough times. I guess I had this deep belief that I could do what I had set out to do, even though the results I was having showed the contrary. I learned to surround myself with positive people who believe anything is possible.

Terry: Part of our plan for ongoing improvement was to pull out positive things from every performance, to assess your focus, and to act on the lessons learned. How did you do that during the years we worked together?

Thomas: The biggest part of evaluating my performances was my race debriefs. Because I was committed to doing one after every race, good or
bad, I learned the hard lessons that usually I would have rather swept under the rug and forgotten. It also showed me that even in a bad race there
are positives, and in a good race there are lessons to be remembered and
improved on. We refocused on a simple game plan based on what I knew
worked best for me. If I had followed my instinct to forget all about my bad
performances without analyzing what had gone wrong, I can guarantee
that I would have never won those two races.

Terry: What kind of a commitment did t take to achieve your goals in your
sport?

Thomas: Every decision I make is weighed on whether or not it will help me
in my quest. If something is not going to help me in this quest, it probably
won't happen. To reach the top of any sport requires a huge time commitment and huge desire.

Terry: I am interested in how your confidence changed since we began working together. Can you comment on that?

Thomas: The biggest change in how I approach ski racing is definitely in my
confidence to focus when I need to. When I started working with you, the
fact that you had such a successful track record, and that you believed in
me and what I was doing, gave me a big boost. Then when we designed
my race plan I knew I was doing all the right things leading up to my races.
The race plan routine set me at ease and allowed me to relax in the start
gate. As I realized the race focus plan worked, I gained more and more
confidence in it. This freed me. It allowed me to really relax so that I could
attack from the first gate all the way to the finish. The more I race, and the
more I put myself in situations that require me to focus, the more I am learning that I can fully focus whenever I choose to.

Part of what allowed Thomas to live his dream was all the work he did on
developing the physical and technical skills required to compete and win at
this level. He had already developed those skills before I met him. The other
part, the part that was missing, was deciding to take full control over his destiny
by focusing in ways that would allow him to live his dream. The final step up,
the one that took him to the top of the podium, came from focusing on the right
things at the right time and understanding that the control switch was always
within his own focus—first run, second run, and every run.

During the time we worked together, Thomas and I had regular e-mail contact to prepare for the season and stay on track during the season. Some key
points from our interaction that he believed helped him achieve the best results
of his life appear here. I hope that they help you on your mission to personal
excellence.

Race Perspective

The perspective and focus that you take into your races or performances sets
the stage for how you perform. In a very real way, your performance outcomes

are dictated by what you do, think about, and focus on before your game, race, or event even begins. You can set yourself up for success or failure based on the perspective you carry into your performance and the extent to which you respect your best focus for the duration of your performance. A positive race perspective allowed Thomas to perform his best.

Thomas: Every race presents a unique opportunity to win, to learn, to grow, to live my dream. My goal for every race, every run, is to seize each opportunity. I race every race with the intention of winning. I race to win! I focus fully on doing what will free me to win. Today's race, this moment, this opportunity will never exist again. Today can never be lived again, so I embrace it with my absolute focus and my heart and soul.

Training Goals

The focus that you take into your training sets the stage for how you perform. The purpose of training is to prepare you to do the great things you would like to do in your races, games, performances, or competitions. Ensure that your training prepares you to do the things you have to do to perform to your true potential in your races or performances. This focus in training allowed Thomas to train his best.

Thomas: I push myself harder in training, not every run, but at least a couple per day. I go past my comfort zone so that I know I can go there and still pull it off. I pick the runs that I want to push hard in, in advance, and then commit to doing it. Going past my comfort zone in training will help me race to my potential more often.

Performance Reminders

In high-performance pursuits, reminders are extremely important. Reminders of what you want to do and how you intend to do it are critically important because they allow you to achieve the consistency you are seeking, in both training and competitions. Your personal reminders are specific to you and your performance discipline. Some athletes benefit from technical reminders during their warm-up before competitions. The following technical reminders worked best for Thomas:

+ Push the line longer and straighter down the hill.
+ Open the stance and be relaxed in the ankles and knees.
+ Stand taller and stay ahead of the course.
+ Anticipate and react well to rhythm changes.
+ Push the line down the hill longer and smoother into the new turn.

To make sure that your technical reminders are fresh in your mind and body shortly before you perform, imagine the feeling of performing that way. Recalling that feeling will free you to perform your best more automatically, without having to think.

Final Prerace Reminders

Thomas took the following final focus reminders into his best races. The purpose of these reminders was to help him focus in ways that consistently brought out his best possible performance. As you read over his race-day reminders, notice that three interrelated themes are present:

1. attack and really go for it,
2. stay relaxed, and
3. trust yourself and your focus.

See what you can find in the following focus reminders that might help you in your personal pursuit of excellence:

+ Trust myself. No matter what happened in training leading up to this day, I can do it on race day when it counts. In the morning, I know that I am going to attack the hill, relax, and do it.
+ Ski relaxed, smooth, and aggressive. Charge down the pitch and keep the skis going down the hill, as clean as possible.
+ Remember how I felt last year. I had a chance to podium, but I watched as others came down and knocked me off the podium. I could have skied faster, but instead I hoped that others would make a mistake. That isn't the way to win. I control my own destiny. Go out there and get it!
+ Out of the start, attack right away. Relax from the first gate right to the bottom. Do a great inspection—know exactly where to go. Get the direction, trust it, and go. Free myself to take the chances I need to be fast.
+ There are no sections on this course that I can't rip. Rip it from top to bottom, with no backing off. Stay grounded, stay focused top to bottom for two runs, and be relaxed and aggressive. Trust myself.
+ Charge out of the start, look for speed, and push the line.
+ Focus forward, keep my body forward, and use a relaxed attack. Don't save anything. Spend everything I have.
+ Go full out from top to bottom. Have relaxed ankles and knees (grounded in my boots) and supple legs. Look for speed.

Race Debriefs

The major purpose of performance debriefs is to help you understand what focus works best for you and what interferes with your best performance focus. When something goes well, you must embrace and remember the lessons related to what made it go so well. When something does not go well, it is equally important to draw out the lessons about why it did not go well.

In two of his best-ever races, Thomas included the following comments in his race debrief:

> The morning of the race I went through my reasons for urgency and really cued in on this: every race is a new opportunity, and my oppor-

tunities are numbered. Had a great warm-up before the race, one free run beside the race hill, and one run in the gates. Ten minutes before my run I flipped the switch.

Before my runs I was so focused I was almost meditative. I had a clear mind and was extremely grounded in the present. I remember thinking when I got in the gate that I'd rather be nowhere else in the world but here. It was my turn for a minute and a half, and I was *on!*

Even when you reach the top of your field, you have to continue to respect and fine-tune your best focus if you want to perform consistently at that level. The following exchanges with Thomas and the lessons drawn from these exchanges provide specific examples of how you can turn disappointment into positive focused action.

Thomas: I was not feeling 100 percent going into today's race. My GS skiing has not been feeling like it should. In training I have been making small mistakes far too often. I am attacking as hard as I can, and I am not very fast.

Terry: You are attacking as hard as you can, but are you also relaxing enough? Are you using your relaxed attack—relaxed ankles, supple legs? Sometimes relaxing a little more gives more fluidity and more speed.

Lesson: Sometimes when you are feeling pressure to perform, you let your focus slip away from what will free you to perform your best. In this situation, the attack was in full force but the relaxing was missing.

Thomas: I was feeling the pressure of being the defending champion and having a lot of supporters out to watch the race. I also drew number 1, which always creates a little more tension. But I skied aggressively. I attacked the hill as hard as I could, but I didn't ski as cleanly as I can. I know that I could have run the last part of the course straighter.

Terry: When you are feeling pressure, shift focus to the doing. The way to the results that you are seeking is to let go of thoughts of results and focus fully on how you are going to race this course. It always comes back to full focus on the doing, on being in the moment, on getting your focus in the right place—body forward, focus forward, relaxed ankles, relaxed attack, straighter line. Free yourself, trust yourself, and trust your focus. When you race, most things happen too fast to think your way down the course, so let your focus lead you, focus ahead, ski by intuition, and go for it—top to bottom.

Lesson: When expectations are high, you must focus fully on the doing and nothing else. Go back to the focus that freed you to perform your best. Remind yourself of that focus. Respect that focus. Keep things simple. Use one or two reminders and go.

Thomas: I skied aggressively. I attacked the hill as hard as I could and relaxed my ankles. I am happy with my approach to stay focused in light of the pressure and distractions. I know that I could have run the last part of the course straighter, but I am skiing really well.

Terry: Great—build on this! Keep working on your relaxed attack. Then everything will be where we want it to be.

Lesson: You can refocus and get back on track even when your focus has temporarily shifted to outcomes. When you bring your focus back to doing what frees you to perform well, the outcomes take care of themselves.

Ups and downs are always present in high-performance pursuits. As long as you keep returning to a focus that is positive and constructive for you, you will arrive at your desired destination. Remind yourself of the focus that has brought out your best in the past. Focus on what is most relevant for you right now and act on that focus.

Simple Reminders to Guide You

+ Decide to do what you really want to do.
+ Once you have decided, connect fully with your performance.
+ Let nothing get between you and your performance. Pure focus, pure connection, is the only place to be.
+ Remember that you are fully capable of performing your best.
+ Free your body to do what it is capable of doing.
+ Free yourself to perform with relaxed intensity.

Essentially, performance excellence is all about flipping the focus switch to absorb yourself completely in what works best for you and doing it consistently, not just for one run, one race, one shift, one class, one interaction, one performance, one period, one at-bat, one inning, one quarter, one round, one shot, or one game but for every experience—top to bottom, start to finish, first second to last second.

Remember, you can choose the perspective and focus that you take into your performances. You can decide to perform with relaxed intensity. You have many reasons to believe in yourself and your capacity. You are fortunate to be out there doing what you love to do. Respect the focus that works best for you and embrace the simple joys of the journey!

CHAPTER 7
Distraction Control

Remove the barriers and distractions of your own making that are preventing you from doing what you really want to do and getting to where you really want to go. A negative and disconnected focus is your worst enemy, and a positive and fully connected focus is your best friend.

Distractions—both internal and external—create the greatest barriers to consistent high-level performance. Maintaining a positive and fully connected focus in the face of distractions is the most important focusing skill required for becoming a great athlete, team, or performer in any high-performance discipline. Developing your skills for positive focusing, positive refocusing, and staying positive and fully connected in the face of distractions is essential for ongoing excellence in any high-performance pursuit. A sustained positive and fully connected focus is also a requirement for excelling at living. If you want to perform your best consistently, choose to be your best in your most important events, challenges, or competitions and choose to live your life fully and joyfully. To perform your best and live your life fully, it is essential that you master the critical skills of positive and fully connected focusing and positive distraction control.

You can begin to master your best focus right now by planning to focus in positive and fully connected ways and by regularly practicing your best focus and most effective refocusing skills. To perform your best in important events, you must learn to respect and sustain your best focus in the face of potential distractions. If your positive and fully focused connection is broken, you must find a way to refocus quickly to regain a positive and fully connected performance focus. Athletes, performers, learners, and teams who remain positive and fully connected to executing their task in the face of ongoing distractions have the best chance of performing their best and winning big or important events. If you want to become one of those winning athletes or performers, work on respecting and sustaining your best focus and continue to work on perfecting your best distraction control skills.

Start by writing down a list of distractions you usually face—or might face—in training, competitions, races, games, or performance contexts. Use the Distraction Control Plan later in this chapter to write down the distractions you will likely face and how you would prefer to focus through each of your potential distractions. Choose a simple refocusing reminder that will help you shift your focus or change channels quickly (from negative to positive, not confident to confident, or disconnected to fully connected). Practice using your positive refocusing reminder to quickly shift your focus from negative to positive or from disconnected to being fully connected with what will free you to perform your best. This simple shift in focus from negative to positive and disconnected to fully connected will empower you to believe in yourself and your preparation, feel your best, perform your best, and fully embrace the opportunities presented to you over the course of your life. Continue to find positive and fully connected ways to get your focus working for you and not against you in all parts of your life!

Potential distractions are an ever-present part of sport and other meaningful performance contexts, relationships, personal development opportunities, and everyday life. Distractions come from a variety of sources—people who are negative, destructive, or not empathetic; negative interactions or environments; your own or others' expectations; winning or losing; injuries; coaches, teammates, or competitors; officials; media; financial concerns; educational concerns; changes in your performance levels or inconsistent performances; making the team or not making the team; changes in familiar patterns; negative thinking before, during, or after practices, games, or performances; maintaining healthy nutrition at home and on the road; and concerns about retirement, transitions, or quality of life after leaving high-performance sport or excelling in other high-performance disciplines.

Respecting Your Own Best Focus

One of the most important lessons you can learn as an athlete, performer, coach, teacher, parent, student, teammate, or person in any other performance field who wants to be the best you can possibly be is how to control, respect, and improve your own best focus. The greatest gift you can give yourself right now and for the rest of your life is to respect your own best focus and make it more consistent. This alone can empower you to become the positive, competent fully connected person and performer you really want to be and have the potential to be, now and for the rest of your life.

In competitive contexts, demanding work environments, and highly charged performance environments, potential distractions can increase substantially. The good news is that you can "**do**cide" whether you let those potential distractions distract you, upset you, lower your confidence, put you in a negative frame of mind, take you out of your best focus, or interfere with your best performance. How you choose to respond to daily challenges and ongoing opportunities is within your control. Something becomes a distraction only if you let it distract you. Otherwise, it is simply something that happens as you go through your day, your competition, your preparation, or your performance. You can choose to be distracted by it or not be distracted by it, to dwell on it or let it go. You decide, and you live with the consequences of your decisions. Remember that your best focus is always within your potential control precisely because it is *your focus* and it lives within you no matter where you are or what you are engaged in.

You don't have to let what you have normally seen as a distraction have a negative effect on your mood, focus, or performance. You don't lose your performance skills because of distractions; you let yourself lose the focus that allows you or frees you to execute your skills fluidly and effectively. You may face situations or decisions that you feel are unfair or experience performances or interactions that do not go as planned. You may find these situations frustrating, but you are not obliged to react by putting yourself or others down, feeling highly stressed, giving up, or questioning your own value as a human being or your capacity as an athlete or performer. Unexpected disruptions may occur, such as schedule changes, delays, incompetent

Darrell Walker/Icon Sportswire

Candace Parker doesn't let distractions shake her confidence. You, too, can choose to overcome distractions.

people, lack of personal space, differences in food choices, or less than best accommodations or facilities. You don't have to let these events or circumstances overcome you or let your positive focus slip away. You probably want to have a great performance, great game, or great result more than anything else, and you are fully capable of doing that. In performance situations there is no value in worrying about the little things you do not control or worrying about outcomes. Simply remind yourself to focus in positive and fully connected ways that will free you to perform your best, given the conditions and challenges you are facing. When you are competing or performing in a high-performance context different from anything you have experienced before, you can still respect your normal preperformance preparation routines and focusing patterns that have worked best for you in the past. Simply respect the focus that works best for you, remind yourself of why you can achieve your goals, and fully embrace the opportunity in front of you.

You can find a way over, around, or through almost all obstacles by committing yourself to remaining positive, turning negatives into positives, drawing out positive lessons, looking for reasons to continue to believe in yourself and your capacity, and maintaining or quickly regaining a positive and fully connected focus. When you react negatively or emotionally to distractions or potential obstacles, you risk defeating yourself. Negative emotions often distract us from our best performance focus and leave us feeling mentally and physically exhausted. This in turn can increase your risk of becoming more distracted, exhausted, or sick, which obviously can hurt your performance and add still another stress factor. Don't waste your emotional energy on things that are not within your control because this will not help your performance, or the overall picture of your life.

When you are facing potentially stressful situations, additional rest is a blessing. If you are well rested, you will cope better, focus better, learn better, and perform better. Take time to relax, rest, and do some simple things that lift your spirits before and after potentially stressful experiences. Set simple daily goals and plan each day to ensure that you get some good rest, have some quiet time to yourself just to relax, do some things you enjoy, and gain a positive sense of control over yourself and your life. This will help you feel more in control, more relaxed, more positive, and more capable of managing potentially stressful people or environments.

At major competitions or in other challenging situations, if you step back and look at distractions from a distance, you realize that most of them are little things that are quickly resolved. They aren't worth the expenditure of a lot of emotional energy. The following pointers will help you stay on a positive track or get back on track quickly:

+ Commit yourself to remaining positive and relaxed.
+ Focus on doing what will help you stay positive and in control. A strong positive focus protects you from distractions.

✦ Get yourself into a positive state of mind before your event and stay fully focused on doing your job within the event; then things will flow smoothly.

✦ Look for advantages in every situation, even if the conditions are less than ideal. Look for good reasons you can still be positive, focused, confident, relaxed, optimistic, and fully capable of performing your best.

✦ Find the positives in the situations you are experiencing. Find the good things in yourself, look for the good things in others, and focus on embracing simple highlights in each day. At the end of the day, record your highlights in your highlight journal. This will keep you on a positive and life-enhancing path.

✦ Remind yourself that distractions do not have to totally consume you. At a tournament, competition venue, game, or performance site, things may happen to you that are unfair or unexpected. You cannot control those circumstances, but you can control how you react to them. Why compound the problem by focusing your positive energy on negative things that are beyond your immediate control? Simply focus on what *you* control and let the rest go!

✦ Expect conditions to be different at important events or major competitions. Expect a faster pace, a busier place, and more delays or waiting around. Prepare yourself to face these potential distractions in a relaxed, positive way. If something begins to irritate you, let those feelings go with as little wasted energy as possible. They are not worth wasting your energy on. Let them bounce off you easily and focus on the good things you are going to do.

✦ Expect people to behave differently at high-stress events, even those who normally are calm, supportive, and understanding. Observe them with interest, but don't take responsibility for their behavior. Look for your own strength. Remind yourself of what you came here to do and where your focus needs to be to do it. Refuse to let anything or anyone get in the way of your best focus.

✦ Know that you can enjoy this experience and perform well, regardless of the circumstances you may be facing. Embrace the simple steps and joys of this journey.

Distraction control skills are a valuable asset in all parts of your life. Prepare yourself to make positive focusing and distraction control your normal way of being. You can do this by acting in the following ways:

✦ Make a commitment to yourself to remain positive and focused every day and act on that commitment every day. Decide to think and act in positive, self-enhancing ways every day. If things are not going well, stop and refocus on something positive. If necessary, take a little time-out to find your own quiet space, do some relaxed breathing, focus on the positives in your day and your life, and then connect fully with something joyful or meaningful within your control.

+ Practice getting back on a positive track quickly. For example, if things don't go well in training, while performing, or in your personal life, take advantage of the opportunity to practice changing mental channels and refocusing into a more positive, constructive, or joyful state of mind.

+ Remind yourself repeatedly that you can change your focus and per-spective to where you want them to be. Then focus fully on doing it. Remember that you are the boss of your focus!

+ Remain open to staying focused on the positives and letting go of stress or distractions. Some athletes with whom I worked found it helpful to imagine themselves surrounded by an invisible bubble or force field that protected them from unwanted stress or distractions at the performance site. Negative comments, distractions, or hassles simply bounced off their protective shield as they focused on moving toward their positive goals step by step.

+ Be the best you can be with your focus today—then draw out the les-sons, learn from them, act on what you learned, and move forward in positive ways. Continue to focus on what helps you do what you want to do and what is within your control.

+ After a mediocre, good, or great day, be proud of your efforts and remember something you did well. Think about where your focus was when you were performing your best. Look for the positive focusing lessons that can help you with your ongoing improvement. Grab the positive focusing lessons from every day. Then start fresh tomorrow—a brand-new day.

+ If you want additional activities that can help you become better at focusing through distractions and finding the positives and simple joys in every day, read *Positive Living Skills: Joy and Focus for Everyone* (Orlick, 2011) and listen to my audio CDs: *Focusing Through Distrac-tions: Positive Living Skills for Tweens, Teens, and Adults (CD 3), Relaxation and Joyful Living: Positive Living Skills for Tweens, Teens, and Adults (CD 4), Focusing for Excellence: Performing in the Zone (CD 4), and Relaxation and Stress Control Activities (CD 1).* For additional information, audio CDs, and recent Zone of Excellence performance and life enhancement educational materials, see Additional Resources in the back of this book, email me at excel@zoneofexcellence.ca, or go to www.zoneofexcellence.ca.

Your best on-site preperformance focus is to focus on preparing yourself for your own best performance and then focus fully on executing your best performance—something over which you have control. Respect and embrace your best focus patterns. Your best performance focus comes from respecting and embracing your best focus for the duration of your event. Choose to fully embrace the focus that works best for you from start to finish and everywhere in between. If you want to perform to your true capacity on a consistent basis, this is the only place to be. You are not asking yourself to do anything unreasonable, only to focus in ways that will free you to perform to your current capacity. Your goal is to simply free yourself to execute your performance the way you want to do it, the way you are capable of doing it! Immerse yourself in the process of doing—that is your primary goal. Your body will follow your focus when you send it clear, positive, focused messages and then just let it happen. Trust your preparation. Trust your body. Trust your focus. Trust your intuition. Free yourself to do what you know in your heart and soul you can do. Release yourself from all other thoughts or concerns, and connect fully with the doing!

Creating a Positive and Effective Refocusing Plan for Potential Distractions

Most people could share an experience from their daily performances or interactions in which they lost their best focus and were not able to regain it quickly. Think of a recent situation at practice or during training; at a competition, performance, or game; in a relationship; or while presenting in front of a group when you lost your best focus. You got angry, distracted, or lost your pure and positive fully focused connection with your performance in some context. Looking back now, how do you think you could have responded more positively, more effectively, or in a more fully connected way in that situation? If you were in a similar situation now, facing a similar challenge, what could you do to not let it bother or distract you? What could you do to stay positive, fully focused, and in control? What could you do to rise above potential distractions? When you get really good at focusing through distractions, almost everything that could have been a distraction bounces off you with minimal or no disturbance. You stay cool, calm, focused, fully engaged, positive, and effective, and if you lose your best focus momentarily, you know how to change channels to get back on a positive track very quickly. This will continue to help you do what you need to do to be your best in your training and performance contexts. Keep reading through this section to find a way to help yourself do this.

Remember that your focus is *your focus*. You decide where you direct your focus and what you need to focus on in different contexts! Your focus dictates whether something becomes a distraction or a problem for you in the first place. How you direct your focus also empowers you to eliminate distractions or potential problems. Essentially, your focus can create problems or distractions or allow you to eliminate problems or distractions. This is why developing and sustaining a positive and fully connected focus is so critical to your performance and life.

Every self-directed positive change is led by three simple steps:

1. Create a positive vision. In this case, create a positive vision of a better way for you to view and respond to potential distractions.

2. Create a positive plan. In this case, develop a positive plan for how you can respond to distractions or potential distractions in positive and effective ways.

3. Make a "docision" to act on your positive plan, again and again and again, until it becomes a natural part of who you are and what you do.

Developing your personal focusing and refocusing plan and acting on it every day will help you make the positive changes you are seeking. It will empower you to be more in control of your actions and more focused on the right things when you face potential distractions in your performances and life. You can begin creating your personal distraction control plan right now by responding to the following questions:

1. What do you want to change or improve about how you see and respond to distractions or potential distractions in your practices, performances, work, relationships, or life?

2. Why do you want to change how you see and respond to distractions or potential distractions in these parts of your performance or life? Why is it important for you to make these changes?

3. Write down a personal distraction control plan today. Docide to act on this plan repeatedly until you gain control over your focus and your distractions. This will help you to make the positive changes you are seeking. Remind yourself of why it is important to have a personal distraction control plan and why it is essential for you to act on your plan in positive and effective ways. The bottom line is that you need an effective plan to control distractions and to focus through distractions in your performance world. Thinking about it is not enough—only positive action counts.

After you have responded to the three distraction control questions from the previous list, you are ready to complete your distraction control plan (see figure 7.1). Many of the athletes I have worked with have successfully used this tool to help them pinpoint their distractions and reminders for focusing effectively with those distractions. Some athletes carry a one-page plan with them to competitions or major events until their reminders and positive actions are automated and inside their heads.

Figure 7.1 Distraction Control Plan

Distractions	Usual response	Preferred response	Refocus reminders

From T. Orlick, 2015, *In pursuit of excellence*, 5th ed. (Champaign, IL: Human Kinetics).

In the first column of the distraction control plan, list the major distractions or refocusing situations you have faced in the past or are likely to face in the future, those that have interfered or could interfere with your best focus or performance. Think about the key distractions that can happen in your performance world or in your mind that prevent you from being your best, feeling your best, focusing your best, and performing your best. The distractions you list and target for improvement can include anything relevant to you in your performance context. For example, you might identify something that happens to you before, during, or after a practice, competition, or performance or what happens at home, school, or work or within your daily interactions or relationships.

In the second column, indicate your usual response to these distractions. Consider what you were thinking, saying to yourself, or focusing on when you faced these distractions.

In the third column, indicate how you would prefer to respond in each of these situations now and in the future. What would you prefer to think, say to yourself, or focus on the next time you face this potentially distracting situation?

In the fourth column, write down a powerful refocusing reminder you can use in this situation to get your focus back to where you want it to be, back to where it is most beneficial to you and your performance. List key reminders you can say or think to yourself the next time you face each of the distractions you listed in the first column. Write down simple reminders that you can use in the heat of the moment to refocus and quickly get back on a positive and fully connected track.

Effective real-world refocusing reminders that can be used in potentially stressful situations often begin with a reminder to breathe. You are probably breathing anyway, so you can just focus on your breathing—take one long, slow, deep breath in followed by one long, slow, deep breath out. Then you can shift to a focus reminder that has personal meaning for you. Here are some examples:

+ Breathe, relax.
+ Focus, focus, focus.
+ Connect, connect, connect.
+ Docide, docide, docide.
+ Change channels. Change channels.
+ Focus only on my preparation—my game plan—my focus plan.
+ Focus only on what is within my immediate control—nothing else matters.
+ This (potential distraction) does not have to bother me—*park it* or *tree it*.

- ✦ Let it go, let it go, and focus on the next step.
- ✦ I can perform well regardless of what happened before this moment.
- ✦ Be totally here. Be in the moment. Nothing else matters.
- ✦ I control my focus—it's my choice. It's my focus!
- ✦ Shift focus back to what will do me the most good—now!

You only need one or two simple but powerful focus reminders that you decide to act on to stay in control or to regain control. Remember that the focus control switch always lies within you. Decide to flip the switch. Decide to change channels whenever you feel it is in your best interest to do so.

Acting on Your Plan

Once you have a refocusing plan that clearly outlines how you would prefer to focus and refocus in specific important situations, your goal is to act on your refocusing plan in positive ways every day. Use every available opportunity to practice fully connected focusing and positive refocusing so you can respond quickly and effectively to situations that may have distracted you in the past. Also consider other situations that could distract you or interfere with your best focus. Practice your focusing and refocusing skills so that you can fine-tune your skills for focusing and refocusing through distractions and improve the overall consistency of your best performances.

The next time something distracts you—a negative thought, comment, or image; a missed move or opportunity; too much thinking; a loss of positive or fully connected focus—challenge yourself to turn it around within that setting. Set a goal to regain your positive and fully connected focus with your performance as quickly as possible. The next time you are about to become upset because of what you or someone else said or did, shift your focus to something that will allow you to respond in a more positive way. Refocusing in positive and constructive ways is one of life's great challenges and great gifts. If doing it was easy, everyone would be great at it, but few of us are because we don't plan and practice doing it.

Nevertheless, each of us has the capacity to significantly improve our skills for sustaining and regaining our best focus in more positive and fully connected ways. Make this your daily goal. Whenever or wherever you are successful, make a note of what you focused on to achieve and sustain that success. Keep doing and learning from the good things that work for you to reach your desired destination.

Changing Focus
Sylvie Bernier

Sylvie Bernier, an Olympic champion in diving, began to work seriously on distraction control about one and a half years before she won her Olympic gold medal. Previously, she had suffered from distractions that resulted in less than best performances, especially on the last dives of a competition. One of Sylvie's main distractions in big competitions was paying attention to the scoreboard (leaderboard) instead of focusing fully on her own dives. In her own words:

> I started to shift away from the scoreboard a year and a half before the Olympics because I knew that every time I looked at the scoreboard, my heart went crazy. I couldn't control it. I knew that I dove better if I concentrated on my diving instead of concentrating on everyone else. It was harder to get ready for 10 dives than to get ready for 1 dive, so I decided to stop looking at everyone else, to just be myself and focus on preparing for my next dive. That was the best way for me to concentrate for my event. I knew I could win, but I had to dive well. I stopped saying, *This diver's doing this, so she's going to miss this one,* or *If she misses one, I'm going to win.*
>
> At the Olympics I really focused on my dives instead of on other divers. That was the biggest change in those two years. Before that, I used to watch the event. I'd watch the Chinese and think, *Oh, how can she do that? She's a great diver.* Then I thought, *I'm as good as anyone else, so let's stop talking about them and focus on my own dives.* That was an important step in my career.

Recovering From Setbacks

Silken Laumann, an Olympic medalist and world champion in rowing, had the unfortunate experience of having a men's rowing crew run right through her boat, breaking it in half, during her warm-up at an international regatta in Essen, Germany. She sustained a serious injury to her lower leg and severed her calf muscle. This happened eight weeks before the 1992 Summer Olympics in Barcelona. She flew home for surgery and rehabilitation and had five reconstructive operations to repair her leg.

Almost everyone assumed that it would be impossible for her to compete in Barcelona. She showed up at the Olympics, limping and walking with the help of a cane. Her competitors asked her if she was there as a media commentator for rowing. She said, "No, I am here to compete." Their mouths dropped open in disbelief. Silken had decided that she didn't really need that leg to row and that she was going to compete anyway, although she had done only limited on-water training over those last eight weeks leading into the Olympic Games.

When race day came at the Olympics, Silken limped down to her boat and needed help to get in. She managed to qualify for the Olympic final. In the final race, halfway down the course, she was still with the leading group. At that point in the race she was feeling so tired that she thought she could not pull another stroke. At that instant, she refocused by deciding to pull 10 strokes. *Anyone can pull 10 strokes,* she thought. So she pulled 10 strokes, and then another 10 strokes, and then another 10 strokes, all the way to the finish line. When she looked up at the scoreboard after crossing the line, there was her name—Silken Laumann, bronze medal.

After the race, she commented, "I was up for a completely committed effort. . . . I'd come so far and thought that if I could commit just a little more energy, I could win a medal." And she did, by breaking her huge challenge into little pieces—only 10 strokes, an effort she thought anyone could get through. Four years later at the 1996 Summer Olympics in Atlanta, Silken won a silver medal and retired from competitive rowing to pursue other meaningful challenges in life.

Lori Fung, Olympic champion in rhythmic gymnastics, provides another example of recovering from setbacks. Her goal in preparing herself for major competitions was to be consistent in all her performances and not to allow one bad move or routine affect the next. She discussed the importance of refocusing between events, especially after making an error:

> If you have a bad routine, you've got to get back to zero again. You just have to say, "OK, that's forgotten. It's totally forgotten. That's it." You go out, do the next one, pretend that the next one is the first routine of the day, and it is going to count. Otherwise, you are never going to get back on track again. You can't do anything about what already happened. You can't do anything about the score you're getting. You can't do anything about why you dropped that one move or how great it was; it's over and done with. Sometimes it's really hard to make yourself forget it, but the more you try, the better you're going to get at it in the future.

Keeping Your Focus

Laurie Graham, winner of many World Cup races in downhill skiing, discovered that to win at the highest levels she had to continue to focus through the potential distraction of small errors within a downhill race:

> Once I push out at the start, I am focused on where I am at the time. A lot of it is "line" in downhill. You don't go right at the gate. You've got the line that you have been running all week, and you just say, *OK, I've got to stay high here, I have to go direct here, I have to jump this jump,* so that you are aware of each obstacle as it comes. If I make a small mistake, often it doesn't even register for me until the end, when I'm at the bottom. At the time you are still thinking about going forward, about speed, about momentum. You don't carry the mistake down the hill. It is shelved until later. Often those mistakes will mean just running them

out, and it really won't cost you that much time if you don't panic, if you just get back on track.

The athlete stories you just read and additional athlete stories later in this book support my belief in the absolute power of a positive and fully connected focus. Focusing through distractions is clearly one of the most important skills for consistently performing to your potential in important challenges or high-level competitions. Perfecting and fine-tuning your focusing and refocusing skills requires a lot of focused practice. What focus do you want to carry today? Think about it. Make it clear in your mind. Know that you can make it happen today and every day. You have the capacity to bring that focus to your everyday pursuits—to live that focus today and every day in different contexts. You have the capacity to take control, to control your own destiny, and to make good or great things happen! Bring that focus into your everyday pursuits!

CHAPTER 8
Positive Images

Imagining positive possibilities can lead you to positive new realities in virtually all your meaningful human pursuits Almost anything is possible if you truly believe it is possible and you focus fully on doing it. Almost everything is impossible if you continue to tell yourself it is impossible. For hundreds or thousands of years almost all human beings believed it was impossible for a wagon or any kind of vehicle to move forward quickly on the ground without horses or other strong animals pulling it. That is, until one person imagined that it was possible and with the help of others turned that positive vision into a positive living reality.

At one time, virtually all people believed it was impossible for human beings to fly, until one person imagined that is was possible and found a way to turn that positive possibility into a positive living reality. Now millions of people are flying somewhere every day and some are preparing to fly to other planets.

Almost everything you want to achieve or explore is impossible if you continue to believe it is impossible. However, if you are able to open your mind and heart to the positive possibilities and believe it is possible for you to accomplish your goals and live your dreams, almost everything becomes possible. This is where positive imagery can become a huge advantage—where you imagine yourself being the way you want to be, performing the way you want to perform, and achieving the goals you want to achieve. Positive and fully focused performance imagery can help you to enhance your focusing skills and turn those positive images into a positive living reality.

Radio was impossible; television was impossible; movies were impossible; computers were impossible; flying to the moon was impossible; and smartphones, tablets, and Skype were impossible. Almost everything we do, see, experience, and embrace today was impossible until one person imagined it was possible and made a full commitment to turn that positive dream into a positive living reality.

Imagine yourself being the person and performer you really want to be, doing the things you want to do, training the way you want to train, performing the way you want to perform, embracing the life *you* want to live, appreciating the people supporting you on your journey to personal and performance excellence, and willfully continuing to embrace the simple joys of your ongoing journey to personal and performance excellence.

Thoughts, images, feelings, and sensations often run through our minds and bodies as we approach significant upcoming events in our lives. This may include something as simple as making or receiving an important phone call; doing something new or challenging for the first time; meeting someone new; asking someone to go out on a date (does anybody do that anymore?); performing for an audition or team selection; and preparing for a presentation, job interview, tryout, game, competition, or any major challenge.

When preparing for an important competition, performance, or event, do you think through, mentally rehearse, visualize, or engage in any positive imagery of you doing what you want to do, saying what you want to say, being how you want to be, or performing the way you want to perform in the specific context you are about to enter? Virtually all great athletes and other high-level performers (including astronauts, fighter pilots, surgeons, musicians, SWAT teams, military units, actors, singers, and business executives) who perform their best consistently do some kind of positive performance imagery before they enter their performance arena, important competition site, or major event. They do this to enhance their chances of respecting their best focus and performing their best in their chosen performance arena.

In your everyday training, daily pursuits, and performance life, your positive thoughts and images can continue to help you create the positive realities you would love to live. If your thoughts, focus, and performance images are negative or distracted, they will clearly interfere with your best performances and reduce your chances of performing your best, reaching your goals, and living your dreams.

You can be your best in all parts of your life by guiding your focus and positive performance images in positive and life-enhancing ways. Positive performance imagery can help you perform closer to the way you would prefer to perform, respond more effectively to expected and unexpected distractions, and become the person and performer you would really like to be. Your positive thoughts, images, and memories of your best experiences can continue to guide your performance and life in positive and life-enhancing ways.

Positive performance imagery provides an opportunity for you to create a better and more positive reality for yourself. It also allows you to practice dealing effectively with potential problems, challenges, or events in your mind before you confront them in real life. If a challenge you have prepared for mentally does arise, you are better able to handle it, cope with it, or focus through it. When you have already prepared for that reality in your positive performance imagery, faced that challenge in your mind, practiced some means of coping with it, overcome the challenge, or seen it from a more positive perspective, it frees you to respond in more positive and fully connected ways in your real-world performance contexts.

Positive performance imagery gives you an opportunity to be successful in your mental reality, even if you have not yet been fully successful in your physical reality. By guiding your mental images and focus in positive and performance-enhancing ways, you can prepare yourself to enter performance contexts, competitions, or any situation feeling like you have been there before and knowing what to focus on to have a successful performance.

Positive performance imagery can help you enter any performance context feeling more positive and in control. Try thoughts like these: *It's no big surprise. There's no reason to panic. I've prepared for this. I can handle it. I belong here. I choose to be here. I want to be here. There is no place I would rather be. I am ready for this. I am focused for this. I am confident that I can do what I want to do and have a personal-best performance! All I need to do is focus fully on the step in front of me, trust my focus, and let the good things unfold.*

Positive Performance Imagery

In sport and other high-performance contexts, you can use positive performance imagery to help you get the best out of yourself in training, competitions, or performances and to open the door to becoming what you have the potential to be. High-quality performance imagery is also effective when you have limited practice time, are making a comeback, or are recovering from an injury because you can repeat many successful experiences (in your mind) in a relatively short time without the physical risk or fatigue sometimes associated with using those skills or performing in the real world.

One of the reasons mental imagery can be so valuable in preparing for performance contexts is that the human brain cannot distinguish between a vividly imagined experience and a real experience. Both are "real" for your brain. The same areas of the brain light up in an imagined experience or performance as in a real experience or performance. For that reason, positive performance imagery has enormous potential.

When you repeatedly imagine yourself doing what you want to do, performing the way you want to perform, and being what you want to become, you are putting yourself on a path to a more positive future. Successfully repeating high-quality skills, moves, performances, or experiences in your mind and feeling those experiences in your body can be as good as doing them in your physical reality because you can do them with perfection and your brain views them as real. You need a certain number of successful repetitive experiences to create an integrated net of nerve cells (called neuronets) in your brain to perform a skill at a high level with consistency.

A fundamental rule of neuroscience is that nerve cells that fire together, wire together. If you do something once, a loose collection of neurons will form a network in response, but if you don't repeat the behavior, it will not "carve a track" in the brain. When something is practiced over and over again, those nerve cells develop a stronger and stronger connection, and it gets easier and easier to fire that network. (Arntz, Chasse, & Vicente, 2005, p. 147)

Creating Personal Advantages

Quality performance imagery training provides an opportunity to create mental, physical, technical, and motivational advantages in your preparation and performance. You can create the mind-set and performance reality that you would like to execute without external interference. Positive images lead to positive realities.

Performance Imagery
Alex Baumann

As far back as the 1984 Olympics, Canadian swimmer Alex Baumann was using performance imagery to help himself win two Olympic gold medals and set two new Olympic and world records in the 200-meter and 400-meter individual medley. In an interview I did with Alex shortly after those races, he spoke about the role visualization or performance imagery played in his success:

> The best way I have learned to prepare mentally for competitions is to visualize the race in my mind and to put down a split time. The splits I use in my imagery are determined by my coach and me for each part of the race. For example, in the 200 individual medley, splits are made up for each 50 meters because after 50 meters the stroke changes. These splits are based on training times and what we feel I am capable of doing.

> In my imagery I concentrate on attaining the splits I have set out to do. About 15 minutes before the race I always visualize the race in my mind and "see" how it will go. I see where everybody else is, and then I really focus on myself. I do not worry about anybody else. I think about my own race and nothing else. I try to get those splits in my mind, and after that I am ready to go. That is what really got me the world record and Olympic medals. . . . I started visualizing six years before the Olympics. My visualization has been refined more and more as the years went on. I see myself swimming the race before the race really happens, and I try to be on the splits. I am really swimming the race. In my mind I go up and down the pool, rehearsing all parts of the race, visualizing how I actually feel in the water.

The split times Alex was swimming in his mind in preparation for his Olympic wins were the times he thought he needed to swim in order to win and to break the Olympic and world records. He never swam those times in a real pool until he swam them at the Olympics.

I have worked with other athletes who have become Olympic champions in other sports (like Alwyn Morris, gold medalist in flatwater kayaking) who have put clocks on their imagery to ensure that their timing and pacing are exactly what they want them to be in major events. They were keen to do the performance imagery training and had fun doing it. Other athletes were not as interested in taking their imagery that far, which was also fine. They looked for other ways to gain an advantage.

Imagining Success: Video Imagery

Imagining in your mind and body the feeling of executing the moves you want and need to do to be successful in a sport or performance domain can help you accomplish those performance skills in the real world. Positive imagery can also enhance your confidence because you are repeating performance skills in your mind and body with a positive and fully connected focus, exactly the way you would like to do them.

Using video imagery is a great way to help make this happen. In 1992 I was part of a 22-week mental imagery study done with 7- to 10-year-old Chinese table tennis (Ping-Pong) players attending a leading sports school in China (Li-Wei, Qi-Wei, Orlick, & Zitzelsberger, 1992). During the study, all the children continued to participate in the same physical, technical, and fitness training they did before the experiment, and they spent the same total amount of time doing physical training during the course of the study.

The children were divided into three equally skilled groups. Group 1 participated in the experimental mental imagery training program, which included relaxation, video observation, and performance imagery sessions. The video sessions consisted of watching a collection of table tennis techniques executed by 12 of the top Chinese table tennis players (all of whom were world champions). The children were asked to choose the player they liked best or with whom they felt most compatible. Then, as they watched the videos, they imagined themselves making the same forehand and backhand smashes as their favorite players were doing on the screen. They did this hundreds of times, and then before they physically practiced with a real table tennis racket, ball, and table, they recalled the feeling of the moves they had watched and imagined themselves doing in the video.

Group 2 watched the same videos as group 1 did, but they were not asked to imagine themselves making the same great moves as the pros. Group 2 also didn't participate in the relaxation sessions. Group 3 did only their normal physical and technical training. The children in group 1 made significant improvements in the quality and accuracy of their shots and performance when compared with the other two groups. Two of the children in this group also placed in the top three in a national table tennis competition held that year against children of the same age from other sports schools in China.

Daisuke Nakashima/AFLO/Icon Sportswire

Watching the technique of a great athlete such as Lionel Messi and imagining yourself doing what he is doing can enhance positive imagery and improve performance. Improve your own performance imagery by watching an outstanding athlete in your sport.

For many years I have witnessed similar kinds of success using video performance imagery with national team athletes. These athletes used video imagery mostly to improve their performance skills, correct technical errors or unwanted performance habits, or be inspired by the outstanding people they were watching. In one case a national team paddler had a technical problem that had been ongoing for many years. He resolved the problem by watching video of one of the world's best technical paddlers, and while watching he tried to make the same movements in his own mind and body (often sitting in his paddling position with a real or imaginary paddle in his hands). This paddler became an Olympic medalist.

In another case a national team skier had been experiencing a technical problem with her approach to gates for many years. She was able to resolve the problem with two weeks of intensive video performance imagery training. She watched video of a technically great skier (whom she admired), skied gates perfectly in her mind, and felt the perfect technique in her body hundreds of times. This skier became an Olympic medalist.

In another situation an Olympic skier was at a training camp where the weather and lack of snow became a concern. She had many things to work on before the first World Cup race and almost no time for training on snow. So she started to visualize a lot more—taking some time each day to keep skiing in her mind, trying to feel the motion through her body, and keeping her body alert to the feeling it should be looking for. For some of her imagery sessions, she put on her ski boots, got herself in her start position (in her hotel room), and focused on feeling the forward pressure on the front of her boots—relaxing her ankles, feeling grounded in her boots, feeling the speed, feeling her skis carving the turns, and skiing fast and flawlessly.

She also watched videos of her own best races and of other great racers so she could mentally "see," "feel," and replicate certain parts of her own best skiing and their skiing in her mind and body. Through her performance imagery she skied with the greatest athletes in the world in her mind and body. In her own words, "Watching those videos and racing my absolute best in my mind and body really helped the consistency of my best performances." More recently, we have used split-screen video technology to see where the fastest skiers, runners, paddlers, swimmers, or triathletes on the course are gaining their speed advantages. A fraction of a second here and a fraction of a second there make a huge difference in final performance outcomes—especially at big events like the Olympics or world championships.

With split-screen video technology, you can line athletes up right next to each other on the computer screen and literally see where they gain or lose those fractions of sections of speed on that course in that event. This technology can be used in virtually any sport, for example, speed skating, running, swimming, and triathlons.

Improving Technique

Most athletes who progress quickly and ultimately become their best, or *the* best, make extensive use of some kind of performance imagery. They are highly motivated to become the best in the world in their sport or performance domain. Positive performance imagery leads them where they want to go. Some athletes use positive performance imagery as a way of directing their day, their training, or their life and as a way of experiencing or preexperiencing their best performances every day.

Performance imagery often starts out simply by thinking through your daily goals, the moves or skills you are working on, your best game plan, and your desired or ideal competitive performances. With practice, you will eventually be able to draw on your senses to fully experience in your mind and body the flawless execution of many of your goals, moves, performances, preferred focus plans, and best refocusing strategies.

For many years, an Olympic figure skater had experienced inconsistency with a particular skill. I asked her to try to visualize herself doing it while I was sitting with her. She was unable to imagine herself completing the skill successfully. She would see herself making an error (the same one she usually made in the real world) and stop at that point, or the image would break up.

After this first attempt, I asked her to practice doing that particular skating skill mentally (through her performance imagery) for approximately 10 minutes every night for a week. I suggested that she take it in steps. First, she tried to get past the point where she usually made the error on the ice or the image broke up, without worrying about her form. She needed several nights of mental practice just to get through that point in imagery. Next, she began working on consistently getting through the complete skill in imagery and refining and improving her form. Finally, she focused on feeling herself do the skill perfectly and fluidly several times in a row.

As soon as she began to feel herself performing the skill flawlessly in imagery, she started to do it correctly in real practice situations. Within two weeks of our initial session, she was doing that skill with more quality and consistency than she ever had before. So performance imagery can work if you are willing to work on it.

This skater usually did her mental imagery in the evening just before going to sleep. She would lie in bed, close her eyes, and try to call up the desired feeling she was looking for on the ice. Later she began to run through the skill in imagery just before doing it on the ice. Finally, while standing in the arena at a competition, she was able to look at the ice, map out her program, and feel herself going through it flawlessly. This set the stage for a clean, focused, consistent, high-quality performance.

Sharpening Focus

Many athletes find it helpful to imagine and feel themselves performing certain skills or movements perfectly before competitive performances. High jumpers feel their ideal jumps, divers feel their perfect dives, skiers imagine their best runs, gymnasts walk through their perfect routines, and archers imagine and feel themselves shooting the center 10, or bull's-eye, with every arrow released. Team sport athletes run through key offensive moves, quick transitions, and great defensive moves and remind themselves (and others) where their focus needs to be to perform their best for the duration of their shift, game, or performance. Let's face it: our ultimate goal is to simply have a great performance every time we are in the performance arena, from start to finish and everywhere in between. This is within your potential control. All you are asking yourself to do is to perform your best. Your chances of doing this are greatly heightened by planning to do this, choosing to do this, imagining yourself doing this, and then bringing your best high-quality, positive, and fully connected focus into your performance. That is the focus that will take you to where you want to go!

Positive performance imagery can help you perform closer to your true potential. Negative performance images usually result in you performing far below your true potential. So my advice to you is simple: go with the positive performance imagery and see where it takes you!

Positive performance imagery can strengthen your overall mental readiness and your confidence in what you can do! It gets you centered on positive possibilities, generates positive feelings, and reminds you to simply focus fully on doing what you need to do to have a great performance.

Memories of previous best performances can help you remember the feeling of connecting fully with what you need to focus on to have a great performance. They can be a great reminder for you to be fully in the moment, focus fully on the task at hand, and connect fully with the step in front of you. Positive performance imagery or positive memories of the best parts of your performances can serve as a last-minute or last-second reminder of the best focus you can carry with you into your game, race, routine, or performance. Choosing to focus in positive ways can quickly shift your thoughts and focus away from worry or self-doubts, which in turn lifts your confidence and gets you fully focused on doing what you came to do. The simple goal that will continue to give you your best performance results is to free your mind and body to perform to their full capacity without any unnecessary interference—nothing more and nothing less! Don't let anything get in the way of you and your performance.

A final reminder that some high-performance athletes use just before their performance begins is to recall the feeling, rhythm, relaxed power, or pace of the movement or actions they are about to perform. Once you get moving, just trust yourself, focus ahead, and go. Clear positive images that are fresh in your mind just before you begin your performance will usually stay with you during your performance. And if they don't stay with you, go to your refocusing plan.

Positive performance imagery can also be used after a successful performance to reexperience and remember the successful aspects of your performance while it is still fresh in your mind. This can help you be more consistent with your future best performances. It is also important to reflect on the unsuccessful or less than best parts of your performance so you can draw out the lessons for ongoing improvement.

Best Images

A lot of "impossible" or amazing human feats or inventions have been accomplished or created as a result of one person's positive vision or image that he or she fully commits to accomplishing. Thousands of impossible things have been accomplished with the help or guidance of positive imagery, including the car, the airplane, space travel, electricity, radio, the telephone and cell phone, television, movies, computers, and books. Almost everything viewed as difficult or challenging, or that has not yet been accomplished, is considered impossible until one person does it, and then everyone believes it is possible.

Positive images can clearly lead to positive new realities. Negative images can clearly lead to negative realities. If you believe it is impossible for you to do something or accomplish a certain goal, chances are good that you will not accomplish that goal unless you change your way of thinking and focusing from negative to positive and from impossible to possible.

The world's best athletes and great performers in other high-performance domains have extremely well-developed positive imagery skills. They use imagery daily to prepare themselves to get what they want out of training, to perfect skills within training sessions, to make technical corrections, to overcome obstacles, to imagine and help themselves succeed in their competitions or high-performance events, and to continue to strengthen their belief in their capacity to achieve their ultimate goals.

The refined high-quality performance imagery used by highly successful athletes, astronauts, musicians, surgeons, actors, dancers, fighter pilots, and other high-level performers almost always allows them to feel like they are actually living the performance and feeling the sensations. Even the best performers in the world, however, typically did not have great control over their performance imagery when they first began using it. They perfected this focusing skill through persistent daily use and ongoing focused practice.

Picturing the Perfect Dive
Sylvie Bernier

I did my dives in my head all the time. At night, before going to sleep, I always did my dives. Ten dives. I started with a front dive, the first one that I had to do at the Olympics, and I did everything as if I was actually there. I saw myself in the pool at the Olympics doing my dives. If the dive was wrong, I went back and started over. For me it was better than a workout. I felt like I was on the board. Sometimes I would take the weekend off and do imagery five times a day. It took me a long time to control my images and perfect my imagery, maybe a year, doing it every day. At first I couldn't see myself. I always saw everyone else, or I would see my dives wrong all the time. Sometimes I would get an image of hurting myself, or tripping on the board, or I would see something done really badly. As I continued to work at it, I got to the point where I could feel myself on the board doing a perfect dive and hear the crowd yelling at the Olympics. I worked at it so much, it got to the point that I could do all my dives easily. Sometimes I would even be in the middle of a conversation with someone, and I would think of one of my dives and do it (in my mind).

Sylvie Bernier, former Olympic champion in springboard diving

Listening to Your Feelings
Brian Orser

My imagery is more just feel. I don't think it is visual at all. I get this internal feeling. When I'm actually doing the skill on the ice, I get the same feeling inside. It is an internal feeling that is hard to explain. You have to experience it, and once you do, then you know what you are going after. I can even get a feeling for an entire program. Sometimes in a practice I get myself psyched into a program that will win. I step on the ice and go to my starting position, and I get this feeling that I'm at the Olympic Games. I get this internal feeling how this program will be. Usually I'm fresh, and usually it will be a perfect program. I don't just step out there in training and say, *Here we go, another program.*

Brian Orser, former world champion and two-time Olympic silver medalist in men's figure skating

Correcting Skills Mentally
Lori Fung

Sometimes I think, *Why did I miss that one move? OK. I know what happened; I pulled my body in too close to the apparatus. OK, now how do I avoid doing that?* Then I try to see myself doing it correctly in imagery. I can actually see the apparatus coming down; I can see the stripe on the club as it rotates, the same way you'd see it when you're doing the routine; that's the best way. Most of the time I look at it from within, because that's the way it's going to be in competition. It is natural because I do the routines so many times that it's drilled into my head, what I see and how I do it. So if I think about a certain part of my club routine, or my ribbon routine, I think of it as the way I've done it so many times, and that's from within my body.

Lori Fung, former Olympic champion in rhythmic gymnastics

The earlier you begin your imagery training, the better off you'll be. I recall a talented eight-year-old gymnast who was capable of incredibly clear imagery. She began doing mental imagery completely on her own with no knowledge that many great athletes practiced it. She would lie in bed at night running through her routines. For her it seemed a natural thing to do. She was able to see the people around her, feel the moves, and experience the emotions.

I remember a 19-year-old college basketball player who had been experiencing difficulty with a particular play sequence in the heat of the game. I asked her to try to imagine herself executing the play properly and driving in for a successful layup. She closed her eyes and sat quietly for a couple of minutes. When I asked what had happened in her imagined scene, she said that she had seen a bunch of Xs and Os on a chalkboard going through the pattern of the play.

Contrast this with the vivid mental imagery that Bill Russell was using when he was 18 years old. Russell became one of the best basketball players ever, winning 11 NBA championships as leader of the Boston Celtics. He describes his use of mental imagery or positive performance imagery in his book *Second Wind* (Russell and Branch, 1979, pp. 73–74):

> Something happened that night that opened my eyes and chilled my spine. I was sitting on the bench watching Treu and McKelvey the way I always did. Every time one of them would make one of the moves I liked, I'd close my eyes just afterward and try to see the play in my mind. In other words, I'd try to create an instant replay on the inside of my eyelids. Usually I'd catch only part of a particular move the first time I tried this; I'd miss the headwork or the way the ball was carried or maybe the sequence of steps. But the next time I saw the move I'd catch a little more of it, so that soon I could call up a complete picture.
>
> On this particular night I was working on replays of many plays, including McKelvey's way of taking an offensive rebound and moving quickly to the hoop. It's a fairly simple play for any big man in basketball, but I didn't execute it well and McKelvey did. Since I had an accurate vision of his technique in my head, I started playing with the image right there on the bench, running back the picture several times and each time inserting a part of me for McKelvey. Finally I saw myself making the whole move, and I ran this over and over in my mind. When I went in the game, I grabbed an offensive rebound and put it in the basket just the way McKelvey did. It seemed natural, almost as if I were just stepping into a film and following the signs. When the imitation worked and the ball went in, I could barely contain myself. I was so elated I thought I'd float right out of the gym. Now for the first time I had transferred something from my head to my body. It seemed so easy. My first dose of athletic confidence was coming to me when I was 18 years old.

Russell immersed himself in the vivid mental replication of a skilled athlete executing a fast-moving play on the court and driving in for the basket; then he acted out that image and turned it into a living reality. Later he began to create many of his own moves in his mind before ever playing them out on the basketball court.

Developing Performance Imagery Skills

No matter how good or how limited your performance imagery skills are now, you can improve them through daily practice both at home and on-site in your training or performance setting. The more quality imagery you do on-site and off-site, the more quickly your imagery will improve.

If you have never done any systematic performance imagery training, start with simple, familiar images or skills. For the next week or two set aside five minutes a day, either before going to practice or before going to sleep, to work on your imagery. Let yourself relax. Close your eyes.

Try to imagine the place where you usually train—what it looks like, how it smells, how it feels when you walk in. Imagine the people there, the first things you do to warm up, the look and feel of the playing surface, and the equipment you use. Try to imagine and feel yourself doing some basic skills in your sport, such as running, skipping, skiing, skating, paddling, rowing, dribbling, kicking, passing, throwing, catching, receiving, rolling, jumping, swinging, stroking, turning, riding, or moving freely. Through your performance imagery, gradually increase the complexity, quality, and free-flowing feeling of the skills.

As a rule, you should get into a pattern of doing about 10 to 15 minutes of quality imagery every day. Most Olympic and world champions do at least 15 minutes of imagery daily. Many do more because they also watch video and do video imagery sessions, particularly when preparing for major competitions, coming back from an injury, or returning to active sport-specific training after taking some time off. They also use mental imagery to practice or run through their race plans, game plans, focusing plans, distraction control plans, and refocusing plans so whatever they need in the performance setting is fresh in their minds when they need to draw on it. Finally, before competing, most great performers call up flashes of confidence-enhancing images from past best performances and projected future best performances.

Besides helping you perfect your physical and technical skills, performance imagery is itself a great focusing exercise. You must focus to create and control the positive images or feelings you want to experience in your mind and body. This focusing exercise can sometimes be tiring, especially in the beginning. So take your time and move into it gradually. Doing short periods of high-quality focused performance imagery at different times in the day is better than doing long periods of low-quality imagery.

Keep in mind that your ultimate objective is to reexperience or preexperience best possible performances using the senses and feelings you usually feel in real best performances. When perfecting performance skills through your performance imagery, try to call up the feeling of the best performance, not merely something visual. The more vivid and accurate the feeling, and the better you perform within that image, the greater your chances of replicating that performance image in the real situation. With regular practice, your performance imagery skills will improve immensely, and your imagined performances will feel real, in the same way that your nighttime dreams feel real.

A good way to perfect feeling-oriented performance imagery is to integrate a piece of your sport or performance equipment and actually move your body while doing the imagery. Instead of lying down, get into your normal starting position for executing the skill. For example, a kayak paddler can sit with her knees bent and arms up, either holding a paddle or as if holding a paddle, and then move her arms through a paddling motion as she imagines and feels perfect stroke execution (using her arms and legs) in her mind and body. In the quiet of his apartment or an empty field, a baseball player can stand up, step into the batter's box, see the windup, swing a real or imaginary bat, and feel the pop of the ball as he imagines and feels his perfect swing and contact. A basketball player can move her body (with or without the ball) and feel perfect shots, beautifully handled passes, and perfect execution of a variety of offensive and defensive skills.

An NHL and Canadian Olympic hockey goalie I worked with prepared for each of his games by going up into the stands long before each game started when no one was in the rink. He sat in the stands behind the goal he would defend to start the game with his stick in his hand. He imagined himself focusing on following the puck so that he could pick it up (visually) early, read the play, make one awesome save after another, and react quickly to stop multiple rebounds off his pads. For key games he anticipated moves the top scorers on the opposing team would make. He stopped all those shots in his mind before the game even started.

When you are first learning to do performance imagery, some physical movement often helps you call up the feelings associated with the skills you are doing. A gymnast, skater, or dancer can run through a completely imagined routine on the floor, ice, or stage by imagining the moves as she walks, skates, or dances across the floor or ice doing slight arm movements, body gestures, turns, and pauses. By combining performance imagery with real movement, you often feel more, and this can speed up and enhance the complete performance imagery learning process. As you become more skilled at feeling imagery, the sensations and emotions associated with best movements will surface more naturally in your imagined and real performances.

Most of the world's best athletes use some kind of performance imagery to prepare for training, games, or competition and to improve the execution of their skills. Before arriving at the training site, they often mentally run through what they want to accomplish that day and "**do**cide" what they will focus on to have their best possible performance. Before performances, they run through key skills or strategies and imagine themselves executing parts of their performance perfectly. They often imagine themselves in the competitive arena—with the sights, sounds, feelings, excitement, spectators, competitors, and coaches—and then focus only on executing their own best performance.

Imagery can also play a key role in familiarizing yourself with a particular competition venue. In many sports—including alpine, cross-country, or big-mountain free skiing; mountain bike or road racing; triathlons; and whitewater kayak racing—internalizing the course is important. The best performers in such pursuits use imagery extensively to learn the course so they know exactly what is coming and feel ready to negotiate whatever lies ahead of them, such as when or where to initiate a change in direction, pace, or strategy.

During the course inspection, they memorize the course and run it through their minds over and over. After they know all the critical markers or landmarks, top racers often imagine themselves going through the course or racing certain parts of the course, seeing key markers, feeling in control, and doing what they want to do in the race. Without this mental familiarization process, the risk factor, especially in speed sports, is dramatically increased. Knowing and preparing for the challenges and obstacles you will be facing increases your confidence and frees your focus on letting it go and giving everything.

Mental Preparation for Potential Obstacles

Mentally preparing yourself to cope effectively with distractions, including potentially stressful situations, negative thinking, or unexpected events, is an important yet largely overlooked aspect of the overall preparation process. If you can see, feel, and imagine yourself responding the way you would prefer to respond to a variety of potential distractions, you will be better prepared to respond effectively in real-world demanding performance contexts. You can mentally rehearse an effective response for almost any situation that might arise or anything you would like to approach in a more positive manner, including a competitor staring at you, a coach screaming at you, a swarm of media people crowding around you, or a stadium filled with 100,000 people. You can prepare a positive response plan and then imagine yourself in that situation seeing and feeling yourself focusing in positive ways and responding the way you would prefer to respond in that context.

Mentally rehearsing or imagining a preferred response plan lets you prepare for and practice effective responses in your mind before you confront that real-life challenge, problem, or distraction. This kind of mental rehearsal can feel real in your mind, without the serious consequences that might occur in the real world. The mental run-through of your preferred response makes it possible to enter a potentially uncomfortable or threatening situation feeling better prepared, less fearful, more confident, and more in control. It gives you something positive to focus on to stay on a positive track or get back on track quickly when you actually face that challenging situation in the real world.

When you reflect on the focus you want to carry into a game, performance, or any other situation, you are taking the first step to mentally prepare yourself to do what you want to do in that performance or specific situation. When you docide to take this preferred focus into your game, performance, or life situation, you are taking the first step to enhance your performance or interaction by eliminating potential problems or distractions and respecting a focus that works best for you.

When you imagine yourself at your performance site (or in any other context) staying positive, feeling relaxed, overcoming obstacles, focusing fully on the task at hand, stretching your limits, and achieving your goals, you are preparing yourself to do this in your real performance world. Whatever you want to do or accomplish in your sport or life, you can turn into a positive reality by imagining yourself doing it, step by step, and then focusing fully on doing it in your real-world context.

A world-class water-skier who I had the pleasure to work with became extremely anxious during important competitions when she passed the first buoy on the way to the slalom run. When she passed this buoy she would say to herself, *Oh no, here it comes*, and a sense of fear and tenseness would overcome her entire body. She decided to try mental imagery to practice using the buoy as a signal to relax. She imagined herself skiing by the buoy and saying to herself, *Relax*, at which point she would relax her shoulders and think, *You're ready—just let it happen*. This process helped her completely alleviate the problem in the real situation and freed her to win the world championships.

A highly ranked figure skater became extremely stressed in important competitions. She was particularly distraught just before starting her program. She tried to imagine herself at the competition site, just as the stress began to rise. As the anxious feelings began to surface (in her imagery), she imagined herself relaxing. She focused on her breathing and said to herself, *Nice and smooth—flow*. She then imagined herself doing her first few moves in a calm, controlled, focused manner. She mentally practiced this refocusing strategy numerous times in her mind to feel the effectiveness of her strategy. She was then able to use this strategy successfully during her competitions and felt fully focused and in control.

Many athletes have used positive imagery to change channels, reduce stress, shift focus, cope more effectively, and improve their performance in a variety of situations. National team archers attending a national training camp shared with me several creative uses of imagery. The following examples from archers who combined simulation and imagery show how you can be creative in putting together workable strategies and how different approaches work for different people.

A world champion archer spoke with me about how she used imagery to transport herself to the world championships from her practice site. Instead of seeing the single target that was actually in front of her (at her practice site), she imagined and saw targets stretched across the field. She was fully aware of her competitors. On her right was the leading Polish archer, on her left a German. She could see them, hear them, and feel them. She shot her rounds under those simulated conditions in the same sequence as she would shoot them in the real competition.

She prepared herself for high-level competitions and distractions by creating the world championships in imagery and by shooting under mentally simulated world championship conditions at practice.

A leading member of the men's national team did just the opposite. In the actual competition he was able to simulate practice conditions mentally. As he prepared to draw his bow to shoot his first arrow at the world championships, his heart was pounding. He glanced down at his tackle box (holding equipment and odds and ends) and noticed the words *Go, go, go*, which one of his hometown buddies had painted on his box in red. That note triggered another reality—a flashback to familiar grounds. From that point on in the competition, he was on his practice range at home, with one small battered target in front of him. He could even hear some of his buddies on the practice field chattering and joking in the background, in place of the chatter of different languages from his competitors who surrounded him. He shot in a steady, collected, and relaxed manner, as if he were at home.

In many cases, performance imagery is a first step performers take to improve certain technical skills and to help themselves overcome anticipated problems or distractions at the competition site. Performance imagery gets you started on a positive path. It is not time consuming, and you can do it yourself, wherever and whenever you choose. Sometimes just doing some positive performance imagery can lead you to overcome a specific problem or challenge and improve your overall performance. The usual sequence is to begin with mental imagery or performance imagery of what you ideally want to happen or want to do, then practice the imagined skill or coping strategy in real-world training situations, then use that fully connected focusing strategy in a simulated competition situation, and finally use it in high-performance events.

CHAPTER 9
Simulation

Simulation training is when you replicate in training, practice, or a simulated performance environment exactly what you have to do in your real-world performance or competition.

If you want to perform your absolute best in important competitions, races, games, trials, auditions, operations, presentations, or any other high-performance pursuit where outcomes count, it is essential to do some kind of realistic simulation training.

Simulation training gives you an opportunity to practice your best focusing and refocusing strategies and your desired performance responses in circumstances as real as you can make them, so you can take them into your real-world situations. Astronauts and military pilots were among the first to make extensive use of simulation training to improve the quality of their performance and their overall effectiveness in real-time situations.

In preparation for each mission into space, astronauts simulate every potential condition they could experience in space, including launch procedures, in-flight and surface activities, and possible malfunctions, so they can practice appropriate responses for each challenge they may face. The cost of error in their performance context is very high with human life and billions of dollars at stake, so no effort is spared to ensure that astronauts are extremely well prepared for their mission before they venture out into space.

Before they leave the launchpad, astronauts feel totally ready, as if they have been there before. They know they can perform extremely effectively and handle any problems within their potential control. Astronauts also do extensive performance debriefs after each mission. They evaluate every aspect of the performance and draw out lessons for improvement after each simulation and mission to space. One of NASA's most respected astronauts, Commander Chris Hadfield, described the critical importance of simulation training and performance debriefs for successful space flights:

We simulate a tremendous amount in preparation for space flight, and we try to make our simulations and our simulators as realistic as possible. We work hard to set up a scenario that is realistic, that is credible, so that the people in the shuttle simulator feel as if they're in a shuttle and the people in mission control feel as if they're controlling a real shuttle. So there's an air of realism to it. Then we will set up the malfunctions so that you drive the system to its edges, try to get into a gray area. What if this failed? Would we know what to do? And so we try to drive ourselves to the edge.

We also debrief in exhaustive detail. The way the debrief runs is that the person who was running the simulation, the flight director or the shuttle commander, has kept major event notes through the whole exercise, whether it's 4 hours or an 8-hour simulation or a 36-hour simulation, or whatever. They will hit every single major event during the simulation, and what went right, and thank the people who did it right. Or if there was a new way of doing something that worked better, we grab that lesson. Then we definitely get into the details of what went wrong or what was inefficient. Then actions are taken to put that into the flight rules or put that into the training from now on. Let's expand our collective brain power here. Let's learn from this thing.

We've flown the shuttle over 90 times, and we've made it look effortless. That is purely through accurate simulation and then incredible attention to detail in learning every lesson we can from every effort and rolling that back into the training flow so that the next one is even better. We implement things as quickly as possible. If it's something that is critical, we'll turn it around in a day.

For my first mission we did an actual full-crew simulation of the docking (with the space station) about 250 times. And then I simulated stages of it, or complete bits of it, in my head. I couldn't count the number of times I did that. I sat out on my deck at home, at night, and thought through it and practiced with it. When we actually got to do it, it was easy because of our detailed planning and detailed preparation. The most important thing is that you have enough representative training that when you get to the real test you aren't relying on chance and you can just focus down and get the job done.

In sport and many other high-performance domains, simulation training can help prepare you to perform closer to your capacity and get you ready to meet the challenges you will likely face in your performance context. Simulation prepares you for the physical, technical, and mental demands through high-quality, high-intensity, focused training that replicates the performance demands of real performances or competition. It helps you prepare mentally for potential distractions so that you are better able to stay focused and get the job done, regardless of the demands of your event or what is happening around you.

Embracing Simulation Benefits

I worked with figure skater Elizabeth Manley for three years leading into the 1988 Winter Olympics in Calgary. Manley (who subsequently became a professional figure skater and is now a coach and motivational speaker) delivered her best-ever international performance, winning the long program and placing second overall. She previously had experienced problems with her long program and often worried before competing about whether she could get through a clean program, especially in major competitions. To perform to her capacity at the Olympics, she needed to feel completely confident that she could skate the whole program with no problems and know that she could maintain a fully focused connection on executing her skills throughout her program—from start to finish.

To prepare herself for her best possible performance, Liz did more run-throughs of her program that year than she had ever done before. In her final Olympic simulations, which took place in an arena similar in size to the Olympic arena, she imagined that she was skating at the Olympic Games. Even though Liz was feeling physically ill in the days leading into those Olympics, she stepped on the ice feeling confident going into her long program at the Olympics, and she executed her program flawlessly and won the long program. Reflecting back on that performance, she believed, and still believes, that the additional simulations and the focus training she did really helped her rise to the occasion at the Olympics.

Eric Heiden, one of the world's all-time best speed skaters, won five gold medals at the 1980 Winter Olympics in Lake Placid, New York. Speed skating is a high-intensity sport that involves lots of pain and discomfort when you are going flat out. To excel in this sport and others like it, you must learn how to relax and push through discomfort barriers. Toward the end of many events, your muscles are burning and screaming at you to stop. You can tolerate very high levels of discomfort once you have "**do**cided" to do something and you know that your success depends on doing it. Focusing through discomfort is within your capacity, and pushing through discomfort helps you achieve your goals. Extending your personal limits is a battle your mind must win over your body because in many sports you must push past discomfort barriers to explore your own limits and live your dreams. Your focus rules your mind, your body, and your results, and your body will obey you if you focus on the right things at the right time.

Eric Heiden often used simulation training to practice pushing forward through personal discomfort barriers. He even included the pain or discomfort in his mental imagery of races and learned to race beyond the pain. By consistently pushing through discomfort barriers in training, he was totally prepared to endure and extend his limits in major competitions. Sometimes he pushed so hard in training that after a hard piece his legs were too shaky to stand up.

Like Eric Heiden, speed skater Gaetan Boucher learned to train with incredible intensity. He used simulation training extensively in preparation for his double gold medal performance at the Olympics, but only after being inspired to step up his training after visiting and training with Eric Heiden. In an interview I did with Gaetan Boucher, he told me the following story:

> I was second in the world for two consecutive years. Heiden was first. I saw him train in the summer when I was with him for a week. He was the guy to beat. When I was second to him at the world championships, I said, "Next year at the Olympic Games I am going to win the 1000 meters, and he will be second." I believed that the whole summer until I went to see him training . . . because his training was so much harder. I thought I was training as hard as I could, and then I saw this guy training even harder. He started with a 10,000-meter warm-up of skating imitations on a small 200-meter track. You are in a skating position, bent over. To do one lap of skating imitations is about the same as doing 400 meters on a track. He was doing that just as a warm-up, and he was going fast. I stopped after 20 laps. My legs were hurting, and that was just a warm-up. Then he did a 5,000, 1,500, and 1,000 all at maximum speed, just like a race.

> We took 5 to 10 minutes to rest after he did the 10,000-meter warm-up, and then he said, "OK, I am doing a 5000." So I followed him and stopped after 3000 meters. After that he did the 1500, fast. This time I did the whole 1500 meters, but he was pulling ahead. Then he did the 1000. I saw him stagger and almost fall from exertion after that interval. It was all in the legs, and it was hard! He said he had started the 5000 too fast, maybe because I was training with him. It was really fast. He was not keeping time. It was just the effort that was so impressive. The 1500 was maximum. The 1000 meters was maximum. Our team would do that same type of training and say, "Well, I have 5 or 10 laps to go. I'll go easier." He was doing the 5000 meters at the same speed I would do a 1500 or 3000. So after that experience I knew I could take more.

> A 1500-meter race hurts most because it is almost all maximum. Heiden got ready for the pain through his preparation. I never used to do that. He even put the pain in his imagery for his mental run-throughs. He would think that it would hurt, and he would be ready to accept the pain, so he knew he could do it. When I raced the 1500 after that, I thought about the fact that it is going to hurt, and I was prepared for it. You have to be mentally ready to accept the pain.

> After my training visit with Heiden, it was not my training itself that I changed, but my thoughts on how much I could take when I train. Before that visit I would do an interval that was supposed to be maximum, and I would think I was going maximum, but I could have taken more. So I changed my understanding of what I had to do to go to my maximum. My training method itself was not different, but the intensity I brought to year-round training was.

At his next Olympics in 1984 Gaetan Boucher won gold medals in the 1500- and 1000-meter races and a bronze medal in the 500 meters.

Replicating Performance Demands

If you replicate real performance demands or competition demands in training, you will be much better prepared to perform to your capacity in the real situation. But you must realize that you can't train with that kind of intensity every day or every interval. You have to pick your times, pick your runs, pick the pieces when you really go all out and when you don't. Find ways to push your limits or replicate competition demands often enough to know that you can do it when it really counts. Remember that rest and recovery are also essential. Find ways to rest as much as possible, physically and mentally, after major simulations and before big performances.

You can overcome many or almost all adverse or unforeseen conditions if you have simulated similar conditions in practice. Performing under simulated adverse conditions is one way of knowing that you can do well in all kinds of circumstances. By anticipating and working through challenges or potential problem situations, you will enter those kinds of situations with less fear, better focus, and more confidence. Simulation helps you do what you are capable of doing in real situations because you know that you can do it and you know how to focus to do it. You also know that you can refocus or adapt to a variety of situations and still perform well. You can perform well regardless of whether you arrive early or late or if you have a brief warm-up or even a poor warm-up. You can perform well whether you are up or down in points, feeling great or not feeling great, on target or slightly off target. All you have to do is focus on doing what you want to do and nothing else!

Simulation of distractions that could occur in your real-world performance contexts can prepare you to overcome all kinds of potential distractions. Think of the kinds of things that happen or might happen in a big meet, major competition, or key game. Consider introducing some of those potential distractions into your practice, training, or preparation settings. If you cannot replicate certain things in practice or in a preparation context, then simulate them through your mental performance imagery so that you have at least worked through some effective responses in your mind. Then, in the real situation, if something does not go perfectly, it isn't a big deal, and you can focus right through it. You can perform well with announcements, interruptions, or distractions going on right in the middle of your performance, presentation, or mission.

Introduce expected competition demands into your simulation training sessions and go through the normal sequence of your competition events in your practice or preparation sessions. For example, enter the gym, arena, rink, field, or performance setting; warm up; get yourself ready; and then play your game, run through your events, or do your presentation, just as you would in your real-world performance context. Consider including judges, officials, audiences, cameras, noises, and other athletes or adversaries at these simulated performances. Some athletes and teams with whom I have worked found that something as simple as wearing their competition

Scott Donaldson/Icon Sportswire

Top athletes like Se Ri Pak are prepared to perform under adverse conditions. Use simulation training to prepare for the unexpected.

uniforms, racing bibs, or performance costumes during time trials, dress rehearsals, or run-throughs made the competition simulation feel more real.

Run through your event, program, game, or race in different conditions you might face in the real world—in the rain, in the sun, in the heat, in the wind, in the cold, when tired, when fresh, before eating, after eating, after missing a meal, in the morning, in the afternoon, and in the evening. Practice overcoming difficult challenges, running different offenses and defenses, responding to false starts, reacting to someone who has passed you late in the race, coming off the bench, or coming on strong toward the final part of the race or game after you or your team has slipped behind. Introduce loud sounds of applause or public announcements over the speakers just when you are beginning to start or are halfway through a routine. Warm up on your own and run through your events on your own, without your coach being there (your coach may be sick, stuck in traffic, or delayed at a meeting). By preparing in these ways you can go into almost any challenging situation feeling at ease and knowing you can perform your best. All you want to do is perform your best—nothing more and nothing less—and performing your best is totally within your capacity. This is the goal of simulation training.

Coaches, officials, or team leaders can introduce unexpected changes that athletes or performers must adapt to. For example, the coach (or a friend role-playing the coach) can tell you that you have an hour to warm up but then start the performance or competition in 15 minutes instead (the bus was stuck in traffic, and your team arrived late). The coach can change the lineup, offense, defense, or order of events at the last minute; unexpectedly bring in judges, unfair officials, important evaluators; and so on. You can practice remaining calm and focused under all these simulated conditions. Just focus on you and what you control and let the rest go! Coaches should openly discuss the reasons for introducing these kinds of simulated distractions before introducing them in a real-world context.

A young figure skater found that while she was waiting to perform in competitions, she often heard other skaters coming off the ice making negative comments like, "It is so hot out there. . . . It was hard to get through the program." As she stepped on the ice herself, she worried about the heat and how it would affect her performance. During the final minute of her last five-minute competition program, she was thinking, *It's so hot . . . my mouth is so dry . . . feels like there's no air . . . I don't think I am going to get through it.* She barely scraped through the last portion of her program and was not at all pleased with her performance. She had never worried about the heat in practice meets or exhibitions; her concern surfaced only in competitions, although the physical setup in exhibitions was basically the same: packed arena, bright lights, and high temperature. This young skater's anxiety about performing well in competitions resulted more from the other skaters' comments about the heat than from the heat itself. This is why having a preperformance plan that gets you focused on the positives and helps direct your focus on how you will perform your best is so important.

With one figure skater who was preparing for the Olympics we discussed the possibility of practicing with an elevated arena temperature just in case the temperature in the skating rink at the Olympics was elevated due to extensive lighting and sold-out crowds in the arena. This idea posed some logistical problems, so we decided to increase the skater's body temperature and leave the rink manager's body temperature alone. We agreed that at the next practice she would dress warmly in heavy clothing and try running through her full free program.

She reported back a few days later and said, "I did my program in practice with a big sweater and leg warmers. I was turning hot, but I didn't have a problem with it. I didn't even think about it." From that time on, heat was not a problem for her in competitions. Even if all the other skaters came off the ice complaining about the heat, she was never preoccupied with it. She knew that she had skated well through elevated heat in practice with no problem. All she needed to do was focus on her skating, which she did. The heat simulation merely provided confidence-enhancing proof that she could do what we all believed she could do.

All performers gain from feeling confident in their ability to do what they are actually capable of doing. They like and benefit from going into their performances or competitions knowing in advance that they are fully capable of performing to their capacity. Simulation training helps build this kind of confidence. Some athletes find it helpful to do more in their simulation training than they are required to do in their real performance or competition. For example, if you know that one five-minute performance, race, or program is required, do two or three in a row; if you know that your game will last an hour, play an additional half hour of high-intensity overtime. When you do more in training or simulations than is required in your competitions, games, or performance, there is a good chance you will be feeling pretty confident.

When you are doing multiple simulations, it is a good idea to build up your performance level by setting progressively more challenging goals and ensuring that you are well rested on the days you choose to do these kinds of extended highly focused simulations. When you become accustomed to doing more than is required in training contexts, doing what is required in real games, races, or competitions is no big deal. If you are accustomed to playing four or five periods of fully focused high-intensity hockey or six quarters of high-intensity basketball in simulated competitive games, you should be able to enter your competitive arena with full confidence in your ability to maintain your fully connected focus and preferred level of intensity for the mere three periods or four quarters. Some of the best Chinese gymnasts in the world have successfully used this approach. I have seen them execute two complete routines in a row before dismounting. This is one reason why their routines are flawless in competition. They know that in their everyday practices they regularly do more than the competition demands. This gives them complete confidence that they can hit clean routines consistently in major competitions. Their single goal is just to go into the performance arena and focus fully on doing it.

Athletes, coaches, and teammates are in the best position to determine what kinds of simulated activities and conditions might help each athlete and the overall team perform their best in their sport or performance domain. The important advantage of relevant and meaningful simulation training is that if you have been exposed to most of the expected and unexpected conditions and distractions you are likely to face at your major events or competitions, you will be better equipped to stay focused on the right things and perform your best under these conditions. If you have practiced focusing through distractions and doing more than is required, you will feel more prepared and more invincible. You will know and feel somewhere deep in the core of your being that you are ready and you will do well. No sweat. Well, some sweat, but you'll know that you can nail it if you just keep your focus fully connected in the right place at the right time for the duration of your performance.

Simulation gives you the added confidence of knowing that you have the ability to do whatever you want to do. Successful simulations help you believe in yourself and in your focus, which is crucial in all sports, performance contexts, and missions to excellence. Your focusing objective is to reach the point where you can face all kinds of challenges, distractions, or potential obstacles and still maintain complete confidence in yourself and your positive and fully connected focus. You know that you have the capacity to perform at a very high level when you focus on the right things and free yourself to perform your best. You have probably performed your best before on certain occasions and certainly have the potential to do it more often. Your best possible performance capabilities live within you, and you will free them to shine as long as you remain positive, healthy, rested, and fully focused on the right things. Your best focus is always available to you—no matter what! You just have to respect that best focus to free yourself to live your potential and perform to your best consistently.

Finding Inspiration From Others

There are lots of ways to become a better athlete, better performer, and more joyful human being by simulating, relocating, or reliving the positive performance examples and positive living examples you see in other performers and people whom you respect and admire. By acting on some of the positive attributes you respect and admire in others, you can begin to improve certain parts of yourself, including your focus and performance. Often when I meet, observe, or get to know a student, athlete, performer, or positive person of any age, I discover in that person some characteristics that I like or admire. That person can be a child, student, family member, parent, teacher, coach, colleague, neighbor, developing athlete, great athlete, performing artist, musician, surgeon, astronaut, business executive, leader, or outstanding performer in any field. You can gain from anyone who has something positive that lives within that person you respect or admire. Winning attributes may be related to the person's physical, mental, or technical skills; commitment; pure connection to an area of engagement; positive and respectful ways of communicating; balanced way of living; or overall positive presence, positive focus, and grounded way of being.

Look for other people's best qualities and strengths to better yourself technically, physically, mentally, emotionally, or spiritually. You can literally attempt to be that positive person in certain respects, and see how it feels for you. You can imagine yourself being that great athlete in stance, posture, and execution. You can tell yourself, *Today I'm going to "be" or pretend to be whoever or however I would really like to be, from the time I wake up and step out the door until the time I go to bed at night. I'm going to walk tall, the way she does, and try to execute my moves as gracefully; I'm going to remain calm and in control just like he does, even if someone starts yelling. I'm going to work really hard just like she does for the whole practice or game. I am going to make a conscious decision to be the way I want to be, and focus the way I want to focus, for a specified period of time. If something feels right for me and helps me in positive ways, I am going to hang on to it. If something does not feel right for me, I am going to let it go and find a more positive way.*

Embrace the special qualities that you like in yourself and admire in others. Continue to nurture your best qualities and your best focus in simple ways every day. This will open doors to being or becoming what you are capable of being or becoming. You can also learn what you do not want to be or become by observing others. For example, you might see a person or performer engaging in a behavior, action, reaction, lifestyle, or way of being that is contrary to your values or the way you want to be. You can "**do**cide" at that moment that you are not going to be like that, perform like that, or go down that negative path. You always have the power of choice.

Choosing to become what you want to become is critically important for excelling in any performance domain and in every part of your life. The only way to reach high-level goals is to be positive and persistent in nurturing your most positive and best fully connected focus. You have to develop these essential focusing skills to become the confident, positive, and fully focused person you have the potential to be.

Successful Examples of Real-World Simulation

Indonesian athletes were world champions in badminton for many years. They had a history of winning when it counted. When they were the best in the world, I watched them play; talked with them, their coaches, and their former world champions; and visited their training camps. One reason they were on top of the world at that time was their extensive use of simulation training. They simulated every aspect of the game—their strategy, coming from behind, bad calls, high temperature, crowd effects—particularly for the world championships. You can adapt the basic ideas underlying this specific simulation program to whatever sport or challenge you are facing.

Long before the match, the top Indonesian players knew everything about their opponents—their strengths, weaknesses, playing style, and technical peculiarities. They studied videos of their opponents and gained from the experiences of teammates who had already faced them. They preplanned a strategy and mentally ran through exactly what they would do when their opponents did A, B, or C. Teammates sometimes role-played the actions of opponents in simulated games. The players knew where they should return the shuttle, or bird, for a particular opponent before they played him, and they prepared to place the bird accordingly before it ever reached them in the actual game.

They also practiced anticipating their opponents' returns, which meant knowing beforehand where the bird would likely go and planning to be there. If this strategy worked on 7 out of 10 shots, it was worth targeting the anticipated return area. In a sport like badminton, speed is closely linked to anticipation. The player must anticipate and move toward the return area before the bird is fully hit, particularly for a hard smash. (A hockey or soccer goalie facing a hard shot must react in a similar way. To be successful, the goalkeeper must anticipate where the puck or ball will go and be there before the player makes full contact with the puck or ball. The puck or ball often moves to the goal faster than a goalie can react; correct anticipation is therefore essential.)

By studying where the bird (or ball) usually goes under various conditions and with different opponents, a player can greatly increase the chances of being in the right place at the right time. The top Indonesian players were undoubtedly quick, but they had much more than speed—they knew where and when to move. They were usually in the return area before the bird arrived, even on blistering shots in doubles play. They targeted their speed, anticipated their opponents' shots, and perfected their own strategies through simulation training.

The Indonesian players also used simulation to improve their performance by preparing themselves for the following performance situations:

✦ **Coming from behind.** Top players built confidence in their ability to come from behind and win a game by simulating specific come-from-behind game situations in practice. A game might start at 14 to 3—a stronger player would begin with 3 or 4 points and a weaker player with 13 or 14 points. The objective for the stronger player was to come back and win the game. For the weaker player, the objective was to prevent this from happening, or at least to have some strong rallies. With a proper matchup, both players could play hard and push their limits, and the stronger player would come back to win. This process gave less experienced players a chance to play the champions and the champions practice coming back from behind. For many years in the Thomas Cup championships, whenever the Indonesian players fell behind they were consistently able to come on strong to win. The fact that they were behind did not seem to distract them at all; they had practiced coming back. They knew that they would come back, they focused on doing it, and they did.

✦ **Bad calls.** Poor officiating—for example, calling a shuttle out of bounds when it is obviously in bounds—was simulated in practice to prepare players to overcome the frustration that can follow a bad call. The purpose of this simulation was discussed and then implemented in some practice games and exhibitions. Sometimes the simulating official would make a series of bad calls. The player's goal was to ignore the bad calls and focus on preparing for the next shot, to shift focus from something beyond his control to something within his control. There were no emotional outbursts or even second looks from the Indonesian players after questionable or close calls at the championships. They simply focused on getting ready for the next rally and got on with the game.

✦ **High temperatures.** For many years, the Thomas Cup championships were held in Jakarta under extreme temperature conditions. The outside air temperature in the evening was in the mid-30s Celsius (mid-90s Fahrenheit), and the humidity was in the 90s. The arena was packed with 12,000 sweaty people, and there was no air-conditioning. Heat-producing television lights were set up right next to the court, and all windows and doors were closed to prevent drifting of the shuttles. Needless to say, it was hot! The spectators, including me, ended up dripping wet just sitting in the stands.

How did the Indonesian players prepare for those conditions? They prepared by living and playing in the heat and by bringing in large crowds to fill extremely hot and humid arenas for exhibition matches. If visiting teams are to play to their capacity under such extreme temperature conditions, they too must prepare for them. The best preparation is to practice and play exhibition games for a couple of weeks in the same time zone, in a similar climate, under similar conditions and then rest well before the tournament. This approach prepares an athlete to walk into that arena and be ready to go the distance.

◆ **Crowd effects.** I have rarely heard fans roar as loudly as the crowd did in Jakarta for the badminton championships. The sound was deafening, and the crowd was definitely partisan. They heckled opponents and roared approval for their heroes' every shot. (The fact that badminton was their major sport and that a lot of private betting was associated with those games may explain some of the fans' enthusiasm.) In some countries a crowd of 12,000 people for a badminton match is unheard of; in Indonesia it was normal. The audience would have been much larger had the seating capacity in the halls been greater. Younger players learned to adapt to those crowds by growing up with them. The junior players and national team members traveled throughout the country giving exhibitions to large crowds. They invited the public to the main badminton hall in Jakarta for simulation matches in final preparation for the championships; the free invitation was accepted gratefully, and the hall was full. This final simulation was aimed at readying the athletes to walk onto the championship court feeling totally supported and completely prepared mentally.

◆ **Longer or more challenging games.** The best players often took on more in their training than was required for their championships. For example, they might play one and a half to two hours straight at an extremely fast pace. They might play whole games in which one player was allowed only to lob, smash, play defensively, or play to the backhand, while the other player could use all his moves. To keep the pace moving, to work on speed, and to develop anticipation, one player might play against two opponents, or multishuttle games might be introduced. In multishuttle games it is possible to play nonstop badminton, with a shuttle always in play, or to practice reacting to shuttles coming rapid-fire from all corners of the court.

As a result of training for more than what was required on the day of the competition, the players were in superb physical condition. They used their fitness to their advantage, particularly in the extreme temperature conditions. They could maintain a very fast pace or deliberately keep a rally or game going for a long time simply to tire out their opponents.

◆ **Taller or different sized players.** When the taller top European players started to play well at the international level, the Indonesians developed a new simulation strategy to train their players to play more effectively against them. They built courts that were higher on one side, so that the players playing on that side were the same height as the taller top European players.

A former world champion and one of badminton's all-time greats believed that following three simple rules, which could easily be applied in practice simulation, gave a player an advantage both strategically and psychologically:

1. Never stop a game to change a shuttle when you are winning. If you lose two points in a row, change the shuttle.
2. Continue to use serves and shots that are working—often—but also use variation in your play. Otherwise, at the higher levels your opponents will anticipate your shots.
3. Never change a winning tactic or strategy.

While still at the top of their game, the Indonesian superstars worked directly with the most promising junior players. The reigning and longtime world champions in both singles and doubles spent about two days a week coaching and playing with younger players. The youthful players had an opportunity to play with their heroes, watch them at close range, learn from them, follow their actions, and be inspired by them. The championship players learned and gained from coaching and working with enthusiastic young players and enjoyed the sessions.

China now has dominant athletes in table tennis (Ping-Pong), badminton, artistic gymnastics, rhythmic gymnastics, diving, volleyball, wushu, and the martial arts and has become a world leader in many other sports as well. The Chinese are masters at simulation training, partly because simulation training originated long ago with traditional training in the martial arts and performing arts and partly because they know from a long history of experience that it works. The Chinese have been doing everything the Indonesian badminton players used to do and more. They now also make extensive use of video imagery training and have a strong central sport development program that supports the overall development of young athletes who have the potential to be great.

China is the only country where I have witnessed in-depth simulation training that surpassed what Indonesia was doing in badminton. In table tennis, a sport China has dominated for many years, the Chinese athletes and coaches used simulation extensively and creatively. Even in the early 1980s, Chinese badminton players were using some of the high-quality simulation procedures used by China's best table tennis players. In the latter part of the 1980s, China became the dominant badminton power in the world. It continued to gain dominance in many sports in the 1990s and is still improving its overall level of sport performance in the 21st century. The Chinese have become the masters of quality repetition and high-quality simulation training and use it to their advantage in sports in which they excel.

Simulation has played a major role in their tradition of martial arts (wushu, for example) for many years. With their most successful teams and athletes, the Chinese went a step beyond what most other countries do in their repetition of skills, moves, and programs in training. They prepare their athletes to perform well when fatigued and when competing against their most challenging opponents. For example, some skilled Chinese athletes have been trained to replicate the playing styles of top opponents from other countries to provide realistic simulation training for their national team members. This kind of simulation training has helped strengthen their overall readiness to face the challenges of high-level competition from around the world.

When countries such as Malaysia, South Korea, Denmark, Sweden, and England began to make extensive use of effective simulation training in badminton, they took a step up and produced some world leaders in that sport. A well-designed, high-quality simulation training program can prepare athletes or performers from any country for the expected and unexpected challenges they will face at the highest performance levels and help them achieve their goals in almost any performance domain or context.

One cautionary note about simulation training is to avoid overloading athletes or performers with too much simulation, too much repetition, too many performances, too much pressure, or too many competitions. Oversimulation, like overtraining, overworking, or overperforming, can burn athletes or performers out physically, psychologically, and emotionally. Excessive simulation can take the joy out of the pursuit, resulting in physical overuse injuries, psychological or emotional fatigue, lowered resistance to common illnesses, and a lack of the spontaneity or creativity sometimes needed for a truly outstanding performance. We have to ensure that simulation training and competition, game, and performance schedules work for us and the athletes and coaches with whom we work, not against us. It is our individual and collective responsibility to ensure that a sense of joy and passion remain within the pursuit and that the athletes and performers with whom we work have adequate rest and recovery time to guard against unnecessary injury, illness, fatigue, or distress. Finally, individual differences must be respected in determining what works best for athletes or performers and how much rest and recovery is required for each athlete to sustain their best focus and gain the best performance.

CHAPTER 10
Zen Experiences

I have a border collie named Zen, and I run with him every morning through the nature trails in the forest next to my house and alongside the lake where I live. Zen is totally in the Zen zone when we are out there running, and most of the time so am I. One of the reasons I love running, walking, paddling, and just being fully in the moment, especially in beautiful nature contexts—on the beach, on trails, in the mountains, and alongside rivers or streams—is being in the Zen zone. There is something very special about that kind of pure, positive, and complete life-enhancing connection. It makes you feel more fully alive and produces a positive energy gain.

What does it mean to really *be* in the moment, to be fully here, to be fully and completely focused with every fiber of your being, to be in the Zen zone? What is the "way," the Zen way, the river of life, the pure fully focused connection? Those descriptions mean everything to one person and nothing to someone else. Words are just words. They have different meanings for different people in different contexts, cultures, languages, and times.

Zen as a way of living, connecting, and performing originated in ancient Chinese characters called ideograms. Each character represents more than just one word; each denotes a concept or way of seeing or feeling things. We might never be sure of the original essence of the ancient Chinese characters that painted the philosophy of Zen. Only when we experience a pure Zen connection ourselves do the characters or words take on personal meaning. We then know what a pure Zen connection feels like from the inside out as an experience, from experience, through experience. Each of us can get to know, appreciate, and find value in the pure Zen connection by experimenting with our own positive, uninterrupted connections in our performances, focus, and everyday life.

Much of what has been written about Zen originates with a little book titled *Tao Te Ching* (*Book of the Way*), written by Lao-tzu in China more than 2,500 years ago. Originally written in ancient Chinese characters, the book has been translated by many authors into English and many other languages, each presenting a slightly different interpretation of Lao-tzu's original meaning. Reading about Zen and experimenting with it yourself make you really reflect on the importance of connecting fully with what you are doing or experiencing and finding ways to avoid being distracted.

You get to know Zen on an internal level by just being in the moment, going with your feelings and intuitions, and fully embracing simple connections. Zen can never be forced, but it can become a natural way of being or connecting fully and joyfully every day in every piece of your life and within every learning and performance context. Zen can also be elusive or beyond your reach if you push it too hard, chase it, or try to apply force to it. For me, pure Zen connections surface naturally when I free myself to connect fully with whatever I am doing, thinking, writing, saying, sharing, feeling, experiencing, or creating.

The Zen connection, or the way to find the fully connected way, lives within you. You experienced it countless times as a child and sometimes more fleetingly in your adult life. It can happen in any context when you choose to open yourself to be fully here and fully connected to what you are doing or experiencing.

One of the intriguing aspects of sports, martial arts, fine arts, and performing arts as they were originally practiced in Asia thousands of years ago was the importance they placed on training the fully focused mind. Zen was initially developed and experienced through play, sport, martial arts, and fine arts, but its ultimate purpose was to enhance the pure connectedness of living of life itself.

Interpreting Zen

For me, the most important lesson of ancient and modern Zen practice is the concept of pure connection and oneness, a concept embraced by many North American First Nations or aboriginal people, including Native Americans (who lived throughout Canada and the United States) and the Inuit people (Eskimos) who inhabited the Canadian Arctic and Alaska.

Entering the Zen zone (in play, nature, performances, relationships, creative pursuits, learning contexts, and ongoing personal interactions) means becoming one with and inseparable from the essence of what you are doing, learning, reading, pursuing, or experiencing for the duration of the time you are doing it. Being in the Zen zone means being all there; totally present; fully absorbed in the moment; one with your body, task, performance, experience, and surroundings.

When you are totally engaged in the process of doing or connecting, you become what you are doing. For those moments nothing else in the world exists for you. You suspend all thoughts or judgments about yourself, others, or your performance. You simply connect fully and absolutely with what you are doing, pursuing, feeling, or experiencing.

When you begin to reflect, deliberate, question, condemn, or judge yourself along the way, you lose the pure connection that frees you to be the person and performer you have the potential to be. When you lose that pure connection, you become disconnected, distracted, tentative, and separated from what frees you to perform your best. The original pure and natural childlike bond between mind and mind, mind and body, mind and task, mind and creation, or mind and nature is broken. There are times when we need to think and reflect but also times when we need to connect totally with what we are doing or experiencing and nothing else. This is what frees best performances to unfold fluidly and naturally. Performance is a time for pure connection rather than ongoing reflection. Excellence is made possible through pure, positive, and fully focused connection.

Think about the value of not thinking or not consciously evaluating yourself during your performances. Think about the value of a pure, positive, and fully connected performance focus. Almost everyone has experienced a Zen connection at some time. Zen is grounded in a fully focused connection—where you choose to be completely where you are when you are there and you are completely absorbed in your performance when you are performing, without any interfering thoughts.

Your challenge is to discover or rediscover what this absolute pure connection is for you, and embrace it, let it be part of you more often, so it can help you most. For me, a Zen connection is a little bit like the wind: you can't see it or grab it in your hand, but you can breathe it in, feel it, and let it become part of you. To enter the Zen zone,

- ✦ let go of forcing things;
- ✦ let go of outcomes;
- ✦ let go of your thoughts about outcomes;
- ✦ connect only to the doing;
- ✦ focus on doing the doing, being in the moment, being all here, being completely present, being fully connected; and
- ✦ become inseparable from what you are doing for the duration of your performance or interaction.

The goal is always pure connection. When you are fully connected no separation exists between you and your performance, you and your experience, you and the person with whom you are interacting, you and nature, you and your dream. You are pure and connected as one.

When nothing is forced, nothing takes you away from the experience or breaks the connection between you and your interaction or you and your performance. You become the performance because you are fully engaged in what you are doing. The connection is so pure and strong that nothing else needs to be done; the performance or interaction takes care of itself. The purity of your connection is what frees you to have consistent great performances or great connections in every part of your life. This is why it is so important to see yourself being or becoming the positive, competent, confident, fully focused, and fully connected learner and performer you have the potential to be.

Zen masters long ago wrote about the importance of softness or suppleness as opposed to rigidity, hardness, or inflexibility in freeing yourself to perform your best. I see this every day in athletes and other high-level performers with whom I work. You can't force performance excellence or best performances; you have to free them to happen. Best performances are nurtured through relaxed power, free-flowing movements, and pure fully focused connections. The way to embrace your life and live your dreams is through pure and sustained positive fully focused connections—which we are all capable of experiencing and nurturing. The way to find and embrace what you are seeking depends on how deeply you connect and how long you can sustain that pure connection. It also depends on how often you disconnect. Pure, positive, fully focused connection leads your performance in positive and life-enhancing ways. The power and pureness of this connection lives within all of us. All we have to do is open ourselves to embrace it. When you disconnect or let obstacles get in the way of your fully connected focus, the effect is like a big dark cloud blocking the sun so that its rays no longer shine down on you. If you open your mind to pure, positive, fully focused connection, pure connections will shine through on you.

Nurturing Pure Connection

You can enter a state of pure connection, or your personal Zen zone, every day in some way. Easy access is the simple beauty and the real benefit of Zen. Pure connection in all parts of your life is the best way to enhance your performance and enrich the overall quality of your life. Here are some reminders that might help you nurture a purer connection within different contexts of your life.

+ Seek moments of pure connection in different parts of your life every day.
+ Practice trying by not trying.
+ Connect fully with the connection.
+ Practice connecting without thinking about connecting.
+ Practice doing by feeling connected.
+ Absorb yourself fully in doing whatever you are doing.
+ Absorb yourself in every experience.
+ Trust your body and intuition to lead you wisely to your desired destination.
+ Trust your pure connection to lead the way.

What do you think is possible for you to accomplish in your sport or performance domain, schoolwork, profession, or life with a pure, positive, and fully focused connection? With a positive, constructive, sustained, fully focused connection, virtually anything is possible. Your focus rules your life and your performance. My focus rules my life and my performance. Our individual and collective focus rules the world we live in because our ways of focusing, positive or negative, connected or disconnected, constructive or destructive, directly affect every person, every experience, every performance, every family, every community, and every society throughout our world—for better or worse.

What would our world look like if no one had a positive focus? What would our world be like if no one had a fully connected focus? If no one had a pure, positive, and fully connected focus, there would be no meaningful learning, no pure connection to fully experience the moment in which you are living, and no possibility of living or performing to your full potential.

I have marveled at the oneness or absolute connection exhibited by the great performers I have had the pleasure to work with and learn from in whatever they are doing, seeing, feeling, pursuing, or creating. They have learned to become one with or inseparable from their performance (through a pure Zen-like fully focused connection). Nothing else in the world exists for them during those special moments. To live your life to the fullest, it is essential that you learn how to enter this positive fully connected state in your training, learning, performances, and personal and professional life. The path to living your life fully and joyfully depends on you bringing this kind of positive and fully connected focus into all parts of your life. Great performers do not allow negative thinking or distractions to get in the way of doing the good things they are doing, sharing, or experiencing. They are usually focused on how to best enhance and sustain the quality of their connections, performances, and lives. To move forward in this positive performance and life enhancing direction:

+ Let your best most fully focused connections lead you.
+ Let your best most positive focus lead you.
+ Let your best feelings lead you.
+ When you are performing, learning, or engaged in doing what you really want to do, let go of any distractions or thoughts that are beyond the connection itself.

Some of my favorite quotes from Lao-tzu's book are presented here. Following each quote I have noted a practical reminder or meaningful lesson I have drawn from it. Think about what each quote means to you and how you might act on it.

+ "Keep sharpening your knife and it will become blunt." My reminder: There is a point beyond which more gives you less. Discover that point to perform your best and live more joyfully.

+ "Care about people's approval and you will be their prisoner." My reminder: Don't let other people's thoughts rule your life or your day.

+ "Do your work, then step back. This is the only path to serenity." My reminder: Take time to relax, regenerate, and dwell in the serenity of silence or the beauty of nature.

+ "Coax your mind from its wandering and keep to the original oneness." My lesson: Stay fully connected in the moment—be one with your mission.

+ "Cleanse your inner vision until you see nothing but light." My lesson: Stay focused on the positives and the positive possibilities and let the negatives go.

+ "Deal with the most vital matters by letting events take their course." My lesson: Control what you can control and let go of the things you cannot control.

+ "Giving birth and nourishing, having without possessing, acting with no expectations, leading and not trying to control: This is the supreme virtue." My lesson: Live a simple, positive and fully connected life without trying to control others. Let simple, positive, and worthy wisdom guide each day.

Zen is centered on fully connecting, fully experiencing, and fully embracing good things each day. You may be thinking about being more positive, more complete, or more connected in the present moment but not acting on being more positive or more completely connected in what you are doing or living. When you move from saying to doing, from thinking to acting, and from reflecting to connecting, you enter the Zen zone and good things will follow.

Transcending Technique

I often wondered how the great fencing masters prepared for duels in the old days, before touches were recorded on an electronic scoreboard. How did the great swordsmen prevent themselves from becoming distracted by outcomes and suffering a fatal performance flaw when the stakes were literally life or death? Many overanxious swordsmen did not live to tell their tales, but what of those who survived and continued to excel?

Daisetz T. Suzuki (1993), in his excellent book *Zen and Japanese Culture*, touched eloquently on this question. Suzuki discussed the connection between Zen and the ancient art of swordsmanship:

> If one really wishes to be master of an art, technical knowledge is not enough. One has to transcend technique so that the art grows out of the unconscious. . . . You must let the unconscious come forward. In such cases, you cease to be your own conscious master but become an instru-

ment in the hands of the unknown. The unknown has no ego-consciousness and consequently no thought of winning the contest. . . . It is for this reason that the sword moves where it ought to move and makes the contest end victoriously. This is the practical application of the Lao-tzu doctrine of doing by not doing. (Suzuki, 1993, pp. 94, 96)

To excel or even to survive, a swordsman had to free himself from all ideas of life and death, gain and loss, and right and wrong and give himself up to a power deep within him. In essence he had to clear his mind of all irrelevant thoughts, follow his trained instincts, and trust his body to lead. The swordsman who performed at the highest level of excellence was likened to a scarecrow that "is not endowed with a mind, but still scares the deer" (Suzuki, 1993, p. 100).

Suzuki continued, "A mind unconscious of itself is a mind that is not at all disturbed by effects of any kind. . . . It fills the whole body, pervading every part of the body . . . flowing like a stream filling each corner." If it should find a resting place anywhere, it is a state of "no thinking," "emptiness," "no-mind-ness," or "the mind of no mind" (Suzuki, 1993, p. 111).

Freeing the Mind and Body to Perform Without Conscious Thought

The following stories provide some examples of how certain high-level performers were able to focus fully in the moment and let go of potential negative outcomes in order to perform their best in what would otherwise be high-stress conditions.

Focusing Lessons for Living: Juan Belmonte

All at once I forgot the public, the other bullfighters, myself, and even the bull; I began to fight as I had so often by myself at night in the corrals and pastures, as precisely as f I had been drawing a design on a blackboard. They say that my passes with the cape and my work with the muleta that afternoon were a revelation of the art of bullfighting. I don't know, and I'm not competent to judge. I simply fought as I believe one ought to fight without a thought, outside of my own faith in what I was doing. With the last bull I succeeded for the first time in my life in delivering myself and my soul to the pure joy of fighting without being consciously aware of an audience.

Juan Belmonte, the great Spanish bullfighter, reflecting on the moment when he first freed his body and mind to dance freely within a performance

Reacting Naturally: Kim Alletson

> For me it was a feeling of separating my body from my conscious mind and letting my body do what came naturally. When this happened things always went surprisingly well, almost as if my mind would look at what my body was doing and say, *Hey, you're good,* but at the same time not making any judgments on what I was doing because it was not "me" that was doing it; it was my body. This way, by not making any judgments, it was easy to stay in the present.

Canadian Olympian Kim Alletson speaking of a similar phenomenon

Professional figure skater Charlene Wong and Olympic downhill skier Kellie Casey became exceptionally good at drawing on the Zen perspective to free themselves in their quests for personal excellence. When Charlene "turned on her autopilot," a wonderful program unfolded. When Kellie suspended conscious thinking and "let her body lead," she had a great run. For the duration of their best performances, they both suspended critical evaluation and trusted the mind–body connection to work without interference from conscious thought.

In the ancient art of swordsmanship, focusing was intimately connected with life. In Suzuki's words, "When a stroke is missed, all is lost eternally; no idle thinking could enter here." A consciousness occupied with irrelevant thoughts and feelings stands in the way of "successfully carrying out the momentous business of life and death, and the best way to cope with the situation is to clear the field of all useless rubbish and to turn the consciousness into an automaton in the hands of the unconscious" (Suzuki, 1993, p. 117).

Distracting thoughts or emotions could result in a swordsman's failing to see or detect "the movements of the enemy's sword with the immediacy of the moon casting its reflection on the water" (Suzuki, 1993, p. 133). Seeing and instantaneous action of body and limbs are essential. This is no place for minds obscured by irrelevant thought or clouded by anxiety. No obstruction should come between mind and movement. As one Japanese Zen master pointed out, you can read the environment much more clearly when you are calm internally, just as you can see the reflection more clearly on a calm lake than on a disturbed one. Stress is like wind that disturbs the image on a calm lake.

Suzuki pointed out that the perfect swordsman takes no cognizance of the enemy's personality, no more than of his own. He is an indifferent onlooker to the fatal drama of life and death in which he himself is the most active participant. The swordsman's unconscious is free from the notion of self. As soon as his mind "stops" with an object of whatever nature, the swordsman ceases to be master of himself and is sure to fall victim to the enemy's sword (Suzuki, 1993, pp. 96–97).

Suzuki went on to say that an idea, no matter how worthy and desirable in itself, becomes a disease when the mind is obsessed with it. The obsessions that the swordsman has to get rid of are

- ✦ the desire for victory,
- ✦ the desire to resort to technical cunning,
- ✦ the desire to display all that he has learned,
- ✦ the desire to overawe the enemy,
- ✦ the desire to play a passive role, and
- ✦ the obsession to get rid of whatever obsession he is likely to be infected with (Suzuki, 1993, pp. 153–154).

"When any one of these obsesses him, he becomes its slave, as it makes him lose all the freedom he is entitled to as a swordsman." Whenever and wherever the mind is obsessed with anything, "make haste to detach yourself from it" (Suzuki, 1993, p. 154). The primary reason these obsessions can impede pure performance or excellence is that they interfere with gaining the purest connection with your performance.

Anthony Bibard/FEP/Icon Sportswire

The performance of a great athlete like Usain Bolt transcends technique to reach a pure mind–body connection.

The following quotations from Yagyu Tajima, the great 16th-century Japanese swordsman, provide some Eastern visions to reflect on (Suzuki, 1993, pp. 114–115):

- ✦ "Emptiness is one-mind-ness, one-mind-ness is no-mind-ness, and it is no-mind-ness that achieves wonders."
- ✦ "Give up thinking as though not giving it up. Observe the technique as though not observing."
- ✦ "Have nothing left in your mind, keep it thoroughly cleansed of its contents, and then the mirror will reflect the images in their 'isness.'"
- ✦ "Turn yourself into a doll made of wood: it has no ego, it thinks nothing; and let the body and limbs work themselves out in accordance with the discipline they have undergone. This is the way to win."

A fencer with whom I worked stimulated my thinking about performing without thinking and without thinking about not thinking. He combined some aspects of Eastern and Western approaches to improve his fencing performance. He developed a precompetition plan that helped him start in a calmer, more relaxed state. What he wanted most was to compete in a Zen mind-set. He wrote out a list of quotations that triggered in him the primary feelings of a Zen perspective. They included the following:

- ✦ Zen is against conceptualization. The experience is the thing. Verbalism often becomes an empty abstraction.
- ✦ If you want to see, see right at once. When you think, you miss the point.
- ✦ When I look at a tree, I perceive that one of the leaves is red, and my mind stops with this leaf. When this happens, I see just one leaf and fail to take cognizance of the innumerable other leaves of the tree. If instead of this I look at the tree without any preconceived ideas, I shall see all the leaves. One leaf effectively stops my mind from seeing all the rest. When the mind moves on without stopping, it takes up hundreds of leaves without fail.
- ✦ To think that I am not going to think of you anymore is still thinking of you. Let me then try not to think that I am not going to think of you.
- ✦ Do not rely on others, or on the readings of the masters. Be your own lamp.
- ✦ You have mastered the art when the body and limbs perform by themselves what is assigned to them to do with no interference from the mind.

The fencer read these quotations to himself several times before competing, as a reminder of the state of mind he sought. He had some initial success but also some subsequent difficulties in maintaining this approach throughout his most crucial bouts. He refined his approach into a series of key words (for example, *It, it . . . be with it* or *Be here . . . be all here*), which he plugged in whenever he experienced too many thoughts or too much stress. As he went out to compete he began to tell himself, *You're here to fence, and nothing beyond the experience of fencing really matters . . . just go out and fence and enjoy yourself*. When he was able to follow these simple reminders, his body took over and he moved in an incredibly fluid way—sometimes making touch after touch without thought. After bouts like that he occasionally found himself wondering where all those great moves came from.

The fencer could not always enter this state, but it began to happen more frequently with less thought in more tournaments. He began searching for competitions to practice improving his focused connection and letting his performance flow. Improving his overall perspective toward competition was his primary goal, but he also found help in backup strategies such as verbal reminders and relaxation when he ran into problems. A Zen orientation is not something that can be accomplished hurriedly, but it is certainly responsive to nurturing, as the fencer's comments make clear:

> For the first few competitions, after reading and talking and thinking, I realized that I was too focused on what was wrong in the bout. I paid attention to what was wrong. To turn that around, I got back into the doing. I went into one tournament thinking, *There's nothing that says I have to be tied up in a competition*. The first two bouts were great. Then I started to tie up. I couldn't let go of the feeling. I was first able to turn it around by becoming interested in what I was doing and experiencing, instead of being so worried about the expectations of others. This took a bit of time. I had to "be in" the competition. With each subsequent competition I had better and better focus control for more and more of the time. The coach stayed away and let me work things out for myself. Telling me technical things at the last minute, or after I'd blown something, just made things worse. I thanked him for staying quiet.

When speaking about his last competition, the fencer said,

> As I stepped up for the bout, I thought, I am here for the fencing . . . nothing else matters . . . get into the experience. At no time did the thought of winning or losing enter the picture. I got into the finals, which was my goal, and we won the team competition. The "pressure situation" didn't faze me. On one occasion one guy did upset me emotionally. I went into the corner, did some relaxation, read my Zen reminders, came back, and won a key match 5 to 0. My primary strategy worked fine, and I gave myself reminders in the bout if I felt I needed them (for example, *I'm here to experience it*). Many people commented on how relaxed I was. I really enjoyed myself and beat four very good fencers. I was there to fence—that's all.

He ended our discussion by saying, "The event is the focus. If I focus on the event, the feeling comes automatically. So I just let my interest get absorbed in the event. I relax and enjoy it. Lots of hits are unintentional. The guy just runs into my point."

Certain things cannot be forced. You must free yourself to let them happen. You don't have to try to be happy. You simply live, connect with your experiences, and embrace the simple joys of life; happiness comes as a by-product. In a similar vein, you don't have to try consciously to focus on winning during a performance in order to win. During the contest you simply become absorbed in the experience. By being in the present, trusting your body, and allowing the performance program that has been ingrained in your mind and body to unfold, the winning takes care of itself.

Before every performance, "**do**cide" what you really want to do and know that you are fully capable of doing it. To be the best you can be, your only goal is to connect fully and to free yourself to perform. When you are totally engaged in the process of doing, you become what you are doing. You, your focus, and your performance are one—this is the Zen zone.

Here are some final focus reminders that will free you to connect fully with your performance. Choose the ones that feel best for you. Before you enter your next performance, remind yourself to carry this focus.

+ Focus by feeling, not forcing.
+ Let your intuition lead you.
+ Stop judging along the way. Focus on the doing.
+ Trust what is already living deep within your body and soul.
+ Become one with your performance.
+ Win by removing all thoughts of winning.
+ Simply connect and trust the connection.
+ Relax. Attack by relaxing.
+ Pure focus is pure connection—this is the only place to be.
+ With pure focus nothing gets between you and your performance.
+ Enter the Zen zone. It is the only place to be!

PART III
Creating Excellence

CHAPTER 11
Perspectives

A positive perspective is your best friend and a negative perspective is your worst enemy. The perspective you are carrying right now is dependent on whether you are focusing on the positives or the negatives.

Your path to embracing your life and living closer to your true potential in both your performance pursuits and the rest of your life lies in developing your ability to focus in positive ways that free you to carry a positive perspective and view the challenges you face in a positive way.

Who is the most positive person you know? What does this positive person do, say, embrace, or act on that makes you feel or believe she or he is positive? How do you feel when you are with this person?

A positive perspective is nurtured when you start to focus on the good things in yourself, the good things in your day, the positives in your life, the good things in others, and the positive possibilities that live within you and the world around you. A negative perspective becomes your reality when you focus on looking for and finding negative things in yourself, in your day, in your life, in others, and in the world around you.

Being or becoming positive or negative is a choice you make every day. A positive perspective comes from focusing on opportunities instead of obstacles, solutions instead of problems, positives instead of negatives, good things instead of bad things, possibilities instead of impossibilities. Here is a simple example. If you have a shopping or to-do list (for your day at home, at work, at school, at practice, or in your performance setting) and you tick off 19 out of 20 things as successfully completed, do you focus on being happy about accomplishing those 19 good things, or do you focus on being negative or upset about the one thing you did not accomplish?

You have the opportunity to embrace a hundred good things—little highlights—throughout every day. Are you fully embracing and remembering those happy little highlights every day? Or are you dwelling on one or two little lowlights from your day? Do you really appreciate and remember all the good things, or do you just focus on the one or two bad things that happened?

Human beings around the world do billions of good, positive, uplifting things for other people every day. We all benefit from embracing and remembering the good things and from continuing to nurture them within ourselves and others. To fully live your life and embrace your own dreams, it is important for you to focus on the positives and not dwell on the negatives, to focus on the opportunities and not the obstacles, to focus on why you can achieve your goals and live your dreams!

Embracing a Positive Perspective

When you focus in positive ways, you become your own best friend. You choose to support yourself and also help others find a way through difficult or challenging times. You encourage yourself to do the good things you want to do, remind yourself of your good qualities, remind yourself to embrace the special moments you have, remind yourself of what you have the potential to be, and remind yourself and loved ones to embrace opportunities and simple things that lift you. This frees you to fully embrace the simple joys in every part of every day and in every pursuit, even when facing extremely difficult challenges. Living with a positive perspective becomes possible when you

+ "**do**cide" to find good things in yourself and your life,
+ docide to find good things in others and their lives,
+ appreciate the good things in yourself and your life,
+ appreciate the good things in others and their lives,
+ rejoice in the good parts of yourself and your life, and
+ rejoice in the good parts of others and their lives.

To continue to move along a positive path, follow these steps:

+ Look for and embrace the good things, the highlights, the magic moments in each situation and day.
+ Look for and embrace the opportunities in each situation, every day.
+ Embrace the positive in positive situations.
+ Find the positives or lessons in negative situations.
+ Focus on why you can do what you want to do (for example, attain your goals, accomplish your mission, or live more positively).
+ Focus on why you can rise to the challenge and how you will move forward in a positive direction.
+ Focus on lifting yourself up instead of putting yourself down.
+ Continue to appreciate the good things you have, the good things you have done, and the good things still to come.
+ Continue to find and appreciate the good things in yourself and others—past, present, and future.

Choosing Your Perspective

When you participate in a competition, performance, or event, thoughts will often run through your head beforehand (and sometimes during and after the event). You may start thinking about what might happen or not happen and begin to feel strong emotions related to those thoughts. Are those thoughts running through your head going to help or hurt your perspective, focus, and performance? Are they going to help you do what you want to do or interfere with you doing what you want to do? Are your thoughts going to make you worry or free you from worry? Are they going to help you feel confident or shatter your confidence? Are they going to help you focus on the right things or lead you to focus on the wrong things?

What triggers your emotional reaction to an event is the way you perceive the event, or what you say to yourself in relation to it, rather than the event itself. A simple shift in your perspective about the importance or meaning of a particular event, or a shift in your belief about your capacity to cope with it positively, can change your focus, emotional reality, and subsequent level

AP Photo/Dmitry Lovetsky

A top performer like Amy Purdy is able to maintain control even in challenging circumstances.

or quality of performance. Nothing changes except the way you perceive yourself, interpret the event, or view your capacity, yet that simple positive change in focus—from negative to positive, from disconnected to fully connected, from stressed to relaxed—can give you inner strength and confidence; release you from stress; and free you to live, perform, and contribute more fully and joyfully. You have the capacity to choose the perspective and focus you carry into your daily life and performances.

Choose Your Focus Wisely

Let's take performance stress as an example. If you take some sportscasters seriously, you might begin to believe that stress is external and inescapable, like rain pouring down from a dark cloud: "You can almost feel the tension out there . . . this is it . . . do or die . . . the world is watching . . . there's real pressure on these athletes here today." Yet some performers are able to enter those high-intensity situations and stay focused on doing their jobs or executing their performances without becoming overstressed. They perform extremely well by feeding off challenging situations to raise the level and connectedness of their performance. How do they do this?

First, these athletes have preperformance preparation plans or routines that ensure they are focused on preparing themselves to do what they came to do. They also have performance focusing plans that keep them focused on doing what they came to do during their performances, games, races, or events. Having effective preperformance focus plans and effective best performance focus plans helps them to perform their best consistently in any context. They don't let anything outside their best focus plan shape their day.

Second, stress, worry, or anxiety doesn't float around out there waiting to pounce on you like some kind of evil spirit or bogeyman. Stress, worry, and anxiety are strictly internal; they do not exist outside your mind. Certain important performance situations or contexts may tend to get the adrenaline flowing, but you are not required to become anxious or stressed in those situations. It is all a question of what you choose to focus on! You can focus on what you control—which is your performance and executing your performance to the best of your ability—or you can focus on what you do not control, which is other people, other performers, or performance outcomes that are outside of your control. If you do begin to feel anxious, overwhelmed, or stressed, you can regain control by shifting your focus (or changing focus channels) back to what you do control—the simple steps of executing your performance, routine, program, race, or game plan.

We become anxious or stressed when we accept a situation or context as anxious or stressful or when we become too concerned with outcomes or consequences of failing or falling short of our goals. Performers who enter the competition or performance arena feeling positive and excited about the opportunity and fully focused on the right things tend to remain positive and in control. Successful performers often create a positive picture in their mind that is uplifting, focused, and filled with opportunity

We experience stress and frustration in performance situations and other areas of life largely because we want to be perfect at everything we do. We expect the performance situations and opportunities we enter to be perfect, which of course they almost never are. We want our partners, children, parents, coaches, teachers, athletes, teammates, colleagues, bosses, and others to be perfect. Sometimes we set ourselves up for stress or frustration because we have impossible expectations of ongoing perfection for ourselves and others. All we can do is be the best we can be on that day and then draw out the lessons for ongoing improvement.

Ellis and Harper (1976, p. 25) identified the following five perspectives or beliefs that can interfere with your capacity to perform to your potential and live a joyful life:

1. The belief that you must always have love and approval from all the people you find significant.

2. The belief that you must always prove to be thoroughly competent, adequate, and achieving.

3. The belief that emotional misery comes from external pressures and that you have little ability to control or change your feelings.

4. The belief that if something seems fearsome or threatening, you must preoccupy yourself with it and make yourself anxious about it.

5. The belief that your past remains all important and that because something once strongly influenced your life, it has to keep determining your feelings and behavior today.

You cannot have the love and approval of all people at all times, no matter what you do or how much you give of yourself; nor can you always be thoroughly competent at all things at all times. None of us is, or ever will be, perfect at all things. We all screw up sometimes, and that's OK. That's being human. The important thing is that we continue to draw out positive lessons from our best and less than best experiences and performances and apply them in our lives and upcoming challenges or performances so we can continue to improve, grow, and move forward on a positive and life-enhancing path.

We all have the capacity to improve our perspective, enhance our focus, and influence our lives in positive ways. We are not locked into the limitations of our current focus, experiences, or ways of being. We can all continue to learn, grow, and improve in our performance domains and all other parts of our lives. We all have the capacity to fully engage ourselves in the process of becoming what we have the potential to become in all parts of our lives. This is what makes life such a wonderful adventure.

Why Worry?

Excessive worry has the capacity to destroy people's lives and create barriers to skilled performances. It usually comes from exaggerating the importance of the outcomes of an event, from viewing performances as if your physical or emotional life is at stake, or from thinking that your entire meaning on earth rests in the balance. We know this is not really the case in most performance situations, but we sometimes act as if it were.

When you approach a performance as if it is the most important event in the world, as if your life will be over or useless unless you do well, you set yourself up for needless stress. If you incessantly worry about how well you will perform or about appearing incompetent, you are probably too focused on negatives or negative possibilities. The worry is almost always worse than the event itself. Your performance rarely turns out to be as terrible as you might have imagined, and it would have turned out a lot better if you did not dwell on the negatives in the first place. The bottom line is not to waste your time worrying about things that are beyond your control. Focus on the positives and the positive possibilities. Focus on why you can achieve your goals. Focus on how you will achieve your goals. Take that focus into your performance arena.

Shifting Your Perspective

You can lessen your worries and improve your performance by shifting your focus to something positive that is within your control and by viewing yourself, your event, and your performance in a more positive light. Consistent high-level performers almost always enter their performance contexts physically and mentally ready: *I've got a job to do; I'm capable of doing it; I know what to focus on; I know what works for me; I'll focus fully on doing it the best I can—step-by-step. Beyond that, I'm not going to worry about it.*

When great performers have a great performance, they rejoice in it briefly, draw out the positive lessons, and move on. If they have a disappointing performance, they soak in the disappointment briefly, draw out the positive lessons, and move on. They have learned to refocus quickly and not dwell on what is beyond their control. They do this to keep things in perspective because if they don't, they will waste a lot of needless emotional energy, which in turn will become another unnecessary obstacle on their path to achieving their high-level goals.

Think about your own situation. At one time you had limited skills in your sport or performance domain—in fact, you hadn't even begun to participate in your sport. Yet you were a valued person then, and those close to you loved you and will continue to love you regardless of your level of performance outcomes. Now that you are much more skilled, is it really so disastrous to achieve a little less than perfection? You are a skilled performer.

You are a worthy human being. You will continue to be an acceptable and worthy human being long after you stop training, working, performing, or competing in this domain.

There are lots of physical skills I no longer have since I stopped training every day, competing and performing in gymnastics. For example, I can no longer do a quadruple twisting back somersault on a trampoline. Does that really matter in the big scheme of life? Probably not! Otherwise we would probably have billions of people wanting to do quadruple twisting back somersaults on the trampoline! Right now I enjoy participating in many outdoor sports and physical activities daily. I also enjoy sharing some of those magic moments with my children and other special people in my life. I also really enjoy writing my books, teaching university students, and consulting with athletes and other high-level performers to help them embrace their lives and live their goals and dreams.

In the end, your overall value as a human being does not depend solely on your performance in your sport, work, profession, or any other high-performance pursuit at any given time. Some athletes and performers in other high-performance domains view their performance as an indication of their overall worth as a human being. I can assure you that our essence and value as human beings extends far beyond our performance on any given task in any performance pursuit at any given time. We are all much more than our performance outcome on any day in any given context and will continue to be.

Flowing Through Stress

Something is stressful only if you view it as stressful, accept it as stressful, and experience it as stressful. Otherwise, it is just something that happens during your day, week, or life. You can choose to feel stressed about it or choose to not feel stressed about it. Choosing to not feel stressed about things that previously resulted in you feeling stressed is within your potential control. You are not required to feel stressed before going into major events, competitions, tests, games, or performances. The best way to avoid feeling stressed in situations that previously resulted in you feeling stressed is to remind yourself that you are not required to be stressed in this situation. Remind yourself to keep things in perspective and then focus on following a positive preperformance focus plan that keeps you focused on you and what you are capable of doing in this context or performance. Focus on slow, relaxed breathing and remind yourself to *relax* as you breathe out in the lead-up time to your performance, test, game, or competition. Slow, relaxed breathing is always a good thing to focus on to relax or turn down the intensity in potentially stressful circumstances or contexts.

Changing channels is another effective way to reduce stress or regain control quickly on-site in performance contexts or other potentially stressful situations. Think of it as changing channels on your TV. If you are on a mental channel you don't like or don't want to be on at this time, a channel that is not helping you, simply press your thumb hard against your first or second finger and change channels mentally. As you press your thumb hard against your finger, think to yourself *change channels, change channels* from stressed to relaxed, from negative to positive, from distracted to fully connected. By choosing to make positive shifts in your focus, you can enhance your positive perspective; make your focus stronger, better, more consistent, or more complete; eliminate doubts or fears; and relax your breathing. All of this can help you channel your positive energy and fully connected focus into the step-by-step process of executing your performance to the best of your ability.

Another effective refocusing strategy I have used with high-performance athletes and other high-level performers is called flowing stream. If you are feeling stressed or distracted before a performance or while you are performing, you simply imagine yourself flowing like a little mountain stream. If you watch water flowing down a mountain stream, you will see that it always finds a path even when there are obstacles like rocks, stones, branches, or tree trunks along the way. The water doesn't get stressed out or stop flowing; it just finds its own path and keeps on flowing to its desired destination. Sometimes it is helpful to remind yourself to flow through challenges, obstacles, or uncertainty in your day or life like a flowing stream.

I have devoted much of my life to creating simple, positive, effective focusing and refocusing strategies to help children, youth, athletes, students, performers, and everyday people reduce stress, enhance relaxation, achieve their goals, and live their lives more fully and joyfully. If you are interested in learning additional simple, effective focusing, refocusing, and relaxation strategies, see chapter 10, "Focusing Activities," and chapter 11, "Relaxation and Joyful Living," in my book *Positive Living Skills: Joy and Focus for Everyone* (Orlick, 2011).

Your first line of stress prevention, stress reduction, and positive focus control lies in focusing on the good things in your life and accepting that your value as a human being remains intact regardless of whether you meet your performance expectations or the expectations of others. You can reduce unnecessary stress in your life by setting realistic performance goals, focusing fully on executing your task, and knowing in your heart and soul that you remain a good and valued person regardless of your performance outcome in any context on any given day. Choose to enter potentially stress-provoking situations with a positive and fully connected focus, and you will greatly enhance your chances of performing well. You may feel your heart thumping or a rush of adrenaline flowing through your body because you are excited and you need a certain level of positive intensity to perform your best in this situation. That's usually a good thing because your body and mind are telling you that you are ready to rise to this challenge.

In some contexts, you may feel more of an adrenaline rush than you would like. If this happens, take a little time-out to breathe in and out slowly and remind yourself to relax every time you breathe out. If you are feeling negative or stressed, ask yourself. *Why am I feeling negative? Why am I feeling stressed out? What am I thinking or saying to myself about this situation that is making me feel negative or stressed? Do I have to feel this way? No, you definitely do not have to feel this way! Do I have to think this way? No, you don't have to think that way! Do I have to get stressed out over this? No, you don't! Is worrying or being stressed going to help me in this situation? No, it isn't going to help you! Is it really worth continuing to be stressed or negative about this? Definitely not!* If being stressed or negative is not going to help you, then why not change channels or shift your focus to something positive that will free you to take control and focus fully on performing your best? Set a personal goal to stop focusing on the negatives and start focusing on the positives.

+ Focus on why you can achieve your goal.
+ Focus on how you will achieve your goal.
+ Act on your positive intentions every day simply by focusing on what you know works best for you. Continue to look for good reasons to believe in yourself and your capacity to meet or overcome the challenges you are facing, whatever they may be. You are fully capable of focusing through these challenges and growing from them.
+ Remind yourself of your strengths. Write them down!
+ Remind yourself to focus fully on the step, move, stroke, or stride in front of you and nothing else.
+ Remind yourself of the amazing power of your fully connected focus.
+ Remember that you are fully capable of achieving your goals.
+ Remember that you are fully capable of carrying a positive and fully connected focus for the duration of your performance.
+ Choose to think and act in positive ways that will free you to focus fully on executing your mission or performance—nothing more, nothing less.

Deciding to be positive and fully focused before you enter your performance context will help you make the positive changes you are seeking. Think about how you would prefer to respond to various situations in your performance arena and other arenas of your life. See yourself responding effectively to situations that may have distracted or upset you unnecessarily in the past. Imagine yourself in future performance situations—thinking, focusing, believing, and acting in more positive and fully connected ways. Focus on bringing this more positive vision of yourself to life in your real-world performance contexts.

Often a simple shift in focus from negative to positive or from disconnected to fully connected leads to a major change in the way you view a situation, your performance, and yourself. As soon as you start to believe that you really do have the potential to do what you really want to do in this performance context, everything changes: *Hey, I'm ready to do this; I can do this; I want to do this; I own my best focus; I control my actions and reactions; just focus, focus, focus, and execute my game plan.*

Continue to act on drawing out the focusing lessons from your best performances and the less than best parts of your performances. Whenever you are able to make a positive change in your focus, perspective, or performance, think about what you did, focused on, or said to yourself to make this happen. Embrace those positive lessons and act on them in your future performances. Try to become aware of self-imposed obstacles to positive change, such as focusing on the negatives, dwelling on distractions, or saying things to yourself that block your own progress, for example, things like *I don't feel ready; this will never work; I can't do this; I'm not good enough to do this; I'll probably mess it up.*

What are you saying to yourself right now about your capacity to improve your focus and make the positive changes you need to make to consistently perform to your capacity? This is a good place to start establishing and nurturing a powerful, positive, fully connected focus. Docide right now to move forward each day with a powerful, positive, and fully connected focus.

Building Confidence

Virtually every athlete or performer you have ever seen or competed against, including the best athletes in the world, experiences a rush of excitement, a feeling of being more fully alive, before an important event. This positive or energized feeling shows that you care and want to excel or do your absolute best. You can make this feeling work for you by recognizing its positive elements and by channeling all of your positive focused energy into executing your best possible performance.

Sometimes simply recognizing the fact that your physical sensations can help you channel your increased energy level into your performance is enough to keep you positive and in control within your performance context. Let's say that your heart starts to thump hard just before your performance begins. You could say to yourself, *Oh, I'm so nervous . . . I don't know what I'm going to do. . . . I'll probably blow it.* Or you could interpret these physical signals in a positive manner and say, *The feeling I have in my body is a good one that can help me perform my best . . . it is the result of positive adrenaline, which acts as a stimulant. My body is telling me that I'm ready and I'm focused. This is positive energy! I am ready! Let's go!*

A certain amount of intensity is necessary for high-quality performances in sport and other mind–body endeavors. You wouldn't do well if you were half asleep, but you don't want to be bouncing off the walls either. You are seeking an optimal energy level or an optimal amount of "upness," the place where your readiness feels just right for you. If you find yourself feeling too pumped up, you can make that feeling work for you by using it as a signal to bring your intensity down a bit, perhaps by shifting your focus to deliberate relaxed breathing or by refocusing on connecting fully with your warm-up or the beginning of your performance.

By thinking about how you would prefer to focus in your performance context and planning to do it, you can enter almost all performance situations focused and in control, even in situations that may have previously caused some unwanted stress or performance problems. A positive focus plan for your preperformance time and your actual performance can help you get your focus where you want it and keep it where it does you the most good.

Suppose that at your performance site your thoughts start to drift to such things as how nervous you are or how terrible it would be if you blew it. What can you do about it? You can use these thoughts as a reminder to shift your focus to something more constructive that puts you back in control. For example, at that moment, you could remind yourself that you are fully capable of executing this performance, recall your simple goal of just doing the best you can do today, focus fully on your preparation or warm-up, and then connect fully and positively with executing your performance. Just before your performance begins, focus on the first thing you will do—your start, your beginning, your opening statement, your first move, or your first action. For the remainder of your performance just stay fully focused on executing your performance, one move at a time, one step at a time, one sequence at a time, one task at a time. This is totally within your control.

Before you begin practicing, training, playing, competing, or performing on a given day, remind yourself of your best performance focus, your best recent practices, your best-ever performances, and your capacity to focus fully on performing well today. Focus on your preparation, your readiness, your commitment, your capacity, and your best focus. Just go out there and focus fully on executing your performance. Trust yourself. Trust your preparation. Trust your focus. Trust your intuition. Everything else will take care of itself. Remember also that your overall value as a person remains intact no matter how you perform today.

Your performance focus and overall life perspective are within your control. When you accept that you can effect positive change in all parts of your life, you will, precisely because all parts are within your control. You can choose to do whatever you want to do by focusing on doing whatever you want to do.

Sometimes important things in our life are beyond our control. It is self-defeating to take responsibility or feel guilty for things that happen to us or to other people close to us over which we have no direct control. You cannot control things that are impossible to control, no matter how hard you try or how much energy you expend trying to do so. You cannot control the past; you cannot control things that occur strictly by chance; you cannot control the actions, reactions, negativity, or incompetency of people around you. But you can control how you view the past, what you learn from the past, how you respond to things that are truly beyond your control, and how you focus on controlling positive things within your control. This shift in focus alone can put you back in control.

You will help yourself, your teammates, and the people closest to you most by focusing on positive things within your control and helping others focus on positive things within their control. Your thoughts are within your control. Your focus is within your control. Your focus directly influences your confidence, perspective, training, learning, interactions, and performance.

If you focus on potential failure or weaknesses you become more stressed. If you focus on errors, they are yours. If you focus on your strengths, you are stronger and more confident. If you focus on why you can and how you will accomplish your goals, your confidence grows stronger. If you focus fully on engaging yourself fully in the doing, the doing will become a positive reality.

Choose to use some of the following positive focus reminders to help you in your ongoing pursuit of personal excellence, or come up with some of your own positive focusing reminders:

+ I am in control of my focus, performance, and life.
+ I choose to excel in my chosen performance pursuit.
+ I choose to focus in positive and fully connected ways to enhance my performance, health, and life.
+ I am fully capable of achieving the goals I set for myself.
+ I learn from setbacks and turn them into positive opportunities for personal growth.
+ I embrace the lessons from my experiences and act on those lessons.
+ I choose to live my life fully and joyfully.

After many years of working with all kinds of people living and performing in all life contexts, I realized that they often want bottom-line reminders of what they can do each day to come closer to living their dreams in their performance domains and ongoing life pursuits. I developed the following positive reminders specifically for that purpose. I often photocopy these reminders and give them to the people I work with. They stick their positive reminder list on their computer or on a wall or mirror where they can see it daily. Their feedback on these simple but powerful reminders has been extremely positive, especially in bringing them back to a positive perspective when they begin to have doubts or drift away.

Positive Reminders for Excelling in Sport, Challenging Performance Pursuits, and Life

+ **Always positive thoughts.** Only positive thoughts help you do the things you really want to do. So think in positive ways, talk to yourself in positive ways, support yourself in positive ways, and focus only in positive ways that will help you live, love, learn, and perform to your true capacity.

+ **Always positive images.** Only positive images of the things you want to do or hope to accomplish will help you to accomplish them. So imagine yourself being the way you want to be, performing the way you want to perform, achieving the things you want to achieve, and doing the things you want to do exactly the way you would like to do them—with full focus, pure connection, and total confidence.

✦ **Always I can.** There is no advantage in approaching your performance, learning, or life situation thinking *I can't* or *I won't be able to do this.* Approach all challenges and opportunities thinking only *I can do this* or *we can do this.* Act as if you can, even if you are not sure you can. The "I can" perspective gives you your best chance of achieving your goals, loving your life, and living your dreams.

✦ **Always opportunities.** Opportunities are present every day in everything you do—opportunities to learn; grow; find something positive or of personal value; know yourself better; overcome challenges; and become stronger, wiser, more focused, more balanced, more joyful, more consistent, and more supportive of yourself and others. Focus on finding and embracing the opportunities in everything you see or do.

✦ **Always focused.** Only when you are fully focused on connecting with each step, experience, interaction, opportunity, or performance can you live and perform to your true potential. So stay focused on the little things that free you to feel your best, be your best, and perform your best. Seek the pure and positive connection in everything you do; it will give you your best chance of living and performing to your ultimate capacity.

✦ **Always lessons.** In every practice, performance, interaction, and life experience there are lessons. Look for the good things you have done, draw out the positive focusing lessons from each of your experiences, and live those lessons every day. Doing this will ensure that you continue to improve, grow, embrace your life fully, and excel in positive and life-enhancing ways.

✦ **Always act on the lessons learned.** You can continue to improve the quality and consistency of your practices, training sessions, performances, personal interactions, and daily life experiences by reflecting and acting on the lessons you learn every day. Thinking about what you want to do or how you want to be is not enough. If you want something to change in your world, you have to act on your positive intentions every day. This will free you to become the person and performer you have the potential to be.

✦ **Always step-by-step.** You will accomplish great things in your life by taking tiny steps forward each day. The step in front of you is all that matters right now. You are always capable of taking that one little step. Take that step, and then the next little step, and the next step. This is the path to your desired destination.

CHAPTER 12
Goals

The biggest problem or challenge with goals is not that you don't have them, it is that you don't act on them in positive and performance-enhancing ways every day. My goal at this moment is to finish writing this fifth edition of *In Pursuit of Excellence,* so I am up at 5:00 a.m. making revisions on this chapter so that I can help *you* achieve your goals, embrace your life, and live your dreams.

To realize a goal, you need to do something every day that will take you one step closer to that goal. What are you going to do today to take yourself one step closer to your goals or dreams? If you don't find a way to act on your positive intentions in some positive, performance- or life-enhancing way almost every day, it is very unlikely that you will perform to your true capacity and turn your dreams into a positive reality.

Acting on your positive intentions is your choice. Before you go to sleep at night and before you get out of bed in the morning "**do**cide" to do something positive that will take you one step closer to your goals and dreams.

I've had students, athletes, and performers in other challenging domains tell me they can't seem to meet or reach their goals. Sometimes discussions about goals go something like this:

Terry: Did you set specific daily achievable goals for yourself?

Student/athlete/performer: Oh, yes—I tried it and it didn't work, so I stopped setting goals.

Terry: What were your goals?

Student/athlete/performer: To make my dream team; to compete in the Olympics; to be a singer, actor, musician, surgeon, military pilot, or astronaut; to finish my thesis by the summer; to get an A in your class.

Terry: Are you setting short-term goals, every day, that are totally within your control, that can take you in the direction you want to go—like what you are going to do today, in the next hour, that will bring you one step closer to being your best or living your dream?

Student/athlete/performer: No, not really.

Terry: Do you have any specific goals for how you are going to get better today or tomorrow or the next day?

Student/athlete/performer: No, not really.

Terry: Before you get up in the morning, think about what you are going to *do* today that will take you one step closer to your goals and dreams. If you really want to be good or great at what you do, *you* have to act on your positive intentions in some small or big way every day. Thinking is not enough. Only positive action counts when your goal is to live your dreams.

People often set long-term, far-off goals without focusing enough on the present. But it is the present—today—that gets you to the future in the way you want to get there. Long-term goals can help motivate and guide you, but you need to focus on achievable daily performance goals that take you progressively closer to your desired destination. Focus your energy on taking small steps forward every day that are within your control to improve your positivity, performance skills, preparation, focusing and refocusing skills, technique, execution, and routines to prepare yourself mentally, physically, and technically to be the best you can be on race day, game day, or performance day.

Some outcomes in competitive or performance situations are not within your direct control because you do not control competitors, teammates, judges, officials, playing conditions, the weather, or chance occurrences—all of which can influence performance outcomes. Focus on controlling what is within your control—your focus and executing your best performance given the conditions you are facing. Stay focused on doing what you can do to be your best every day. Every day ask yourself, *What am I going to focus on today to take myself one step closer to my goal as a performer and as a human being?*

Accomplishing Everyday Goals

To get where you want to go, set specific, relevant, daily goals and then focus fully on acting on those goals, one step at a time. Encourage yourself, compliment yourself, and smile to yourself as you achieve each short-term goal and move toward long-term ones. You want to get from point A to point B efficiently and joyfully, and the only way to do that is to focus on the little steps that get you there. Let's say you want to become the best performer you can be or you want to write a book. Great! What are you going to do about it in the next five minutes, hour, day, week, month, or year? Setting specific daily goals and pursuing them in a systematic, focused way separates those who want to meet challenges and excel from those who actually do.

Let's take writing the fifth edition of this book as an example. I could simply write whenever I feel like it, or whenever I have free time, and finish whenever the book is complete (if ever). Or I can commit to accomplish specific, concrete writing goals for myself, within a specific time frame, saying that I want to finish the revisions to this chapter today, before eating supper; write the revisions for the following two chapters by the end of the week; finish the next three chapters by the end of the month; and complete all the book's revisions by the end of the summer. I've tried the "do it when I feel like it" approach, but I never seem to advance very quickly toward my goals—not because I don't want to do it but because a hundred other things pull on my time. When I commit specific time to write (usually early mornings when there are no distractions) and set specific short-term goals that will take me to my long-term goals, things begin to roll along nicely.

In my case, the book process goes something like this. First, I think about whether completing a fifth edition of this book is important to me or you or anyone else. This first step is critical, because only if I have a meaningful reason to do it will I be truly committed to the goal and have a realistic chance of achieving it in a timely manner with quality. I decide that this goal is important to me because I like writing, creating, and reflecting, and I want to share my most recent thoughts and experiences with you and others in hopes of helping you achieve your personal goals. I know more now than I did when I completed the fourth edition of this book eight years ago. I know that this book will be a much improved edition because the experiences I have gained over these past seven years have crystallized the essence of focusing for excellence for me.

Sharing meaningful and practical ideas that can actually help you improve your performance and enhance your life makes me feel that I am doing something worthwhile. Also, I love to see the visions or ideas that are floating through my mind become typed pages that are then transformed into a real book you can hold in your hands or read on your computer. It's very concrete: I can see what I'm accomplishing, and in the end I can feel it and touch it. Thinking about the outcome (in this case finishing this book) and why it is important to me inspires me to do the work required to turn this dream into a positive and concrete reality. Achieving the outcome always comes back to focusing on the doing, focusing on the process—which means acting on the day-by-day, step-by-step goals that will take you to your desired destination.

The concreteness of progress in most sports is obvious. New tricks, better technique, faster times, higher jumps, better plays, improved focus, improved rankings—all can be seen and felt. You know exactly where you are, and you can see progress in a way that is often not possible in other aspects of life. When I teach a class or make a presentation to a group, for example, I rarely know whether I've really accomplished anything. I don't have anything concrete that tells me I have affected any positive change in the lives of the members of the audience, unless people come up to me after a presentation, workshop, or class and tell me how great it was. On the other hand, sport, performing arts, big adventures, and my one-on-one consulting work with athletes and other high-level performers offer indisputable proof of progress and positive influence, which can yield much personal meaning and add joy to their lives and my life.

Let me return to my example of writing this book. Having determined at the outset that writing the book is important to me and to others, I begin to set some goals that are realistic in terms of my time, abilities, and motivation. Just the process of thinking about specific goals gets my mind moving in positive directions. Writing my goals and projected completion dates on paper usually helps even more. During the process, some things take longer to finish than expected, but that is no reason to panic. I simply readjust the goals to bring them in line with my reality. At times I move ahead of my stated goals, usually when I am totally focused—in a zone—and things just seem to flow along by themselves. Some days I really need a break from writing. I take that break because it allows me to return refreshed with a clearer mind. The next day I usually work twice as well—particularly if I know that my goal is to complete a certain amount by the end of the week. I also take short breaks every day when I am writing—to run or paddle or exercise or play because doing so helps me feel better, be better, focus better, and write better.

I gain great satisfaction from fulfilling my goals, even the small ones. Meeting my goals makes me feel more alive. It shows me that I can decide to do something that is important to me and then do it. Reaching a goal feels good, even if it is only a short-term one. Often this feeling is enough to keep me moving toward the next goal, as long as I believe it is a worthy one. If the goal has been difficult to meet or if I'm tired or need a lift, I take a few days off, go to nature, spend more time with my family or friends, run, ski, kayak, see a movie, or just relax. I treat myself well when I think I need or deserve a treat. We all need and deserve an occasional extravagance.

When *you* decide that something is worth pursuing with passion and persistence, you can apply your positive and fully connected focusing skills to reach a high performance level in virtually any area of your life. Whether you want to improve your focus, win a championship, excel in school, start or grow a business, excel in the performing arts, enhance your health, start or improve a relationship, or balance your life, the basic path is the same. First, you need a good reason to do it. Second, you need a high level of commitment. Third, you need to develop and nurture a positive and fully connected focus. Fourth, you need to identify and act on specific daily goals that will take you where you want to go.

Committing Fully to Your Mission

We all start with one constant: each day has 24 hours! If you are training or working toward a specific goal for a limited period of time each day, you might as well dig in and do as much quality work as you can during the time you are there. If you mentally prepare yourself to complete every task as well as you can, with a positive and fully connected high-quality focus, you can achieve your daily goals and still have some time to relax alone or with your family or friends.

Plan your workout or training session, set specific daily goals, and focus fully on executing or achieving the goals you set every day. This will free you to accomplish more with quality while you are working out, practicing, or training. Schedule in some relaxation time, some fun time, and some free time to embrace other simple joys in life. Quality focus, training, work, and rest are all important to get to where you want to go in your performance life and life outside your performance.

Three of my university students observed some local gymnasts at practice. They used a stopwatch to record the actual time that each gymnast spent performing on the apparatus during a two-hour workout. The average time they spent physically and mentally engaged in performance tasks was 15 to 20 minutes. How much time do you think you spend fully focused on high-quality training during a practice or workout session? Do you think you could extend the time you are fully connected in positive ways? Could you be using your training time more effectively to replicate the focus you need to perform your best in your real-world games, competitions, or performances? The answer is probably yes.

To perform your best, you have to bring your best focus into your practices and performances. This is a choice you have to make for yourself. Do you really want to be the best you can be, or is that not an important goal for you at this point in your life? If excelling is not important for you right now, focus on getting what you want out of this experience—fun, fitness, confidence, social interaction, the wind and sun on your face, or whatever you are seeking. Making that decision is perfectly OK. But if you want to excel or be the best you can possible be in a high-performance field, then you need to make a major commitment, set specific goals, and maintain a positive and fully connected focus throughout the course of your journey.

Often we know intuitively whether something is worth pursuing with a high level of commitment. At other times we are not really sure. If we are not really sure, it may help to ask ourselves some questions or discuss our feelings with people close to us. Think about each of the following questions and respond to them honestly (perhaps in writing).

+ Are you involved in this sport or performance pursuit because you really want to do it or because someone else wants you to do it?
+ Is this something that gives you ongoing joy and satisfaction?
+ Is this something that makes you feel more fully alive?
+ Why do you want to do this?
+ What do you expect to gain from being engaged in this sport or performance pursuit?

✦ What do you expect to lose from being engaged in this sport or performance pursuit?

✦ Do you think the time and focused effort you put into this sport or performance pursuit will be worth it when there are no guarantees of the outcome?

When you recognize that you do have a choice and that you can make a conscious decision about whether you want to continue in this pursuit or do something else, you can often approach things in a positive light. If you decide to go for it and are dedicated to that choice, you will have a greater capacity to endure the demands that follow. Friedrich Nietzsche wrote, "He who has a reason why can bear with almost any how." If you decide to let this pursuit go and pursue something else of perhaps greater interest, then you are free to explore and embrace other, perhaps more meaningful, pursuits.

Setting Short-Term and Long-Term Goals

Establishing a series of short-term goals, with specific target dates for achievement, that are directly relevant to your long-term goals is important for ongoing improvement. Achieving a goal, even a short-term one, makes you feel competent and inspires you to pursue your next goal, thereby helping you maintain commitment and build self-confidence.

Short-term goals might include mastering a certain skill, focusing on quality work or quality execution, getting adequate rest, or completing a certain number of moves, plays, programs, workouts, or assignments—today, by the end of the week, or by the end of the month. Your short-term goals can help you improve not only physically, technically, and tactically but also mentally; thus, you should set daily goals for mental readiness; positive imagery; positive, fully connected focusing; distraction control; relaxation; and drawing out positive lessons from your experiences and acting on them.

Long-term goals may include becoming more positive with your overall attitude, less stressed, or more consistent with your best focus; reaching your highest level of excellence in your sport or performance domain; mastering a particular routine, program, race plan, or game plan; deciding on the speed, distance, time, or performance level you want to attain by the end of the current year and in the following year; or achieving a personal best in an important assignment, performance, or competition.

By writing down your goals in concrete terms (I will accomplish this goal by this time), you have a greater chance of accomplishing your objectives more quickly than you otherwise would. How many preparation days remain before your next performance, presentation, trials, audition, assignment, championship, or event? Write down your goals and the number of days remaining before your next key event. This simple activity is often enough to stimulate ongoing positive action.

Curtis Compton/Zuma Press/Icon Sportswire

Jordan Spieth didn't achieve success overnight in the PGA. Great performers use short-term as well as long-term goals to achieve their dreams and you can, too.

Many high-level performers keep daily logbooks for training and performances to direct, monitor, and continue to improve the consistency of their best performances. They list goals set and met, record their training programs, and keep track of what they focus on during best and less than best practices and performances. This process of ongoing reflection and acting on the lessons learned speeds up their learning and makes their best performances more consistent because they continue to learn more from each of their experiences and continue to act on the lessons learned.

Think about tomorrow's goals tonight before you go to sleep or first thing in the morning before you get out of bed. Just lie there for a few minutes and run through your mind what you want to accomplish that day. This simple positively focused action sets the stage for doing the good things you want to do every day.

A respected coach or seasoned performer may be able to assist you in establishing realistic but challenging goals by helping you translate your overall aims or long-term goals into specific concrete actions, moves, plays, times, programs, routines, scores, or performance requirements.

Ultimately, you must set and commit to your own goals rather than have someone else dictate them for you. When *you* make the decision or completely agree with the decision, your commitment to go after that goal is *greatly* increased. Shared goal setting—between you and your coach, you and your trainer or supervisor, you and your parents, or you and your teammates or partners—is valuable as long as you have personally weighed the situation and feel that this goal is what you really want to pursue and achieve.

Identifying your own goals and having input into your preparation or training program is a very effective means of reaching your potential. This has been true for most of the high-performance athletes with whom I work, and it is probably also true for you. You know better than anyone else. You know what you have done and know what you want to do. You also know what will help you and what you need to focus on at a particular moment. So trust your intuition when it comes to respecting the focus that works best for you.

You can sometimes strengthen your commitment to pursue a goal by talking with family members, trusted teammates, coaches, friends, or focus enhancement consultants like me about your reasons for making a commitment to pursue a specific goal or mission. Some athletes go so far as to make a public statement about their goals in an attempt to increase their own commitment to pursue them. Not all athletes gain from making their goals public, but we all gain from the support and constructive encouragement of important people in our lives when we are pursuing high-level personal goals.

Making Adjustments

When you fall short of the goals you set, remember that unmet goals, plateaus, times of seemingly little or no progress, and even periods of backsliding are natural. Everyone faces these experiences at some point in their sport or performance life. Progress is a series of ups and downs; it is not all clear sailing. Even when you see no obvious signs of improvement, you may still be laying the groundwork for future progress. Think of the best performers in your sport or performance discipline. All have been discouraged at times.

All have struggled to overcome certain problems and failed to meet some goals. But somehow these performers persist through the setbacks, learn from them, and find ways to overcome the obstacles. Such trials are part of the path to ongoing excellence and part of the path to joyful day-to-day living.

Falling short of a particular goal in your sport or performance domain or in your personal life is not a tragedy. You grow from the experience and learn from it. You refine your focus, adjust your goal, and stick some short-term goals or intermediate steps in front of it. A temporary setback doesn't mean you have to quit or give up on your goals or dreams. It means that you draw out the lessons, work on setting additional appropriate short-term goals, improve your focusing and refocusing skills, and readjust your goals to meet the needs of the new challenges and opportunities you now have in front of you. Your goal today may simply be to cope or be the best you can be today. Or to find and embrace some simple joys today. Or to choose to make better and wiser choices today.

When I first started working in the performance and life enhancement field, I used goal setting haphazardly. Now that I am more seasoned, I am better able to set specific meaningful goals and adjust my goals to bring them in line with me, rather than trying to force myself in line with them. When a discrepancy exists with my goals, the goals are usually off target. I am being who I am. I am doing the best I can at this moment, given the complexities and challenges of life. Goal setting doesn't provide all the answers to living your dreams, but when used properly it nudges you in the positive direction you would like to go.

Regardless of what you want to accomplish in your life, setting meaningful goals, being positive with yourself, and focusing on the step in front of you are very important. What are some short-term goals you would like to start working on today? Put your goals up on your bathroom mirror and on your bedroom wall and on your computer or mobile phone as a reminder to do what you want to do today and every day to move forward in positive and performance-enhancing ways. Try it and see what happens! You've got nothing to lose and lots to gain in terms of living and performing closer to your true potential.

Believing in Yourself and Your Capacity

Your performance is largely a result of how you see yourself, what you expect from yourself, and your capacity to focus in positive and fully connected ways. If you see yourself as someone who has something valuable to offer, someone who has a meaningful contribution to make, someone who has great potential, and someone who can focus fully on executing your best performance, then this will be your reality.

If you see yourself as having little or nothing to offer, then this will likewise be reflected in your performance, unless you choose to change your perspective—from negative to positive and from disconnected to fully connected. Don't sell yourself short! You can accomplish much more than you or most people recognize. How can I say that? I don't even know you, right? Well, if you are anything like other members of the human species with whom I have had the opportunity to work, you have all kinds of untapped potential. You have no idea how good *you can be*, and if you are still reading this book, you probably have visions of realizing some of this potential, and you are probably ready to act on some of the focusing for excellence lessons I am sharing with you. This potential will lead you to where you want to go!

Excellence in any field depends largely on

+ knowing where you want to go (having a big-picture vision),
+ really wanting to get there (making a full commitment to get to where you want to go),
+ believing in your ability to arrive at your desired destination (believing in your capacity), and
+ connecting fully with the step in front of you (sustaining a fully focused connection).

I once worked with a young athlete who was overflowing with natural talent. But he didn't believe he could be a great athlete because he had no "proof"—that was the word he used to describe what he needed before he could believe in himself. One way of providing proof in your potential is to chart your progress systematically so that you can see your ongoing improvement. Another way to find proof in your potential is to practice, train, interact, observe, or compete with some high-level performers you really admire or respect so that you can see that they too are human and that you can hang in there with them at least for certain pieces, workouts, practices, assignments, or parts of training or competitions.

Look for the good things in yourself and in your performances instead of just looking for what is lacking. Remind yourself of the things you do well, and give yourself a pat on the back for the good things you are doing. Make suggestions to yourself for ongoing improvement in a positive and constructive manner. Walk into the performance arena and be positive with yourself. Act as if you can do anything. This will make you feel better, focus better, and perform better.

With the teams and individuals with whom I work, I ask athletes, coaches, and other performers to respond in writing to questions about three key goals. I do this to inspire personal excellence (the big dream), to target realistic goals, and to address the critical issue of personal acceptance. Your dream goal opens the door to pursue your stretched or unlimited human potential, your realistic goal keeps you grounded and focused in what you can realistically achieve, and your goal of self-acceptance reminds you that you are a valued human being and will continue to be a valued human being apart from your performance on any given day.

Goal Questions

✦ **Dream goal.** What is your dream goal? What would you really love to do, achieve, or accomplish in your sport or performance domain and in other parts of your life? What do you think is possible in the long run if you remove all barriers, focus fully on doing what you want to do, and continue to challenge yourself to stretch your limits?

✦ **Realistic goal.** What do you feel is a realistic best performance goal that you can accomplish or achieve this year (based on your present skill level, your motivation to improve, and your commitment to focus fully on making those improvements)?

✦ **Goal of self-acceptance.** If you really go after your dreams with a positive and fully connected focus every day, there is a great chance that you will achieve your realistic goal and a good chance that you will achieve your dream goal. But just in case you do not achieve those goals, it is important that you make a commitment to accept yourself as a worthy human being and grow from the experience, regardless of whether you achieve your dream goal or realistic performance goal for this year.

Dream big so you keep the door open for accomplishing big things.

+ Focus fully on attaining your realistic best performance goals in training and in competitions or performances.
+ Accept yourself as a valuable and worthy human being regardless of whether you reach your dream goal or attain your realistic best performance goal this year.
+ Remind yourself that personal excellence is a challenging journey and sometimes it takes a while to get to where you want to go!
+ Embrace the simple joys and sometimes not-so-simple steps of your journey every day.
+ Find something to smile about every day!
+ Start a highlight journal where you write down your highlights at the end of every day.

Alwyn Morris, a talented First Nations former athlete, won a gold medal with his equally talented paddling partner Hugh Fisher in the K2 race at the 1984 Summer Olympics in Los Angeles. ("K" stands for kayak and "2" signifies two paddlers in the kayak.) I invited Alwyn to speak at an international sport psychology conference I was hosting in Ottawa to share his journey to personal excellence. I had worked with Alwyn for many years through the ups and downs of his journey to excellence, and we had become good friends. He mentioned in his talk that he first started to believe he could be an Olympic champion (and set it as a goal) when he met me at the Canadian national canoe–kayak team training camp in Florida. He specifically said that writing down his dream goal on paper—*Olympic champion*—had somehow made it seem possible. Because he had a dream goal, a realistic goal, and a goal of self-acceptance, he had all the bases covered no mattered what happened. Once he had these three major goals in place, everything else he did in his sport revolved around setting daily goals for mental readiness, bringing his best focus into every training session, and giving his best effort to build the physical, technical, tactical, and focusing skills he needed in order to be his best and to be the best in the world in his sport.

I encourage you to do what Alwyn did. Write down your dream goal, your realistic goal, and your goal of self-acceptance, regardless of how you perform on any given day. Then choose to bring your best focus—your most positive and most fully connected focus—into your everyday training and performance pursuits.

CHAPTER 13
Commitments

I have been fortunate to work with many Olympic champions and world champions in a variety of sports. I have learned many valuable lessons from each of these athletes, which I have shared with others and applied to my own positive life pursuits—including writing this book.

When Beckie Scott "**do**cided" to become an Olympic champion in cross-country skiing and be the best she could possibly be, she made a choice that many other great performers make. She described it as "putting your heart and soul into doing everything it takes to accomplish that goal." This is the kind of focus and commitment required to excel at the highest levels in any high-performance pursuit.

Long before Sylvie Bernier won an Olympic gold medal in diving, like many Olympic champions, she docided she was going to do everything in her power to win at the Olympics. Her dream goal came to her "like flashes all the time. Every day I would see myself doing perfect dives, walking down and getting the medal. When it actually happened, it felt like I had already done it before."

To achieve your full potential or live your dreams, somewhere deep in the core of your being you have to choose to go after your dreams. You have to create or develop an underlying belief within yourself that you can actually do it. When you dream big dreams and focus fully on embracing the little daily focused steps that will take you to where you want to go, you continue to nourish your long-term commitment, enhance your daily focus, strengthen your confidence, and give yourself good reasons to believe in yourself and your mission.

Even if you fall short of attaining your ultimate goal, your dream of getting there inspires you to become far better than you otherwise would have been. Most great and noble human accomplishments begin with some kind of positive vision or dream. Every great human feat flashes through someone's mind before it surfaces as concrete reality, whether it be flying to the moon; landing on Mars; becoming a great student, artist, writer, director, or performer; making a positive difference in the world; healing yourself; excelling in a relationship; building a dynasty; or building a tree house. Positive dreams precede positive realities; they nourish, direct, and even create them.

Our dreams of personal excellence, personal accomplishments, and meaningful contributions are forward reflections into a positive future where we see ourselves doing the things we want to do, being the way we want to be, and freeing ourselves to get to the places we want to go. Visions of excellence, creative accomplishment, and joyful and harmonious living are themselves stimulating and uplifting. They provide us with hope, meaningful positive direction, and sustainable ongoing positive energy. Dreams of attaining our highest levels of personal and performance excellence often become memories of the future, waiting to unfold, for those of us who choose to push beyond the sometimes limiting boundaries of past and present experiences.

All people who have excelled at anything had dreams of making a meaningful contribution, stretching their limits, accomplishing things important to them, becoming their best, or reaching their potential in whatever they were pursuing. People who excel dream big and go after their dreams. They begin with a positive dream and focus on the step-by-step process of living or creating a better reality.

Some people dream big but do not act in concrete ways that will lead them to more positive new realities. Their lack of positive action is their essential disadvantage. Dreams do not become a reality unless you act in positive ways every day to turn those dreams into positive living realities.

Some people remain stuck where they are because they don't dream of a better way, a better life, a better performance, or a higher level of humanity. Equally important, they don't act on their positive intentions because they don't believe in the possibility of living at a better or higher level. But we know people can turn things around by seeing and accepting that it is possible to accomplish things previously viewed as impossible. Few things are impossible when you believe strongly enough in the positive possibilities and focus fully on turning them into positive new realities.

Think about your own dreams. Visit them often in your mind. Let them lead you. Pursuing your dreams is the best chance you have of moving forward on a path of self-fulfillment, joy, and personal excellence. One life, many opportunities! Turn every opportunity into a positive new reality now rather than looking back and wishing that you had.

Qualities of Excellence

Excellence is embodied in a variety of shapes, sizes, shades, languages, and cultures. Personal excellence is largely a question of believing in your capabilities and fully committing yourself to be the best you can possibly be. Success is grounded in finding a way to make it happen—regardless of where you live, where you come from, what language you speak, or what kind of support system you have. If you really want to excel badly enough, you will find a way.

Commitment and focus are the most essential keys to personal and performance excellence. To excel in any field, you need a high level of commitment and a fully connected sustainable positive focus that allows you to perform your best under a variety of challenging, distracting, or stressful circumstances.

Excellence in sport, school, the performing arts, business, medicine, teaching, coaching, and every other high-performance profession begins with a dream or goal to which you must bring a high level of commitment or passion, an optimal level of intensity, and a positive and fully connected focus. At some point you have to say to yourself, *Hey, I really want to be great at this; I am going to do everything I can possibly do to be as good as I can be; I am making this mission to excellence a priority in my life.*

To be your best, choose to live this commitment with your heart and soul and focus on finding ways to continue to improve and stretch your limits every day. Act on your positive commitment by bringing your best focus into your everyday pursuits for ongoing improvement. Remember also that a lack of commitment or fully connected focus guarantees you will fall short of your potential.

The solid leaders in every sport and high-performance discipline are great examples of the kind of commitment and focus required to become the best that one can be. Their commitment and focus are reflected by the incredible intensity they bring to training, practices, simulations, performances, games,

Franck Faugere/DPPI/Icon Sportswire

Lindsey Vonn exemplifies the kind of commitment and focus needed to make success happen.

and competitions. When they are training, preparing, and performing, they are focused on doing their best and accomplishing their goals. Their primary goal is to be fully focused in positive and fully connected ways every second out there. In important games, performances, or competitions, they are positive, energized, and superfocused. Nothing less than their best fully connected focus is enough to perform their best consistently.

Your Personal Commitment

Your personal level of commitment is something you have to determine for yourself. No one can tell you how important it is for you to excel in your sport or your life; that is your decision. But clearly people who excel in their sport or performance domains are extremely committed to those goals. Excelling at living and achieving the goals you want to achieve in your life requires a high level of personal commitment.

Rate the importance of excelling in your sport, life, or performance domain on a scale from 1 to 10. A rating of 10 indicates that this pursuit is the most important thing in your life (very high commitment), a rating of 1 indicates that it is not important at all (very low commitment), and a 5 indicates a middle position between the two.

How important is it for you to live your life fully and joyfully?

| 1 | 2 | 3 | 4 | 5 | 6 | 7 | 8 | 9 | 10 |

Not important at all   Most important focus in my life

How important is it for you to excel in your sport or chosen performance domain?

| 1 | 2 | 3 | 4 | 5 | 6 | 7 | 8 | 9 | 10 |

Not important at all   Most important focus in my life

When a large group of marathon runners were asked, "How important is it for you to excel in your running?" it became clear that those with the highest levels of commitment (scores of 9 and 10) became the fastest runners. As your commitment level increases, your performance level increases proportionally. As your commitment level decreases, your performance level decreases proportionally. This holds true for virtually all performers in all high-performance disciplines.

When members of a number of national teams were asked what they thought the main difference was between them and other athletes who did not make the national team, their first response was commitment and focus ("wanting it more," "being willing to train harder or smarter," and "training and competing with more focus"). The most committed athletes who became the best performers sometimes stayed after practice, focused on learning by watching the best athletes play or perform on-site or on video, practiced with more focus and intensity, and did extra work when required. They were willing to make sacrifices, and they believed that they would one day be excellent performers. Most important was their commitment to be totally focused within their training and performance arenas.

In a study we did with the National Hockey League (NHL), we interviewed top NHL coaches and scouts. We asked them what they looked for when drafting a player into the NHL and why they thought that some players who were selected didn't perform well at the NHL level. Commitment (desire, determination, attitude, heart, self-motivation) and focus were the crucial ingredients that tilted the balance between making it and not making it at the professional level. Making their hockey careers a top priority, maintaining personal pride, constantly trying to improve, and always investing maximum focus and effort were named as the key indicators of the kind of commitment necessary to succeed at the highest levels.

The chief scout for one of the NHL's top teams expressed it this way: "The main thing is that the player is willing to give that little extra when it's needed. . . . He's preparing himself to give that little bit more . . . even when he might be dead tired. . . . This separates the great hockey player from the good hockey player."

Physically talented athletes who do not make it in the major professional leagues are described as lacking in the area of commitment, focus, or distraction control and unable to cope with the stress of the pro situation on or off the field, court, or ice ("could not cope with pro demands," "choked under pressure"). The difference between making it and not making it was highlighted in a discussion of the drafting of one of the NHL's most celebrated players—Bobby Clarke, former team captain and general manager of the Philadelphia Flyers hockey club.

> We drafted Bobby Clarke on our second round, but there was a boy we drafted on our first round who was bigger and stronger, could skate and shoot better than Clarke, but Clarke made it and he didn't. He never had the heart for the game. He wasn't willing to sacrifice that little bit extra that you need to be a professional hockey player. In practice, Clarke would be there 10 minutes longer and he would work harder. In a game, he got himself mentally prepared to give the extra effort. . . . The other player didn't do that. Result—one went ahead, the other fell behind. Clarke did extra work on the ice, where he had to give a little more to check the man, where he had to bear down. Where it showed more than any place is coming back. . . . Gotta give a little bit more. If you lose possession of the puck, now you have to dig down to your bootstraps for extra adrenaline to come back and check the man. Bobby Clarke would always show that. The other boy would put his head down and sort of give up. That's the difference between the two.

A commitment to do quality work and quality training is a prerequisite for excellence at any level in every discipline, but unless you also master the art of focus control you will continue to fall short of your goals or dreams.

Excellence requires that you develop a strong and positive fully connected focus, as well as an ongoing openness to learn from others and your experiences. If you really want to excel at whatever you are doing, continue to learn from your best and less than best experiences and continue to act on the lessons learned.

Scotty Bowman, a highly respected NHL coach who guided his teams to many Stanley Cup NHL championships, offered some interesting advice in this regard:

✦ **Accept criticism.** "Our superstars can handle constructive criticism. . . . They can even handle unfair criticism. . . . If they make a mistake, they acknowledge it and do everything in their power to not make it again. . . . A person with star potential will not become a star if, when I criticize him or point out a mistake, he tries to fight me."

✦ **Don't be afraid to fail.** "If a superstar ever sees a slight opening, zip, he has the courage to go for the small hole. He won't hold back because he's afraid to fail."

✦ **Maintain composure.** "The best players maintain their composure . . . when there's a call that goes against them, maybe even a bad call. They stay cool, look to correct, and try to calm down the other players."

Being Your Best

To become the best you can possibly be, the first essential ingredient is your commitment to focus on doing the right things at the right time. It takes a strong commitment to train and rest your body so that you can perform under demanding conditions over long periods of time. It takes a strong commitment to train your focus so that you can execute your best performance skills under the most demanding or distracting circumstances. If you really want to be or become the best you can possibly be, acting on the following basic guidelines will help immensely:

✦ **Set specific daily goals.** You need to know what you want to accomplish every day, every practice, or every workout or training session. Before you begin, take some time to prepare yourself mentally so that you actually do what you want to do and get the most out of yourself during that practice, workout, or performance session. Commit yourself to execute your skills with full focus. In practice sessions, simulate what you want to do in your performance setting. Run through complete, clean routines, programs, plays, moves, races, or events on a regular basis. During workout sessions, scrimmages, or run-throughs, focus 100 percent, every step of the way. Positive images of what you want to do can help you prepare your mind and body to perform closer to your potential. Imagine and feel yourself successfully executing the skills you are trying to perfect before you do them, and then focus fully on executing those skills.

✦ **Listen to your body.** When preparing for an important competition, series, or performance, rest well and avoid overworking or overtraining so that you go in rested, strong, and healthy. Your commitment to rest well is as important as the commitment to train well. Without proper rest, the mind–body system falters and eventually breaks down.

✦ **Discover and respect your own best focus.** Discover what focus works best for you in different high-performance contexts. Where is your focus when you perform your best? Respect that focus. If it drifts away, click back or shift back to your best focus. Remind yourself to bring your best focus into your preparation or training sessions and into your performances, and shift or click back to your best focus whenever you encounter obstacles or distractions in performance contexts.

✦ **Decide to remain positive.** Practice overcoming distractions on a daily basis. Avoid wasting energy on things that are beyond your control. Choosing to stay positive and fully focused will lead to higher-quality training, better performances, and more joyful living.

✦ **Respect your best focus.** Before important events, remind yourself to respect the focus that works best for you. Mentally prepare yourself to connect fully with "the doing" for the entire performance and be prepared to refocus through potential distractions in the heat of the moment. Follow the preevent preparation patterns that have resulted in your best performances. If you feel it might be helpful for you, imagine and feel yourself executing your perfect performance or key parts of your performance before you actually begin your game, routine, race, or performance. Some athletes find that this helps them keep their best performance program fresh in their mind and body. They then close off their thinking and connect totally with executing their performance.

Draw the lessons out of every event, game, race, competition, or performance. What went well? What needs refining? Were you able to maintain your best focus for the whole performance? Were you able to refocus quickly if you got off track? What do you want to do in the same way next time? What do you want to change for your next performance? Where do you want your focus to be in your next performance, game, race, event, or competition? How can you remind yourself to respect the focus that works best for you? Make a note of key reminders that can help you feel totally prepared—mentally, physically, and emotionally—for your next challenge.

The following reminders for high-performance excellence are quotes drawn from individual interviews with leading NHL coaches and scouts. Think of how you can adapt and apply some of these positive reminders to your sport or situation.

Prerequisites for Excellence

✦ Do constant work on the ice; be in on the action, always after the puck, the check, or the goal; make things happen; give a little extra when it is important.

+ After a mistake, goal against, or a coach's criticism, come back with a strong shift, make the right moves, stay in the play or game, and try harder to correct or make up for the mistake.

+ Never give up (for example, take a check, get back into the play quickly, try and try again).

+ Plan, evaluate, and correct with linemates on the bench; encourage others; pass to better-positioned players on the ice.

+ Take tips, ask questions, listen, admit errors and correct them without excuses, and show that you want to continue to learn and improve.

+ Pursue activities both in and out of season to maintain conditioning and improve skills (for example, by fitness training and power skating).

+ Learn how to perform in a big game as well as in a normal game; come through in tight situations or close games; make the big play when needed.

+ Learn how to stay motivated, come back, and play well after a setback, mistake, missed chance, call against you or your team, or bad penalty.

+ Learn to control your temper (for example, do not needlessly retaliate after a hit or setback). Learn to react to referees, coaches, teammates, and fans in a mature and positive way, particularly in big games.

+ Learn to adapt to the stress of success, travel, and playing with different players (for example, line switching) without negative effects on your attitude or play.

+ Learn to stay cool, confident, and focused under pressure (for example, avoid being moody or worrying excessively; maintain focus on getting the job done in pressure situations).

Lessons in Commitment
Chris McCormack

Chris McCormack is one of the world's best ever Ironman triathletes. Chris has won more than 130 triathlon races globally, at all distances. In this interview he sheds light on the commitment and focus required to bring the highest level of excellence to this extremely demanding sport. My graduate student, Karine Grand'Maison, conducted interviews with Chris and a number of other leading Ironman triathletes for her master's thesis. I extracted portions of Karine's interview with Chris to share an excellent example of what commitment to excellence looks like at the highest performance levels.

Commitment to Training

I guess the biggest challenge for Ironman racers is the volume of work, the training, the time that needs to be committed to the sport for the three disciplines. The volume of work uses up a lot of time. I'm a very hard trainer. I think anyone who trains with me knows that. I have four or five training partners, and I recycle them. I like standing at the start line thinking, *There's not a person here who's trained harder than me.* So for me that's a positive, when I'm standing at the start line, in there swimming, fighting in the water going, *OK, we've got eight hours of pain, but no one here has been through what I've been through.* Everything I need to do for every race, I do. It gives me confidence, and it gives me the edge when I'm meeting those obstacles during the race. If there's someone up the road, I can remind myself, *I've hurt like this a thousand times before, and he hasn't trained as hard as I did. You're ready for this, don't be soft.*

When I've had good training I'm standing on that start line and going, *OK, there's nothing more I could have done to be more ready for this phase, and physically I think I'm the best in the world. So there's no one here who should beat me. So anyone who's in front of me shouldn't be there, and the only person who's stopping me from winning is me.* When I have an obstacle I deal with it; I deal with this thing. Otherwise, this guy is going to beat me, and he doesn't deserve to beat me because he's not as good as I am. That's how I deal with things. Self-doubt is the biggest killer for anyone. That's why I like to start every race feeling that I've done everything I can to be ready for it. Self-doubt can kill you and take away a win.

Commitment to Your Plan

The swim. I'll place myself among the good swimmers and get ready to go. Once the gun goes, it's long strokes, like I've done so many times in training. That's all I think about. I'll pick up my rate [turnover of the arms] and think, *Long strokes, long swim strokes, come on.* The first part is fast. I'll usually position myself next to the best swimmer. He's going to be the first out of the water, so all I have to concentrate on is his suit. Obviously, I look up every 10 or 15 strokes, but I just focus on swimming next to him. So I don't look up for maybe the first three or four minutes. We start to get into clear water, and then he might start to pull away because he's a bit stronger. The group starts to establish itself, and then my focus is just staying where I am, staying with the front guys. My aim is just to keep my tempo, the things that I've trained, the pace I've trained at, which is usually in the front group.

Two hundred meters out from the transition, I'm starting to think about the bike. I might be kicking a bit more to get some blood into the legs, and I'm thinking, *OK, where's my bike?* I picture where it is. And I'll start to look at who's around me then, what competitors are there. Then I'm concentrating on the bike, getting out, getting my wetsuit off. You've walked the transition chute so you know where stuff is. You get out of the water and just follow your path that you've done in training.

The bike. My thoughts getting on the bike are, *Let's go! Now we're on the land, this is where I'm good.* So boom, I'm immediately shoes on and ready to rock 'n' roll. I set a really good tempo, and I try to draw people into my pace, especially the younger guys, because I want to have people with me if I can. When you're solo all day for hours on the bike, it's just lonely. It's good to have other people around. Also, if they tend to have bad patches, you drop them. You take their energy and you feel good about it. You sort of steal their energy. I like having people around me and battling with people. I draw from that; I get energy from that.

On the 180-kilometer ride I keep repeating the circle. For me, it's like 500 calories in per hour. I'm going to have a Clif Shot every 15 minutes; I'm going to drink that bidden [bottle] of water within this hour. Every 15 minutes you're riding along and you're like, *OK, there's an aid station: Clif Shot, drink*. And then it's 120 calories, and when you start counting calories it's amazing how quick that part goes, because you're thinking in small increments all the time. You're like, *OK, there's an hour, have I got 500 calories in? Yep, boom, start again. Have I got enough water? What gear am I pushing? Is the pace good?* You're thinking so many things. In my first Ironman, I remember thinking, *What am I going to think of for 8 1/2 hours? How boring!* And I was absolutely amazed how quickly it went.

The run. I'm a runner. But the run still intimidates me. Every Ironman I've done, I have led off the bike. So the two where I've failed, I failed on the run. So in the last five kilometers on the bike I always think, *OK, that felt good*. I get off the bike, and the first thing I'm thinking about is how the legs are feeling. Then my whole race for the run is structured around my watch. I go, *OK, boom, start the watch*. Now I'm going to run four minutes a kilometer. I've done it one million times in training, I know I can do it comfortably, I know I won't be in any trouble, and if I run four minutes a kilometer, no one will catch me. A 2:48 marathon will win it for me, no matter what, because the guys who can run quicker will be too far behind. So I start my watch. After the first kilometer I ask myself, *Too fast or too slow?* And usually it's too fast, because of the hype, so I just adjust my pace and take my fuel in. The run is quite easy for the first 10 miles. I focus on staying controlled, staying on the pace, and staying relaxed.

I want to know where my competitors are, but I'll never look back for them. I always try to think, *I'm in the lead; everyone is feeling equally as uncomfortable as I am*. I consider myself one of the best guys in the world at this, so anyone who is behind me is behind me because they're not as good as me. And they're feeling just as bad as I am. So to catch me, they've got to run quicker than I am running right now, and they can't do it. These are the things that I think to myself.

Sometimes you get to a turnaround point and you'll see your competitors for the first time. You always try to look good. And you just keep saying to yourself, *OK, they're four minutes back. OK, we're 20 kilometers from home. He has to take one minute out of me every 5 kilometers, and he can't do it, man! If I'm hanging on to this pace, he can't do it.*

I'll never think about my competitors when I have a bad patch. I'm thinking, *How am I going to get out of this? OK, fuel, caffeine. I need sugar. OK, let's slow it down a bit, slow the pace, and I'm in the circle, I'm expecting it to happen.* I'm not going into this race expecting not to have any bad patch. It's going to happen. You just think, *OK, this is a bad patch, I expected this to happen. I've done this 50 times before in races, and I wonder how long this is going to last.* And sometimes you think, *Oh, here we go, 5 or probably 10 minutes of this, so it will probably be that bridge down there.* You're like, *I'll probably feel uncomfortable up to that bridge; let's just run to that bridge.* Your body will adjust, and you'll come out of it. It's amazing how it does it! When you show your body that you're not going to stop, it says, *OK,* and goes back to being good again. You have to avoid giving in to your body, because if your body senses that your mind is going to be weak and give in to it, it will shut down! When you're feeling good, you capitalize on it, and when you're feeling bad, you can slow it down. If you're capitalizing when your competitors are going through a bad patch, it ends up helping you out. At the end of the day, it's the person who has the fewest bad patches who wins the race.

Commitment to Staying Positive

In the Ironman at the elite level, everyone's physically well conditioned. Your mind is important, and not just in the race. It's the whole package—the training too because it is such a monotonous sport, with monotonous workloads. Mentally, I look at my Ironman failures and successes and try to determine the causes. In the ones that went bad, I allowed outside sources of negativity to move into my race. Things weren't going my way, I went for hard sections, the pace was fast, it was hot and windy, it wasn't what I expected, and I allowed those things to influence my race. Once you start down that path, it's like the dark side of the force in *Star Wars*. Once you start with the negative, it's easy to quit mentally. If you switch off mentally in the Ironman, it's over.

In an Ironman, especially when it gets hard and tough, it's important to be mentally tough. You have to remain positive. The way I try to think of it is this: in my perfect scenario, I lead out of the swim by 5 minutes, I have a 10-minute lead out of the bike, I run great, and I win. That's a perfect scenario, but it's not going to happen. So I think of it like a circle: no matter where I am in that circle I'm going to have obstacles, and I deal with those obstacles as they arise. So if I'm swimming and I'm behind, I deal with it: *OK, I have to make up the distance and focus on the now, not the future or the past.*

In the swim, my plan is to swim off and go with the front people. If that's working, great; I focus on that. If it's not, then when I am in "the now," I think, *OK, let's lengthen my stroke. How can I get back to where I want to be?* and I focus on those things and meet those obstacles as they arise. I look at those races where I did badly, and I didn't deal with "the now." I was like, *Ahhhhh, it's over, it's finished,* instead of focusing on meeting the challenge in front of me. I think many people do that. That's where the mental side as opposed to the physical side is more important, because I think in those bad races, physically I could have been successful, but I allowed the negatives and those obstacles to stop my progress. Instead of meeting the obstacles and fixing them or dealing with them by going, *OK, this has happened, so let's focus on what we're doing and deal with this*, I allowed the obstacles to become an issue so I couldn't get past them. I never completed the circle (back to the positive action focus).

You either deal with the problem in the race now, or you don't. And if you don't, it's going to finish you. The race is going to finish, and there's nothing worse than being in the car driving home after the race thinking, *If only I'd sprinted earlier, if only I'd eaten that food, if only. . . .* I never like to have "if onlys."

To complete the circle and not let the negativity affect my performance, if I'm on the bike and I'm behind, I look at my pace and my gear and think, *OK, this is my pace. This guy is going well; maybe he's going too fast.* Obviously, you have to revert to what you're physically capable of doing. If I'm behind on the bike and everything is going well, then I just reassure myself that this is good: *He's going too fast for me at the moment. It's a long day. We have eight or nine hours. Maybe he's pushing too hard.* So I deal with what I can control, my variables. If I'm going through a bad section, if it's tough and I'm losing because it's tough, then I'm constantly saying, *It's OK.* Your body is not too smart, but your mind is amazing. Your body starts to do what you tell it to do. If you start thinking that you're tired and it's hot, your body will react so as to make you tired. It's actually lazy, I think. It wants to stop, and it doesn't want to be there, so it constantly sends these messages that it's uncomfortable. So you keep telling yourself, *I feel good. This is a problem, but we'll deal with it. It's OK.*

Your body is not the smartest thing. It will do anything your mind tells it to do. You've seen these athletes start wobbling during a race. They're physically shutting down, but their minds keep telling them, *Everything is good, everything is good, keep moving forward, keep going forward.* You're still mentally alert. You know what's going on.

If I am tired and I'm losing time, the first thing I can control is fuel. *Let's get some fuel, let's drink, let's shift the gears. Maybe I'm pushing too big a gear. Rest the back.* Just control the things you can control and ride out the storm. When you're tired, you might be running out of fuel. You need to get out of the saddle and change gears. You try to control the things within that environment to take your mind off what isn't helping you. You keep telling yourself, *It's normal, this is normal, this is an Ironman. It's a long day, eight hours.* It's biorhythms. You're going to have good times and bad times, and you expect that. You think, *I'm going through a rough patch at the moment. I'll come out OK.* Maybe you get some caffeine in and spark yourself up, and 9 times out of 10 you ride out the storm. Boom! You're back!

I've been in some races where I truly think I'm going to die and then 10 minutes later, I am Superman again; my body is OK. You just have to remain in a positive frame of mind. And positive is not just saying, *Great, I feel great, I feel great,* because you're not stupid. You don't feel great. Positive is like, *OK, it's an obstacle, but I'm going to make it. I've felt great all day, and suddenly I'm starting to feel tired. Let's deal with this problem now.* Sometimes it could be 10 minutes or 20 minutes. Sometimes it could be a hill, 30 seconds. And after you've ridden that out, you actually feel stronger because you think, *Wow, I just dealt with that. OK. I'm back! Now let's get back in our race plan,* which is to pick up the intensity, pick up the pace.

I'll start riding to pick up the tempo, and I'll work. When I feel good, I capitalize on it. When I feel bad, I'll deal with the problem. I'm prepared to lose time when I feel bad. When I feel good, I'm on the attack, I'm racing my race. I'm an aggressive racer. I think that's why I'm successful. Bang! From the start I'm aggressive. Go! Catch me if you can. I'm usually leading all the time. I always like to be in the front of the race, always in control, putting the pressure on everyone else.

When you race with that mind-set, there's only two ways of thinking: you're on the attack or you're on defense, and the only time that you're on defense is when you're feeling bad. And you're going to feel bad because you're pushing a lot harder than the guys who start out slowly. They're not going to have a bad patch until very late in the race, maybe 10 kilometers from home on the run.

Commitment Through Pain

I think anyone doing an Ironman knows that it's going to be uncomfortable. You know that you're going to get sore, it's going to be painful, but you're going to be close to the finish. That's how I always think. When the pain is coming, the day is nearly done. Honestly, in the Ironman 70 percent of it is comfortable. The swim is easy. The first half of the bike is controlled—you can talk and you feel good. Then the pain starts to come, but you're halfway through the race. I always think, *OK, I'm here in the circle. I have to complete the circle. I've done so much. I only have a little bit to go.* That pain I actually enjoy. I like that part of the race. That's sort of the whole reason you start doing it, to push yourself. You can be in pain or uncomfortable but still in control, and that's different from a bad patch where you can be feeling great and then suddenly feel terrible. You just have to deal with it and take fuel.

At the later part of the races you have painful periods, but you can be in pain and still be in control. The greatest part of the race is when you're on this line and you push yourself and push yourself and push yourself, but you're somewhat in control of it. The endorphins are flowing. It's like a high—that's the buzz of Ironman racing. Mentally, that's not tough. Mentally, it's tough when it's painful and you have one of those bad patches. That's the toughest combination you can have later in the race, maybe on the run 5 kilometers from home. Your legs are very tired, you're physically exhausted, you've been pushing yourself and pushing yourself, and suddenly you run out of glycogen. You have no fuel left, and suddenly you feel terrible, absolutely terrible—weak and tired as well as in pain.

I always tend to suffer the last 30 minutes, because I'm so aggressive early in the race. A lot of the time you're so tired physically, mentally, and emotionally at this point of the race that everything becomes sort of a blur. Because I'm close to the finish I just think, *It's nearly home, it's nearly home, it's nearly home.* I'm thinking, *It's 15 minutes, 15 more minutes and this is over, we've finished this.* I'm always saying that to myself. *Complete the circle, complete the circle, finish the circle, 15 more minutes and we're done. We'll pack it up, go home, it's done.* And if it's half an hour from home, it's a *Seinfeld* episode. Or 30 minutes from home I might picture my favorite training runs, where I always do my long runs in Sydney. I always say to myself, *You're at the Springs, 30 minutes from home. How many times have you run home from the Springs?* I visualize that run from the Springs: *I'm at the Springs. I've done this a million times. Today it sucks. I don't feel good but just run home from the Springs. Put one foot in front of the other.* And bang, bang, bang—it's like a trance.

Commitment to Finishing Strong

In a race in Germany, I had my toughest competitor (Lothar Leder) right beside me for the whole latter part of the race. I'm always trying to think, *Come on, let's get home, let's get home, you're at the Springs.* But my competitive instincts are there. I'm looking across at him, and the whole time it was a really strange sensation because it was a real cat and mouse game. I was trying to look great even though I felt terrible. Speaking to Lothar after the race, he said the same thing; he was absolutely destroyed. He said that with eight kilometers to go, he had nothing left, but at the time I thought he looked great. During the race, I just put my chest out, and it was a big mind game between the two of us. I remember thinking, *OK, when we get four kilometers from home, that's it.* I took my belt off. *I'm racing; I don't care how much this hurts.* And for me that last four kilometers was just a blur. I don't remember anything. I just put my head down and ran. All that I remember is seeing Lothar's arm side by side with me the whole time. I just focused on the run. I don't remember the people coming the other way. I just kept running and running.

I remember, like in flashes, coming down the hill and working together side by side. The hill went to the left, and Lothar had the inside. I remember immediately thinking to myself, *It's because it turned left and I was on the right-hand side. I guess it's because he raced there so many times.* We came out of the corner, and he had one step in front. It stayed like that the whole last 500 meters, one step in front. The whole way to the finish. At that point, I remember I was looking, pumping my arms, thinking, *Just run past him, run past him. Come on, run past him, just go, run past him!* But I couldn't catch him, and he's just one step ahead the whole way. All the people were going nuts. I learned some things from that race that made me a better Ironman racer.

Commitment to Learn From Every Race

I always do evaluations of my races and my preparation. I like to write everything down—all my training, my races, what works, what doesn't. For the successful races I can look back at the good things. If I have a bad race, I look at what went wrong, why, and when I felt bad, just so I can replicate the good things. You form the model for your training and competitions, so you're always trying to find what works and what doesn't. Your body is an amazing instrument.

If mentally you know that something worked in the past, replicate it. I have done that in my short-course career. Through my whole career, people have asked, "How are you so successful?" I won a race doing something, and I did it again. I won again, just did it again, and did it again. It's simple, and some people and coaches try to complicate things. Find something that works for you and just replicate it. You obviously adjust your training and your focus, but you stick to the patterns that work.

Commitment to Pushing Your Limits

I've had some races where I've got the wobbles a lot. And you're alert, even though it may not look like it. I see this as a mental and physical challenge. I enjoy putting myself in that position and pushing myself. I get immense satisfaction out of it. I don't know why. I get a buzz, I think. If I was going to do these Ironmans and it didn't hurt, I don't think I'd do it. There would be no buzz to it.

All the winners, all the people who have been successful in Hawaii, have taken a chance. They've gone, *You know what, it's the world championship, and I want this more than you, and I'm going to ride and race like that.* So a lot of people have "died" trying, and they don't become stars, but I respect them more than the guy who is racing for fifth. The person who wants to win Hawaii, the person who ultimately wins Hawaii, arrives thinking that he can. And I think there's only a handful of guys that turn up in Hawaii each year thinking that they can win. I think that of the 100 pros competing, only 10 think that they can win. The rest are there for fifth place.

I would never do that. I'd rather die trying than never try at all. It's just the way I am, and I guess in Hawaii I've blown up the last two years trying. The first one I had a 10-minute lead off the bike, first ever in Hawaii, but I blew the pace in the marathon. Last year, I attacked the last half of the bike. And I got away, took my chance, and blew up six miles away. And everyone keeps saying, "You should wait, you should relax, you have to pay your dues. You need to come in 10th, 5th." Forget that! I don't want to come in 10th. I'm a competitor. I'm a racer. It's in me. I don't train as I do, and go without spending time with my family, and live this harsh lifestyle to come in 10th, you know!

The big obstacle that I'll be working on for Hawaii will be having no doubts. I'll be ready to race. I'll be doing everything I can. I'll be training in the heat. I'm going to Hawaii on a training block for 10 days to race the course, run the course, learn the course, and know the course. I'm going to have rough patches and challenges in that race, and these are the issues that I'm going to deal with. It's all about preparation, visualization, and convincing yourself that everything is good.

Commitment to Be the Best

I'm hard on myself because I think I'm physically good enough to win. If I were riding the Tour de France against the fastest rider in the world, I wouldn't be hard on myself if he rode 20 minutes faster than I did. But in this sport I'm hard on myself because I think I'm good enough to win. If I don't win it's because I've done something wrong, or the other person was better and I need to adjust and make changes so that it doesn't happen again. There's no one in the sport I have seen yet who scares me, about whom I think, *You're better than me.*

In short course triathlon (Olympic distance), Simon Whitfield a great Canadian triathlete is a better runner than I am. I've trained with him, he's one of my best friends, and I know that if we ever came together off the bike and had to run side by side, he would beat me every single time. It's a hard thing to swallow as an athlete. It's the first time ever in my sport where I've had to acknowledge that someone is better than me. I cannot beat him in the run. But in the Ironman if I was racing Simon, I would never let myself be in that position. In Ironman, there's no one I've seen whom I cannot swim with, I cannot bike with, and I cannot run with. So for me it's a big positive, and I try to start the race thinking that way. It's something I take with me every day in training.

Commitment to Achieving Goals

When I first started triathlon I had a list of all the things I wanted to do. I wrote down that I wanted to be a world champion, win the World Cup series, win the national championships, and win the French Iron Tour (Iron Tour is like the Tour de France for triathlon in seven days). I wanted to win Chicago, win Wildflower, and win Alcatraz. I wanted to win the Hawaiian Ironman, and I wanted to break eight hours. That was it. And I ticked them off. I won the worlds, I won the World Cup, I won Alcatraz, I won Wildflower, and the only two left for me are Hawaii and eight hours. I still have the list on a piece of paper in an old training diary. It keeps me motivated.

Until I achieve those goals, I will continue to be hard on myself. I will continue to assess races, continue to learn from what I am doing wrong. I will continue to fly to training camps, go to different places to meet with sport scientists, and spend time away from my family. I think that when I'm done, I will have accomplished things that I can be really proud of. It's better to die trying than never to try at all. That's how I like to think. Catch me if you can. And if you do, well done!

Since this interview, Chris ran two sub-eight-hour Ironmans to win the Quelle Challenge in Roth, Germany, in 2004 (7:57:50) and 2005 (7:58:45) and won the Australia Ironman in 2005 and 2006. In 2007 and 2010 he won the Ironman World Championship in Hawaii. Chris also won a World title in 2012, claiming the ITU Long Course World Championship and has had recent wins in 2013 and 2014 in Italy and Dubai and across the United States and Asia.

CHAPTER 14
Connections

One night as I was driving down a little dirt road in the countryside near my home, something darted out of the darkness onto the road right in front of me. My heart pounded as I lurched for the brakes. A large rust-colored wild cat was in pursuit of a little gray field mouse. The cat focused on that mouse as if nothing else in the world existed, as if a radiant energy beam connected the cat to the mouse. If I had not hit the brakes instinctively, I would have run over the cat—but she pursued that mouse as if I didn't exist. Only after she had the mouse firmly clenched in her teeth did she acknowledge my existence and saunter off into the woods. This is an example of fully connected focusing, the pure uninterrupted connection between you and something you are doing or pursuing, a cat and a mouse, a cheetah and its prey, a performer and his or her performance, or an athlete and his or her goal.

If you watch young children playing, you will notice that the only thing that exists in their world during that play time is the action, interaction, or movement they are engaged in at that moment. They are totally unaware of the chaos around them. You can call out their names, yell at them, or drop something on the floor next to them, and they don't even notice. The intensity and pureness of their connection or focus is similar to the pure connection of the cat with the mouse or a great performer when he or she is fully engaged in a free-flowing fully connected great performance. This is something you and I are capable of doing right now. You just have to free yourself to do it.

A fully focused connection is the most important skill in life because it affects everything we experience, do, accomplish, achieve, or fail to achieve over the course of our lives—all learning, all performance, all relationships, all potential contributions, and all joy in life. With a fully focused connection (see figure 14.1), everything is possible. Without a fully focused connection, very little of real value is possible. A fully focused positive connection makes the difference between a great performance and a poor performance, between really living your life and just dragging yourself through another day. Millions of opportunities are lost every day because people are present physically but

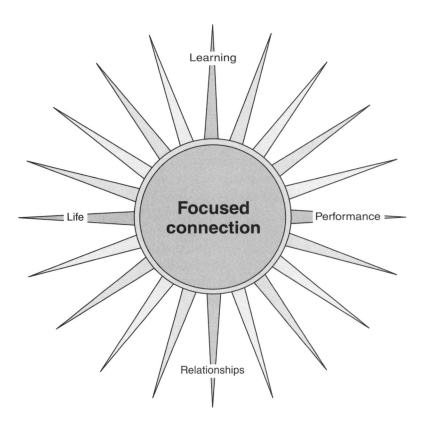

Figure 14.1 A positive and fully focused connection is the center of ongoing learning, performing your best, and living your life fully.

not fully present mentally or emotionally. Their bodies are there in the room, but they are not taking full advantage of learning opportunities, performance opportunities, connection opportunities, or opportunities to continue to learn, grow, and embrace positive lessons and simple joys every day. You put yourself at a disadvantage when you do not bring a positive and fully connected focus into your ongoing daily experiences, interactions, training, performances, and pursuits.

The more I have come to fully understand the role of focus in life and performance contexts, the more I have come to believe that focus is every-thing—in all life- and performance-enhancing pursuits. A positive and fully connected focus channels your positive hopes, dreams, and commitment into a series of positive actions that make your personal journey to excellence possible. A positive and fully connected focus releases you from everything negative or irrelevant and connects you fully, firmly, and positively with your learning experiences and performances. Fully connected focusing is a state of mind, place of mind, or way of mind where nothing exists apart from your pure connection with whatever you are engaged in or experiencing at that moment. Positive and fully connected focusing is the most important mental skill associated with ongoing positive learning, positive relationships, and consistent high-level performance. Challenge yourself to discover and respect the focus that frees you to live, learn, and perform your best. Embrace that fully connected focus in some positive way every day so that you continue to feel fully engaged in every important task, activity, interaction, or performance every day.

The connectedness of your focus, or the depth of your focused connection, affects every learning, performance, and relationship situation you will ever have. It determines your rate of learning, quality of learning, quality of performance, and quality of life. By guiding your focused connection in positive and fully connected ways, you can control the intensity, direction, duration, consistency, and joyfulness of your daily experiences, actions, and reactions. Your focus is the leader. Where your focus goes, everything else follows. Let your focus lead you wisely, happily, and productively.

Turning Off External Worries

If a preschool child happily and fully engaged in playing begins to think about being judged by all the big people around him or her, do you think that child's fully focused connection will remain the same or be broken? A young competitive figure skater recently came to see me because she had lost her fully focused connection. When she performed in her first major competition at age 11, she "just went out and let it happen." She skated in the same way that young children play, totally absorbed in her performance and oblivious to the outside world.

Only later, when she started to worry about judges, other skaters, the audience, her results, her parents, and being evaluated, did she start to feel stressed and lose her fully focused connection: "When people said I was expected to win, the feeling of pressure started." Her thoughts began to drift to others' expectations of her. She began to worry about her performance and about how it would affect her acceptance by others: "What if I fall or mess something up?" As her stress began to rise, her performance began to slide not because she lost her physical or technical skills but because she lost her fully connected focus—her pure and natural connection. To help regain her pure and natural connection, she tried to recall the focus and feelings she had taken into her previous best skating performances. What worked best for her was to free herself to connect fully with her own performance and forget about everything else. This same focus works for her now—she just frees herself to do what she knows she can do and lets go of everything else. It is just her skating her program—connecting fully with her performance—nothing else matters.

Stop dwelling on the expectations of others. Stop thinking about possible failure. Focus on the step or stride in front of you and know in your heart and soul that you will continue to be a valuable human being regardless of how this performance turns out. Unnecessary worrying is one of the greatest inhibitors of skilled performance because it interferes with the fully focused connection that frees you to perform your best. View your games, competitions, programs, or performances as opportunities to connect fully with your performance in ways that free you to perform consistently at or close to your optimal level.

A pure fully connected focus is something you feel and experience in your mind, body, spirit, and soul. It is something you can initiate and have the power to direct, embrace, and control. A fully connected focus creates an inseparable connection between you and what you are doing or experiencing or between you and the person you are with. A pure fully connected focus is also something that others in your presence can sometimes feel or see—like some kind of positive energy beam radiating from your presence. Feeling that pure connection, embracing the power of that fully connected focus, and feeding off that powerful focus is inspiring for you and those around you.

Do you ever wonder why you spend time worrying about things that are beyond your control when all it does is interfere with your effectiveness in doing or accomplishing what is within your control? Worry creates unnecessary stress, drains positive energy, and distracts us from our best performance focus. You can reduce unproductive worry by shifting your focus to concrete positive actions that will help you do the constructive things you would like to do or connect you fully with executing your best possible performance.

You can reduce or eliminate most or all preperformance worry or stress by actively engaging yourself in preplanned preperformance warm-up routines. Most performers find that once they are actively engaged in focusing on doing positive things that fully absorb them, such as following a preperformance warm-up routine or executing the performance itself, worries disappear. Find a way to shift your focus away from worry to a more positive, productive, and absorbing focus. If your focus is fully connected to warming up, preparing yourself to perform, and thinking about the good things you are going to do, you cannot be worrying at the same time.

To shift your focus away from worry, refocus on something more constructive that you would prefer to be doing or thinking about, such as running through a specific play, move, strategy, or technique that you want to use today; reviewing your game plan or race plan; thinking of one of your best previous performances; remembering something positive—a positive life experience, positive thought, or positive image; focusing on relaxing your shoulders or relaxing your breathing; remembering that you are fully capable of having a great game or performance; and reminding yourself to bring your best focus into this event. This positive shift in focus will help you stop worrying about what is beyond your control at this moment and get you fully focused on what is within your control. Stop comparing, doubting, evaluating yourself, thinking negatively, putting yourself down, thinking about outcomes, or projecting into the future. Support yourself, remind yourself of your readiness, and then completely absorb yourself in the process of doing

Fully Connected Focus
Chris Hadfield

An interview I did with Chris Hadfield, former fighter pilot, test pilot, engineer, and commander of the International Space Station, and one of the world's most respected astronauts, offers some insights on the value of a fully connected focus. Chris provided the following insights about the role of focus in his life and performance in space:

> When you're flying an airplane at 500 miles an hour, there's all kinds of things that don't matter, and there's a few things that really, really matter. What's in front of you for the next kilometer really matters because you're going to be there in a few seconds. The whole rest of your world doesn't matter; what's going on with your car or at home, or what just happened 30 seconds ago, or whatever. What really matters is what's going to have the biggest impact on you in the next 30 seconds. In a high-performance airplane things happen quickly, especially when you're flying down low or flying with another aircraft. So you need to completely compartmentalize and just be ready to disregard things that don't matter and worry about them later. Even though it may be life or death later, for now it doesn't matter and you can't pay attention to it. You need to focus fully on what is in front of you right now.
>
> There are times when if you don't focus right down to the critical items right there, you don't give yourself a chance to succeed. So you've got to learn to put things into their boxes and drawers and compartments to be able to succeed. I think I learned to focus that way incrementally over my whole life. I was a downhill ski racer as a teenager, and there's a lot of focus required in that. In downhill racing, you have the next 30 seconds to do it right—either you're getting a medal or you're falling and maybe breaking your leg. So that's a good opportunity to focus. You can begin by doing it on a very small scale. Focus for this length of time to get something done that's difficult. Challenge yourself to do something that you can just barely do, and then learn how to focus on it until you can do it well. Then slowly expand that.

the good things you want to do and are capable of doing. Nothing more and nothing less.

When one of my daughters, Skye, was five years old, she asked me, "Daddy, when will I be grown up?" Her question made me reflect on what being grown up actually means. Physically, we are grown up relatively early in life, but mentally and emotionally, and in terms of our focus, we can continue to be in the process of growing up for our entire life. You can choose to continue to improve the depth and quality of your best focus in different parts of your life at any age. You can choose to be more positive, be more supportive, feel less stressed, cope better with stress, find more simple joys, relax more fully, and live every day with a happier and healthier perspective. There is no end line for growing more positive mentally and emotionally or for enhancing the quality and consistency of your best focus.

Focusing for Total Connection

The goal of a world-class archer is to hit the center of the target with each arrow. He trains himself to find the middle of the middle, to see only one center. Genge (1976) described the process the highly skilled archer uses:

> In this state of full focus, she or he could be anywhere in the world and remain fully focused and undistracted. The great archer shoots each arrow as a separate entity, concentrating fully for the short period required to release that shot. The periods between shots are times to relax, in which all tension, muscular and mental, is dissipated and the mind is freed from the last arrow in preparation for the next one-arrow effort.

One world champion archer described focusing in the following way:

> I block out everything in my world, except me and my target. The bow becomes an extension of me. All attention is focused on lining up my pin [sight] with the center of the target. At this point in time, that is all I see, hear, or feel. With the bow drawn and sight on target, a quick body scan can tell me if anything is off. If everything feels right, I hold focus and simply let the arrow fly. It will find the target. If something feels off, I lower the bow and draw again.

When a person has trained his muscles and nervous system to shoot an arrow into the middle of a target, theoretically he should be able to put it into the center every time. What prevents him from doing this? As with most performers, worry, distracting thoughts, and a loss of that totally connected focus with the target prevent archers from achieving their true potential. They have the program in their mind and body to perform the skill flawlessly. They can do it without thinking. Their challenge, like yours, is to free their body and mind to connect totally with the goal—for every shot, for every move, from start to finish—especially in situations that really count.

What all the world's best performers seek, and work to perfect, is a fully connected focus that will free them to achieve their goals and live their dreams. They clear the mind of irrelevant thoughts and focus only on what is important at that moment. Outside distractions are absent. Their focus is centered on a specific target—first the preparation, then the doing—a total pure connection between one's body and one's performance.

When you are fully focused in any sport or other high-performance pursuit, you are totally connected to what you are engaged in to the exclusion of

Peyton Manning and other great athletes possess the ability to tune out their surroundings and fully connect with their performance.

everything else. In a real sense, you and your performance become one, and nothing else in the world exists for that period of time. In many individual sports, best performances occur when athletes are totally connected or riveted to their performance, trusting their bodies and their preparation, often to the point of performing on autopilot and letting their bodies lead without conscious interference. In some circumstances they may use conscious reminders to maintain, regain, or sustain their best focus or best technique or to push through discomfort, pain, or adversity. They find and nurture positive ways to fully reconnect or sustain their best focus so that they are able to consistently have their best performances.

In team sports, best performances likewise occur when players are totally focused and absorbed in the crucial aspects of their performance. They are aware of the flow of relevant play around them, completely trusting in their capacity to automatically read and react to that awareness, and totally connected to executing their moves. Their focus remains adaptable, like the lens on a camera, capable of zooming in and out quickly. For example, a point guard in basketball, a quarterback in American football, or a ball carrier in soccer (World Cup football) needs a wide-angle perspective to read the field for an open player and then must zoom in on the open player and make a crisp, accurate pass. For best performances, a total connection or reconnection to your ongoing changing tasks or choices is required through the constantly changing demands of the game or performance. This could be viewed as a flowing focus or adapting to the changing demands in front of you—like a stream that continues to flow freely regardless of the possible obstacles along its path.

Your goal is to discover what kind of focus works best for you under various circumstances. Initially, you may experience a completely connected focus (on the right things) for only short periods. Work on freeing your best focus to become a natural part of how you connect your focus during practices, games, and performances.

If you want to perform your best, you cannot afford to focus on things or thoughts that interfere with your best performance. Discover what kinds of focus or thoughts free you to perform your best and respect that focus.

A fully connected focus is absorbing, natural, free flowing, and intense. It is simple and magical—a focus that you lived often as a young child. Your ultimate goal is to enter this fully connected focus on a consistent basis. Connect fully, trust your connection, and free yourself to let outside worries go so that you can live and perform closer to your capacity in everyday interactions and in all performance situations that count. The key to experiencing and sustaining this fully focused connection lies in absorbing yourself in the present, in the here and now, and gradually increasing the consistency, quality, and duration of your fully connected focus.

Developing and Nurturing Your Best Focus

Your best focus may at times feel like a nonfocus because you are letting the performance unfold automatically and freely—often free from conscious thought, directives, or self-evaluation. In many contexts, connecting fully just means tuning in to your body, trusting your body, connecting to the step in front of you, and remaining totally connected for the duration of your experience, performance, game, or task. Training to improve your focus involves making a commitment to stay fully connected to what you are doing, discovering what frees you to perform your best, not letting irrelevant or distracting thoughts interfere with your best performance, trusting or freeing your mind and body to do what you have trained them to do without needing to force anything, and reconnecting your mind and body when either begins to tire or deviate from a fully effective performance focus.

To improve your focusing skills and make your best focus more consistent, set some personal goals to free your best focus to surface more regularly. Here are some practical tips to choose from to help make this happen:

✦   When you walk into the gym or onto the field or step into your practice or training setting, performance context, or work arena, leave everything else behind. Nothing that happened before you arrived here matters. During the time you are here, choose to be totally here and totally focused. Make the absolute best of this day, this practice, this opportunity.

✦ To get the best out of yourself during this practice or training session, think about what you want to accomplish here today and imagine your doing some of the things you want to do, refine, or improve. Try to imagine yourself doing some of the skills, moves, programs, plays, or performances you would like to do or improve. Then focus fully on executing some of those key skills, positive actions, or positive reactions in your practice or performance setting. Let them unfold freely and naturally in your training session, without any negative or interfering thoughts.

✦ Whenever you are training, practicing, interacting, working, studying, or performing, focus fully on being totally connected with whatever you are doing or trying to do. Take a few minutes to think about what you want to do or what you really want to accomplish today (physically, technically, tactically, and mentally) and then focus fully on doing it.

✦ If your sport, work, or performance domain requires awareness of your teammates (with whom you are working, training, interacting, or playing) or other players with whom you must connect, focus on connecting with them in positive ways. Then totally connect with what you need to focus on here today to execute your best moves, best actions, and preferred reactions. Practice reading and reacting fluidly and naturally.

✦ Free yourself to execute your skills, actions, reactions, moves, or tasks without conscious thought or evaluation. Just do it: just connect fully with the doing, be totally in that moment, and see what happens. Go by feel. Trust your instinct. Free yourself to let your moves flow freely and naturally. Don't question. Don't evaluate. Just be totally in the doing. See what it feels like. See where it takes you.

✦ When you train, work out, or perform, "**do**cide" to respect the focus that you feel allows you or frees you to perform your best.

✦ Find some simple, powerful focus reminders that can help you enter or reenter your best performance focus and use them every day, in every training session, in every interaction, and in every performance.

✦ Practice sustaining your best, most fully connected focus for as long as you can—even if you start by doing it only for very short periods. Commit yourself to achieve a gradual increase in the time you are fully connected in ways that free you to perform your best. The ultimate goal is to be able to sustain your best focus, your absolute connection, throughout your entire performance—every move, every step, or every stroke of the way, from start to finish.

✦ When you step out of your training site, performance arena, or work space, take a couple of minutes to reflect on what went well and why it went well and on what could be improved and how it could be improved. Then leave it behind. Shift focus to connecting with something or someone else less demanding, more relaxing, or more joyful. This positive and relaxed shift in focus will free you to enter other contexts of your life in a positive and fully connected way.

✦   Tonight, before you go to sleep, when you are lying quietly relaxed in your bed, think about what you would like to do tomorrow. Think of a couple of key things you really want to accomplish. When you wake up in the morning, while you are still lying quietly in your bed, think about the key things you would like to do. Then get up and do them, with a positive and fully connected focus. Make this part of your regular presleep and early morning routine.

Only Focused Actions Count in the Real World of Performance

The following focused actions will help you improve your positive and focused connection within your performance setting:

✦   Stand or sit quietly, let your shoulders relax, and think about doing a particular skill or movement. Try to imagine and feel the perfect execution of that skill. Then perform the skill, freeing your body to perform automatically.

✦   Seek the feel of the movement or performance. If the feel is right, everything else will be right.

✦   If you are feeling stressed before an event or performance, try pressing your thumb hard against your first finger. This is the slow-motion button you can use anytime to slow everything down. Move slowly, talk slowly, stretch slowly, and breathe in and out slowly in a deep and relaxed way.

✦   If you are feeling distracted, try clearing the distractions from your mind by focusing on positive little reminders that can free you to perform your best.

✦   If you make a mistake, first breathe, then quickly shift focus to your next move or next step that is within your control.

✦   Prepare yourself to stay focused in the moment—one shot, one stroke, one swing, one step, one glide, one stride, one corner, one lap, one move at a time. Stay in the present moment—the only one that counts.

✦   Use simple reminders to keep your positive and fully connected focus on target (for example, *focus, connect, relax, be here, be all here*).

✦   Choose to be what you want to be. Choose to become what you want to become.

✦   Embrace the simple joys and magic moments in everything you do—every day!

+ Choose to become inseparable from what you are doing or experiencing.
+ Relax your body, relax your focus, and free your body and mind to move forward in free-flowing ways without forcing anything.

The world's best performers experience their best results when they connect fully with their performances and clear their minds of thoughts about outcomes during performances. It is not that they never think about outcomes, but thinking about results, scores, or outcomes during a performance often becomes a distraction that interferes with their best performance focus. A top Olympic shooter offered this perspective:

> For my best performances, I'm thinking about how to shoot correctly, letting shooting sequences run through my head, seeing myself in control and totally confident. It is very important for me not to start adding the score and projecting what the score might be. If during the last few ends [rounds] I become nervous and start to worry about blowing it, I have to work hard to keep my shooting sequence in mind (*form, form, form*) and not the glory of shooting a high score.

Another top Olympic athlete shared, "I'm not nervous in a negative sense in advance, because I remain who I am, myself, so that it is impossible for other competitors to have a harmful effect on me." She doesn't go through a big comparison scene, worrying about how well others are performing. She simply focuses fully on doing her own thing. That's when she has her best results.

Another great athlete shared:

> For my best performances, I empty my mind and I feel as though it isn't me performing, but at the same time I feel totally connected with the feelings in my body. It's as if my subconscious is doing the performance. I imagine the perfect movement in my head, and the rest follows automatically.

After the event, she evaluates why her performance was good or bad. If it was good, she asks herself, *How did I get my mind and focus working that way? How can I duplicate it the next time?* If her performance was not up to par, she draws out the lessons for ongoing improvement and moves on. In her own words, "I probably work harder and learn more when something goes wrong."

Respecting and Reconnecting to Your Best Focus

The difference between best and less than best performances lies within your focus. In poor performances, you allow negative or distracting thoughts (about other performers, your preparation, doubts, others' expectations, fatigue, a bad warm-up, a mistake, a previous performance, the weather, or final placing) to interfere with a fully connected focus. In best performances, you are able to stay in the moment, which is the only moment you can influence anyway. If you find yourself losing your best focus, try one of the strategies I have already discussed or use one of the following strategies:

✦ Return to basics; go with the focus that has worked best for you in your past best performances.

✦ Focus on following your game plan, race plan, shot plan, focus plan, or performance plan.

✦ Break your challenge into manageable parts—one section, one shift, one rush, one shot, one hurdle, one stroke, one step, one piece, one inch, one day at a time.

✦ Focus only on the step immediately in front of you, which is the only step you can control at this moment. Then focus on the next step, and the next step, and then on the next step.

✦ If you have trained or prepared well, remind yourself that you have trained well and are totally ready (for example, say to yourself, *I have done this skill, this routine, this movement, this sequence, this play a thousand times before—I am fully capable of doing it well*).

✦ If you have not trained or prepared as well as you had hoped, remind yourself that anything is possible if you focus fully on bringing out the best that you have to give: *I am fully capable of performing well or playing well if I just focus fully on doing it.*

✦ Remind yourself of your best past performances and recall the feelings and focus that allowed you to perform so well.

✦ Remember that your goals are realistic. All you want to do is perform as well as you are capable of performing—nothing more and nothing less.

✦ Imagine yourself executing your skills or game plan perfectly; then focus fully on doing what you are fully capable of doing when you enter your performance arena.

✦ Remind yourself to stay fully focused in the moment. Forget the past, the other athletes or performers, and the final score. Focus only on doing your job or executing your performance.

✦ Connect your fully connected focus to executing the little steps, one step at a time.

✦ Remind yourself that anything is possible in this game or performance if you just focus on the doing. Let your best fully connected focus lead you.

✦ After every game, competition, or performance, do a careful postperformance analysis. Reflect closely on where your focus was when you were performing best, where your focus was when you were performing less than your best, and where you want your focus to be. This focus evaluation process is extremely valuable for learning how to be and perform your best consistently.

✦ Do everything you can to keep the joy in your pursuits, training, games, performances, relationships, learning opportunities, and life outside your sport or high-performance domain. Embrace the positive parts. Find lessons in the difficult parts and continue to appreciate the joys, challenges, opportunities, and lessons in your ongoing pursuit.

Practicing Focus

Choosing to continue to develop your ability to connect fully with the important little steps in your performance and hold it there is critical to consistent high-level performance. Fully connected focusing is a skill you must practice to perfect. There are many opportunities to practice improving your focusing skills inside and outside your performance setting. Take advantage of these opportunities for two important reasons. First, they will help you learn to connect more fully in your life outside your performance domain, and second, they will help you improve your focus within your performance domain. Here are some general focusing exercises to get you started:

✦ When you are sitting in a classroom or talking with someone in person or on the phone, try to clear your mind of everything else and connect fully with what that person is saying, sharing, or experiencing. See how long you can hold a fully connected focus. If you start to drift away, see how quickly you can refocus to regain a fully focused connection.

✦ When you are reading, studying, writing, doing puzzles, watching TV, hammering nails, doing homework, or performing some other task, practice focusing fully only on what you are doing. You can also try focusing fully on doing something like this when other people are watching, making noise, or talking. Breathe, relax, and then focus or refocus fully on doing what you were doing. If you lose focus, see how quickly you can regain a positive and fully connected focus.

✦ Look at the page in front of you right now. Pick the third word from the end of this sentence and focus on it. (That word is *focus*.) Focus on this word *focus* until it stands out more than anything else on the page. Remember this word and use it whenever you want to reconnect your focus in any context.

✦ When you are doing something physically active today or tomorrow, see how it feels to focus on different kinds of thoughts or feelings. Go for a run today or tomorrow, and as you extend your leg, think *stretch* or *float or relax*. Do this 10 times in a row. See what happens. Then try thinking *power* when your left foot pushes off the ground and again when your right foot pushes off the ground. Do this 10 times in a row. See what happens.

✦ Do some body scans at different times during the day. Focus on the sensations you feel in different parts of your body. How does your back feel right now as you sit here reading this page? Are you sitting up straight? You are now! Are your hips forward, in line with your shoulders, or are they back in your chair so that your shoulders are hunched forward? How do the soles of your feet feel right now? What parts of your feet are touching the ground? Are you warm or cold? Are your calves relaxed or tight? What does your behind feel like right now? Is it warm or cold or tense or relaxed? Now focus on your shoulders. Are they loose and relaxed? Probably not. Let them drop down a little. Tell your shoulders to relax. Wiggle them a bit. Roll your head around in a circle. Let your head and shoulders relax.

✦ Sit quietly, relax your breathing, and focus on looking at something in front of you, such as what is on your computer, your wall, or your table, or look closely at a pen, a flower, a piece of paper, a painting, a piece of fruit, a leaf, the bark on a tree, a friend's hand or face, or a cloud. Really focus on looking closely at the object; look at its shape, texture, design, and feel; focus on one thing to the point that everything around it disappears. Good. Now you know what is around you and in front of you!

✦ Sit quietly, breathe in slowly, breathe out slowly, and let yourself relax. Focus on listening to the sounds in the room, the sounds outside the room, the sounds of nature—birds, the wind, the leaves—or other sounds you hear around you right now. Connect fully by listening to one of those sounds; then let it fade away by absorbing yourself in another sound or focus.

✦ Line up several targets or objects on a table, a desk, or the floor in front of you. Become aware of all the objects. Then begin to narrow your focus until you are aware of only one object. Focus on the center of that object, and finally focus on the center of the center of that object. Let everything else blur into the background; let all external sounds disappear. Connect fully with the center of that object and nothing else.

✦ Close your eyes and focus on a specific positive thought, image, action, or performance that you would like to become your positive reality. Focus on trying to make this positive thought, image, action, or performance clear in your mind.

✦ Before you go to sleep tonight, do some relaxed breathing—breathe in and out slowly for 10 slow, relaxed, deep breaths. Then try to recall a specific positive thought, image, action, or performance that you would like to become your positive reality. See how that feels.

The key to consistent high-quality performance and high-quality living centers on choosing to focus in positive and fully connected ways. Let those positive and fully connected images and feelings flow through your mind and body. Let them lead you to your true potential.

CHAPTER 15
Challenges

Challenges are an ever-present part of life. They always have been and always will be. Sometimes getting up early in the morning is a challenge, or doing all the things you want to do in one day is a challenge, like going to practice, training, school, meetings, teaching, learning, coaching or being coached, or getting enough rest and recovery. Eating well, drinking enough fluids, and staying healthy are a challenge. Performing your best when it counts most is a challenge; doing all your training, homework, or assignments at work is a challenge. Nurturing or sustaining positive long-term two-way loving relationships when you are away a lot is a challenge. Failing to perform to your capacity consistently at home or away from home is a challenge, and missing or losing important supportive people in your life is definitely a challenge.

You have probably encountered challenges in your sport or performance domain or in other parts of your life that felt enormous, overwhelming, or almost insurmountable at the time, and you will likely face other challenges like this in the future. How well do you feel you were able to respond to some of these challenges in the past? Were you able to shift your focus from something negative to something positive? Were you able to learn and grow or gain something of value from these challenging experiences? If you worked through some of these challenges successfully, you probably found a way to shift your focus away from something negative to something positive or you were able to free yourself from your own negative thoughts and redirect your focus to connect fully on the step in front of you, both of which are within your control.

Two factors—your perspective (positive or negative) and your present focus (fully connected or disconnected)—determine how well you perform in the face of major challenges. Prepare yourself to accept big challenges as positive opportunities—choose to embrace a positive perspective. Choose to remain fully connected on the step-by-step process of totally engaging yourself in the experience or performance. Excelling or performing your best in challenging contexts, whatever or wherever they may be at this point in your life, depends almost entirely on bringing the best positive perspective and fully connected focus into your chosen pursuits.

Most athletes or performers fail to reach their goals in their most important performance contexts for two main reasons. First, they fail to respect their best focus or the focusing patterns that work best for them. They do this by changing or not respecting the focus that has worked best for them in the past. If you fail to respect your best focus or fail to prepare yourself to deal effectively with distractions, there is a very good chance you will perform below your capacity.

Every important performance context we enter has potential distractions that could take us away from our best performance focus. Performance problems often surface in this context when we shift focus away from fully connecting with our performance and begin to focus on doubts, concerns about outcomes, or consequences of failure. Distractions in any challenging context can take you places you don't want to go, so prepare yourself to stay fully focused on what best works for you and let go of everything else.

In certain contexts, sometimes we fail to do our best because we don't try hard enough, but in a high-stakes context we often try too hard. At a recent Olympics one of the world's best long-track speed skaters, who was favored to win, faltered in his races and finished far off the podium. In a subsequent World Cup race shortly after the Olympics, he was back on track as a world leader. What was different? On the World Cup circuit, he returned to familiar territory, took the load off his shoulders, and simply focused on following positive patterns of thinking, focusing, and performing that worked best for him. His focus was back where it needed to be and he was fully connected with the right things at the right time. The bottom line is that you cannot force good or great things to happen; you have to free them to unfold naturally.

Your Most Challenging Performance Context

When you enter your most important performance context, what do you think will be the same and what do you think will be different from other events you have competed in? What do you think you have to focus on to have your best results in that context? What kind of focus might interfere with you having your best results? The performance demands in challenging or important performance contexts are no different from the performance demands in other contexts in which you have played, performed, or competed. So you just have to focus on respecting your best focus and free yourself to do what you know how to do—nothing else matters.

Have you ever walked across a wooden beam lying on the ground or along a train track? Try to imagine what it would be like for you to walk across that wooden beam or along that train track if it were suspended between two buildings 100 stories in the air. The performance is exactly the same, the task is exactly the same—you just focus on walking across the beam or track. If you can do it on the ground, you can do it on a beam or track suspended 10 feet or 100 stories in the air. The same is true for performing in big events where millions of people are watching you. You just have to focus on freeing yourself to do what you know how to do and nothing else.

You can do it if you believe that you can do it and if you choose to focus fully on putting one foot in front of the other—step-by-step. The consequences of failure, however, are dramatically different If you lose your focus and lose your balance at extreme heights, even momentarily, the fall will be long and severe.

Raising the height of the beam or track gives a little flavor of what some athletes and other performers might feel when walking in to perform within their most important event or their Olympic context. The task is the same, but the context and consequences are different. When you have dreamed of this moment or trained extremely hard for this opportunity, and the expectations are high, and millions or billions of people are watching, including everyone important to you, the challenge and consequences may feel different.

The best way to perform your best, when consequences feel critically important, is to focus fully on executing the task before you and nothing else. Doing this may not always be easy, but it is possible if you keep things in perspective and prepare yourself mentally to keep your focus centered only on what needs to be done at that moment.

At some levels and in some sports, the hopes and dreams of nations and sponsors ride on the backs of athletes. For example, at the 2002 Winter Olympics in Salt Lake City the powerful Swedish ice hockey team was unexpectedly eliminated after a strong showing in the preliminary round. The Swedish media tore into the players and described their loss as one of the most devastating events in Swedish history. On the other hand, the Canadians were ecstatic when they won the gold medal after a poor showing in the preliminary round. More Canadians watched that game than any other televised event up to that time in Canadian history.

Some differences often found in higher-profile performance contexts include more spectators, large numbers of people in and around your performance venue, more noise, an increased media presence, multiple security checks, increased travel time, lots of traffic, delays, crowded restaurants, noisy lodgings, and reduced training time.

If you prepare yourself in advance to deal with various kinds of distractions that you will likely face and make a commitment to yourself to stay focused on the positives and use your focusing and refocusing skills to stay on a positive path, your chances of performing your best within this high-profile context will be greatly enhanced. When you prepare yourself well for the kinds of realities or distractions you will likely face in your most important or highest-profile performance contexts, you immediately increase your chances of performing to your true capacity in that context. Plan to do what *you* want to do, and plan to focus through distractions so that you continue to move forward in positive ways that free you to do what you came there to do.

To perform your best in high-performance contexts, perhaps after feeling somewhat intimidated, "**do**cide" to take control. This can begin with a simple step—plan your day! How do you want your day to unfold? Make good choices that respect your best performance focus and your primary reason for being there.

When do you want to get up, eat, sleep, practice, rest, take a break, or find some quiet time for yourself? When do you want to make yourself available to the media and others, and when do you want to restrict access? When do you want to eat together as a team, and when do you want to eat on your own or with a friend, family member, coach, or a couple of favorite teammates?

In one Olympic context, a national team of basketball players who were accustomed to eating as a team reported that never eating together as an entire team at the Olympics took away from their sense of team unity and had a negative effect on their performance. This highlights the importance of respecting familiar, positive patterns that have worked well for you and your team in the past. Decide what you want to do or not do each day as a human being, an athlete, a teammate, a friend, and a person who wants to perform your best. Choose to do what will help you feel your best, focus your best, rest or recover your best, and perform your best!

Athletes or performers who do not perform to their potential at the Olympic Games or other high-profile events usually fall short not because the performance demands are different but because they have not prepared themselves

Ryan Gormly/STL/Icon SMI

The 2002 Olympic Canadian ice hockey team persevered and overcame challenges of a poor preliminary round to win the gold medal.

well enough to deal effectively with the high-profile environment, the Olympic or championship expectations, and the many distractions surrounding their performance. Those who perform to their capacity plan their own best path, commit themselves to stay positive through the many challenges, and focus fully on executing their best performance. Anything is possible when you prepare well, see the challenges as great opportunities, embrace the positive energy in your performance context, and channel your focus into connecting totally with your performance.

When you are playing, performing, or competing in high-stakes performance contexts, your performance outcome will depend almost entirely on how well you maintain or sustain your best performance focus. Your simple goal is to connect fully with your performance, your game plan, or your race plan to the exclusion of everything else. Focus on being fully connected with each stride, each stroke, each move, each shift, each opportunity, and each little step forward. Let your best on-site performance focus rivet you to executing your best performance, step by step, stride by stride, stroke by stroke, shift by shift. Give everything you have so that when you finish your game, race, competition, or performance, you have no regrets.

Phases of Preparation

Preparing to be your best in your most important performance contexts includes four distinct but interrelated phases:

1. your preevent preparation phase,
2. your on-site familiarization phase, which includes adapting to the new environment and dealing with multiple distractions,
3. your on-site performance phase, and
4. your postperformance reflections and transition phase that allows you to draw out important lessons for ongoing improvement and move on in a positive way.

Each of the four phases affects the quality of your focus and the quality and consistency of your performance. If you are well prepared and fully focused during each of these phases, you greatly increase your chances of performing to your capacity in your Olympic or most important performance contexts. If you do not respect and embrace each of these four phases, you heighten the risk of falling short of your dreams, goals, and potential.

1. Preevent Preparation Phase

Within a short period you will be in the midst of the excitement of playing, performing, or competing in an event, game, audition, race, or other performance context. To perform your best, plan your preparation phase so that you are feeling your best when it is time to perform, race, or compete. Respect the training and rest patterns that work best for you in the time leading up to your event, game, or competition. Prepare yourself mentally to remain positive and fully focused on the right things at the right time at your event, game, or competition. Your primary goal in the final preparation phase is to do everything you can possibly do to be at your best physically, mentally, technically, and emotionally, without feeling overtrained or overloaded.

Leading into this performance, fine-tune what already works for you rather than trying to overhaul your training or performance program. Remember what got you where you are now. Keep doing the good things that have worked for you and continue to refine the things that will make you even better.

Focus on quality training and quality rest in the lead-up time to major events. Avoid overworking or overtraining. Trying to do too much within a limited period before important events is an error that has led to many disappointing performances. Go in rested and ready, knowing that you can give your absolute best. Being well rested and mentally ready for the challenges or demands you will be facing is a critical part of excelling in your important competitions or events.

2. On-Site Familiarization Phase

The more familiar you are with the environment in which you will be performing or competing, the more comfortable, relaxed, or normal you will feel within it. Talking with athletes, coaches, sport psychology specialists, or focus enhancement consultants who have firsthand experience in big events like the one in which you will be competing can be extremely helpful. Ask them for details about what to expect, their own experiences, and their suggestions for preparing to perform your best in this context. I often ask former Olympic athletes to come in and share their Olympic experiences with the current athletes, coaches, and teams I am working with who are preparing for major competitions. Their personal stories help the athletes and coaches prepare themselves for their biggest challenges. These kinds of mental preparation or focus enhancement meetings have always been an empowering experience for everyone involved.

Many world championship or Olympic events have websites that provide photos and updates about facilities, competition venues, and so on that can help you get a feel for the context in which you will be living and competing. You can also request updated information from your coaches and team leaders, former athletes, and sport federations or associations. They may be able to provide answers to some of your specific questions, requests, or concerns. Every championship venue is unique in certain physical or structural ways, but there are many common challenges, distractions, and opportunities that athletes and coaches can prepare themselves for.

If you have been through an event similar to the one you are now preparing for, be sure to draw out the important lessons from your previous experiences.

Carefully reflect on what you did well, what you were focused on when you were performing your best, and what you can improve or do differently to be better prepared and more focused for your upcoming performance.

If possible, go to the competition venue to train or compete sometime before the actual competition. Many athletes with whom I have worked have had personal best performances and won medals at the Olympic Games after visiting, training on, or competing on the Olympic course or in the Olympic arena before doing it under the lights in the real Olympic Games. Those experiences made them feel more in control and more comfortable, as if the venue was their place. In addition, they were able to continue preparing mentally for competing at that specific competition venue when they were away from it. For example, they could recall details of what it looked like, think through their race plans or game plans, and imagine themselves performing their best on that specific course or in that particular arena.

After you arrive on-site for your big event, gradually familiarize or refamiliarize yourself with the various areas, arenas, or competition venues where you will be staying, training, and performing. Make sure you know the location of everything that might be important to you (for example, where you will be staying, transportation options, cafeteria options, food, drinks, bathrooms, live-feed television rooms, warm-up areas). After you settle into your lodgings, become familiar and comfortable with your competition venue. Even if you have trained or competed in that venue previously, check it out carefully. Some changes in the course or venue will likely have been made for the current event. For example, for the triathlon event at the 2000 Sydney Olympics, large concrete barriers were erected to restrain the many spectators who lined the course. These barriers dramatically narrowed the course in some sections, resulting in a number of crashes in the bicycle portion of the race. You should be aware of and prepared for these kinds of changes in advance, rather than be disappointed by a circumstance or crash you might have been able to avoid or manage. The more prepared you are for everything you will face, the better and more confident you will feel, the better you will focus, and the better you will perform.

Many athletes I have worked with have found it helpful, when possible, to go to competition venues when no one else was around just to get the feel of the place; to feel good in that place; to make it their place; to walk through or think through their performance plan, game plan, or race plan; or to trace the steps they wanted to follow on their competition days. Some of these athletes walked from their warm-up area into the performance arena just as they would in the competition. Others got into their starting position or imagined themselves performing the way they wanted to perform while being right there in the place they would actually do it with millions of people around the world watching. Anything that helps you feel more ready, more relaxed, more confident, more focused, and more in control of what you are doing can enhance the quality of your best performance on the big day.

3. On-Site Performance Phase

The task that lies before you at your big event is the same task you have performed many times before. The most important part of performing to your capacity within this bigger context is to respect the patterns that have worked best for you in the past—during the lead-up time, on-site at your venue, just before you compete, and during your performance. Follow your normal precompetition routine and do your normal warm-up. Then focus fully on executing your performance—step by step, shift by shift, move by move, stroke by stroke, stride by stride, section by section. Follow your best or preferred focus plan to stay on track every step of the way. Use your best refocusing plan to get back on track if you start to drift away. Decide to follow your best focus plan. Then follow that plan because it will take you where you want to go.

Expect to feel different when you enter your Olympic or most important performance context and know that you can perform to your capacity within it. Know that after you begin performing, playing, or competing, everything irrelevant will fade away. You will focus only on connecting fully with what frees you to perform your best—just you and your totally connected focus, you and your performance. Nothing else matters.

Remind yourself to follow the same focusing patterns that freed you to perform your best in previous events. Rest well. Carry a positive perspective. Feel your relaxed intensity. Focus on what is within your control. Connect totally with your performance. Just focus on doing your job and executing your performance, which you have done many times before. Plan your own path. Follow your preferred precompetition routine. Focus on staying fully connected. Take it step-by-step. Give everything that you can possibly give today. You are not asking yourself to do anything unreasonable—only to perform as you are capable of performing.

Many athletes and performers I have worked with who performed to their capacity in their Olympic context found that responding to the following two questions in their final preparation phase helped strengthen their confidence and direct their focus:

1. Why I can. What are the reasons why you can achieve your goal in this event?
2. How I will. Outline how you will achieve your goal in this event. What will you focus on to achieve your goal?

If you prepare the way I have suggested, when your big event is over and you return home, you will know that you prepared as well as you possibly could, given the constraints and complexities of your life and the world around you. You will know that you gave everything you could, and you will have no regrets. And if you know that you gave everything you could on that day at this point in your life, you have won a personal victory.

4. Postperformance Phase

You achieved one of your lifetime dreams just by representing your school, your club, your university, your family, your friends, your neighborhood, your city, your region, your state or province, your country, and yourself at your competition. Regardless of where you placed in this performance context, you need to keep things in perspective. You know that you tried your best within a very challenging context, regardless of your performance outcome. You have done what many other people have never done, and you have grown as a person and a performer through your efforts in this pursuit, although you may not yet fully realize it.

Just competing among the best in what you are doing is a great accomplishment. Few people reach the high level of skill that you have attained, in any field or endeavor. The people who know you and love you are extremely proud of you for what you have done and for how you represented your family, your community, your school, your region, or your country.

Think about all the wonderful experiences, opportunities, friendships, and accomplishments you have gained from committing yourself to this pursuit. Think about the lifelong friends you have made and the many lessons you have learned on your journey. You will carry these memories with you for the rest of your life. Take a well-deserved time-out to rest, relax, and embrace the simple joys in your life before moving forward to one of the many other exciting challenges that lie ahead.

Implications for Your Future

Much of what you have learned about the importance of remaining positive and fully focused in pursuing and embracing the big challenges you have faced or are facing right now is relevant to what you do with the rest of your life. The same positive focusing and refocusing skills are equally relevant in your future pursuits when you will be performing, living, learning, and embracing life's other big challenges. The challenges that lie ahead may be even bigger or more important than the challenges you have already faced—such as competing in more prominent performance events; being more consistent with your best performances; overcoming injury or sickness; learning to relax; maintaining your health; giving birth; dealing with setbacks, loss, or failure; rebounding from the death of a loved one; or being your best when it counts most in relationships, parenting, teaching, coaching, your studies, your profession, or any other chosen performance pursuit or life domain.

Important life contexts, inside and outside of your sport or performance domain, are sometimes highly charged emotional events, because during those moments you sometimes feel as if your life, mission, reputation, relationships, or self-worth is on the line. Before you enter these kinds of contexts, plan your path, and when you are immersed within these challenges, continue to draw on your best focus. With a focus plan to remain positive and fully connected and a refocusing plan to deal with distractions effectively, you will conserve energy, carry a more confident perspective, enhance your learning and performance in any context, and contribute more to your team's performance, your quality of life, and family harmony. The outcome of positive planning, detailed positive mental preparation, and being fully focused in any important performance or life context is success.

We all face challenges at some point in our lives where the demands are high, the outcomes are important, and our ability to remain composed and focused in positive and fully connected ways is put to the test. When entering these kinds of challenges, pause for a moment to think about what you would really like to accomplish, how you would prefer to live and focus to make good things happen in your life and the lives of your loved ones, and why doing whatever you are doing is worth doing well.

Remember that small, positive shifts in your focus make a huge difference when working through obstacles, trying to perform your best in challenging or stressful situations, or living within emotionally charged contexts. Anything that makes you feel better, happier, more relaxed, more connected, more confident, more fully alive, more appreciated, or more focused on what you control inside or outside your performance context can enhance the quality of your focus, the quality of your relationships, the joyfulness of your life, and the quality of your overall performance. Moving forward along this path is a choice only you can make. Choosing to move from where you are to the place you want to be is a powerful and positive step-by-step process. Choose to make your best focus more consistent! This will give you your best chance of living your life fully and arriving at your desired destination.

CHAPTER 16
Actions

If you want to be your best, feel your best, focus your best, perform your best, and live the best life you can possibly live, you have to act on your intentions in positive ways every day. You can begin to do this right now in your training, learning, and performance contexts in some of the following ways:

✦ Create a sense of urgency.

✦ Choose to take advantage of every learning opportunity, race, game, training day, qualifying session, competition, or performance opportunity.

✦ Seize and embrace every performance opportunity like it was your last.

✦ Bring your best performance focus into every race, game, learning opportunity, or performance context so you can perform your absolute best consistently.

✦ Continue to act on your positive intentions by continuing to respect your best focus.

✦ If you continue to respect and nurture your best focus, you will put yourself in a positive position to achieve your goals and live your dreams.

✦ Performing your best does not have to be a "sometimes" thing.

✦ You can perform your best consistently by focusing on what works best for you.

✦ Get into your best positive and fully connected focus zone so you can free yourself to perform your best consistently.

✦ You are capable of doing all the great things you want to do by simply respecting your best focus.

✦ It's your focus! Choose to make it work for you and not against you—every day!

If you remember the essential focusing and refocusing strategies that are most important to you, you are ready to move forward to your highest levels of personal and performance excellence. As soon as you begin to apply these positive focusing strategies, your options for personal growth will become clearer and your chances of reaching your personal goals will increase significantly. To achieve the positive changes you are seeking, you must act on your positive intentions in some small or big way every day. Thinking is not enough. Without positive action, nothing changes.

Initiating sustainable positive changes usually means practicing a positive strategy long enough and often enough for its positive effects to surface in a consistent and natural way. Even when no signs of improvement are immediately evident, you can be laying the foundation for future use or ongoing personal growth. The following three actions will free you to live, love, and perform closer to your potential:

1. "**Do**cide" to act on your positive decisions or positive intentions.
2. Persist in acting on your positive intentions by focusing through the obstacles.
3. Retain and sustain your sense of purpose. Remember why you are pursuing your goals and dreams and why you are capable of living them.

Docide

From what you have already read in this book, it has probably become clear to you that the doing side of deciding has the greatest positive effect on your performance and your life. Three critical steps are present in dociding.

1. First, decide what you want to improve, change, or act on and why you want to do it.
2. Second, decide to do the things you believe will help you make positive changes and ongoing improvements.
3. Third, actually *do* what you decide to do. Doing the good things you decide to do is what will bring meaningful positive change and feelings of success and joy to your life.

Some great examples of the power of dociding have already been presented in this book. Olympic champion Beckie Scott, in the last cross-country race of her World Cup career, decided to focus beyond the extreme fatigue and exhaustion she was feeling and focused all her energy on the step or stride in front of her to win her final World Cup race. Thomas Grandi, after 12 years of competing on the World Cup circuit, decided to focus fully on his first World Cup victory, and then "**do**cided" to do the same thing in his next race for consecutive World Cup wins.

Space shuttle commander Chris Hadfield decided to become an astronaut by taking every step required to become one, even though at the time it was considered an impossible dream because there was no astronaut program in his home country of Canada and there were no opportunities for non-U.S. citizens to be accepted for training to become an astronaut in the United States.

A final example of deciding is the story of my father's decision that saved his life. I took one of my graduate students from China and her family to visit my father on his farm in Maryland when he was 82 years old. My student was an expert in qigong, one of the ancient martial arts. Shortly after her arrival, she led us through some basic qigong exercises, which combined deep abdominal breathing (breathing through the diaphragm) and slow synchronized arm movements. This way of breathing allows a person to get more air into the bottom part of the lungs. Many classical singers, musicians, and endurance athletes use similar breathing techniques. We stood out there by the cornfield, feeling the warmth and freshness of the morning air, and did these qigong breathing exercises for about half an hour.

Six months later, my mother called to tell me that my dad had been in a bad car accident and was in the intensive care unit at the hospital. He had collapsed lungs and a broken sternum. I jumped on the first plane I could get, flew to the nearest airport in Washington, DC, rented a car, and drove to the hospital. By the time I reached his room, he was coherent and I was able to speak with him. He told me what happened.

He was driving down a two-lane country road to pick up some supplies. As he came over a hill and started down the other side, a car in the wrong lane was speeding straight at him. The two vehicles collided head-on. The impact drove the steering wheel and dashboard into my father's chest. At that point he could not breathe, no matter how hard he tried. His first thought was that he was going to die because the pressure of the steering wheel on his chest prevented him from getting any air into his lungs.

In the heat of that moment, when his life was hanging in the balance, he remembered the breathing exercises we had done together next to the cornfield—qigong. He instantly focused on trying to breathe with his lower abdomen, which was not being crushed by the steering wheel. He focused on breathing in slowly and feeling his stomach rise and extend. He was able to get some air into the lower part of his lungs, which kept him alive until the emergency medical team arrived on the scene and was able to extract him from the car and rush him to the hospital.

His deciding to do the abdominal breathing saved his life and gave him another 10 years to live, love, learn, and grow. He worked vigorously on his rehabilitation and paid special attention to strengthening and expanding his breathing capacity through breathing exercises. During his recovery he had every part of his wheel of excellence working for him—focus, commitment, mental readiness, positive images, confidence, distraction control, and ongoing learning. And it worked wonders for him.

These examples show the power of dociding to act on your positive decisions when it really counts—the power of putting the *do* into your decisions. My father probably would have died within minutes right there in that car if he had not docided to take that one deep abdominal breath, the next one, and then the next. We can extract a positive lesson from his decision: one deliberate breath, one deliberate positive action, one positive step forward can change the course of your life. In my father's case, taking one positive breath and then another and another literally gave him the gift of another 10 years to do the things he loved to do, to reconnect with family, to meet grandchildren he would never have met, and to embrace the simple joys in his life.

The same is true for Thomas Grandi when he won his first back-to-back World Cup alpine skiing races, for Beckie Scott when she won her Olympic gold medal and then World Cup medal in cross-country skiing when she was sick and completely exhausted, and for space shuttle commander Chris Hadfield when a farm boy from Ontario became one of the most highly respected astronauts in the history of the NASA space program. Without the help of a deliberate and sustained positive focus and without dociding to pursue their goals and live their dreams, they never would have arrived at their desired destinations. This is the power of focus!

I know that you or someone close to you probably has or will have a story about the power of his or her own fully connected focus and positive docisions. If you feel so inclined, e-mail me one of those happy docision stories at excel@zoneofexcellence.ca. I know I will learn from it, and perhaps I will be able to share it with others who can also learn or grow from it.

- ✦ Docide to pursue your dreams.
- ✦ Docide to make the improvements that you are seeking.
- ✦ Docide to become the best person and performer you can be and have the potential to be.
- ✦ Docide to fully live your gift of life and embrace the simple joys to the fullest every day.

Persist

A big part of the challenge of pursuing excellence is to be persistent in pursuing your goals and in accepting yourself as a worthy, competent human being throughout the ups and downs of the journey. When you apply specific relevant positive focusing strategies to your personal life situation or ongoing challenges, expect improvement, but don't expect instant miracles. Sometimes positive changes occur instantly, but often they take time. For example, if you've been highly stressed in competitive situations for years, don't be disappointed and give up on a strategy if you are not totally calm and in complete control by tomorrow. Although I have witnessed dramatic—

literally overnight—improvements, personal growth is often a progression of simple steps. Take it step by step, day by day, and moment by moment, and be persistent.

You may have ups and downs in training and guiding or refining your focusing skills, just as you do in physical training. Sometimes you will feel mentally strong, totally positive, totally focused, and totally in control; other times you may temporarily slide back into less constructive ways of thinking or focusing and thereby upset yourself or fall short of your potential. But as soon as you get your focus back to where it should be, totally connected and totally focused on the doing, you will roll back into control. With persistent practice you will become more fully focused in ways that free you to perform your best more frequently and you will gain greater control over your life and your performance.

In some contexts or situations persistence involves noneffort rather than more effort. Did you ever try to go to sleep and end up tossing and turning for what seemed like hours? You keep telling yourself, *I have to get to sleep; try to go to sleep*. Then as soon as you stop trying hard, or stop thinking

Years of persistence have led Alex Morgan to the heights of soccer. Remember to keep going through the ups and downs of your journey.

Andy Mead/YCJ/Icon Sportswire

about *have to*, you slip effortlessly into a deep, restful sleep. In some cases, noneffort, or less conscious effort, yields results that forced effort continually chases away. You can achieve some things more readily, easily, or fluidly by "trying easier," by taking your time, or by moving forward toward your goal in a more relaxed or unhurried way.

Persistence means giving something enough time to work. Don't be too quick to say, "I tried that and it didn't work." How long did you try it? How often did you practice it? How fully did you focus on it? Did you gradually introduce the strategy, first in a relaxed setting and then under more stressful circumstances? Did you provide yourself with enough opportunities to free the feeling, focus, or relaxation to surface naturally without forcing it or rushing for instant results?

A focusing strategy may fail due to a lack of a fully focused connection or an absence of full focus on the task at hand or because more persistent practice is required to make the connection you are seeking feel pure and free.

For example, practicing a refocusing strategy a couple of times and concluding that it doesn't work is like trying out a new skill or performance program a couple of times or for only one minute and then claiming it doesn't work. One minute of training may not work, but extensive, high-quality fully focused training does work. Falling short of achieving immediate success with a focusing strategy does not mean that it will never work for you. Imagine if you had approached the refinement of your physical or technical skills in that way! How skilled would you be today?

Some strategies may not be compatible for you, and you should not waste much time on them. But if you select a strategy that feels right for you, even a little bit right, give it a chance to work for you. Remember these points when trying a new approach for personal growth or improved focus control:

+ Go with what seems workable for you.
+ Don't overload yourself with strategies; start with one or two simple strategies.
+ Try the focusing or refocusing strategy in less stressful situations until you sort things out.
+ Create a reminder to help you bring on the desired response or focus (for example, *focus, power, flow, control, relax, connect, be here, be all here, free yourself to perform*).
+ Practice using your favorite reminder as a way of entering or getting into your best focus.
+ Before the day or event begins, think about how you would like to feel that day or how you would prefer to focus in that event; remind yourself of the perspective and focus you want to carry.
+ Choose to let positive feelings and a fully connected focus surface naturally.

✦ Prepare a backup refocusing plan in case the feeling or focus doesn't surface or you lose that best focus at some point in your event or performance.

✦ Give your chosen focus strategy or positive reminders a chance to work. Try easier!

✦ Expect improvement but not overnight miracles.

✦ Be willing to lose a little in the short run to gain a lot in the long run.

✦ Remember that experimentation, persistent refinement, and keeping the joy in your pursuit are necessary for ongoing progress.

When you are trying new strategies or experimenting with different ways of focusing or refocusing, guard against thinking too much about what you are thinking about or focusing on. A female fencer made this comment:

> In the first two bouts of the tournament I was thinking so much about what I was thinking that I didn't fence. It took losses in those two bouts for me to realize what was happening. I was expecting everything to just happen, and it didn't. Once I started to focus on fencing my opponent, things slowed down. I began to relax, and I won the next two bouts. The latter two wins were against much stronger fencers than the first two losses.

An important lesson was gained from this fencer's experience: during the event, focus on the doing. A cat pursuing a mouse is not concerned with what she should be thinking about. She is focused on the doing. The purpose of your fully connected focusing strategy is to get into that fully focused, fully connected mind-set.

The best time to evaluate (or think about what you focused on during that performance) is after the event, unless an immediate change in focus is required within the game, race, performance, or match. If an immediate shift in focus is required during the event, do a brief evaluation and refocus quickly in the heat of the moment. If your thinking begins to interfere with your best, fully connected focus during the event, change channels by focusing on something more absorbing, constructive, and concrete that will immediately get you back on your best fully connected track.

The process of learning to be consistent in connecting fully in your best possible way can take some practice. Sometimes refining your focus, channeling your emotions in positive directions, or focusing on the right things at the right time is a bit like learning to walk on a beam, fence, or wire. You may wobble or even fall a number of times before you become fully focused, stable, balanced, and in control. Sometimes you need persistence to learn how to walk, run, or fly freely with your fully connected focusing skills, just as you sometimes need with your physical skills.

Setting daily focus goals, writing down your best focus reminders, and rejoicing in positive steps along the way can help you become better and more consistent at whatever you want to do. To do anything really well, you must willfully make a commitment to continue to improve your focus, your performance, and your life. Everything begins with your commitment to focus in positive and fully connected ways that lead to positive changes and ongoing improvements. No one can force you to want to grow to be better, happier, kinder, or more fully focused. This decision must come from within you. Once you have made a decision to do something you would really like to do and you docide to act on it, persistence does not guarantee that you will achieve your ultimate goal; it does guarantee, however, that you will continue to learn, improve, and grow along the way. Embracing a journey that you choose can give your life substance and meaning, even when you do not arrive at a specific destination.

Retain Purpose

Why are you doing what you are doing or pursuing the goals you are pursuing? What do you want to experience or accomplish in your performance domain? What do you want to experience or embrace in the rest of your life?

If you continue to move forward in a purposeful direction that you have chosen, you will add joy and meaning to your life, but the task or direction you have chosen requires that you retain a sense of purpose. If you want to get to where you want to go, you need some really solid personal reasons for wanting to get there. Your ability to retain a meaningful sense of purpose in pursuing your mission is a key factor that keeps you going through the challenges, obstacles, and ups and downs of your ongoing journey.

Some athletes and performers retain a sense of purpose in their mission because they love their experience and pursuit. It feels great to be fully connected to something challenging and meaningful and to become really good or great at something. It feels good to be accepted, valued, and respected as an integral part of a team. It feels good to wake up knowing you have something that you really want to do and enjoy doing and a meaningful challenge to pursue. It feels good to be part of a mission, to accept challenges in positive ways, and to push beyond what you have previously done. It feels great to be strong and fit and to have a familiar life-enhancing activity pattern or routine that you follow every day.

Sometimes embracing the ongoing simple joys or highlights in your daily experiences or pursuits is enough to sustain your love for what you are doing or pursuing. Often, fully engaging yourself in your pursuit makes you feel more fully alive and takes you to special places you have not gone before. Sometimes you also need to remind yourself to appreciate the good things you have, the good things you have done, and the good things you have the potential to continue to do. All of these personal attributes can help you to retain your sense of personal meaning and meaningful purpose.

The time you are living in now, the moment you are experiencing, and the opportunity you have in front of you this day, this hour, this minute, and this second only exist right now and will never exist for you in exactly the same way again. Embrace your gift of life, your gift of time, your gift of opportunity, and the gift of living this moment. Choose your own path to sustain your personal sense of meaning and purpose so that you come as close as possible to living the life you would really love to live. This will give you your best chance of doing the things you really want to do and experiencing your life fully and joyfully, given the time that you have to live on this planet.

Chris Hadfield provides an excellent example of retention of purpose. As a nine-year-old Canadian farm boy, Chris watched the first man walk on the moon on a live black-and-white television broadcast. From that moment on, he wanted to be an astronaut. That vision drove every major decision he made for the rest of his life. At that time becoming an astronaut was an impossible dream; Canada didn't even have an astronaut program. Still, he persisted while many other youngsters let their dreams fade away. I asked Chris how he was able to persist through the many challenges and seemingly insurmountable obstacles that he faced along the way. His response was simple—retention of purpose.

> If you want to achieve a very challenging goal, you have to have a reason for doing it, you have to really want to do it, you have to persist through a series of obstacles, and you have to keep your focus centered on why you are doing it and why it is important in your life. This retention of purpose or passion is what keeps you going toward your goal. There will be seemingly insurmountable setbacks if you set yourself any sort of difficult goal. You'll get to a stage where the whole horizon is black and you don't see any way through. That happened to me several times—I mean, I chose as a kid to be an astronaut when I grew up. It was a black horizon from the beginning; there was no way; it was impossible at the time. But things always change, given time. There are always new possibilities.
>
> The important part in achieving, or even coming close to what you dream of doing, is retention of purpose. Every day you're going to have a choice to go a little bit closer to where you want to get, every single day. And then there will be some break points in your life where you really fundamentally choose whether you're going to head in that direction or not. And if you don't make that choice, if you don't change direction, you will end up where you're headed. Guaranteed. So you need to fundamentally choose which direction you want to go, start heading that way, and maybe you'll get where you want to go.
>
> The purpose that I chose for myself, the goal I wanted to achieve as an adult, I internalized deliberately at nine years old. I was by no means a robot headed that way, but I always had choices and I thought, *Well, someday, maybe, I'll get to be an astronaut, and if I am, I really should know about this; I better study this; I should do this*. I was lucky enough

that when I got to the point in my life where I was qualified, the opportunity arose, and I was in a position to take advantage of it. I think that basic retention of purpose through a whole life not only gets you to your goal but also makes life more interesting and fulfilling because you're headed in some direction that you like. And your life loses its random and therefore unfulfilling nature. I really enjoy it.

Note: Chris Hadfield recently retired from his career as an astronaut and commander of the space shuttle at NASA. He excelled at what he did, he loved what he did, and he loved and lived his life fully—with no regrets!

PART IV
Living
Excellence

CHAPTER 17
Confident
and Composed

Confidence and composure are positive assets that can free you to feel your best, be your best, connect your best, perform your best, and interact more freely and positively with anyone in any context. Look for good reasons to be confident in yourself and confident that you can live and perform to your true capacity. Write down some positive reasons for you to be confident in yourself and in your capacity to achieve your goals and live your dreams. Look at those positive reminders every day and add to them as you find additional good reasons to be confident in yourself and your mission.

To perform your best, continue to remind yourself of your good reasons to be confident in yourself and your mission. In your performance contexts, focus fully on executing your performance and nothing else. Nothing else matters for those moments in time. Your chances of performing to your true potential are greatly enhanced when you choose to believe in yourself and your mission and focus fully on doing what you are doing and nothing else.

Every spoke on the wheel of excellence can help you to strengthen your confidence and free you to perform consistently closer to your potential in any context (see figure 17.1). Your focus, commitment, mental readiness, positive images, confidence, distraction control, and commitment to ongoing learning and improvement all work together to free you to perform your best and live your dreams in your performance domain and all other parts of your life.

Ways to Become Confident

✦ Confidence grows when you choose to see yourself as competent, committed, and caring and as a skilled athlete, performer, or person capable of doing what you really want to do.

✦ Confidence grows when you remind yourself of your best experiences, best training, best performances, and best focus in your everyday pursuits, training, practices, performances, games, auditions, shows, competitions, and other life-enhancing pursuits.

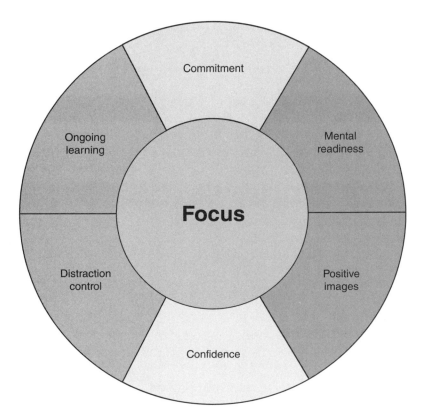

Figure 17.1 The wheel of human excellence.

The fact that you have already performed very well in some training, performance, or educational contexts is proof that you are capable of performing at least that well again. You just have to remind yourself of what you have to focus on to do it!

✦ Confidence and composure in competitions, races, games, recitals, tryouts, or any performance context are often enhanced by reminding yourself of your previous best performances and accepting the fact that if you performed that well in a previous performance context, you can definitely perform at least that well again—and probably a lot better. All you have to do is focus fully on doing it!

✦ Best performances and sustained high levels of performance excellence come from respecting your own best focus, choosing to believe in yourself and your potential, and choosing to focus in positive and fully connected ways that free you to perform your best consistently.

Ways to Continue to Enhance Your Confidence and Composure

✦ Choose to look for and find the good things in yourself.

✦ Choose to look for and find the good things in your performances.

✦ Choose to believe in yourself and your capacity.

+ Choose to remind yourself of your good reasons to believe that you can perform the way you want to perform—today and every day.
+ Choose to continue to remember your best performances and best parts of your performances
+ Choose to believe in yourself and your positive possibilities.
+ Choose to be positive and fully connected in doing whatever you are doing or pursuing.
+ Choose to remind yourself of your good reasons to believe in yourself and your capacity.
+ Choose to breathe in and out slowly whenever you need to relax or before you perform.
+ Choose to let go of any unnecessary stress, doubts, or worries. Let them flow away like water flowing gently down a stream.
+ Choose to be confident in your focus and confident that you are totally capable of doing what you want to do.
+ Choose to go out there and connect fully with the doing—nothing more and nothing less.

Ways to Continue to Perform Your Best

+ Choose to perform with confidence and composure.
+ "**Decide**" where you want your focus to be before you start performing.
+ Embrace the challenge.
+ Plan your positive path.
+ Anticipate potential obstacles or distractions.
+ Create a positive plan to focus through potential obstacles or distractions.
+ Create a backup refocusing plan to get yourself back on a positive track if needed.

To avoid potential problems and perform your best in any game, race, or performance context, consider these reminders:

+ Embrace the challenge you are about to face as a positive adventure worthy of you and your focus.
+ Plan to do what you believe will take you to your goals.
+ In preparation for your performance, run through your focus plan in your mind so that you know what you want to do and how you want to do it.
+ Create a backup focusing or refocusing plan to deal with potential obstacles.
+ Begin your performance by focusing fully on flowing through the first few moves.

✦ Stay fully connected with what you are doing for the duration of your race, game, audition, competition, or performance.

✦ If an obstacle surfaces, focus on finding a positive way through that obstacle, for example, by refocusing on the next step, move, or opportunity within your control.

You have a much better chance of staying in control or regaining control quickly if you catch things early, as they are surfacing, and remind yourself to breathe, relax, and focus on what you control.

If you know you will be entering a situation that has challenged you or created stress in the past, prepare yourself mentally to be your best in that context. Plan your path and best focus and do something that relaxes you before you walk into that setting. This will free you to begin in a calmer, more relaxed, or more focused state. Direct your focus to do what works best for you.

Creating a Focus Plan

Performing your best when it counts most requires that you focus on doing what is ultimately best for you and your mission. Maintaining your best focus is easier if you bring a positive perspective into the overall situation, focus fully within your performance, and have a prepracticed plan for overcoming obstacles. Know what you want to do and how you are going to focus to do it—before you do it. Decide that you are going to carry your positive mindset and bring your best focus into the competition, game, or event. Know what you are going to do if something pulls you out of your best focus so that you can get back on track quickly.

To be as prepared, confident, and composed as possible and to experience as few setbacks as possible, top performers develop effective on-site focus plans and refocusing plans. An on-site focus plan usually includes your preferred preperformance focus and your preferred best performance focus. In some cases, athletes and other performers also outline the sequence of key steps they will go through from the time they arrive at the performance site to the time they finish their performance. Your refocusing plan should include a list of potential problems or distractions that could arise and your plan to avoid, minimize, or focus through each of them.

Performers in all disciplines can gain from personalized, relevant on-site focus plans. Every world champion, Olympic champion, and top performer with whom I have worked has developed an effective way of preparing mentally for competitions or major performances. They have learned how to maintain their best fully focused connection by focusing consistently in ways that are effective for them. They know what their best focus is. They know how to enter that focus. They know how to maintain or sustain their best focus when it counts most. You probably already have the beginnings of a good or great focus plan that only needs refinement or fine-tuning to take you where you want to go consistently.

Answer the following questions to help develop or refine your best focus plan:

✦ How do I want to focus in this performance? (What focus is going to give me my best chance of performing to my true potential consistently?)

✦ What should I do to get into my best focus? (What am I going to say to myself, think about, focus on, or do to ensure that I enter my best focus?)

✦ Why should I bother doing it? (Why should I bother getting myself into my best focus?)

✦ What should I do if I can't do it right away or it doesn't work? (What am I going to do to refocus in positive ways if I can't get into that focus on the first attempt or can't maintain that focus?)

✦ After your performance, ask yourself how it went. How effective was I at implementing and maintaining my best focus? When was my focus best during this performance? Why was it best at that time? How can I improve the quality or duration of my best focus? How can I act to make those improvements?

To determine how you want to focus and how to get into that focus, think about what you would ideally like to do when you arrive at your performance site so that you will feel the way you want to feel, physically and mentally. List your preferred preparation activities in the sequence in which you would like them to occur. You may want to use the Sample On-Site Focus Plan (figure 17.2) as a guide. Some athletes or performers prefer, and gain from, detailed descriptions of activities, focus reminders, and positive actions they want to engage in. Others prefer more of a sketch, image, feeling, or simple focus reminder to guide them into their best and most fully connected focus. To recall or remember the perspective, feeling, or focus you want to carry with you, think about your focus in a previous best performance and then remind yourself to simply connect fully with the performance in front of you. Free your performance to unfold naturally by connecting fully with your performance.

What you choose to focus on is your choice. You can direct or redirect your focus any way you want. Practice focusing on what helps you connect fully and perform your best. Ideally, your best on-site focus will become automatic so that you will need only a simple reminder to "focus," "flip the switch," or "change channels" to activate and sustain your best focus in training and other important events.

After you have outlined your preferred on-site preparation activities and your best focus reminders, remember why they are important to you.

Figure 17.2   Sample On-Site Focus Plan

Event: Track Sprint

What is my best focus? Focus on the doing—one step at a time.

What should I do?	Why should I do it?	What should I do if it does not work?
General warm-up: long, slow stretching	To feel loose, relaxed, and calm	More stretching, relax, use reminder—*I can run well no matter how warm-up feels*
Event preparation: keep warm, active; stretch periodically until event time	To stay loose	Extra sweatsuit, run loose, relax
Replicate part of race at full speed, short duration but intense enough to sweat	To feel confident in speed	Visualize best previous race; feel it; then simulate first 20 meters
Simulate start with preceding heat with cue words	To feel ready for explosive start	Simulate in imagery if not possible physically—think explosiveness in imagery
See myself, feel myself run the way I want to run	As a last-minute reminder before letting my body do it	Remind myself how I want to feel and run
Approach blocks: breathe; relax; be ready, alert, strong	To feel 100 percent ready	Remind myself of past best, of untapped potential—*I need to feel butterflies; I'm going to run well*
In blocks: ready position, breathe out, relax	To feel that everything is under control	Let my shoulders relax, focus on breathing
Set position, think blast off, blast off	To fly off the blocks as fast as lightning	Explode, uncoil, spring like a cat

1. How did it go? What went best? What can I improve?

2. What improvements or refinements can I make in my focus plan for next time?

From T. Orlick, 2015, *In pursuit of excellence*, 5th ed. (Champaign, IL: Human Kinetics).

What can each of these activities or reminders contribute to your confidence, composure, best feelings, best focus, and best performances? Knowing why they are important to you and your performance will motivate you to act on them consistently in important performance situations.

Whether a preparation activity or focusing strategy worked well or did not work the way you wanted it to in your real performance context, draw out the lessons from your experiences and improve by acting on them. Think about what worked well and why it worked well. Think about what didn't work as well as you had hoped and why it didn't work. Think of a refocusing strategy or reminder you could use within your performance context that can quickly bring your focus back to where it will do you the most good. An effective refocusing reminder can be a simple word, thought, breath, or image. Find something that works for you and practice using it before, within, and after an event. Keep refining your focusing or refocusing reminders until they work effectively for you or until you find something else that works better to get your focus where you want it to be.

Backup refocusing strategies can sometimes also be helpful. You normally bring them into play only if your original focusing strategy or refocusing strategy is not doing the job. For the most part, backups remain in reserve, but it is good to be able to call on them if needed. Your best focus plan consists of the following five action steps that can help you prepare to perform your best and maintain your focus and composure throughout your performance:

1. Choose to focus in positive ways that make you feel fully connected and confident in yourself and free you to perform your best. Do this before you begin your performance, race, or game.

2. Choose to focus in ways that free you to maintain your positive and fully connected focus for the duration of your performance, race, or game. Your primary and most important goal is to respect your best and most fully connected focus from start to finish.

3. Choose a refocusing strategy to use, if needed, to shift your focus back to your most positive fully connected focus. You only use step 3 if you are having difficulty getting into or maintaining a positive and connected focus or if it momentarily slips away.

4. Choose a backup refocusing strategy in case your first refocusing strategy is not working for you.

5. Carefully evaluate and reflect on your best and less than best focus after every performance (and after some practices or training sessions) to continue to make improvements in the quality and consistency of your best focus for your best performances. Think about what focus works best for you and what focus works against you in your training and performances. Think about how you can continue to improve and sustain your best focus for longer periods of time.

Every time you train, practice, work out, play, compete, or perform, you can draw out meaningful positive lessons and act on them to continue to improve your best focus and the consistency of your best performances.

After every game, performance, or event, take some time to assess the overall effectiveness of your focus plan. How did it go? How was your focus during your preperformance or warm-up phase? Was it where you wanted it to be? How was your focus during your performance? What parts went well? What were you focused on when you were performing your best? Was there a time when your best focus drifted away from where you wanted it to be? If yes, what was going on then? What can you do to continue to improve the quality, consistency, and duration of your best focus and best performances?

Many elite athletes and great performers in high-performance disciplines who perform their best consistently in high-intensity challenges or events engage themselves in positive preplanned activities or routines right up to the moment they begin performing. Then they zone in to their best performance focus and connect totally and completely with their task from the start to the end of their event. You might enjoy reading some detailed focus plans of great performers engaged in various high-performance pursuits in my free online *Journal of Excellence* (available at www.zoneofexcellence.ca) where you will find hundreds of articles and interviews with some of the world's greatest performers in a variety of high-performance domains.

Turning Fear Into Focus

Many athletes and other performers who enter situations in which they are being watched, evaluated, or judged or in which the risks of serious injury are high have confided in me that they sometimes feel very nervous or afraid before those races, games, performances, or adventures and that sometimes it "isn't a good feeling." Shifting your focus away from worry to total engagement in your performance (or connecting fully with the doing) is the fastest way to release unnecessary fear or turn fear into focus. Totally engaging yourself in the pure and absolute connection with the step, stride, stroke, or challenge in front of you is the best way to clear your mind of all unnecessary thoughts and relax your body enough to have a great performance. A pure and positive fully focused connection works wonders in any challenging performance pursuit.

If you are feeling stressed or worried before your game, race, competition, adventure, or performance, consider some of the following options and reminders:

✦ Before you enter your performance arena or before you begin to race, compete, dance, sing, or perform, let go of the outside world and any fears or worries you might have about the outcome because those worries are not going to help you or your performance. If you don't

Contra Costa Times/Zumapress/Icon Sportswire

Outstanding athletes like Steph Curry are effective at maintaining their composure even when under pressure. Plan a strategy to help you maintain focus.

like the channel you are on, change channels (just like you do with your TV's remote control).

✦ If you are feeling fearful or worried about the outcome, slow down your breathing. Breathe in and out slowly, and as you breathe out say to yourself, *Relax . . . relax . . . relax*. Then think only about the good things you are going to do.

✦ Nothing else in the world matters at this time.

✦ Just connect fully with what you are going to do.

✦ It's just you and your connection, you and your performance.

✦ Concentrate on your fully focused connection.

✦ Your fully focused connection will free you from tension and worry and free you to perform your best.

✦ Focus only on fully connecting in ways that free you and your body to perform.

✦ When you are calm, focused, and in the moment, your performance will run freely.

To eliminate doubts about your ability to do what you want to do or perform the way you want to perform, read the following reminders:

+ I totally belong here.
+ I am totally committed to making this as good as it can possibly be.
+ I am in control of the feelings and focus I bring into this performance or pursuit.
+ I choose my focus.
+ I choose to focus fully from start to finish.
+ I decide to make it great.
+ I decide to fully embrace the challenge.
+ I decide to draw out and act on the positive lessons from each of my experiences.
+ I am so lucky to be here doing what I love to do.
+ I choose to focus fully and continue to embrace the simple joys of the journey.
+ Everything is cool.
+ Nothing else matters.

Developing a Refocusing Plan

Everyone can gain from having an effective refocusing plan for dealing with potential distractions. Without an effective refocusing plan you can waste a huge amount of positive energy trying to control things that are beyond your control. Some things are within your control, and some things are beyond your control. No matter how hard you try, you can never change some people, some rules, or some contexts.

Focus on yourself and on what you can control. A refocusing plan is the best way I know of for letting go of unnecessary stress, worry, or negativity and regaining a positive, fully connected, healthy, happy perspective and an overall sense of personal control and composure.

To develop your own refocusing plan, start by listing the things that usually bother or concern you at home, at training, at competitions, or in other parts of your life. Let's say you are preparing for an important event that may only come along once or twice in your life. You want to be as prepared as possible to cope with or focus through both expected and unexpected circumstances or distractions that you may face at this event. A first step might be to find out as much as you can about what these events have been like for other performers or athletes in the past. You may be able to speak with and learn from former competitors, athletes, coaches, support staff, focus enhancement consultants, and others who have lived in those challenging contexts. Based on your own experiences in certain performance contexts and the experiences of others, you can make an intelligent guess about what that event might be like for you and how you best can prepare for it.

Think about the distractions, obstacles, or hassles that have affected you in the past, as well as specific things you feel are likely to happen at your upcoming event. Include distractions that could arise in the week or two leading up to the event. Make an educated guess about what might occur when you are traveling; what it will be like at your lodgings and training site; what kind of food will be available; what it will be like at your competition site before your event, on the day of the event, and within your performance; how it will go between halves, periods, or performances; and what will happen after the competition. Develop a simple refocusing plan for circumstances you might face that could create stress or pose problems.

Your goal is to be as prepared as you can possibly be for what you might face, to avoid as many potentially bothersome or energy-draining distractions as possible, and to be prepared to cope effectively with circumstances you cannot avoid. You may prefer that no dark storms blow your way, but should they come, you need to know how to avoid them, how to focus through them, and how to overcome them.

You can divide your refocusing plan into major if-then components:

+ Plan A. If this happens, then I do this or I focus on doing this.
+ Plan B. If this doesn't work, then I do that or focus on doing that.
+ Plan C. If that doesn't work, then I take a time-out to relax or I talk with my coach or a member of my support staff about how to avoid that unnecessary distraction.

Plan your refocusing strategies in detail. Write down positive reminders that will help you do what you want to do. Use your reminders in practices and simulated conditions. Become familiar enough with them so that you can call on them naturally in challenging or high-stress situations.

If you practice staying calm, relaxing your pace, changing channels, channeling your focus in positive ways, accepting uncertainties, and embracing ongoing challenges, you are less likely to become upset over various distractions, changes in schedules, long waits, outside pressures, unfamiliar conditions, regimented procedures, or demanding expectations.

Unexpected circumstances often occur at major performance events. Although you cannot anticipate every possible adversity or distraction, you can prepare an effective on-site focusing and refocusing response to use in the face of almost any unexpected happening. If you feel yourself starting to react negatively to someone or something, use these thoughts or feelings to signal a shift in focus. Saying *shift focus* or *change channels* several times in a row will generally break you away from the distracting thoughts long enough to refocus on something more positive or constructive.

The whole refocusing sequence might unfold as follows: *I don't like these feelings, and I don't have to stay with them. Shift focus, shift focus, shift focus. This doesn't have to bother me! It's no big deal. I can still do what I want to do and what I came here to do. So relax and focus on doing what you came here to do!*

When facing unwanted or unproductive distractions, focus fully on doing something within your immediate control—performing the skill you are currently doing, preparing to do the skill you are about to do, or doing something else that is positive, absorbing, and constructive. If a distraction occurs just before your performance begins, shift focus to your final preparations for executing your performance—the feel of it, the form of it, the flow of it, or the game plan you want to follow. Take a deep breath in, relax as you exhale, imagine yourself doing what you want to do, and then do it with full focus.

When you focus your energy on things you can control and let go of things you cannot control, you become the master of your own destiny. You cannot control other people's thoughts or actions, the caliber of competition, the media, or the past no matter how hard you try. You can, however, control your preparation, your focus, and your performance. You can choose to focus in ways that free you to do your personal best. No one can ask for more than that; no one can do more than that. Nothing beyond your sincere commitment to focus your best and do what will help you perform your best matters. Other competitors are who they are, and you are who you are— you're separate entities. Focus on your own preparation and performance, and let everything else go.

Your on-site focus plan and refocusing plan free you to enter your performance arena with a greater sense of confidence and composure. You have a positive and effective plan to help make things go well and a refocusing plan in case something goes wrong. You are ready and fully focused. That's when great things happen! Embrace the journey.

CHAPTER 18
Balanced

If you are pursuing excellence in any area of your life, you are probably experiencing a sense of overload or imbalance, just like millions of other people. This chapter will help you to reduce the overload and enhance the balance in your life. Almost everyone I have worked with who has been in pursuit of excellence in virtually any field has experienced overload. There are just too many things to do and not enough time to do them. Even our children and youth are overloaded, with going to school; doing homework after school; participating in sports, physical activities, or creative pursuits; doing things with their friends or classmates; and spending a huge amount of time on their computers, mobile phones, and other electronic devices. Many adults and children do not have much uninterrupted time to do joyful things together as a family or with friends. They are too busy working, studying, training, and trying to meet multiple demands even at an early age. People from all walks of life engaged in a variety of professions or pursuits around the world suffer from overload—too many demands and not enough time in the day to meet those demands.

Overload. What does it feel like for you? What does it mean to you? Do you feel yourself becoming stressed because you are being pulled in too many directions at the same time? Does your focus begin to drift away from what you are doing or you want to do to something else? Does your tension or stress level begin to rise? Do you feel stressed when you begin to think about how you can possibly meet everyone's demands, including your own?

Keeping some sense of balance in your life is important for a lot of good reasons. The consequences of ongoing overload without enough rest or recovery or embracing simple daily joys include becoming more stressed, losing your sense of inner harmony, letting things bother you that would normally not bother you, and becoming more distracted, less focused, or less tolerant. You may become more irritable toward yourself and others, especially people you love, not because they are the ones placing the demands on you but because they just happen to be around. A daily diet of overload or too many demands, combined with failing to respect your personal needs for rest, relaxation, recovery, and embracing daily simple joys is not conducive to ongoing performance enhancement or joyful quality living.

One positive thing about feeling overloaded is that it is a great reminder for you to pause long enough to think about how you want to live your life, how you want to feel every day, and how important it is for you to schedule in some quiet time, joyful time, and relaxation time every day just for you.

Life is not a race to get to the end before anyone else. The journey of your life is something you want to fully embrace! Your life offers many opportunities to embrace the simple joys in every day in every context. Find a way to embrace some of those simple, relaxing, joyful life-enhancing moments every day.

When too many people want too many things from you, or when you feel that too many demands are being placed on you at the same time, stop, breathe in slowly, breathe out slowly, and remind yourself that you can only do a certain number of things well in one day, one week, one month, or one year. You may be superchild, superwoman, or superman—but even super-people need time to relax and recover. Most people perform their best when they are well rested and focused fully on executing one task, one assignment, one move, one stride, one stroke, or one mission one step at a time without having to worry about other demands.

Given the complexities and challenges of your life and the fact that there is only one *you* on this planet, *you* can choose to do what you feel is reasonable every day and let the rest go. Focus on doing the things you believe are most important for you to do right now and focus fully on doing them really well. Choose to not worry about anything beyond your control because worrying about things not in your immediate control will only cause unnecessary stress and slow you down. Focus on doing something positive for you today so that you feel good about you, more relaxed, happier, or more fully alive because of the happy or fun things that you actually did today!

Coping With Overload

Let's assume that right now you are already feeling overloaded or pulled in too many directions at the same time and are feeling more stressed than you would like. You might be thinking, *I don't like being in this overloaded state or situation even temporarily. I don't like feeling pressured or rushed to do something. I feel better and perform better when I am more relaxed. It is ridiculous to get caught up in overloaded or stressed-out feelings because it is not helping you feel or perform your best.* Remember that you do have the power to "**do**cide" to take a time-out to relax and do your best *to prevent overload situations in the future.*

You can choose to avoid or say no to additional demands. You can choose to find a quiet place to escape where you don't have to answer to anyone. You can remove yourself mentally or physically from situations or people who create feelings of overload and give yourself permission to relax and reflect on what you are feeling. Taking little relaxation breaks can usually put things back into a positive perspective pretty quickly. Doing some things you love to do can put you back in control of your day and your life. Allow yourself to embrace some simple joys and moments of relaxed silence to regain a more balanced or positive perspective.

Breathe, relax, focus. Focus on doing one little thing at a time. Focus on taking that first step. When you complete that step, focus on the next step. Then breathe, relax, and take your next step. Let each step fill you with positive energy, focus, and purpose.

Even if you can't complete something right now or are late on a deadline, don't beat yourself up over it or blow it out of proportion. Maybe at this time you can't do it all, or it will be late. Not meeting this deadline or not completing this task right now is not going to kill you or anyone else.

Take a time-out! Relax. Breathe. Slow down. Learn something from this experience about how you can best control your schedule. Try to plan your time and your path to prevent overload circumstances like this from happening in the future. Worrying, putting yourself down, stressing out, or punishing yourself more than you already have won't help anything.

Take a break. Go for a walk, a run, a swim, or a massage. Spend some time in nature. Do something you really enjoy doing. Embrace a few moments of silence. Draw out the lessons from your experiences and move on in positive ways.

Listen to your feelings, listen to your body, and listen to yourself. Slow down and relax. You usually know when things are getting out of balance. There are physical signs, emotional signs, and changes in feelings that can tell you that you are overloaded or need a little break. Tune into those signals or signs and do something about it. You may start to feel tense, grumpy, negative, or irritated by things that normally don't bother you. You may begin to feel physically drained or exhausted, easily distracted or upset, not fully focused, or lacking in motivation. Your body, mind, and emotions are telling you to slow down, relax, and respect your need for balance in your life, but you are not listening.

When you begin to listen to your personal signs and relax your pace before the overload becomes too heavy, you can save yourself a lot of unnecessary grief. You don't need to rush everywhere or through everything. Slow down. Take it easy. Move in a confident, unhurried fashion. Focus on connecting fully with each of your experiences. When you sit down to talk with someone, be there, relax, focus, listen, and then relax again for a few moments before responding. *Slooow* down when you walk, eat, drive, or cycle from one place to another. Walk relaxed. Run relaxed. Think relaxed. Rest relaxed.

If your mobile phone or other electronic device rings, relax for a few rings before responding, or if you want to avoid additional demands, don't answer it at all. Relax in the shower; in front of a fire; in a sauna, hot tub, or warm bath; in a beautiful nature setting; or any favorite place.

Eat relaxed and drink more slowly. After eating, take a little time to do nothing but enjoy some quiet time alone or with people you love. Do something relaxing every day. Do something you love to do every day—listen to music; get yourself into an uplifting mental space or relaxing environment; relax the muscles in your body; stretch out on the grass, the sand, or the beach; or walk quietly in a park or other nature setting such as along the beach. Do anything positive and healthy that makes you feel good, uplifted, and happy to be alive. Plan to relax before entering any potentially stressful setting. If you feel it might help, take a 5- or 10-minute time-out from any stress-related situation to relax, be alone, and refocus in positive performance- and life-enhancing ways.

If people you love may be feeling neglected because of your overload or busy schedule, talk with them about your feelings. Reassure them that you love them and care dearly for them. Let them know that your overload is making you more irritable or distant and that you are working on getting it under control. They will appreciate knowing that they are not the cause of your increased stress, short temper, irritable responses, or possible unhappiness. Just talking openly with people who are close to you may reduce your load and help you put things in perspective. The long-range challenge is to prevent overload, embrace the different loves of your life, and live your life more fully and joyfully every day. You can begin to live your life with less stress, more joy, and more balance right now. Docide to do the following:

+ To live this day free from stress or worry
+ To live this day free from anger
+ To live this day free from overload
+ To do something today that you really enjoy doing
+ To do something you love to do with someone you like, admire, or love
+ To live your day with a positive and fully connected focus
+ To find some time to relax in silence today and every day
+ To live this day fully; then do it again tomorrow, the next day, and every day after for the rest of your life!

Respect your own needs for personal space and accomplishments, daily exercise or physical activity, good nutrition, adequate rest and relaxation, meaningful interactions, positive focus, and embracing simple joys every day. Make these priorities in your life. In the end they will be the greatest gifts you can give yourself and others over the course of your life.

Before you accept an additional request, assignment, or demand, ask yourself these questions:

+ Do I really want to do this?
+ Do I really have to do this?
+ Do I really have time to do this?
+ Will this be an energy gain or an energy drain for me?

If three of your four responses to these questions are negative, respectfully decline the request—don't do it. Decline in a positive way: *Thank you for the request. I would love to do it, but unfortunately* [or fortunately for you] *right now I have too many other commitments to take on anything else. Check back with me later.*

Preventing Overload

As you become more skilled, proficient, well known, or respected as an athlete, teacher, coach, performer, writer, or expert in any field, people and circumstances will place more demands on you. The better you become at doing what you do, the greater the demands will likely be. People and performers who excel at what they do often face additional requests. Lots of people want a piece of you, and if you accept too many requests or demands, you risk overloading yourself, which is an energy drain that in some cases leads to having no quality time or relaxation time left for you or your loved ones.

Even if you never gain a high profile in your sport, career, profession, or life, you will encounter times when the demands in your life seem to overwhelm your capacity to meet them. This situation is common among high-profile and developing athletes, well-known actors and performing artists, teenagers facing multiple demands, university students, parents with

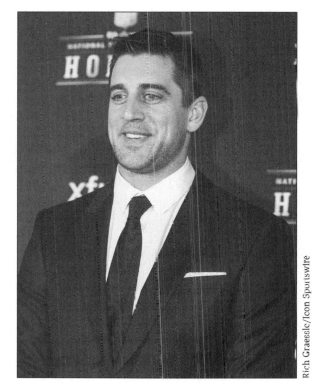

To be successful, NFL MVP Aaron Rodgers must balance the demands on his time off the football field. To prevent overload, carefully assess the demands on your time.

young children, teachers, coaches, doctors, business executives, managers, secretaries, waitresses, and anyone else who feels overloaded in their work life or performance field.

To prevent overload, first think about your priorities and what balance means to you. What are your priorities at this point in your life? What are your priorities in your studies, work, or performance domain? What are your priorities in your relationships? What are your priorities in the time you have outside your school, work, or performance domain? Are you able to take on additional commitments and still fully embrace the highest priorities in your life with quality focus and pure connection?

Assessing Demands

If you find yourself in a situation where the demands on your time exceed your hours available to fulfill them, you have to take control of your life. No one else can do this for you. Decide how many requests you can accept or how much of your time you can realistically give to others and how much you want to take on. Maybe you feel that you can reasonably handle one or two additional demands this month (for example, outside requests, social events, interviews) but nothing next month before your most important events. At some point in your career or life you may find that you cannot answer all your e-mails, letters, requests, or calls, so you can either get someone to help you carry that part of your load, answer only the most important ones, or not answer any of them. Sometimes you may benefit most from just taking a little break to go some place relaxing where there are no demands, nobody knows you, and nobody wants anything from you. Just chill out, relax, and regenerate for a few days.

You are the one who must set realistic priorities for yourself and follow them. Otherwise you may surrender too much of your independence and positive energy—essential in your ongoing pursuit of excellence and the achievement of your goals—to people who demand a lot but do not give much in return or to people with good intentions who don't realize how challenging it is for you to meet your current commitments to your training, performances, work, rest time, and loved ones.

Before saying yes to anything that creates additional demands on your limited time, think about what the positive gain will be and what the cost will be in terms of your time and energy. You can be sure that almost every task you are asked to fulfill will take longer than you have been told. A 10- to 15-minute interview often ends up taking at least an hour or two out of your life—talking on the phone, making arrangements, thinking about what you want to say, getting there, waiting until everyone is set up and ready to go, getting home, and so on. Before agreeing to a request, indicate exactly how much time and commitment you are willing or not willing to give. Set your conditions and call the shots before you accept.

If you are not sure whether you want to do it, my advice is simple: don't do it! Remember the word *no*. Saying no can be difficult at times, but it is often the only way to maintain the high quality in your performance and preserve some balance in your life. Usually if you are respectful and honest in turning down a request, people will understand and you will reduce your load and level of stress. You can simply say, "I would love to do it, but I already have so many commitments that I simply can't fit it in." Your life is not likely to suffer, or be any less fulfilling, for turning down a request. On the contrary, your life will probably be better because you will have more time for yourself, your loved ones, and the things you love to do.

If you are not sure whether taking on an additional commitment will help you, at least delay committing yourself. Give yourself a few days to assess the relevancy of the request to see how it fits with your overall schedule and priorities.

If you are a busy person and want to say yes to some other opportunities, choose to say yes to things that are personally uplifting (for example, going to exciting countries or experiencing different cultures, time doing relaxing things for you, quality time with family or friends, or time doing things you really enjoy that are energy gains, uplifting, exciting, or relaxing). Balanced excellence is not a question of working any less diligently while you are training, studying, working, preparing, or performing; it is a question of lightening your load and relaxing more fully outside of training, performing, or working hours. Choose to accept the things you really want to do and respectfully let the other things go. Choose to do things that give you positive energy, make you feel good, or make a positive and meaningful contribution to you, your loved ones, or a cause you believe in.

Occasionally, you may still find yourself feeling momentarily overwhelmed by too many demands. However, most of the time you can predict how much you can handle comfortably and choose to adjust your pace, your choices, or your commitments before getting into trouble. This may mean saying no to certain people, situations, or requests, but it also means saying yes to living your life fully and joyfully.

Managing Stress

The good news about stress is that it is often within your control. You can choose to be stressed or not stressed in a variety of situations or contexts. What you focus on and how you view or interpret certain situations are huge factors in determining whether or not you feel stressed. You are not obliged or required to feel stressed in performance situations or other challenging life situations even if you might have viewed them as necessarily stressful in the past. You do have a choice: you can choose to be stressed or choose not to be stressed. You can choose to focus on what makes you feel happy, optimistic, confident, fully connected, and more fully alive or choose to focus on what makes you feel worried, stressed, hopeless, or less than fully alive. These are choices you can make every day in every part of your life.

You can choose to direct the course of your own performance and life in positive ways by focusing on being positive with yourself and others and by remaining fully connected with the good things you are doing or want to do. This alone will reduce or eliminate a lot of unnecessary and destructive stress in your life.

Keeping Life in Balance
Laura Christian

Stewart Event Images

I asked a wonderful and talented athlete with whom I had been working in some capacity for many years if she would be willing to share part of her challenging journey with you and others reading this fifth edition of *In Pursuit of Excellence*. She responded positively to my request and agreed to allow me to share her reflections with you:

> I first became aware of Terry Orlick almost 10 years ago. I was qualified for my first national agility competition with my young border collie and heading into a very intense atmosphere so I purchased a variety of motivational books in my preparation. *In Pursuit of Excellence* quickly became one of my favorites, which I read and reread many times. I called it my "success manual."
>
> It was during this time that I first spoke with Terry, and his calm and confident advice was just what I needed to hear. He suggested listening to his CDs, which I did. I was thrilled when we came in second and third place out of a very large field of talented teams.

Terry helped me believe in our ability to succeed. Really believe it.

Competition has been a consistent theme throughout my life, including a wide range of sports such as bowling, basketball, track and field, tennis, golf, and 5K and 10K runs. Sometimes these involved working alone, other times with a partner or several teammates. As an adult, I first teamed up with equines (horses) and now with canine partners (border collies). It's truly a unique challenge to partner with a different species (who does not speak your language), which introduces a completely new angle to teamwork.

What I find most helpful with Terry's books is their universal relevance regardless of the competition venue.

I first met Terry in person when he was given to me as a birthday gift! (No, he did not pop out of a cake.) But he did attend a local agility competition in which I was running with three of my dogs. He was able to observe several of our competition runs, and later we reviewed some video replays and analyzed them together.

We then continued to remain in contact to devise a plan for our upcoming national event to which I was taking two different dogs. It was during this time when a new challenge came to light. I was diagnosed with breast cancer. This occurred during the summer, and I underwent first one operation, then 10 days later, another. Then a third major surgery was necessary. The first two surgeries and recovery periods caused me to miss several events, and I was not yet qualified for the nationals. As the qualification period neared its completion, I asked my doctors if I could delay surgery long enough to get in one last trial with my dogs. They agreed. So we went and were able to win enough classes to qualify. I was thrilled. We had some fantastic runs and everything just flowed.

I could now go into surgery with peace of mind. I had the surgery and needed a few months to recover. Just when I returned to practice I encountered a major setback by an infection. Up until the day before we had to leave for the nationals, I was hooked up to IVs with antibiotics fighting to get well enough to run.

Terry kept me refocused and confident that we could stay in our flow of what we knew, in spite of the circumstances.

I had used the National Agility Competition (NAC) as the focus goal to survive and minimize my diagnosis and surgery, determined to have a chance to run with each of my two talented teammates.

We approached the nationals as a learning experience, with realistic optimism, fully acknowledging that we were not at our peak performance level.

Terry helped coach me, encouraged me to maintain a positive attitude, and helped me to be confident and focused in our success routines.

The National Agility Competition environment was charged and challenging. Stepping to the starting line with each of my canines was exciting: they were explosive and eager. We handled the courses well and performed well but not to the necessary perfection that is required at that level. We had the potential, gave it our best effort, gained experience and inspiration, and strengthened our teamwork. Fundamentally satisfied, we arrived home to immediately begin working toward out next competition.

Competitive agility racing with dogs is a game of hundredths of seconds, volatile with all-or-nothing results. Winning requires perfection. It is a constant test of the combination and balance of physical and mental skills and attitude. This is further complicated by working with a teammate who speaks another first language. Working with my enthusiastic partners is an ongoing joy—a *super* joy.

Navigating a technical course of challenging obstacles and turns by working together, at a winning speed, is the ultimate goal and achievement for us.

Terry's guides and books continue to help me and my three border collie teammates to embrace all the essential elements necessary to continue finding the joy in "the pursuit of excellence." We do what we do because we love it!

I have a new appreciation for the joy in our journey and the joy in my life. I will continue to strive to learn and expand my potential for reaching for the podium position and embracing my gift of life with Terry's help. It is truly a privilege to work with such a wonderful team—canine *and* human. Thank you, Terry!

Managing Ongoing Commitments

Challenging demands often occurs in waves. This day or week may be extremely heavy, which is fine as long as other days or weeks are lighter. If possible, spread out your workload over a reasonable period of time and schedule in happy spaces for simple joys between your multiple demands. Plan meetings, presentations, workshops, social or work commitments, travel, and other scheduled activities so that they are not back to back, with one still incomplete while another is starting or with no time between one and the next. Accepting a series of back-to-back commitments that seem far in the future can come back to haunt you when you actually have to do them today, tomorrow, and the next day.

Be realistic in making additional commitments. Overestimate the time it will take, rather than underestimate the amount of time, energy, and work involved in meeting this commitment and doing it with quality. Start preparing earlier to meet deadlines by setting daily short-term goals. Leave earlier for appointments, classes, meetings, practices, or other commitments so that you arrive early without having to feel stressed or rushed. Accept the fact that when you have multiple commitments, at a certain time you will have to stop working on one commitment or mission and move on or shift focus to complete another.

Remember also that a constant diet of stress and overload will inhibit or weaken your immune system, make you more susceptible to illness, and make your life less joyful. Reducing the unnecessary stress and negativity in your life will make you a better performer and a happier person. If you only have one life to live (or maybe two), why not make wise choices and choose to live your life fully and joyfully? Relax your schedule enough to fit in some quiet time for yourself between whatever demands you are facing every day. Set priorities so that you can say yes to those things you really want to do. Choose to do more positive things that lift you and fewer things that drain you. Schedule regular meetings with yourself to do simple things that relax you, lift you, reenergize you, and make you feel more fully alive. If you feel your stress level rising, remind yourself to take in one long slow deep breath and breathe out slowly. As you breathe out, let all the stress or tension flow out of your body. You can take a one-breath relaxation break anywhere and anytime! To put things back in perspective, relax for a few minutes—with no calls, e-mails, TV, text messages, computer, or negative thoughts—just you and your breathing.

Scheduling Positive Time for You to Balance Your Life

A critical part of preventing overload and maintaining physical, mental, and emotional health is scheduling time to do some healthy things you love to do outside your work or performance domain. Run, walk, play, swim, slide, smile, find a quiet place or quiet time, or do anything quiet and relaxing that gives you a feeling of peace, harmony, or pure positive connection. Take some time to reflect on the good things in your life, on the positive things that lift you, make you feel joyful, or make you feel more fully alive. Simple, positive, uplifting experiences can help you enter any context feeling more positive, more confident, more connected, more in harmony, more balanced, more resilient, and less likely to react negatively to whatever challenges you may be facing.

Balanced excellence becomes possible when you reduce the stress in your life and add more joy to your life. You can add or increase the joy and balance in your life by positive actions inside and outside your performance domain:

+ Reduce the unnecessary stress in your life.
+ Connect your focus in positive and fully connected ways.
+ Find and embrace simple joys in your performance domain, work, school, relationships, and daily living.

✦ Relax more fully and continue to find more simple and super joys in your performance domain.

✦ Appreciate your gift of life.

✦ Set a goal to maintain a sense of appreciation and harmony every day of your life.

✦ Practice relaxing in the face of stress.

CHAPTER 19
Consistent

Performing their best consistently is one of the biggest and most important challenges for athletes, coaches, teachers, dancers, musicians, singers, actors, surgeons, astronauts, military units, corporate leaders, and performers in virtually all high-performance domains. The key to performing your best consistently is to respect the focus that works best for you in your training, practices, simulations, preperformance preparation, and real-world performances. For consistent high-level performance you also need to respect your ongoing needs for rest, relaxation, recovery, adequate sleep, simple joys, healthy nutrition, and positive interaction with others.

The moment you enter your performance arena, your best performance depends on how well you can attain and sustain your best fully connected focus. You will perform your best consistently when you bring your positive and best fully connected focus into every performance and sustain that focus for the duration of your game, race, mission, interaction, or performance.

When you understand or discover what focus frees you to feel and perform your best, your challenge for consistency rests solidly in respecting your own best focus consistently. This holds true regardless of what your best performance might be at this point in your sport, performance domain, personal interactions, career, or life.

When your performance or parts of your performance falter or fall short of your potential, you are probably at least momentarily failing to respect the focus that works best for you to bring out your true potential. You do not lose your physical, technical, or communication skills from one moment to the next, from one day to the next, or from one week to the next. What you lose, or what you are missing when you are not performing your best, is almost always the fully connected focus that frees you to perform and interact to your true capacity. Less than best performances can also be influenced by a lack of adequate rest or recovery time between games, races, performances, or missions. So do your best to make sure that you rest and relax as much as possible between major competitions, races, missions, or performances.

You will win your quest for consistency by finding and sustaining a positive, fully connected focus that works best for you. Over the course of your life or performance career, continue to refine and improve the focus that brings out your best performance consistently. There is always a way of focusing that brings out the best in you and your performance. There is also a way of focusing that prevents you from being your best or performing your best. Part of your quest for consistency in pursuing and sustaining excellence is to continue to discover, respect, and fine-tune your best focus.

If you consistently perform close to your potential, you have probably learned to do four things effectively:

1. Direct and connect your focus in positive and fully connected ways
2. Channel your thoughts and emotions in positive directions
3. Bounce back from setbacks quickly and efficiently
4. Act on the positive lessons you are learning and apply them in your next performance situation

Consistent high-level performers continue to respect, improve, and refine their focusing skills so they can focus completely on what they are engaged in to perform their best consistently. If they are momentarily distracted, they quickly shift focus from negative to positive, from off target to on target, from disconnected to fully connected, so they can successfully face and overcome challenges, self-doubts, stress, errors, or setbacks they may be experiencing.

You can also choose to do this to increase your chances of getting the most out of your preparation and getting the best out of yourself when it counts most. If you practice focusing and refocusing in positive and fully connected ways, you will become better in many ways that will free you to perform your best more consistently. Now is the time to begin!

Focusing Through and Growing From Setbacks

Many people react to setbacks by becoming upset with themselves, getting angry at others, or losing control emotionally. This often results in them losing their best focus, ceasing to perform well, backing off, or giving up. The sooner you learn to react to life's obstacles, setbacks, or challenges in less negative or more positive and focused ways, the better off you'll be. A positive and optimistic focus can lead you through things you never thought you could get through and take you places you never dreamed you could go. The good news is that you always have the potential to direct or redirect your focus in positive and life-enhancing ways even in the face of loss, setbacks, or unjustifiable treatment. This is true not only in your sport or performance domain but also in relationships.

A setback within a game or performance (for example, making a mistake or failing to perform your best when it counts most) can drag you down, but it can also serve as a positive reminder to focus fully on the next step, redirect your energy in a more positive and productive way, and analyze errors at an appropriate time (which is usually not in the middle of a performance or argument). After best and less than best games, performances, and interactions, choose to find lessons that will help you focus better for your next game, performance, or interaction.

Carefully reflect on what went well and what you can improve. You may be disappointed or frustrated with certain parts of your performance or interactions, but you can move through it quickly by extracting and acting on constructive lessons you have learned that can help you be more fully focused and happier in the future. As one of the world's best athletes said, "As a less experienced player I reacted more emotionally; I was angry at myself. Now I concentrate more on being in the game, and later I analyze errors or losses at an appropriate time, replay key shots and turning points, draw out important lessons, and act on them."

One player experienced real problems with emotional outbursts during games. "If I lost a rally, I hated my opponent. . . . I would get so angry that I could lose eight points in a row because of that. I had problems controlling my temper to the point of shouting and breaking rackets." He made a strong effort to get his temper and focus under control. When he played with controlled focus, he played as well as anyone. One strategy he used when he became angry was to try to take advantage of his anger by constructively directing his burst of energy into the next rally, to focus on reading and reacting, to hustle more, to move faster, and to smash harder. He shifted his focus away from anger (at himself or his opponent) and reconnected it to playing the game with renewed focus and positive energy. Focusing your mind forward on the attack, even after making an error, is obviously preferable to focusing backward on something you can no longer control.

The problem with becoming angry, upset, negative, or out of control is that those emotions usually interfere with your best performance focus and your best chances of nurturing positive and loving relationships. If you are in a performance context and mentally putting yourself down because of the last shot, shift, or move, you cannot at the same time be focusing fully on the present skill or preparing for your next move. You can't dwell on how you blew the last shift, gate, or routine and at the same time be fully focused on performing your best in the current moment. The only way to free your body and mind to perform fully in the present is to clear your mind of all negative thoughts about the past or future and focus fully on connecting to the remaining tasks you can control.

Someone who has a tendency to lose control, fly off the handle, or dwell on the negatives might say, "Oh, it doesn't matter that much if I do it during practices or my daily life." Ah, but it does matter. If you become accustomed to negative thinking, getting angry, or losing emotional control, chances are good that you will carry that into your performances, competitions, and relationships. In addition, negative ways of thinking and acting take much of the joy out of sport, relationships, work, and life. The journey to personal and performance excellence already has enough obstacles; so don't add negative thinking, anger, putting yourself down, or putting others down. There are no advantages in being negative or putting yourself or others down. Choose to stay positive, relaxed, and fully focused on your mission because this focus is within your control and will give you a great advantage for performing your best consistently. It will also help you to sustain or regain a sense of flow in your performances or interactions, particularly after experiencing a negative thought, an error, an argument, or a setback.

Think about how you would prefer to respond in challenging situations you may face in the future. Set some personal goals for improving the quality and consistency of your best focus and work toward achieving those goals. The next time something begins to go wrong in a game, performance, routine, mission, or relationship, use that feeling or experience as a signal to immediately shift your focus back to doing what you know will enhance the rest of your performance, mission, or interaction. For example, if during a performance routine, program, game, race, or mission, you lose your best focus even momentarily, use it as your signal to focus fully on the next move and the next move and the next move, each of which are within your control.

Lessons From High-Performance Military Pilots
In Their Own Words

In high-performance military aviation contexts, simple errors can be deadly. Here I share some direct quotes from elite pilots on the strategies or perspectives they use to stay on a positive and fully focused track. For additional information on this study see Hohmann and Orlick (2014).

> I think you can choose to perform well. . . . I think you can choose to at least set yourself up for success. You can't control everything, but you can at least put yourself in the best state of mind so you are emotionally and physically ready to perform.

> I remember we had a blast. [The training exercise was very successful] . . . it was very exhilarating, knowing that you made it work, and it's fun. It's very challenging.

> There's no way to simulate [an engine fire] in real life, but in the simulator . . . I'll do the maneuvers . . . I don't take it nonchalantly . . . I try and keep it as close to as if I would do it in real life.

I visualize everything from what I see outside to controls in the cockpit. I even go over what ATC [Air Traffic Control] will say/ask and what I will verbalize to myself when I need to do checks in the cockpit.

I would just sit in a room for about 5, 10 minutes just to think about the flight and just to try to relax a little bit, especially before an airborne test, because those are stressful. It would help me relax and get more in control. Just think positive.

Your focus narrows and you're not thinking about other stuff. I can have outside stresses at home and it won't affect me . . . as soon as I get into the plane I don't think about it anymore until I'm on the ground.

You can have a plan, but the plan can change very, very quickly. So having situational awareness throughout changing environments would probably be the number one thing. Everybody [can learn] the hands and feet, but it's the thinking part that's the most important.

On one trip, I was just all over the place. I wasn't settling in. And I was flying with this guy, he told me "just talk yourself through it." And I started to do that, and I'd say "plane, line, hinge," . . . . It's almost like you worry about it up until the moment [of the flight], but then when the moment's there you kind of go "you know what, I just have to go and do what I've been taught to do or do what I've trained to do."

Following every flight, the military pilots engaged in a detailed debriefing in which the various segments of the flight were analyzed, mistakes were pinpointed, and corrective measures were suggested. Many participants noted that the tools or strategies for "how to improve" were the most valuable product of the debriefing, as they were frequently well aware of their mistakes as soon as they had made them. The idea of owning one's mistakes was also important to all participants.

I look at what happened, what I did, what could I have done better so that I can learn something. But I also take into consideration that it's always easier after the fact to analyze because I also think about the information that I had at the time, and the time that I had to respond or react. Failure may happen from time to time—none of us are perfect—so the guys who can bounce back from that, actually use that to feed on, they tend to be quite successful.

Reprinted from M. Hohmann and T. Orlick, 2014, "Examining the psychological skills used by elite Canadian military pilots," *Journal of Excellence* 16: 4-19. [Online]. Available: www.zoneofexcellence.ca.

Some sports and other high-performance contexts have brief breaks in the action, so at those times there is no need for a constantly intense focus. This is true in sports like tennis, table tennis, badminton, volleyball, baseball, and golf where it is possible to quickly analyze the reason for certain errors, make mental corrections, and quickly move forward in a positive and focused way. For example, in tennis, while walking back to receive the serve or preparing to serve a ball, it is possible to take a deep, relaxing breath (in and out slowly) and focus fully on what you want to do next.

A top tennis player learned this lesson through experience. As a rookie he quickly discovered that as soon as he became upset, he couldn't play well. After learning this important lesson about himself, he grew into a veteran who chose to focus only on what worked best for him in real-world game situations:

> I practiced reacting the way I wanted to react, which changed my feeling going into the game. I could go in with more confidence. . . . I tried to think about what caused a mistake and corrected it. I thought about what made me lose and analyzed it. I was disappointed at the time, but I tried to learn from it.

And he acted on the lessons he was learning! This athlete's early recognition of the critical importance of focus control, along with his commitment to make continual improvements, allowed him to become one of the best players in the world.

Learning Self-Control

The ongoing lessons from the journeys of many high-performance athletes and high-level performers in many other domains clearly show that the most important influence on your performance is your control over your focus going into your performance and your ability to sustain and sometimes regain your best focus while engaged in executing your performance.

What sets you up for a great practice or great performance is usually a positive focus or focusing in positive ways. If you remain positive and fully connected, you are capable of performing at least as well as you have ever performed before.

If you focus on your real capabilities and think about why you can do what you want to do, and about how you will focus to make that happen, at some point something will click inside your mind and you will say to yourself, *Hey, that's true! If I focus fully on doing what I am doing right now and focus on doing it the best I can, I can really do this.* This simple acceptance or willingness to believe in your capacity may seem like a small step, but in reality its effect can be gigantic because you are taking control of your focus and performance.

You still may catch yourself focusing on something negative from time to time (for example, *I messed that up, so I'll probably mess this up too*). But when you know how unproductive that kind of thinking can be and you choose to take control by focusing or refocusing on something positive or constructive, you can turn things around right on the spot. For example, you might say to yourself, *Stop. Refocus on the positive. I can do this. I want to do this. I will do this because I am capable of doing it and I am choosing to do this. I can do as well here or better than I've ever done before. Just get focused on doing it.*

Focus fully on your first step, your first move, your first positive action, and nothing else. Focus forward, connect fully, and free yourself to go. Let your positive and uplifting thoughts and images lead you and remind you of what you can really do. Then focus fully on doing it. Nothing more and nothing less!

Greater Personal Control
Pat Messner's Journey

Pat Messner, former world champion in water skiing and a professional musician, reflected on how she went about gaining greater personal control in practice and in competition:

> I began competing when I was 10 years old. At that time, I felt that having days when nothing goes right and everything goes wrong, days when I felt I was the worst competitor on earth, and days when I would be mad at anything, was all part of the competitive life. I was wrong, and it wasn't an easy thing to find out. It happened because of an experience I had in the Western Hemisphere championship in Mexico. It was in March, and that was during our off-season. During the practice session, I couldn't do anything right. I felt like I had never skied as badly. This practice session made me believe that there was no way I was going to place, let alone win! I decided I might as well relax and enjoy myself.
>
> Before the actual event, I went through my usual stretching and warm-up. The only difference was that I wasn't thinking about what was to come. I just sat down on the grass, listened to some music, and waited for my turn. This was very unusual for me, because I'm usually very nervous. I just didn't seem to care. I listened to the music and relaxed. Believe it or not, I've never had a better tournament. I skied better than I ever had before. Not only that but I became Western Hemisphere champion. What did all this prove? It proved to me that if I could stay relaxed and calm and focused at all my tournaments, maybe I'd always ski better.
>
> Since that time I have learned many things that may be as helpful to you as they were to me. I've tried a number of different methods of relaxation. The method I found best is a simple thing anyone can do anytime, anyplace. Sit down or lie down and listen to some relaxing music. I can take my music right down to the dock and listen till it's time for me to ski. I let my mind do what it likes. I don't take responsibility for my thoughts. I just let them pass by. If you don't like music, then try reading a book. I also found this to be very helpful.
>
> Another important thing for me is running through my event mentally just as if it were real. I try to feel as if I am actually doing the run. If you find it hard to "feel" yourself or you can't picture yourself, watch a video of yourself or someone you admire. Sometimes it helps to give yourself audio cues as you go. I also try to simulate as many tournament conditions as possible in practice so that if unusual conditions should occur, I won't be as affected by them.

Sometimes it seems that the better you are, the easier it is to get upset by little things. I found that if I moved my focus away from what was making me angry and thought about something else, I'd feel better. Sometimes I set a goal for myself, like the next two out of three times I get a chance to get mad, I won't. Most days it worked pretty well. On other days, the more I tried not to get mad or upset, the madder I got. It's days like that when I'm probably better off having a day of rest rather than practicing. Continuing to practice when I'm upset accomplishes absolutely nothing.

To try to improve her focus control during practices, Pat followed the mission to excellence process outlined in chapter 5 of this book. Her goal was to make the best of as many practice sessions as possible in preparation for the world championships. Here are three self-control strategies that she chose to implement to improve the consistency of her best performances:

✦ **Relax.** Try to relax yourself physically. Calm yourself. Take deep breaths and feel your body get loose as you exhale. Pat and her coach tried a little experiment. "Each time I frowned he'd tell me, and I'd try to correct the situation by relaxing. I found that when I did, my whole body felt more relaxed and I could do the trick easier."

✦ **Focus on correction.** Focus your attention on how to correct mistakes instead of getting mad at yourself. If you make any errors, repeat the move mentally and correct the errors in your mind before trying it again. When practice is going well, write down what you think might be some of the reasons for your success. Refer to this list to improve future situations.

✦ **Encourage yourself.** Avoid statements such as *You dummy; you can't do anything right; you will never make it to the championships; give up*. Remind yourself of the facts. It's not that you can't do anything right; you're simply doing one little thing wrong. Praise yourself for all the things you are doing right.

Pat experimented with each of these strategies, sometimes stopping practice for five minutes to attempt to change her focus. She said, "If you do not change the way you feel, the rest of the practice will be a waste of time." This acknowledgment gave her a good reason to refocus. She found all these strategies worked well most of the time, but she still got upset every now and then, no matter what she tried. Under those circumstances, Pat sometimes found it helpful for her coach to remind her of what she had accomplished or to point out that she was being silly. "My behavior either got corrected, or he convinced me to take the day off." She found it helpful to have a coach "who makes me realize that I'm only human."

If, after multiple attempts, Pat could not rectify a problem, she could leave practice knowing that she had given it a good shot. Her positive focusing skills improved greatly over time. She also realized that almost everyone has a bad day, or even a bad week, at some time. Bad days usually happen when you need a break mentally or physically. Getting upset about it doesn't help. Refocus. Relax. Take the rest of the day off. Learn from it. Come in fresh tomorrow.

Mood Control
Sandy's Journey

Sandy, a talented young female gymnast, had just made the team to compete in Europe. Immediately afterward, she had two weeks of consistently bad workouts. She and her coach had been arguing regularly, and then for the last couple of days her coach had not spoken to her at all. Two weeks remained before Sandy would depart for her first international competition.

The coach called to ask whether I could help. Sandy and I stretched ourselves out on a blue mat in the corner of the gym and had a nice little talk. She spoke about the poor workouts and arguments and expressed sincere concern about not being ready for her big meet in Europe. She told me that workouts usually started out OK but that she became upset when the coach said something negative, such as "That's terrible," "You don't listen," or "You don't try." At that point the workout would begin to slide, which led to more negative comments by the coach or no interaction at all, bad feelings, some tears, and a lousy workout overall.

"Sandy," I said, "we know that the coach isn't perfect, but then not many of us are. She says some very negative things, and I've talked to her about giving more positive comments. She's improving a little, but it's a difficult thing for her to do. An important point for you to keep in mind is that this is her way of trying to help you. She does care, and she does want you to improve—to be ready for this meet—and you want that too. At this point I think it is easier for you to control your reaction to her than it is to hope that she will change. You can, in fact, control your own moods if you really want to."

Sandy said that she really wanted to improve the gloomy practice mood and agreed to try the self-control approach.

"What do you think about before a bad mood begins?" I asked.

"I think, *The coach hates me; she thinks I'm no good; she's mean to me; I'm never going to do this right.*"

"What do you feel when a bad mood begins? Are there physical sensations that you are aware of? Are there certain emotions that begin to surface? Do you know when it's starting to happen?"

Sandy had specific thoughts and personal signals of an impending mood change, although she had never thought about them before. She discussed some of them, and I gave her this advice: "OK. When you start to experience these thoughts or feelings—these personal signals—take a deep breath. Say to yourself, *Relax.* Then say to yourself, *Turn this thing around. I want to have a good workout. She's here to help. I am not going to waste the night feeling lousy. I can control this.* Then immediately focus on the trick or move that you're trying to do or the routine that you're trying to improve. Run it through your mind. Then do it.

"Your challenge for the next week is to look for any signals of a bad mood coming on and then turn it around before it gets to the destructive stage.

Don't let it ruin your workout, and don't let it drive you to tears. You may not be successful in turning around every bad mood or every bad thought right away, but if you can do it even half the time, that's a big improvement. That's success. Even doing it once is better than what is happening now. Your ultimate goal is to be able to turn potentially bad situations into good ones all the time. You have the capacity to do this, and you are the only one who can do it because you are the person who controls your thoughts and your focus."

We devised a little mood chart with various "mood faces" to help Sandy assess her feelings and record her progress through the next two weeks. At the start of each practice she recorded her prepractice mood on the mood chart. For each event, she also recorded her mood at the start of the event, mood changes within the event, and her mood at the end of the event. If her mood changed within the event, she indicated what had happened by marking the happier or sadder face that it had changed to. If her mood changed more than once during the event, she drew an arrow from one face to the next to indicate the changes that had taken place. At the end of practice Sandy recorded her postpractice mood.

You can adapt this chart to suit your needs, in sport or in another part of your life. A personal comments section should also be part of the chart, primarily to help you (athlete or coach) discover what influences your mood. If your mood begins to decline and you are able to stop the slide or improve your disposition, then jot down what you did, focused on, or said to yourself to turn things around. This process will help you discover what works best for you and what does not work. You will then be in a better position to use things that work (key words, positive images, positive thoughts, focus reminders, or actions) whenever you need them.

Let's look at what happened to Sandy's mood control during the first week:

✦ Day 1. We discussed Sandy's concerns and the use of the mood chart approach.

✦ Day 2. She started practice feeling happy and ended feeling so-so. Her pattern the previous week had been to start practice feeling happy and end feeling sad.

✦ Day 3. She started practice feeling so-so and ended feeling very happy. She demonstrated to herself that she could lift her mood.

✦ Day 4. She started practice feeling sad, mostly because she was feeling sick. She was able to work through this and end feeling happy after a productive workout.

✦ Day 5. She started feeling happy and ended feeling very happy. This was wonderful for all of us because it showed that Sandy was starting to get things under control.

At the end of the week Sandy and I went over her mood charts. Both of us were pleased with her progress. Sandy's mood charts showed even more improvement the following week, and she left for Europe feeling excited and more in control. Happily she then had one of her best-ever performances in her first international competition. As her self-awareness and focusing strategies for mood control continued to improve, the necessity for conscious attempts to control and chart her moods declined. She learned to maintain her best focus more of the time and to solve many problems before they arose. If her mood did occasionally start to slide, she knew from experience what she could focus on to control it (almost always).

Positive Perspective and Focus
Karin's Journey

Karin, a teenage gymnast, was inconsistent in both practice and meets. One day she could do everything well, and the next day she could blow everything. Karin told me that she knew whether it would be a good day or bad day before she got into the gym. If she had had a long day or felt at all sluggish, she would take those thoughts or feelings and that mood into the workout with her. Karin's pattern of being up one day and down the next was not restricted to training sessions. In her last competition she fell on every routine, although she had done the same routines with no problems in practice. Why? She explained, "I knew I would have a bad day because I had a bad warm-up."

"Karin," I began, "unless you are seriously overtrained or ill or totally exhausted, no matter how you feel or the way into the gym, you can turn things around to have a productive workout. Haven't you ever felt sluggish before practice and still had a good workout?" She had. "How is that possible? It is possible because you have the same body and the same skills that you had yesterday, when you had a good day. On your sluggish day, if your life depended on it, you could not only mount the beam but you could jump over it and still have enough reserve energy to do everything you want to do."

"The next time you 'know you're going to have a bad day,' surprise yourself. Leave your negative thoughts in your locker. When you step through the gym door, decide that you are going to have a great day. When you see that apparatus, challenge yourself to feel strong, feel energetic, feel radiant. Remind yourself why you are here. If you are here, you might as well make the best of it. Why waste two or three hours? Focus fully for at least one event so that you leave having had a good workout on something. If you can do it once, even in one event, you know you can do it again. When you do energize yourself on a sluggish day, or turn a negative feeling into a positive focus, try to be aware of how you did it so that you can do it again and again. You may not always have a super workout, but most days can be good days, and you can make those not-so-good days better than they might otherwise have been."

Karin worked on bringing a more positive perspective and more complete focus into her practices and competitions. As a result she made significant strides in the consistency of her best performances. It wasn't that she couldn't do the moves or routines. She was simply letting her negative focus get in the way of or interfere with her best performances.

Controlling Moods

Mood control means finding a way to focus on the positives consistently and choosing to not upset yourself needlessly over things that don't really matter, including circumstances or events that are beyond your control. When athletes or performers compete or perform in places or countries culturally different from their own, those who perform best do not allow the food, the accommodations, or the system they are in to have a negative effect on their performances. They view these differences as relatively unimportant in the big picture (which they are) and rely on the thoroughness of their mental and physical preparation to take them to where they want to go.

Thinking in positive ways before you even get out of bed in the morning, particularly on an important performance or game day (and they are all important), is a great way to start out on a positive track. Try focusing on thoughts like the following while you are still lying in bed: *Today is going to be a great day. I'm going to focus on why I can and how I will have a great day. I am going to focus on doing some things that lift me and make me feel good* (think about what they are). *I am making a choice right now to accomplish what I want to do today. I feel strong. I'm loaded with positive energy. I'm totally focused. I'm completely ready, and I am going to give everything I can give and really live this day.*

Positive, action-oriented focusing can get you into a positive and fully connected frame of mind, no matter how you are feeling when you first open your eyes to the daylight. Choose to feel the way you want to feel today. Choose to direct your focus in positive and fully connected ways. Choose to consistently focus on the good things and positive possibilities in yourself, your situation, and your world. Continue to find opportunities in the obstacles and the beauty and gentleness in the storm.

If you have a history of focusing on the negatives, remember that you can learn to shift your focus to the positives. One of the benefits of focusing on the positives is that it leads to positive emotions, which in turn have a positive effect on you, your performance, and your relationships. One of the downsides of focusing on the negatives is that it leads to negative emotions, which in turn have a negative effect on you, your performance, and your relationships. Ongoing negative emotions have the potential to fuel the flames of your own destruction. The sooner you shift away from a negative focus to a positive focus, the sooner you will control the quality and consistency of your own performance and life.

People who become the best at what they do experience setbacks, fatigue, fear, stress, and self-doubts, just like anyone else. However, at some point on their journey they develop effective focusing skills that free them to let go of negative thoughts and refocus on positive ones. The sooner you begin to do the little things every day that free you to feel your best, be your best, focus your best, and perform your best, the sooner you will perform your best consistently.

You are one tiny focus shift away from gaining or regaining a positive perspective. One simple positive thought or positive action can do it. By making that focus shift sooner rather than later, you will save yourself and others unnecessary anguish. At some point you will probably make that positive shift in focus anyway, so why not plan to make it now and save everyone a lot of energy?

Positive perspectives are vital because they inspire us, energize us, and bring meaning and joy to our pursuits. They generate positive emotions that free us to do the good things we want to do, alone and together. Negative perspectives do the opposite. They drain emotional energy that we could otherwise channel in positive directions. So dwelling on the negatives has no value. If you can simply change the thought, perspective, focus, or interpretation that led you to the negative emotion, you can usually move quickly to a more positive new reality. You gain control over negative emotions by taking control of your thoughts and focus. You have a choice here. Positive changes in your focus begin with you. If you find yourself slipping into a negative focus and you would prefer to remain more positive, consider the following actions:

Free Yourself to Become the Most Positive Person You Can Be!

+ Start by getting enough sleep or more rest. Slipping or sliding into a negative focus is much more likely to occur when you are tired, overloaded, or fatigued, so find a way to get enough rest or relaxation, either for short times during the day or at night.

+ Reduce the stress or overload in your life. The more stress you allow into your life, the more susceptible you are to negative shifts in mood.

+ Do at least three positive things each day that are just for you—things that you really enjoy doing. This will definitely lift your spirits and enhance the joy and quality in your day.

+ Start a highlight journal where you write down simple joys that lift you in simple ways every day, in and out of your performance domain. The more positives you can find and appreciate every day, the happier you will be or become.

+ Embrace and appreciate the successes in your life—the small ones and the big ones. Soak in them for a while. Remember them often. They can keep you focused on the positives.

+ Embrace the positive emotions of good people around you. Celebrate their simple joys and successes with them. Grow from their positive energy, inspiration, and perspective.

+ Sometime each day, ask yourself, *Am I focusing on the positives today, or am I dwelling on the negatives? Choose to focus or refocus on the positives!*

Choose to Free Yourself From the Negatives

+ Stop dwelling on the negatives. Start dwelling on the positives.

+ Stop dwelling on things that went wrong in the past in a performance, a relationship, or any other part of your life.

+ Start dwelling on the positives and positive possibilities you have in front of you.

+ If you find your focus slipping back to something negative, change channels to something more positive or uplifting.

+ If you can't let a negative thought go, shift your focus to something positive—a memory that reflects a positive reality or an experience that clearly demonstrates your capacity to perform well or confirms that you are skilled, competent, special, appreciated, and loved.

+ If the negative thought returns, shift your focus to a positive vision of the future or a positive action you can engage in right now to move in the direction you want to go.

Plan for Positive Focused Action

+ Develop a personal focus plan for remaining positive more often and for getting back on a positive track more quickly (if you drift away), with as little self-inflicted pain as possible.

+ Set a specific short time limit for remaining negative or moping around. Then shift to a positive focus and move on in more positive performance- and life-enhancing ways.

+ If you are not feeling the way you want to feel or not focusing the way you want to focus, take a little break. Do something that you really love to do. Find your own quiet or special space. Clear your mind of clutter or anything negative. Clear your mind to see a positive path. Then focus fully on the things you really enjoy and love to do.

+ Pause long enough to breathe, relax, and reenergize. Let your mind and body relax. Free your focus to center on positive thoughts, positive images, positive possibilities, positive parts of your life, positive experiences, positive performances, and a positive future.

+ Practice focusing on the positives and shifting your focus from negative to positive whenever the opportunity arises—every day.

+ Plan a positive path. Act on your positive plan. Continue to follow your own best path.

+ Choose to live the life you want to live and embrace the simple joys and super joys in every day!

CHAPTER 20
Coachable

We can all gain from competent and supportive coaches, teachers, parents, family members, friends, and teammates who believe in us and what we can do and inspire us to reach for our goals and live our dreams. Choosing to be the best you can possibly be is critically important whether you are pursuing excellence in sport or any other part of your life, including coaching, teaching, parenting, education, leading others, living joyfully, or performing to your true potential in any worthy human endeavor. Once you have made the decision to excel, attaining and sustaining high levels of excellence in any pursuit is largely dependent on doing something positive every day to take yourself one step closer to your goal. Cooperation, respect, and positive collaboration play a huge role in nurturing successful relationships and enhancing high levels of performance in all areas of life. Coaches, teachers, teammates, focus or performance enhancement consultants, and other support staff can play a meaningful role in helping you become the best you can possibly be.

Whether you are a coach, athlete, parent, teacher, student, leader, consultant, or performer in any domain, your chances of achieving your highest levels of excellence and making a meaningful contribution in your chosen pursuit are largely dependent on three factors:

1. Finding and pursuing something you love and find meaningful, challenging, and life enhancing.
2. Feeling accepted, valued, positively challenged, respected, and more fully alive as a result of being fully engaged in this meaningful pursuit you have chosen.
3. Choosing to focus and refocus in positive, meaningful, and fully connected ways whenever you think about yourself performing or whenever you are actively engaged in training, practicing, or performing in your chosen pursuit.

Performing Your Best

I have never worked with an athlete or performer in any domain who entered the performance arena with the intention of performing poorly. However, some coaches, fans, and managers respond to athletes who do not perform well as if it was their intent to not perform well. Great coaches and focus enhancement consultants support their athletes and other high-level performers through the ups and downs of their journey and try to help them to understand and embrace the focus that frees them to feel and perform their best consistently. Putting down athletes or other performers when they don't perform their best is counterproductive because it just makes them feel worse and lowers their overall confidence in what they have the potential to achieve.

The best option is to find something positive in the performances of athletes or performers, give them constructive feedback on the things they did well, and ask them what they were focused on when they were performing their best and less than best. Constructive feedback on what athletes or performers did well and what they can focus on to continue to improve the quality and consistency of their best performances is the best option for ongoing improvement.

+ Best coaches continue to believe in their athletes and performers through the ups and downs of the journey.
+ Best coaches continue to find positive ways to help their athletes and performers continue to improve so that they can become the best they can possibly be.
+ Best coaches know there is always something that was done well or a positive lesson you can find in both best and less than best performances.

To keep the joy and passion in the pursuit, athletes, students, performers, coaches, teachers, and support staff members should answer the following questions:

+ What do I love most about what I am doing?
+ What are the things I like least about what I am doing? (Can I do anything to change that?)
+ Am I continuing to experience a sense of personal growth and meaning from the efforts I am putting in and the contributions I am making?

Coaches, teachers, performance enhancement consultants, and supportive parents can play an ongoing critical role in helping make personal growth and ongoing excellence possible.

All human beings grow when they feel loved, accepted, valued, and supported in positive ways. They also grow in meaningful ways when they learn to focus in positive and fully connected ways that free them and others to become the competent, supportive, respectful, and caring human beings we all have the potential to be. This is true for coaches, athletes, teammates, teachers, students, support staff, administrators, parents, family members, and people in all contexts in all parts of the world. People have a much greater chance of blossoming in positive ways and becoming the best they can possibly be when someone believes in them, encourages them, and supports them in positive and life-enhancing ways.

Most people don't really know what they are capable of doing until they actually do it because before you do it, there is no concrete proof that you actually can. It is your belief in yourself and in your capacity to accomplish whatever it is you want to accomplish that frees you to do it. A critical role that best coaches, teachers, parents, and support staff play in helping athletes, students, and performers do the wonderful things they want to do begins with helping them believe in themselves and their true potential.

The roots of excellence begin to grow when athletes or students feel accepted, valued, respected, and supported inside and outside their training and performance contexts. We can all become our best in sport or any other life-enhancing pursuit when respected people believe in us, respect us, encourage us, and challenge us to become the best we can possibly be. In almost all meaningful performance and life pursuits, belief is the mother of reality!

This is why it is so important for coaches, teachers, teammates, classmates, performance enhancement consultants, parents, and support staff to continue to help athletes, students, and other performers to believe in themselves, their mission, their teammates, their coaches, and their capacity to become the best they can possibly be and live their dreams.

When people fail to find a way to believe in themselves and their true capacity, their chances of performing at a high level or achieving to their true potential are greatly reduced. This is why it is so important for all of us to continue to focus on the positive possibilities and fully embrace the step-by-step journey to personal excellence, especially when things may not be going as well as you would like.

Ten Characteristics of Best Coaches

1. Best coaches care about their athletes as people and performers.
2. Best coaches believe in their athletes and what each athlete has the potential to do, accomplish, or become.
3. Best coaches continue to support and believe in their athletes through the ups and downs or highs and lows of their ongoing journey to personal excellence.
4. Best coaches challenge their athletes to become their best and perform their best consistently.
5. Best coaches make sure that each athlete knows the kind of commitment and focus required to live his or her dreams.

6. Best coaches try to make sure that athletes know their coaches believe in them and their capacity to become great athletes, performers, or the best they can possibly be.

7. Best coaches support their athletes when they are injured, struggling, or going through difficult or challenging times or transitions.

8. Best coaches often follow up with injured, sick, or recently retired athletes by letting them know they are thinking about them and wishing them the best. This kind of positive contact is important, even for busy coaches, because it can make a huge difference in the lives of athletes. It is always a highlight to know that some important person in your life still really cares about you as an athlete, performer, and worthy human being.

9. Best coaches are positive people who love doing what they are doing.

10. Best coaches and best athletes know or discover that belief is the mother of reality. If you really believe that you have the capacity to do something at a very high level, and you are willing to pour your heart and soul into doing everything possible to live your dreams, there is a very good chance you will get there. Even if you do not live your dream goal, you will still gain immensely from the journey and from moving forward in positive ways.

Aaron Josefczyk/Icon Sportswire

Coach Tom Izzo epitomizes the characteristics of a best coach.

Which coaches, teachers, authors, or performance enhancement consultants have had the greatest positive influence on you and your performance? What did they do or share that separated them from other coaches, teachers, or consultants? The best coaches I have worked with helped their athletes continue to love what they were doing and encouraged them to continue pursuing their dreams. They believed in their athletes, helped them believe in themselves, helped them overcome difficult challenges, and made the journey to excellence as enjoyable as possible. Positive coaching facilitates personal growth and makes the pursuit of excellence and joyful living a realistic possibility.

Great coaches and focus enhancement consultants are committed to doing what is best for the athletes or performers with whom they are working. Great coaches are secure enough within themselves to respect and listen to the people with whom they are working. They value relevant input and act on good suggestions from their athletes, coaching staff, and support staff. They respectfully listen, even when they do not totally understand or agree with another point of view. They respect the experience of athletes and support staff and value their input. They believe in their athletes to the point that athletes can feel the strength of that belief in their gut. Best coaches care about their athletes as people and performers and challenge them to push their limits so they become the best they can possibly be. They support their athletes every step of the way, especially through the big challenges, difficult times, injuries, or setbacks.

At the high-performance level, almost all coaches are competent in their technical, tactical, and training skills. What separates great coaches from the rest is often their people skills. Best coaches are masters at communicating in positive and fully connected ways, believing in people and their potential, challenging people in positive ways, and building meaningful, respectful, and trusting relationships.

Truly great coaches significantly influence the lives of athletes and performers in positive ways and help them grow as performers and people. They have mastered the art of coaching people largely because they made a commitment to fine-tune their capacity to see beyond the surface, and to listen, respect, challenge, support, and believe in positive possibilities. In the preparation or lead-up to important competitions or events, observing closely, listening attentively to what is being said and not said, respecting athletes' personal space and preparations patterns, and challenging athletes or performers in positive ways are critically important. In the on-site performance phase, best coaches project their belief and confidence in their performers, support them in simple ways, and occasionally remind them of where their best focus needs to be. These factors are central to facilitating performance excellence. Believing in people and their capacity to perform at least as well as they have performed before is important in all phases of development and within all performance contexts. Belief is the mother of reality, and it needs to be constantly nourished through the ups and downs and ongoing challenges of every meaningful journey.

Best coaches continue to give athletes good reasons to believe in themselves, their team, and their capacity. They seize opportunities to enhance their athletes' or performers' confidence and avoid speaking or acting in ways that undermine confidence. They challenge athletes and performers to push or extend their limits, and they do it in positive and respectful ways rather than negative or disrespectful ways. A positive approach is very empowering. Best coaches and best focus enhancement consultants constantly look for ways to become more effective at meaningful communication. The best-case scenario for any coach or team is when all athletes or performers, all coaches, and all support staff work together to bring out the best qualities and performances in everyone.

When athletes, team members, coaches, support staff, or professionals in any performance context feel truly valued, supported, and respected, they give more of themselves, give more to others, and perform at a higher level on a more consistent basis. Great coaches, directors, and team leaders recognize the immense value of positive and respectful collaboration. They respectfully engage in positive, ongoing collaboration with those with whom they work or play. It is important that we all recognize the value in respectfully challenging ourselves and team members to become the best that we can possibly be and that each of us chooses to be a key player in shaping a positive vision of our own destiny.

In high-performance contexts or major performance events, coaches and support staff, like the athletes or performers with whom they work, face higher levels of stress, more demands, higher expectations, and more distractions than they are accustomed to. They have less personal control over their environment than they normally do. To be your best when it counts most, as a coach or member of the support staff, you can also benefit from having positive focus plans, effective refocusing plans, and distraction control plans. Positive focus plans can help coaches and support staff remain calm, confident, and fully focused on the right things in times of increased stress. Positive focus plans can help coaches and support staff by reminding them to continue to project belief in the athletes and performers with whom they work, through the good times, big challenges, and difficult times in their journey.

Initiating Positive Communication With Your Coach

As an athlete, it is advantageous to initiate positive communication with your coach so your coach knows where you are at in this stage in your journey, where you want to go, and how he or she can help you get there. Most coaches do their best to help their athletes do their best. However, at a certain coaching level, coaches also have other commitments outside their training and performance contexts. If you want to continue to improve and build the best possible relationship with your coach, take some positive steps to communicate with your coach. A great starting point would be to tell your coach what you liked about today's workout or training session and thank her or him at the end of the practice for the positive things the coach did or said that you liked or found helpful. If there are some things your coach said to you about improving something and you are not sure how to do it, ask your coach for specific details on what you can do or focus on to improve whatever it is you want to improve. This helps the coach to know you are interested and keen to continue learning and improving. If there are other issues you would like to discuss or share with one of your coaches, ask her or him if you can set a quiet time to talk openly and constructively after your practice or performance.

Ask questions or talk constructively about what he or she thinks will help you and the team continue to improve. You can discuss with your coach what you feel contributes to your best practices or workouts and what helps you perform most efficiently in games, performances, or competitions.

If you have a good working relationship with your coach, you could also share what kind of communication you prefer, what upsets you, and what you feel interferes with a good workout or a best performance. Remember that coaches are there to help you! The better you perform and feel, the happier they are. If you both communicate openly and honestly, you should be able to help each other more forward in positive ways that will improve your effectiveness, the coach's effectiveness, and the overall team performance. If you don't feel comfortable meeting one-on-one with your coach, take a chance—try it and see what happens—or bring a teammate with you to the first meeting.

When the coach does something that you find helpful (before, during, or after practices or performances), let him or her know about it right away. For example, if the coach's comments are helpful or constructive, offer a thank-you. Tell your coach that his or her feedback, support, or comments helped you! Coaches like to be appreciated too! If your coach has contributed to a good workout or a best performance and is giving you the kind of support and feedback you like, tell your coach this before leaving the practice or performance site. Help your coach to feel good about what she or he is contributing and better understand how he or she can help you continue on your positive journey.

Another way to show your coach that you want and appreciate her or his feedback is to ask for additional help or further clarification on feedback (for example, "Coach, I'd really like to improve this; what specifically should I focus on doing?"). Asking for clarification will help you get the specific feedback you need for technical, tactical, physical, and focusing improvement. To show your coach you are really committed to your goals, choose to practice and perform with a positive and fully connected focus—every day! The more you demonstrate your commitment to improve through your positive and determined actions, the more likely it is that your coach will continue to help and support you in your ongoing mission to personal excellence.

To continue to move toward your positive goals, do the following:

1. Think about what works best for you (physically and mentally) to bring out your best performance.

2. Work on improving your positive communication skills with your coach and teammates.

3. Take full responsibility for focusing fully on doing what works best for your best performance and your team's best performance.

4. Work on improving your capacity to direct and sustain your own best focus.

5. Learn from the positive and fully connected focus used by the best athletes and performers in the world and the athletes you admire most on your team. Always remember that *you* have the capacity to direct your own focus in positive ways. *Choose* to make *your* focus work for you and not against you every day.

Maintaining Respect

The challenge of every coach is to bring out the best in every one of his or her athletes. The challenge for athletes or performers is to get the best out of themselves with the help of their coaches and support staff. So the overall challenge becomes one of getting the best out of each other regardless of whether there is a natural bond or perfect fit among athletes or between coaches, athletes, and support staff. Everyone on the team or connected with the team has something of value to offer, so why not focus on getting the best out of what each person has to contribute and move forward in positive ways from there?

Problems with coaches rarely result from a coach's lack of technical knowledge. From the athlete's perspective, coaching problems are usually related to communication problems or athletes feeling a lack of respect or support from their coaches. Athletes or performers who experience problems with their coaches usually feel that their coaches do not listen to them, understand them, respect them, challenge them in positive ways, believe in them, care about them as people, or support them in positive and meaningful ways. When athletes and other performers experience these kinds of negative feelings within any kind of performance or relationship context and the coach or team leader does not address them, declines in motivation, confidence, and overall performance are not far behind.

Performances and relationships are enhanced most readily when coaches and athletes or performers work together to create a positive environment and share the responsibility for successfully pursuing their mission and improving ongoing positive communication. Whether you are a coach, athlete, student, or performer in any high-performance domain, to get the best out of yourself, your teammates, and your situation, you have to commit fully to the mission and work together to solve the problems along the way in a mature, collaborative, responsible, positive, and respectful manner. The reminders in figure 20.1 can help you and your coaches create a positive environment that fosters excellence.

We are all human beings first. Most of us appreciate support or recognition for the good things we are doing, and we like to receive constructive

---

Figure 20.1   Athlete and Coach Excellence Reminders

Believe

1. Share your vision.
2. Project your belief.
3. Believe in your mission and your team.
4. Help team members to believe in themselves.
5. Identify positive roles and goals with team members.
6. Become the most positive coach or athlete you can be.

Challenge

1. Challenge your team.
2. Challenge everyone to be what they can be.
3. Challenge team members to focus on what brings out their best and the team's best.
4. Challenge team members to draw out and act on the lessons from each performance.
5. Challenge yourself to be what you can be—as a coach or athlete.
6. Commit yourself to ongoing learning and improvement.

Support

1. Value people and their contributions.
2. Listen to people and their different perspectives.
3. Be positive and respectful in your interactions.
4. Act in positive ways every day.
5. Give honest and constructive feedback.
6. Continue to support and show respect for others.

(continued)

Figure 20.1 *(continued)*

Remember

1. Remember to focus on what brings out your best.
2. Remember to act in positive ways, especially through the tough times.
3. Remember to act on lessons learned and suggestions for improvement now.
4. Remember your commitment to ongoing learning and ongoing improvement.
5. Remember that everyone on this team wants to win.
6. Remember that everyone needs time to rest and regenerate.

Appreciate

1. Appreciate the small steps and simple joys.
2. Appreciate the opportunities you have in front of you.
3. Acknowledge good effort.
4. Rejoice in simple successes.
5. Keep the love in the pursuit.
6. Help all the athletes and coaches keep the love in the pursuit.

Focus

1. Bring your best focus to every pursuit.
2. Focus fully on the step in front of you.
3. Wherever you are, be totally where you are.
4. Take care of your own needs.
5. Seek balance in excellence.
6. Connect totally to bring out your best and the best in others.

From T. Orlick, 2015, *In pursuit of excellence*, 5th ed. (Champaign, IL: Human Kinetics).

comments about ways to become even better or more consistent. If the suggestions for improvement come from genuine care, love, or respect, they are always better received. Although coaches often focus on results because their jobs depend on results, they too are people dedicated to a mission. You can create stronger bonds with your coaches when you talk with them individually and realize they are thinking, feeling human beings dedicated to nurturing high-level performance who also have lives outside their sport or performance domain.

Respectful communication is a two-way venture. Both you and the person with whom you are interacting are responsible for making it work. Communicating openly and constructively is not always easy, especially in conflict situations or power struggles. A helpful approach in some situations may be to initially share your thoughts in writing, perhaps through a handwritten letter or card or a diplomatically written e-mail that you review carefully before you send. You may want to share a page or chapter in a book like this that outlines the benefits of a certain approach and follow up with a face-to-face discussion about it. Communication is sometimes a delicate process, but it is an important life skill that you should learn, develop, and continue to refine. Over the course of your life, it is definitely worth the effort.

Communicating Your Preferences

To optimize your chances of performing well in important events, consider communicating your on-site preferences to your coach. Good coaches are interested in helping athletes perform to their capacity, so they will usually accept and act on this information. Talk with your coach about what you would like him or her to do, or not do, at the performance site. Be specific in your instructions (for example, "I'd prefer to be left alone," "Remind me that I can do it," "Talk calmly," "No last-minute changes," or "Give me corrective feedback only during time-outs").

Often, athletes will not share information that influences performance outcomes when they feel it is too risky to communicate honestly with their coach. This reluctance to share information applies to both training or preparation sessions and performances or competitions. For example, every player I interviewed on one professional football team felt that the coach's pregame pep talk, as well as the last-minute changes he made in the game plan, either were a hindrance or did nothing to contribute to the players' mental preparation for the game. One athlete said, "I'm not motivated by it. I know my job. I'm ready, and I don't need him to make me ready. Rah-rah stuff is of no benefit." As one of the more accomplished players stated, "The standard pregame speech that so many of us have heard before is simply not doing the team or individual players any good. However, it may be a method of tension release for the head coach. Having been in the locker room on many occasions, I think it is. If this is so, he should find another way of doing it, away from the players."

Performers in a variety of disciplines report that their best focus or confidence may be shaken if the coach makes too many changes or places additional demands on them just before a game or performance. The moment before a game or performance is not the time for the coach to add new moves or strategies, change well-established routines that work, make detailed comments about improving technique, give complicated instructions, or even require athletes to sit and listen. Last-second changes before important competitions tend to be more detrimental than helpful in almost every sport, unless athletes have been extremely well prepared or trained to adapt to them. For certain athletes, last-second instructions can spell disaster. Players don't need lingering thoughts such as *Maybe I'm not as well prepared as I thought. . . . Maybe the coach doesn't have confidence in me. . . . Maybe the coach doesn't have confidence in the game plan that we practiced all week. . . . Maybe I (or we) won't be able to perform that well.* My advice to you is to stay positive, respect your best focus, and stick with what works.

As game time approaches, the coach's job of preparing athletes for the contest is over. He or she must shift gears so as not to interfere with the athletes' last-minute mental preparation. Some athletes appreciate a word of encouragement, a simple reminder, or a reassuring comment, but beyond that most prefer to be left alone during their final focus preparation for the event. If athletes could be totally honest with their coaches, most would say, "Leave me alone so I can concentrate," "Watch from a distance so as not to distract me," or "I'll come to you if I need you." At high levels in sport, athletes know what they want to do and have a focus plan to do it. At all levels in sport, the time just before the event is the athletes' time to focus on their performance and the coaches' and support staffs' time to free them to do it.

If you, as a player, have an assistant coach whose temperament or style of communication fits best with your precompetition needs, request that he or she interact with you on-site in place of the head coach. I suggested this strategy to some high-level coaches whose team was preparing for an important tournament. The head coach was high-strung, whereas the assistant coach was calm and low-key. Before the sudden-death elimination match, the two most hyper players on the team interacted only with the calm and reassuring assistant coach. They both played the best games of their lives and were instrumental in determining the final outcome, which was in their favor.

Sylvie Bernier also used this best-fit approach when winning her gold medal in diving at the Olympic Games. At Sylvie's request, her personal coach, who was at his best during regular training, sat in the stands during the final on-site Olympic practices and competition, while another member of the coaching staff who was calmer, more supportive, and less inclined to give last-minute technical input interacted with her on deck. Her personal coach agreed to this arrangement because he knew that Sylvie would be calmer and more fully focused on executing each dive, and she was.

Common Coaching Errors

Every coach, athlete, and performer makes errors. We would all be better and improve a lot faster if we were able to identify those errors, learn from each of them, and act in more positive or constructive ways because of them. Too often coaches, athletes, leaders, and team members keep making the same errors over and over, day after day, month after month, year after year. The errors can become habit and create a major obstacle to the attainment of best performance goals. Every performance error, every bad choice, every loss of focus, and every flawed interaction is an opportunity to get better in some way. You should learn a lesson from every error and act on it because it is your direct path to ongoing improvement.

If you do not learn from and improve as a result of an error, you are wasting an opportunity. If you do not act on that error to improve yourself, your relationship, or your performance, you are wasting an opportunity. Experience is of value only if you learn from it and get better because of it. Regardless of whether your performance was good or bad, you can learn from that experience and get better from it but only if you act on it.

If coaches or athletes make an error at a performance site, they should have a preset refocusing plan that frees them to get back on track and shift focus back to something positive within their immediate control. After the performance, coaches and athletes should draw lessons from their errors so they are not repeated. Coaches must ensure that they do not become a distraction for athletes, and athletes must ensure that they have an effective focus plan and refocusing plan in order to execute their game plan, regardless of what happens.

Athletes can improve the consistency of their best performances by preparing themselves for all potential distractions. Some coaches have a tendency to become uptight or wired in the final preparation phase before an important competition. At a time when athletes might gain most from a coach who boosts their confidence and frees them to get focused on executing their task, an athlete might be faced with the opposite. A common coaching error is trying to get athletes pumped up before an important competition. For example, instead of saying, "Let's just focus on following the game plan, one step at a time," a coach may say something like, "This is a crucial event. Everything is riding on this. All of our work was for this; don't blow it."

If an athlete or performer takes this to heart or starts to stress out about it, and does not have a solid refocusing plan to get back on track quickly, that athlete could easily become overactivated or distracted, which could result in a disappointing or certainly less than best performance. In times of stress or uncertainty you should always come back to your own best focus and what works best for you and your team to bring out your best and the team's best, regardless of what the people around you are saying or doing.

Another common coaching error leading into major events is overtraining, overloading, or overworking athletes and not giving them enough time to rest, relax, and recover. As an athlete, during the final training phase leading into a major competition, you might feel overloaded or like you're cramming for an exam. Guard against overtraining or overworking by making sure you rest more away from the training site and talk with your coaches about reducing the load or increasing the recovery time so you feel strong, healthy, and ready going into the event.

Overload in the final preparation phase, excessive technical input, demands for last-minute changes in familiar performance patterns, and an overall increase in stress are major reasons why many athletes and coaches perform below their potential during major events. When you have executed a program or performance or played your game well hundreds of times without a major problem and then screw it up in the biggest game, competition, audition, or event of the year, everyone wonders why. The reason is directly related to not respecting your best focus, along with feelings of fatigue or overload, heightened demands, increased stress, and the need to perform under a different set of circumstances. At times like this, you do not gain from additional outside demands or stress from management, media, your coach, or anyone else. To get back in control and stay on a positive track, you simply need to respect your best focus, your need for rest, and the preparation patterns that worked best for you in the past. Nothing more and nothing less!

Another common coaching error at all performance levels is failing to build the confidence of all team members. Confidence can be a fragile thing, especially if expectations are high and some things have not been going well. Coaches can help athletes perform their best by helping them focus on good reasons to believe in themselves and their chances of performing well. Ask your athletes and performers to write down or tell you their good reasons to believe in themselves and their capacity to perform to their true capacity in this game, audition, or performance. Coaches should be the first and biggest believers in their athletes because athletes and performers often feed off their coaches' beliefs, actions, or inactions.

Coaches may be quick to tell athletes or performers that something was wrong but often do not give them specific advice about what to do or what to focus on to make things right. Pointing out how things can be improved is valuable, and equally important is pointing out things the athlete or performer did well and acknowledging the progress and positive contributions they have made. Likewise, athletes or performers may fail to express appreciation for the good things their coaches do. Both athletes and coaches benefit from positive feedback, support, and encouragement. Without the positives, the road to excellence can be long and lonely. We all like to be acknowledged for the good things we do and contribute, and most of us are open to specific suggestions about how we might continue to become better and more consistent at what we do. Start by pointing out the good things and then target an area for improvement.

Positive feedback motivates us, makes us feel good about ourselves and our efforts, and enhances our self-confidence. Statements like "You should have been better" or "You should be more confident" rarely instill additional confidence. But when coaches, teammates, and support staff remind us of the good things we have done and demonstrate their belief in us, our confidence continues to rise. Putting people down or dwelling on the negatives usually undermines self-confidence, whereas focusing on the positives does just the opposite. Even the world's best athletes and performers, who are generally confident in their abilities, gain from positive feedback, ongoing support, and knowing that someone they value, admire, or respect really believes in them and what they have the potential to do.

One of the major coaching criticisms relayed to me by experienced high-performance athletes and performers in other high-performance disciplines is that their coaches sometimes fail to listen to and act on their input and suggestions. Best coaches are open to athletes' input and often do act on their experienced athletes' wisdom when it is clearly communicated to them in positive and respectful ways because they respect their athletes' experience and want the best possible performance results for their team. The same holds true for most really great athletes or performers. They are not afraid to at least listen to and reflect on advice from experienced high-performance or focus enhancement coaches and other respected support staff. Other athletes and performers who could benefit from this input may sometimes dig in their heels and resist. The resisters are often not taking advantage of the collaborative human resources available to them.

Even if you as an athlete or coach meet resistance from good suggestions you make, at least people are thinking about positive possibilities, and they may eventually act on some of those positive suggestions. Keep working on improving and sharing your positive communication or ideas; people do change, and miracles do sometimes happen!

As an athlete, your last option, if you are simply incompatible with a coach, is to consider a coaching change that may bring the joy and motivation back into your pursuit and improve the overall quality and consistency of your performance. If you decide to go this route, talk with other athletes about their relationships with prospective coaches and visit some practices, training sessions, or workouts run by coaches with whom you think you might be compatible. Talk to coaches you like, and then make a decision.

CHAPTER 21
Team-Oriented

Nothing builds team spirit and harmony better than a group of positive people, such as teammates, performers, athletes, or coaches, who continue to support and encourage each other through the ups and downs and ongoing challenges of every meaningful journey. Working together to help all team members reach their potential frees teammates to live their dreams or become what they have the potential to be.

What can your teammates, coaches, classmates, teachers, friends, or family members do to help you feel your best, be your best, and perform your best consistently? What can *you* do to help your teammates, coaches, classmates, teachers, friends, or family members feel their best, be their best, and contribute their best? Simple positive comments or supportive actions can make a huge difference in the way people feel, act, interact, and perform.

Think of a time when a person did something for you or said something to you that made a difference in your day, your performance, or your life. Think of a time when one of your friends, teammates, classmates, teachers, coaches, family members, or another person was positive, caring, and supportive of you. How did that make you feel? Can you recall a time when someone was negative or destructive toward you? Maybe the person tried to put you down, excluded you, or humiliated you. How did that make you feel?

There is no advantage in negativity, but there is a huge advantage in positivity. By simply choosing to eliminate negativity and embrace the positives in yourself and others, you can make a huge difference in how you and other people feel, interact, and perform.

We all have the capacity to be positive and supportive toward ourselves and others. We are all capable of finding and embracing something positive in the different contexts of our lives. All we need to do is focus on looking for the positives and appreciating the positives in everything we see or do.

Continue to remind yourself of why it is important to be positive and supportive with yourself and others through the ups and downs of your ongoing personal journey. When you focus on finding and embracing the positives at home or school, in your community, in your sport and performance contexts, when doing leisure activities, and in your daily interactions with others, everything in your life improves. So continue to focus on the positives and let go of the negatives. Following this path will continue to help you open doors to enhanced daily interactions and performances; increased team harmony, cohesion, and support; and more joyfulness in your everyday living.

There are no winners when people dwell on the negatives or live in a sea of hate, negativity, distress, destructiveness, constant conflict, put-downs, or unnecessary stress. Ongoing negativity or conflict can break the spirit of even the best athletes, performers, teams, families, or organizations. Those who embrace a positive spirit of mutual respect and ongoing support open doors to positive missions that can lift the spirits of every member of the team. Teams, relationships, families, and organizations that are positive and mutually supportive bring out the best in everyone and inspire people to become their best and give their best for their team, family, relationships, and positive mission.

Negativity and conflict have a toxic effect on individual and team spirit within families, organizations, relationships, and teams of all kinds. Every comment you make and every action you take has the potential to affect the spirit and performance of those on your team in positive or negative ways, whether you are a team member, athlete, coach, support staff member, or administrator. Positive actions drive positive results; negative actions drive negative results. So choose to be positive with yourself, your teammates, your classmates, your teachers, your coaching staff, and your family members. Challenge yourself and others to find positive ways to bring out the best in everyone. Encourage all team members to make a commitment to be as positive and supportive as they can possibly be.

The first team goal should be to be as positive as you can be (with yourself and others). The second team goal should be to do no harm (to your own performance or your teammates' performance). Achieving these two goals requires carrying a positive perspective into your own performances and projecting a positive attitude, message, spirit, or belief onto your teammates. If you are not ready to focus on the positives in yourself and others, then at least refrain from being negative. You do not have to love or like everyone on your team, but you do have to execute your job the best you can and free or encourage your teammates to do their jobs the best they can without interference. Refuse to become an obstacle that interferes with the achievement of your personal goals or your team's goals. You can achieve great things within any team context when team members put the team mission above everything else.

Fostering Team Harmony

One of the most satisfying experiences in sport or any other domain is being a member of a team that gets along well and works as a cohesive, collaborative unit. When you live, work, and play together in harmony, the chances of enjoying the journey and achieving mutually beneficial goals increase significantly. By committing yourself to interact in simple, positive ways that make teammates feel valued, appreciated, respected, and supported, you go a long way toward improving team spirit, harmony, and performance. Team spirit grows when all team members feel that they have a meaningful role to play, are challenged to be what they can be, and experience something positive and have some fun in the process of getting where they want to go. Help your teammates to believe in each other and genuinely encourage each other to

Bob Martin/BPI/DPPI/Icon Sportswire

Rugby is just one example of many team sports where having a strong team spirit and sense of unity can help the team perform better as a team.

become whatever you have the potential to be, individually and as a team. Working and playing together can create a positive atmosphere, a feeling of acceptance, and a sense of unity. Direct your individual and collective focus toward helping each other to accomplish your collective mission. This will help you to have better practices or workout sessions and consistently move you toward higher-quality performances.

Harmony grows when you look for the good qualities in teammates and they look for yours, when you take the time to listen to others and they listen to you, when you respect their feelings and contributions and they respect yours, when you accept their differences and they accept yours, and when you choose to help them and they choose to help you. Harmony and improved team performance are rooted in positive focus, a commitment to excellence, and ongoing mutual trust and respect.

When you know that someone needs you, cares about you, appreciates you, respects you, believes in you, values you, and accepts you—with all your imperfections—trust, harmony, and best performances are nurtured. When you help others and they help you, you begin to appreciate and respect each other. When you move beyond the surface and begin to understand other athletes' or performers' problems, feelings, challenges, or perspectives in a more intimate way, you begin to feel closer or more connected to them. Opening the door to real feelings, as difficult as this may be for some people to do, creates more intimate or real connections.

When Olympic and professional team performance enhancement consultant Cal Botterill studied the link between mood and performance in highly skilled team athletes, he discovered that team harmony was a key factor in performance. Each athlete's mood had a direct effect on his or her performance, and athletes on the road often cited positive interaction with their coaches, roommates, and teammates as having a positive influence on their mood and performance.

Some of the Olympic and professional teams I have worked with have had more than their fair share of disharmony and interpersonal conflicts. Some team members felt ignored or left out, some athletes believed that the coach did not respect them or believe in them, some athletes refused to room with others, and some team members withdrew emotionally or physically from the group. In one case, I witnessed firsthand two Olympic athletes physically fighting on-site just before an important international competition. Fortunately we were able to help them refocus to get back on a positive track in time for their event. Rarely do teammates or coaches intentionally try to create conflict or resentment or set out to hurt their teammates' feelings or performance before races or competitions. No one gains from that process. Both parties go through unnecessary and unpleasant turmoil and experience stress and distractions that can ultimately hinder their focus and team performance. The root of many interpersonal conflicts within team contexts is a lack of commitment to the overriding team mission, a lack of awareness of other people's feelings, or sometimes a misinterpretation of the actions or intentions of a teammate, colleague, or coach.

Merely being together at meetings, work, practices, training camps, games, competitions, or team parties does not necessarily increase mutual liking or performance harmony among team members. For a genuine positive team spirit to develop and grow, individuals must commit to a common mission or goal and be linked in some positive interdependent way so they know that they have to rely on and help one another to have a chance of achieving their individual and collective goals.

Harmony or compatibility sometimes flows or grows naturally among members of a team. When this ideal circumstance is not present, it is important to discuss the commitment required from everyone on the team to put the bigger mission above any conflict or disharmony so that everyone gives his or her best and supports one another to achieve a worthy, higher-level goal. When all team members make a decision to be supportive, remain flexible, be their best, find good qualities in their teammates, and work together to accomplish mutually beneficial goals, collectively they put their team on the path to harmony and excellence.

Open communication is an important step in preventing and solving conflicts or problems among team members. Respecting another person's needs, feelings, and perspective is difficult when you do not know or understand what they are. It is never too early or too late to move along a more positive path, turn a negative into a positive, transform a wrong into a right, or turn an error into a positive lesson. The best time to begin this performance- and life-enhancing process is right now.

Staying Positive

Building positive team spirit is in itself a worthy goal because of the way it makes you and other people feel and because it leads to improved performance for all team members. Whenever people are linked together in pursuit of challenging, mutually beneficial goals, several action points become essential for individual and group success.

+ Find the good qualities in each team member.
+ Recognize the good things each member of the team can do or contribute.
+ Commit to remaining positive through adversity; remember that all challenges, great and small, demand that you focus in ways that free you to overcome setbacks, adversity, or obstacles.
+ Embrace the challenge of getting along and finding a way to make things work.
+ Focus on doing your job the best that you can.

✦ Help teammates accomplish their individual goals and the overall team goals.

✦ Put the mission above the conflicts, obstacles, or potential setbacks.

✦ Remember that when you embrace a positive perspective, you can tolerate or work with almost anyone in any context for short-duration missions.

Teammates are in a great position to help one another learn, provide positive challenges or positive rivalry, help each other believe in themselves and their mission, constructively analyze one another's performances, provide a positive lift or word of encouragement when needed, and share actions and perspectives on how to focus in positive ways that will benefit all team members. You can feed off the great things your teammates or training partners do in practice, training, and performances and be inspired to continue to improve because of their intensity, execution, determination, and skill level. Teammates are also in a great position to identify what actions or inactions are interfering or helping with individual and team goals. If you think someone on the team or in the organization is doing something that is negatively affecting the team's performance, consider talking with that person, either directly or through a team representative (the team captain, coach, assistant coach, or manager or a trusted member of the support staff). If there is even a small chance that your intervention will be helpful, it's worth a try. Respectfully share your appreciation with others for the good things they are doing and your thoughts on what could lead the team to even better and more consistent team performances.

Team members, support staff members, and others associated with the team should become aware of which of their actions may help or hurt their performance and the team's performance. If coaches or teammates do not know they are doing something that is interfering with the team's best focus or team goals, there is little chance that they will change their behavior. If they are aware of what helps you or other members of the team prepare best for your tough challenges or performances, they will be in a position to help you set the stage for your consistent best performances or at least not inadvertently interfere.

Positive, meaningful communication among teammates and between coaches and athletes is extremely important for attaining best possible performances, nurturing positive team spirit, maintaining overall personal well-being, and sustaining consistency of best performances. How many times was the coach's communication positive and helpful today? How many times was the communication between you and your fellow athletes positive and helpful today? How many times was your communication with yourself positive and helpful today? Can you or your teammates or coaches make it happen more often tomorrow? What actions can each of you take every day to enhance team spirit, team harmony, and overall team performance?

Athletes offered the following suggestions for promoting more positive interaction among teammates:

+ Get to know your teammates well and focus on what you like about them.
+ Talk with your teammates on-site and off-site.
+ Listen to your teammates and their ideas or point of view.
+ Avoid putting down teammates.
+ "**Do**cide" that you will get along well with everyone.
+ Take responsibility for yourself and do whatever you can to improve the consistency of your performance and the team's performance.
+ Encourage your teammates in positive ways every day.
+ Accept individual differences or different ways of seeing things.
+ Include everyone.
+ Show others that you care about them.
+ Become a positive example for others to follow.
+ Believe in your teammates and let them know you believe in them and appreciate their positive contributions.
+ Believe in your coaches and support staff and let them know you believe in them and appreciate their positive contributions.

Respected athletes and performers in other high-performance domains are in an ideal position to lead by their positive example, which can in turn encourage others to give their best and build the best team possible. The following best focus rules and reminders can help you and your teammates build strength, spirit, positivity, and unity on your team.

Follow Best Team Focus Rules

+ Focus on why we can accomplish our team goals (not why we can't).
+ Focus on opportunities (not obstacles).
+ Focus on solutions (not problems).
+ Focus on helping each other move forward (not putting each other down).
+ Focus on the positives and positive opportunities (not the negatives).
+ Focus on turning lessons learned into improved performance.
+ Focus on continuing to move forward step by step, day by day.

Strive for Positive Personal Excellence

+ Become the most positive person you can be, with yourself and with others.

+ Decide to be your best—as an athlete, student, teammate, and positive person.
+ Focus on doing what brings out your best every day.
+ Focus on executing the step in front of you to the best of your abilities.
+ Focus on finding the positives and the positive lessons during the tough times.
+ Make a commitment to yourself to embrace ongoing learning and improvement.
+ Lead by setting a positive example.

Challenge and Support Your Teammates

+ Challenge your teammates to be what they can be—as athletes, teammates, and human beings.
+ Challenge your teammates to focus on what brings out their best and the team's best.
+ Challenge each other to act on lessons learned from each training session, game, or performance.
+ Share with your teammates that you value them and their contributions.
+ Acknowledge or praise teammates for their great focus and impressive effort.
+ Remember that all your teammates want to perform their best and win.
+ Continue to help each other find a way to win.

Keep the Joy in the Game or Pursuit

+ Find ways to keep the love and joy in your pursuit of excellence.
+ Appreciate the simple joys and opportunities you have every day.
+ Rejoice in the little victories, small steps, and simple successes.
+ Help your teammates to keep the love in the pursuit.
+ Keep things in perspective; what you are doing or pursuing in your sport or performance domain is part of your life, not your whole life!
+ Take time to rest and regenerate.
+ Take time to enjoy or appreciate other opportunities or pursuits.
+ Take care of your own needs and the needs of your loved ones.

Respect Your Core Values: Respect and Support Others

+ Respect your own potential.
+ Respect your teammates' potential.
+ Respect your own best focus.
+ Learn something from every experience and act on those lessons learned.

- Support your teammates and loved ones through the ups and downs and challenges along the way.
- Respect the contributions others are making to help you live your dreams.
- Work together to bring out the best in everyone.

Finding Advantages in Differences

There are vast individual differences among members of all teams—different experiences, different perspectives, different responses to stress, different ways of focusing or coping with distractions, different strengths, and different challenges, doubts, or fears. These differences can work to your collective advantage and strengthen your team if you are willing to learn from each other, work together, help one another, and share your strengths. No coach, athlete, or performer knows everything. But when individuals and teams put their heads and best thoughts together, they can know almost everything that is important for individual and team success. You and your team, coaches, and support staff will become much stronger and better if you follow these steps:

1. Decide as individuals and as a group that you are going to excel at what you do and become the best you can possibly be.
2. Help one another to excel by sharing your experience on how you gained certain strengths, how you mentally prepare yourself to perform your best, and what you focus on to perform your best consistently. Share your positive experiences, visions, best focus, or questions about how to continue to improve the quality and consistency of your best individual and team performances.
3. Encourage each other to be your best and congratulate your teammates when someone makes a small or large improvement or gives a great fully focused effort.
4. Support yourself and your teammates before and after practices, games, competitions, or performances. Support each other for taking positive small steps in the right direction. Continue to improve the quality and consistency of your physical and technical skills by focusing fully on the right things at the right time. Make sure your thoughts, focus, and emotions are working for you, not against you.

Resolving Conflicts

Imagine that you are going on a space voyage to another planet or rowing across the biggest ocean in the universe in a small boat. You must live, work, train, perform, and interact together within a space about the size of a space shuttle or small rowboat. You must remain with your team in this space for a minimum of three months and possibly as long as a year. You have no chance of leaving until the mission ends successfully. Living, interacting, and working together in harmony would be critical to your survival, the survival of your teammates, and the success of the overall mission. Who would you want with you on this mission? What would you do to avoid conflict and maintain a sense of harmony and mutual support on a mission like this?

Crew members for long-duration space missions have to be well selected for compatibility and adaptability; otherwise, communication might break down and destroy the essential human links that allow them to succeed. Sport and performance teams rarely choose their members based on their natural compatibility or ability to work in positive and supportive ways with others. Selecting athletes or performers based on a natural fit among all team members could be an advantage but is improbable. So we have to make the best of what we have and help athletes and other performers learn to adapt in positive ways to challenging situations to complete their ultimate mission together successfully. Everyone who wants to be a contributing member of a great team has to be willing to adapt a little so that everyone on the team can gain a lot.

As athletes or performers we do have several advantages over our long-distance space explorers or ocean voyagers. We do not have to leave behind our family, friends, and everything familiar or comforting for many months or years at a time. We have the advantage of being able to step away from our teammates, coaches, or performance domain to enjoy a beautiful natural world and rejoice in many other simple joys. Positive breaks or time-outs with no pressing demands make our challenges more manageable and allow us to return to our daily focused missions with renewed energy and greater tolerance for those with whom we are linked in our high-performance pursuits. Getting away and enjoying some quiet time or personal space frees us to come back refreshed to make the best of the opportunities we have at and away from the performance site. Every day is a new opportunity to embrace something positive or magical in and away from your performance context.

When a communication problem arises, regardless of who is more responsible for creating it, both people usually end up upset by it and need to share the responsibility to implement a workable solution. Coaches and athletes can reduce conflict and improve team harmony in the following ways:

+ Work on improving your positive communication skills.
+ Set a goal to become a better listener and work on expressing your feelings in positive, respectful, and constructive ways.
+ Work on improving your skills at respectfully helping others and receiving help from others.
+ Set a goal to give assistance to others more readily and to receive suggestions from others more openly and enthusiastically.

✦ Work on improving your positive and fully connected focusing skill in different contexts. Set a goal to focus in ways that free you and other athletes or teammates to achieve your best results, and work on refocusing to stay positive or constructive when things don't go your way.

One of the many instances in which I've been asked to help resolve conflicts within a team context involved a team of young athletes who trained every weekday. Coach X called me with some urgent concerns about interpersonal conflicts on the team. The atmosphere was filled with tension, practices were degenerating, and spirits were low. Conflicts existed between the coach and certain athletes as well as among some team members. The problem had escalated to the point where practices were being ruined and many people left practice feeling upset. The coach was fed up. The athletes were fed up. Coach X described the situation as desperate.

I agreed to go in to try to help resolve the situation. I began by asking the coach and each athlete to write their responses to the following questions, hoping that their answers would provide some insights into the situation and some possibilities for resolving the conflicts.

✦ What is the main reason you come to practice?

✦ If you could change anything you wanted about practice, what would you change?

✦ Is there anything the coach or other athletes could do to make you feel, work, focus, or perform better in practice? What about at competitions?

✦ What would make practice more uplifting and productive for you?

✦ When the coach is at his or her best, what does he or she do?

✦ When the coach is at his or her worst, what does he or she do?

✦ What are two things in your life that you like to do more than anything else?

✦ What are your overall goals in your sport or performance domain?

✦ What will help you achieve those goals?

After reviewing the athletes' responses to these questions, I spoke to the group and shared their overall views (without mentioning any names). Everyone, athletes and coaches, said that their involvement in this sport was one of the things in their life that they liked best. They all wanted to improve their skills and have positive and productive practices and performances. They felt great when they learned a new move or perfected an old one, and so did the coach. The overall goals of the coaches and athletes were similar, but sometimes a lack of clear and positive communication got in their way of achieving their goals, and as a result none of them achieved their goals. During those times, nobody enjoyed being there and nobody learned much.

I suggested that the quickest way they could all have more uplifting and productive practices or workouts was to work together and help one another get to where they all wanted to go. Based on their responses to my questions, I created some positive workout suggestions to pinpoint exactly what each of them could do to make their practices more like they all wanted them to be. I wrote these workout suggestions on index cards and gave them to the athletes and the coach as reminders they could use for subsequent practices (see figure 21.1, *a* and *b*). Their goal was to do as many of the actions listed on one card as possible in one practice or performance session and to do the remaining ones at the next practice or performance.

Figure 21.1a   Coach Reminders

Coach Reminders—Card I

1. Absolutely no yelling—no matter what happens, stay cool.
2. Smile—show that you are in a good mood. Let athletes know that you are happy to be there.
3. Point out what athletes do well and then correct constructively.
4. After giving correction, briefly explain why.
5. Say something positive not related to the sport.
6. Be encouraging and reassuring with words and actions.

Coach Reminders—Card II

1. Give positive feedback every chance you get.
2. Lighten up a little—loosen up.
3. Give specific instruction and encouragement.
4. Tell the athletes what they did well tonight.
5. Say goodnight and leave the gym happy.

Coach Reminders—Card III

1. Show that you care and want each athlete to be there.
2. Say hello to everyone sometime today.
3. Give everyone some positive individual feedback sometime today.
4. Listen closely when athletes give input or express a feeling.
5. Respect and act on the athletes' input.
6. Feel good about your own progress.

From T. Orlick, 2015, *In pursuit of excellence*, 5th ed. (Champaign, IL: Human Kinetics).

I gave them several reminder cards because I did not want to have too many reminders on one card but wanted to include all the key reminders from their written responses to my questions. I wanted to respect their input and suggestions but not overload them with too many reminders during any one practice or performance session. You can create your own positive reminder cards to make your practices or performances the best they can be. Write down the focus reminders you think might work best for you. Then try them to see what works best. Select the best reminders to keep with you in case you need them in practice or performance situations.

To find out how these attempts to improve team harmony affected interactions, we observed Coach X's team before and after the intervention. The

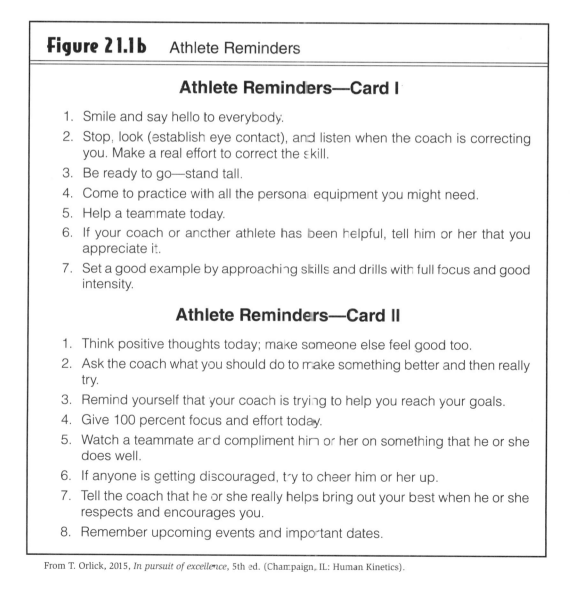

Figure 21.1b   Athlete Reminders

Athlete Reminders—Card I

1. Smile and say hello to everybody.
2. Stop, look (establish eye contact), and listen when the coach is correcting you. Make a real effort to correct the skill.
3. Be ready to go—stand tall.
4. Come to practice with all the personal equipment you might need.
5. Help a teammate today.
6. If your coach or another athlete has been helpful, tell him or her that you appreciate it.
7. Set a good example by approaching skills and drills with full focus and good intensity.

Athlete Reminders—Card II

1. Think positive thoughts today; make someone else feel good too.
2. Ask the coach what you should do to make something better and then really try.
3. Remind yourself that your coach is trying to help you reach your goals.
4. Give 100 percent focus and effort today.
5. Watch a teammate and compliment him or her on something that he or she does well.
6. If anyone is getting discouraged, try to cheer him or her up.
7. Tell the coach that he or she really helps bring out your best when he or she respects and encourages you.
8. Remember upcoming events and important dates.

From T. Orlick, 2015, *In pursuit of excellence*, 5th ed. (Champaign, IL: Human Kinetics).

rate of positive verbal interaction (for example, praise, compliments, and encouragement) doubled. More important, negative criticism (for example, yelling and put-downs) ended almost completely. The coach commented to me, "Everything is working out much better now. Everyone seems to be more happy and relaxed. All the athletes seem to be really working and trying hard."

The lesson from this story is that everyone on a team, even in individual sports, is linked together like a family. What you do or don't do and how you interact with or respond to others affects how others feel, how they perform, how you feel, and how they respond to you. To ensure that our sport or performance family remains positive, happy, and productive, each of us has to do our part. If you give a little extra positive effort in the beginning, it will be worth it in the end. When we encourage our teammates, classmates, family members, friends, teachers, coaches, colleagues, and others by helping each other, listening to each other, respecting each other, supporting each other, and interacting with each other in positive, respectful, and constructive ways, everybody feels better, works harder, and contributes more. We all enjoy living, learning, training, playing, performing, or working in a positive and life-enhancing setting. When we eventually transition out of that positive team setting or performance context we will be not only better performers but also better, happier, more positive, and more compassionate people.

Teams can participate in a number of activities that help create a positive environment. One activity I have found to be successful with athletes, coaches, classmates, workmates, playmates, or families involves simply sharing the good qualities we see in each other. To do this, write down the name of each athlete, student, coach, and support staff member at the top of a separate piece of paper. Then pass these sheets around the room from person to person and ask everyone on the team to write down one thing they like, love, admire, appreciate, value, respect, or enjoy about that person. This activity can also be done orally, but writing things down on a piece of paper adds a special dimension. Everyone leaves the room with a positive piece of paper, which is a collection of uplifting comments from teammates, coaches, and support staff that the person can refer to when he or she needs a little lift. People often share positive comments about their teammates, classmates, colleagues, or family members in this context that they would never otherwise share. It is a very uplifting experience! Reading over those positive comments definitely feels good. It helps to create a more positive and respectful environment where athletes and other performers are able to work together and respectfully deal with conflict more successfully when it does occur.

Inspiring Others

When one person on a team takes a big step up in performance, others on the team are usually inspired to do likewise. If she can do it, I can do it! If he can do it, I can do it! Everyone on the team can gain from the inspiration provided by one person, even in individual sports. There is true power in leading by example. When a few more people take a step up, their actions often inspire more teammates to step up. When a whole team docides to take a step up, magical things happen because those athletes or performers choose to give everything they have—individually and collectively. This is the true power of belief and focus in both team and individual sport contexts.

When Canadian Beckie Scott took a step up and won an Olympic gold medal and started winning World Cup races in cross-country skiing, her teammates began to follow her example, even though no one from Canada had ever done these things before. Her teammate Sara Renner started to reach the World Cup podium and won an Olympic silver medal. Then their younger teammate, Chandra Crawford, only 22 years old at the time, won an Olympic gold medal. After winning that gold medal, Chandra commented, "It has been so awesome having Beckie and Sara and having their leadership and success to learn from. I was so inspired by them." She went on to say, "On those days where I got my butt kicked, I learned so much and knew I could do something about it next time."

The biggest positive change that occurs when one athlete on your team takes a step up to the top of the world is the belief that you can do it too. It is no longer an impossible dream. You train with these people every day, and you stay with them in training (at least sometimes). You begin to think, *If they can do it, I can too.* That belief can work magic for you. Nothing changes except your belief that you can actually do this if you really want to do it. You learn what it takes to perform at that level, and you commit to doing what it takes to get to where you want to go!

When Thomas Grandi took a step up in alpine skiing by becoming the first male athlete from Canada to win a World Cup in a technical event in alpine skiing, others on his team also took a step up. They could race with him and sometimes even beat him in training, so that enhanced their confidence or belief that they could actually do it! They thought, *Why not do it in a race?* I have witnessed this phenomenon with athletes in many sports and in many countries, and I am still amazed at how fast this belief transition can move athletes to the top ranks in their sport. One teammate's accomplishment creates a whole new positive spirit of believing, which in turn leads to a positive new reality for others associated with the team. Nothing changes but their belief, but their belief changes everything. This is the true power of belief and of leading by example. You feed off the belief, intensity, success, and positive example set by a teammate or a member of another team who you know is like you in many ways.

This stepping-up-to-the-challenge phenomenon also occurs during championship team events when everyone on the team decides to believe, play, or perform with full focus and intensity every second out there. When a team of fully committed athletes is on a fully focused mission, every single one of them, they end up beating teams they are not supposed to beat because of the belief, commitment, and riveting focus they bring to their game or performance. They never let up; they never give up. They just keep coming at you, creating their own opportunities and giving everything they have from start to finish. When every single player chooses to believe in the mission and gives everything he or she has every second out there, the effect on overall team performance is extremely powerful.

CHAPTER 22
Self-Directed

I have never worked with an athlete, student, or performer in any high-performance discipline who intentionally went into a performance arena and tried to perform poorly, nor have I ever met a person who intentionally went out to have a miserable, unhappy, or unproductive life. But people do make mistakes, go down negative paths, or fall short of their ideals, most often because they have not learned to focus fully on the positives and positive possibilities. If you choose to make positive choices and focus fully on acting on those good choices every day, you will begin to move forward in the positive direction you want to go.

Positive self-direction centers on making life-enhancing choices that will take you where you want to go in the manner in which you would like to get there. Positive self-direction becomes possible when you choose to drive your own life by making positive, life-enhancing choices and by acting on your positive intentions. To move along this positive path, think about the direction in which *you* would like to go in different parts of your life and *act* on those positive choices in some positive way every day. Continue to remind yourself that thinking is not enough. Only positive action in your real-world training, learning, preparation, and performance contexts will lead you happily in the direction you want to go.

Finding your own best path in life is sometimes like being in a kayak on a challenging white-water river. You have to make choices about your own best course, best focus, and best path. You can't trust the river or other people to make your choices for you. If you let a fast-moving white-water river direct your course for you, instead of taking control of your own course, you risk being swept off-course or plunging over a falls.

The point I am making here is that *you* have to choose your own best course to guide yourself in positive and life-enhancing ways. This will put you in control of your own course, your own choices, your own life, and your own destiny, as much as is humanly possible.

Many things are within your control. You can make good choices that will help you overcome challenges and live your dreams. You can find a way around, through, or over most obstacles that may or may not be within your control.

Reflecting in positive ways, making positive choices, and acting consistently on your positive intentions will give you your best chance of focusing in ways that will free you to perform your best and live the life you would love to live.

Positive performance, positive self-directed actions, and positive living involve not only choosing your own best path but also choosing to move forward in the manner in which you would prefer to travel. How do you want to perform? What do you want to focus on doing or improving every day? How do you want to live your life today and every day as a learner, friend, teacher, teammate, family member, or performer?

Choosing Self-Direction

The following are 10 simple—or perhaps not-so-simple—questions to ask yourself to help you move forward in positive and self-directed ways to improve the quality of your performance and joyfulness of your life.

1. How do you feel about yourself as an athlete or performer?
2. How do you feel about yourself as a human being?
3. What do you feel is good or great about how you are performing right now?
4. What do you feel is missing in your performance right now?
5. What is good or great on your team right now?
6. What is missing on your team right now?
7. What is good or great in the relationships you have right now?
8. What is missing in your relationships right now?
9. What is good or great in your life right now?
10. What is missing in your life right now?

If everything is good and nothing is missing in your life right now, then stay on this wonderful, positive, life-enhancing path. Keep doing what you are doing. If something is missing in your life or your focus that could bring you a step closer to your goals or dreams, think about what you can do about it and do something about it!

+ Choose to do the things you want to do.
+ Choose to live the life you want to live.
+ Choose to be the person you want to be.

✦ Choose to be the athlete or performer you want to be.

✦ Choose to live your life to the fullest with no regrets!

The path to personal excellence is full of ups and downs, progression and regression, great steps forward and plateaus. As long as you maintain control over your choices, you can continue to guide the direction of your life in positive ways. Positive choices free you to do the things you want to do and allow you to achieve the goals that are important to you.

The pursuit of personal excellence is challenging and fulfilling. Relish its intensity, cherish its beautiful moments, and accept its challenges, lessons, and risks. Many people's lives lack a sense of passionate absorption in something that is personally meaningful—the charged-up feeling, the flow of adrenaline, your body telling your mind, *I'm ready, let's go*. Embrace these opportunities. Experience them fully and let them work for you.

When you gain positive control of your focus, competing or performing no longer needs to be the fearful experience it can be for some athletes or performers. Challenges that you joyfully or willfully accept can provide unique opportunities to embrace the excitement, raise the level of your performance, fully experience the experience, be stimulated by others, feel the effectiveness of your fully connected focus, and stretch your personal and performance limits. All of these experiences can continue to enhance the quality and joyfulness of your life.

Dan Sanger/Icon Sportswire

On the journey to personal excellence, Clayton Kershaw and other great athletes learn to enjoy challenges and important performances.

Embracing meaningful challenges in positive and fully focused ways will lead you to your personal and professional goals. Every challenge embraced can help you to live and perform better and more fully than you have before. Continue to focus through the challenges in positive ways, and remember to draw out the positive lessons from each of your performance and life experiences. This will help you to continue to improve the quality of your life and the consistency of your best performances. Choose to bring your best and most positive focus into your sport and performance pursuits and into all other parts of your life and you will be forever grateful.

The essence of excellence is choosing positive self-direction and directing the course of your own actions and life in positive and life-enhancing ways. You decide whether to embrace an opportunity or not to embrace it, you decide to do something with quality and passion or to not do something with quality and passion. No one can do this or make these decisions for you.

I challenge you, encourage you, and strongly advise you to "**do**cide" to do the following:

+ Embrace the positive people, the positive activities, the positive opportunities, and the positive pursuits that are important to you.
+ Fully embrace your life and your passions right now.
+ Choose to live, learn, perform, and embrace the simple joys in your life right now.
+ Choose to live your life with no regrets now and in the future.

To move forward in a positive, self-directed way, docide to do the following:

+ Pursue the positive things that you love to do and in which you find personal meaning.
+ Respect the personal choices that bring out your best.
+ Put yourself in positive situations where you feel valued, respected, accepted, or loved for the good person you are.
+ Make positive, self-directed choices that are in your best interest and that will help you live your dreams.
+ Trust your intuition about what is truly best for you as an athlete, performer, and human being.
+ Help the good or supportive people with whom you live, work, train, play, interact, or perform feel loved, valued, and respected.
+ Bring your best positive focus and the best you into your different life pursuits.
+ Fully embrace each positive step of your ongoing journey to personal and performance excellence.

Following Your Best Path

When pursuing our performance and daily quality-of-life goals, we must be careful not to fall into the fatal trap R. M. Pirsig (1984) described in *Zen and the Art of Motorcycle Maintenance*. The following excerpt recounts an incident that occurred on the author's cross-country motorcycle trip with his teenage son. They stopped in the mountains to do some hiking on steep mountain trails that had switchbacks (trails that go back and forth across the mountain because the slope is too steep to go straight up or down). His son saw the switchbacks above him as he was hiking and continually complained because he was here and not there, and even when he got "there," he still complained because he always wanted to be somewhere else.

> He's here but he's not really here. He rejects the here, is unhappy with it, wants to be further up the trail but when he gets there he will be just as unhappy because he will be "here." What he's looking for, what he wants, is all around him but he doesn't want that because it is all around him. Every step's an effort, both physically and spiritually, because he always imagines his goal to be external and distant. (p. 206)

Wherever a pursuit involves only a distant destination (for example, getting to the top of a mountain) with little or no regard for embracing the simple joys in the step-by-step process of moving toward that goal, a harsh reality is not far behind. The real value in pursuing a noble goal lies in finding and embracing an abundance of positive simple joys and the occasional super joy and continuing to love or appreciate the simple joys or discoveries of your journey. To fully embrace your life, you do not necessarily have to arrive at a specific place or predetermined destination, but you do have to immerse yourself in the simple joys of your daily experiences and really embrace them. This is one of the great values in learning to become fully absorbed in the simplest joys of your ongoing experiences.

In a book titled *Love*, Leo Buscaglia (1996) wrote about the importance of embracing a fully connected focus in different parts of your life. As you likely know, I strongly believe that a positive and fully connected focus is the most important mental skill required for enhancing the quality of your learning, your performance, and your life. When you choose to be positive and fully focused in any context of your life, your life immediately becomes a better place to be. Buscaglia writes:

> Live now. When you are eating, eat. When you are loving, love. When you are talking to someone, talk. When you look at a flower, look. Catch the beauty of the moment. (p. 22)

> There is only the moment. The now. Only what you are experiencing at this second is real. This does not mean live for the moment. It means live the moment—a completely different idea. (p. 73)

> Change is inevitable. Feelings change, attitudes change, desires change, love changes. We cannot stop change, we cannot hold it back. (p. 92)

We cannot stop change, but we can always embrace the positives in our life. So let's embrace positive change, positive growth, positive actions, positive lessons, positive opportunities, and positive possibilities. Positive changes, life-enhancing transitions, or charting new paths toward love, respect, self-growth, and positive personal and performance enhancement is always good. We can choose which paths we go down or avoid going down, we can willfully choose some of the positive changes we want to pursue, how we negotiate those changes, and whether we choose to focus on the positives or negatives, the opportunities or the obstacles, over the course of our lives.

Carlos Castaneda's (1985) Don Juan speaks of the direction and choice of change in *The Teachings of Don Juan: A Yaqui Way of Knowledge*:

> You must always keep in mind that a path is only a path. If you feel you must now follow it, you need not stay with it under any circumstances. Any path is only a path. There is no affront to yourself or others in dropping it if that is what your heart tells you to do. But your decision to keep on the path or leave it must be free of fear and ambition. I warn you: Look at every path closely and deliberately. Try it as many times as you think necessary. Then ask yourself and yourself alone one question: Does this path have a heart? All paths are the same. They lead nowhere. They are paths going through the brush or into the brush or under the brush. Does this path have a heart is the only question. If it does then the path is good . . . if it doesn't then it is of no use. Both paths lead nowhere, but one has a heart and the other doesn't. One makes for a joyful journey; as long as you follow it you will be one with it. The other will make you curse your life. One makes you strong, the other weakens you. (p. 107)

Choosing a path with heart is great advice for all of us. When we follow a path with heart, we are choosing a path that feels right for us, that resonates with our inner being, that intuitively feels like the right choice. Our intuition or gut feeling is usually right for us, and even if it is not always the best choice, we can always choose to change our path. My experience is that when I embark on a path, it always leads to many other paths and opportunities I never anticipated when I started down that first path. Where I started my career path is certainly not where I ended up, because so many other exciting and meaningful options opened up for me along the way, and I embraced them fully. New and exciting or meaningful paths always present themselves to us over the course of our life. As long as you remain open to the positive possibilities that feel right for you, you will find multiple paths with heart. Embrace those paths and continue to grow from them in positive and life-enhancing ways.

The depth of my understanding about what is required to excel in any sport, performance domain, or other part of life has changed over the years. When I first started working in the performance enhancement field, I thought the path to the highest levels of excellence was to work, work, work; train, train, train to shut out the rest of my life; and to live only for that one dream. I was wrong! You do have to train or work extremely hard, but you don't have to shut out the rest of your life and you don't have to live only for the future. You can achieve the highest levels of personal and performance excellence in virtually every field by developing and refining a positive, high-quality, fully connected focus and still have a balanced, happy, and productive life in the here and now. The path to personal and professional excellence is totally dependent on developing, refining, embracing, and respecting your best possible focus and willfully following a path with heart.

A great friend with whom I was fortunate to share many adventures was a renowned filmmaker, artist, and outdoor adventurer. He was a living example of embracing a balanced life and following a path with heart. When he worked, he was totally absorbed in his work, but he always left room for embracing simple joys in his play and the joyful other parts of his life. In fact, nothing—and I mean nothing—got in the way of his play. His pure connection in his playtime enriched his life as much as any achievement or honor ever bestowed on him did. His play and his love for the outdoors gave him something to look forward to with great enthusiasm every day, and it let him return to his work with a fresh perspective and lots of positive energy.

He set high goals for himself and pursued them vigorously, but on a day-to-day basis he never failed to appreciate the time that he lived with his family, friends, and nature. In some ways he was like a little kid who just wanted to go out and play. I can remember him banging on my door on many occasions, and as I opened the door, hearing him say, "Hey Orlick, can you come out and play?" Of course, I always said yes, and I grabbed my play clothes and playing equipment—whatever they might have been for that day—and we went outside and played! He appreciated each simple playing experience and each simple joy so much that his enthusiasm and positive energy radiated onto all those around him. I wondered about how he managed to keep that playfulness at the center of his life—a life that otherwise revolved around perfection and the pursuit of excellence. A near-fatal heart attack, which almost grabbed his life early in his career, helped teach him this lesson. He was thankful for another day of living, then another, and another. We are all given only so many days to live, experience, and fully enjoy. Why not fully embrace them!

He did pass away some time ago, and I still miss him, but I know he lived his life fully and joyfully, and for that I am eternally grateful. The lesson I learned, remembered, and respected was to live every day of my life fully and joyfully while I can. A gift of life! I encourage you to do the same. Choose to fully live your gift of life!

CHAPTER 23
Adaptable

Many performance and life challenges that at first glance may appear to be impossible or insurmountable can be overcome with a simple shift in focus. All you have to do is find a way to see the challenge, obstacle, or opportunity in a different way or view it from a more positive perspective. A simple personal example is when I first started running up and down hills on trails through the woods with my border collie Zen. Zen is superfast and superfocused. He taught me some important lessons about staying focused on the positives and remaining resiliently adaptable.

One early morning when we had been out running up and down trails together for well over an hour, I slowed down just as we approached a long steep hill. At that same moment, Zen looked at me as if saying *What are you doing?* and he started running up that hill like he was flying down a hill. I reflected on what Zen focused on to fly up these long hills. At that moment, I made a conscious decision to approach all hills in a different, more positive light—from a *Zenlightened* perspective.

I chose to look at hills as opportunities rather than obstacles, to see them as positive challenges, as if they were not really hills but flat land on a slant. As soon as I began to see those hills and other potential challenges in positive and manageable ways, I could approach them in totally positive ways. I just put my head down and focused on looking at the step directly in front of me and putting one foot in front of the other until I arrived at the top of the hill or overcame the challenge I was facing.

I discovered that by focusing only on the step in front of me, which is totally within my control, hills and other uphill challenges don't really look or feel insurmountable. They look, feel, and become totally manageable, even at the end of a long day or run. I have learned to focus fully only on my step-by-step stride or day-by-day progress in whatever I am doing because I know it will take me to the top of whatever hill or challenge I choose to embrace. I am always joyful when I complete a meaningful challenge, attain a worthy goal

I chose to pursue, or help someone else attain a worthy goal (big or small). I choose to engage myself in joyful, fully connected moments whether I am running up a hill, paddling across a lake, living magic moments, sharing time with special people, or finishing a chapter in this book. Connecting fully in positive and life-enhancing ways keeps me happily and fully engaged in the good things I am doing or pursuing every day.

The bottom-line lesson is to shift your focus to positive—in how you view yourself and others, how you view your personal potential, how you view your capacity, how you choose to overcome challenges, and how you live the life you want to live. This simple shift in focus can make a huge positive difference in how well and how quickly you adapt to ongoing challenges in positive, productive performance- and life-enhancing ways. The power of this positive shift in focus holds true in sport and all other performance contexts as well as in relationships and other meaningful ongoing life challenges. Change your focus and you will change your reality.

Do yourself, your friends, your teammates, your classmates, your coaches, your teachers, your colleagues, your family, or your students a great service by choosing to find the positives and by working together in positive ways to find a path through potential challenges, negatives, setbacks, or bumps in the road. This will free you and others to continue to learn, grow, and benefit in positive ways from your ongoing challenges and daily experiences. Every day you can learn or do something of value that can help you become better, wiser, more positive, more resilient, more adaptable, or more fully connected with the right things at the right time.

Choose to view challenges in positive ways and you will reduce the unnecessary stress in your life and free yourself to live your life more fully and joyfully. Open yourself to positive opportunities and positive opportunities will open to you. Choose to embrace positive possibilities every day. This will free you to live the life you want to live—the life you are capable of living.

Choose to live the way you would ideally like to live with an open mind, a loving heart, a positive focus, and no regrets. The more positive, resilient, and adaptable you are or choose to become, the better your chances of loving your life, living your dreams, and supporting yourself and others in ongoing positive, life-enhancing ways.

Opening Yourself to Positive Opportunities

Choose to fully live the life you want to live by continuing to embrace ongoing positive opportunities! The more you open yourself to simple positive opportunities, the better your chances of living the life you would love to live. The more you embrace positive opportunities, the better your chances of achieving the goals you would love to achieve.

Continue to open yourself to the positive possibilities, and your chances of living your dreams and embracing your true potential will be greatly enhanced. If you do not open yourself to positive opportunities or choose to not pursue your dreams, how happy, meaningful, joyful, or fulfilling do you think your life will be?

Choose to make a commitment to yourself to act on your positive intentions in performance- and life-enhancing ways every day. Only *you* can do this for *you*! If you act on your positive intentions, the quality of your life will continue to blossom and your chances of living your dreams will be hugely increased.

Choose to be fully focused, resilient, adaptable, and open to ongoing positive opportunities. Choose to do everything you can possibly do to make the best of your years, months, days, and special moments. Choose to live, love, train, learn, perform, appreciate, and interact in positive and life-enhancing ways with special people who enter your life. Open yourself to fully appreciate the good people in your life whom you love, like, or admire. Choose to fully embrace the simple positives in your everyday life and the magic moments in your chosen performance pursuits.

To fully embrace your life, choose to do the following:

+ Live the life *you* want to live.
+ Do the positive and life-enhancing things *you* want to do.
+ Connect fully with positive people who love and support you just for being you.
+ Fully embrace the time and pure connection you have with special people in your life.
+ Free yourself to live your life with no regrets (or as few regrets as possible).
+ Fully embrace the simple joys in every part of your day and life.
+ Recognize that your one life offers many opportunities—choose to embrace them fully!

It is better to do what *you* want to do right now, while you still have the opportunity to do it, rather than waiting and looking back on your life wishing you had.

Choose to find and embrace positive people and opportunities in the different parts of your life. This will free you to continue to experience deeper levels of connection, more meaningful learning, purer feelings of love, and appreciation for the opportunities you have throughout your life. Choose to chart a positive path that will continue to open doors to more positive living, more joyful and meaningful learning, and more consistent best performances.

Open yourself to the possibility of finding, nurturing, and sustaining a special two-way positive, life-enhancing relationship with another positive, caring, and compatible human being (hopefully the love of your life). It is never too late to find your true soulmate.

By opening yourself to connect fully in positive and life-enhancing ways you can enhance the depth and quality of your positive connections in virtually all pursuits: with friends, family members, classmates, teammates, and loved ones in nature, sport, music, fine arts, dance, acting, coaching, teaching, learning, or traveling while fully embracing simple daily joys with positive people and experiences in all parts of your life. Ongoing positive personal-growth experiences are available to you and others through meaningful educational experiences, positive interactions, experiences in nature, and all positive performance pursuits.

The possibility of finding, nurturing, and developing positive and sustainable two-way life-enhancing relationships with positive people and adventures is enhanced when there is a feeling of mutual trust and ongoing respectful, positive, caring, or loving interactions. It is very difficult or impossible to find ongoing joy in a relationship with a negative person—trust me on this one! Genuine mutually supportive relationships and ongoing positive interactions can lead to special, inspirational, or life-enhancing feelings that have the potential to be sustained over time.

Positive adaptability can be nurtured by embracing good things and good people and opening yourself to positive possibilities or opportunities that can free you to live your life more fully and joyfully. Positive adaptability can free you to live the different parts of your life fully and joyfully and help you to pursue your goals and dreams in positive ways with no regrets. Embarking on this journey means finding, embracing, kindling, or opening yourself to the possibility of deeper levels of love, passion, pure connection, and sustained commitment to a mission, person, or chosen performance pursuit.

Passion and pure connection can be discovered through nature, sport, music, dance, acting, coaching, teaching, learning, reading, writing, helping others, speaking, or any other positive and engaging personal or performance pursuit. Positive two-way compatible relationships that are mutually uplifting, beneficial, natural, supportive, and respectful also have the potential to be sustained over time. The challenge lies in finding, nurturing, and sustaining a meaningful and joyful loving relationship that is mutually positive, uplifting, and supportive. One-way relationships that are controlling, selfish, or dishonest do not tend to last very long, so choose wisely.

Positive adaptability is all about embracing our lives fully and remaining open to the simple daily positive opportunities presented to us (sometimes by chance) so that we can truly live our lives fully and embrace them joyfully with no regrets. Choosing to fully live your life and then actually living it fully is what makes life such a special and inspiring journey for anyone who chooses to follow this positive path.

The more positive you are and the more adaptable you become, the better equipped you will be to live, train, learn, perform, and enjoy your life fully. The more you look for and embrace the positives, the better you will feel and the less stressful your life journey will likely be.

The lifelong advantages of embracing a positive, fully connected, adaptable focus are huge. Positive adaptability greatly enhances your chances of loving your life, embracing your journey, adapting in positive and life-enhancing ways, performing your best, and living your dreams.

✦ Choose to make positive choices that free you to do what you really want to do.

✦ Choose to follow your own best path.

✦ Choose to live your own dreams.

✦ Choose to act on your positive choices or positive intentions every day!

This will lead you along a positive path, a path with passion and heart, a path that will take you to places you really want to go.

Choose to support yourself and pursue your own positive dreams. Embrace your life-enhancing choices. These choices will free you to become the person and performer you really want to be. Act on your positive choices. They will direct the course of your life in positive, meaningful, and life-enhancing ways.

If you make a mistake, experience a setback, or lose your best focus in some context, choose to learn and grow from that mistake or lapse in best focus. It will make you better, wiser, more joyful, and more fully human if you do. If you open yourself to do what *you* need to do to get to where *you* want to go, *you* will probably get there. If you don't open yourself to do what you need to do to get to where you want to go, you probably won't get there.

Adapt your focus and your actions to do what *you* need to do to get to where you really want to go. Give yourself the best possible chances of being the person you really want to be and getting to where you want to go. Personal excellence is your choice, and you will live with your choices for the rest of your life, for better or worse.

When you make good choices and act on them in positive ways every day, your chances of leading yourself and others to the positive places you want to go are greatly enhanced. So continue to make positive choices and act on those good choices. They will direct your personal interactions, your performances, and the course of your life in positive and life-enhancing ways.

If you do make a mistake or a less than best choice, simply choose to learn and grow from it. Turn it into a learning opportunity. Act on the positive lessons you learn from your mistakes or bad choices and continue to learn and grow from your successes and good choices. This will free you to continue to become better, wiser, happier, and more consistent in your performances and more fully human in all parts of your life.

The more positive, focused, adaptable, and resilient you are or become in any context, the less stress you will feel and the better your performances and personal life experiences will be. Make a personal commitment to yourself to continue to move forward in simple positive ways every day in your sport or performance domain and in your everyday life pursuits. Willfully choose to move forward in a positive and focused way even if you have to move beyond your comfort zone to get to those places you really want to go. Dream big and focus on the little steps that will take you to your desired destination.

Decide to continue to try to move forward in your sport or performance domain and in your personal life in small positive ways every day. Choosing to be positive, focused, resilient, and adaptable is the only way to live your dreams and get to where you really want to go. Sometimes we have to take risks when we choose to become more focused, resilient, and productive and when we choose to stretch our perceived limits to get to where we really want to go in challenging life or performance pursuits. Developing skills that free you to be positive, focused, resilient, caring, and adaptable is essential for living the highest levels of excellence in sport or other high-performance or high-risk pursuits. The importance of being positive, focused, resilient, caring, and adaptable also holds true for developing, nurturing, and sustaining a high quality of living and high-quality positive interpersonal relationships outside of your work or performance domain.

There may be someone with whom you would really like to share something special—a thought, feeling, worry, wish, dream, fear, or hope—but you don't do it because you are afraid the person might misunderstand your intention or think less of you because you shared this feeling with him or her. However, that simple and yet not-so-simple step, or simple and not-so-simple positive action, could in fact open doors that lead you to where you would like to go with this person and help you become the friend, partner, teammate, or performer you really want to be.

If you really want to do or share something, then do it, even though you may feel uncomfortable at that moment. If you really don't feel ready to do something, then don't do it. Choosing to be positive and adaptable is dependent on directing your focus in positive ways every day, choosing the activities you want to do, and adapting your focus so you do the positive things *you* really want to do. Positive adaptability also requires that you adapt your focus to turn negatives into positive lessons and embrace positive opportunities that will help you move forward on your positive journey to personal and performance excellence.

Acting on positive choices and minimizing negative thoughts, focus, actions, and people in your life is a big part of positive adaptability, positive focus, positive resilience, positive performance, and ongoing positive living. If someone has a negative effect on you or your performance, try to talk with that person in a positive way (away from the performance site) to remedy or improve the situation. It is also important to develop effective on-site focusing and refocusing plans so that you can deal effectively with negative or distracting people and also your own negative thoughts or other negative distractions you might face.

Your primary goal is to be completely prepared to respect your own best focus and be totally ready to maintain or regain that best focus regardless of the challenges you may face in your performance world or life outside of your performance.

Do your best to free yourself to live your dreams by

+ focusing on doing what you really want to do,
+ focusing on doing what works best for you,
+ refocusing or shifting focus away from anything that might interfere with your best performance focus, and
+ avoiding unnecessary distractions or dwelling on anything negative that could drag you down.

The more positive, prepared, fully focused, and adaptable you are in any challenging performance context, the freer you will feel, the less stress you will experience, and the better your experiences and performances will be.

Your performances and your life outside your training and performance contexts consist of many possible choices you make every day. Almost all of these choices are within your control. Positive adaptability grows when *you* make positive choices and act on those positive choices every day.

Positive possibilities become positive realities when at the performance site you choose to

+ focus on the positives,
+ focus on being fully connected with what you are doing, and
+ focus on being resilient and adaptable to the challenge you are facing.

Positive possibilities become positive realities when away from the performance site you choose to

+ live the life you want to live;
+ act in positive and life-enhancing ways every day;
+ respect yourself, your best choices, and your true capacity;
+ respect your best focus;
+ follow your positive convictions;
+ do the good things you want to do;
+ follow the positive path you want to follow;
+ see and feel the positives in yourself and in the good people around you;
+ see and feel the positive possibilities in everything you do;

+ bring your best focus, heart, and soul into your training and performances every day;

+ choose to be the person and performer you really want to be; and

+ choose to be positive, focused, resilient, and adaptable every day.

You are given one life with many opportunities—embrace them fully.

Pursuing Your Dreams

You can accomplish pretty much anything you want to accomplish in your life if you set positive, meaningful goals and have the courage to relentlessly pursue those goals that are important to *you*.

Sometimes we really want to do something, try something, change something, improve something, embrace someone or something, meet someone, share our real feelings, thank someone, work with someone, collaborate with someone, help someone, ask someone for advice, or ask someone out. But often we don't do it—sometimes because we lack the confidence to do it or are afraid of potential failure or rejection. Stepping outside our comfort zone can be difficult at times, but failing to step outside our comfort zone often prevents us from doing what we would really like or love to do.

To excel or live our lives fully, we have to some way, somehow, sometime find the courage to move beyond the uncertainty. Sometimes this means taking chances or having the courage to step outside your comfort zone to follow your convictions, embrace meaningful challenges, and take yourself one step closer to living your dreams. If you try to do something and it doesn't work, what's the worst thing that can happen? You try and it didn't work, but at least you tried, and there is always a lesson you can learn from trying anything. You learn from it, adapt because of it, continue to move forward by reflecting on that lesson learned, and then you try again and again and again until you get to where you want to go or reach the place you want to be.

Choosing to be adaptable by continuing to move forward in positive ways is a huge part of personal performance excellence, fitness excellence, health enhancement, positive relationships, and overall quality of living. If you want to live, love, learn, perform, and continue to grow and adapt in positive ways, make a commitment to yourself to continue to look for the positives, embrace the positives, share the positives, create new positives, learn from the positives, love the positives, turn negatives into positives, and continue to adapt in positive ways that will free you to turn negatives into positive lessons and positives into more positives.

Gaining Confidence
Theresa Jenn Lopetrone

davelaus.com

Theresa Jenn Lopetrone, a leading fitness model, began her positive journey to personal excellence when she was a long way from being the confident, amazingly fit, and eloquent woman she chose to become. Theresa shared the essence of her positive journey and agreed to allow me to share it with you. Theresa's life is a great example of how each of us has the power to choose how we can adapt our life and direct our focus and choices to become the person and performer we really want and deserve to be.

What did I gain over the last 10 years? Confidence! That person that I used to be always wanted to do what the person who I am now is doing, but I felt helpless and insecure and didn't believe in myself as much as I do now. If you want to become a better version of yourself then you need to take small steps every day in the right direction. Yes, there will be days that you are unmotivated, upset, or frustrated. These feelings do not have to become your permanent future. You *can* escape these negative feelings, and you *can* become stronger mentally and physically. Ten years ago I didn't know this is where I would be today, but here I am because I never gave up on myself for too long. Once you begin to change on the inside you *will* begin to change on the outside. This could mean something different for each person, but chances are your smile will become brighter, your skin will glow, you will feel better in your own skin, you will treat others with more respect, and most importantly you will treat yourself with more love and respect. Decide today what you want your future to look like and proceed in that direction. Life is waiting for you. Until you value yourself, you will not value your time. Until you value your time, you will not do anything with it.

The more positive and adaptable you are or become, the better, more focused, more joyful, more fulfilling, and less stressful you and your life will be.

A lifetime of joyfulness can be lost or never found when people are not encouraged to follow their dreams. You have to find a way to believe you are capable of living in positive ways and achieving your dreams. You have to find the courage and confidence to begin pursuing your dream. For most people who don't live their dreams, it is not because they can't live their dreams but because they don't believe they can live their dreams or accomplish high-level meaningful goals. To help others live their dreams, we need to encourage them to find a way to step outside their comfort zone and adapt their focus in positive ways so they are empowered to see, feel, and believe they can actually do what they would love to do. Positive beliefs grounded in positive reality create positive change.

Human beings are adaptable creatures. Every day we adapt to something in some way: time changes, schedule changes, people changes, request changes, demand changes, mood changes, venue changes, weather changes, expectation changes, food changes, health changes, loss changes, win changes, support changes, relationship changes, happy changes, sad changes, nothing-to-do changes, too-much-to-do changes, and every other possible kind of change you can think of.

Some changes can drag you down, and other changes can free you and lift your spirits. Flowing through and finding meaningful lessons in changes (with as little self-inflicted pain, worry, stress, or negativity as possible) is a good life-enhancement plan. The more positive and adaptable you are, the less stress, worry, or pain you will bestow on yourself or others.

Do your best to let go of negative things you cannot control and embrace the positive things you can control. Support yourself and the people you love most through the ups and downs and ongoing challenges of your performance or life journey.

Choose to adapt in the best way you can to continue to move forward in positive and life-enhancing ways. This is a great gift you can give to yourself, your friends, your teammates, your colleagues, and your family and loved ones.

One of the best ways to continue to adapt to ongoing challenges and embrace your ongoing life journey in positive and life-enhancing ways is to continue to look for the positives and positive opportunities that live within you, your performance pursuits, your friends, and your loved ones.

Positive adaptability in any context is greatly facilitated by continuing to look for, embrace, and share simple highlights with others every day. Keeping a highlight journal where you write down your highlights at the end of every day is a great way to stay on a positive path.

Remember that regardless of the situation or challenge you may be facing right now or later in your life, it's your life, your mind, your focus, your body, your choice, and your decision, and you can choose to continue to embrace your life, enjoy your life, pursue your dreams, look for simple joys, and live your life as fully and joyfully as possible every day. Docide to live your life fully and joyfully in positive, healthy, happy, and life-enhancing ways every day!

Adapting to Adversity
Noella Klawitter's Story

Noella Klawitter was born on Christmas Day; that's why her parents named her Noella. Noella is a Canadian visually impaired high-performance track athlete. She started losing her sight at the age of 22 and has overcome many adversities along her path. As a high-performance athlete, she holds four Canadian records, three gold IBSA (International Blind Sports Federation) Pan American Games medals, and a sixth-place finish at the world championships. While pursuing her dream in high-performance sport, Noella went back to school and completed her master's degree in human kinetics at the University of Ottawa with a specialty in sports psychology. Noella is happily married to her supportive husband Derek and is very appreciative of her guide dog Zeke. She plans to continue her positive dream of pursuing excellence in academia and sport and shares her story here.

Adversity can be life-changing, whether positive or negative, and it can have severe implications for our lives. My challenges began at a young age, at 13 to be exact. My family had uprooted from the northern pines of Manitoba to Prince Edward Island. It was a chance at a new beginning for my parents, and it all went downhill from there.

The company with which my father was promised work went bankrupt on the day of our arrival. My father found himself unemployed and unable to find work. We became a family on social assistance.

As a relatively shy 13-year-old, I embarked on our journey to Prince Edward Island feeling sad to leave my friends but excited at the opportunities that lay ahead: new friends, a new school, and new experiences. My bubble of elatedness was suddenly burst when I entered high school. I was excited for high school, but I soon learned firsthand the degree to which people can be nasty.

The bullying I endured was so bad that I would often stand in the snow barefoot when my parents weren't home in the hope of being sick the next day. A few girls made up a bunch of rumors about me, and my situation at school declined from there: teasing, heckling, and put-downs. I was isolated and alone, and my fellow students often cornered me in the hallways. I came to hate PEI. I felt so vulnerable and insignificant every time I walked down the hallway at school or someone heckled me. There came a point as a friendless, unpopular misfit that I felt life was no longer worth living. I was very hopeless and at my wits' end.

On a day when I didn't think I could handle the teasing anymore, I saw one of the girls who was on the basketball team. She approached me as I ate my lunch alone. When I saw her walking toward me, I thought, *Here we go, I can't take this anymore,* but, to my surprise, this basketball player came up to me and asked me how I was doing. She went further to tell me she thought I had done a good job on the basketball court that day. She said nothing mean. This turned my thinking around almost instantly: there were nice people on PEI.

It's amazing what a positive impact a simple gesture can have on a person. That basketball player had the potential to make me or break me that day. I really couldn't take any more teasing. Instead of grief, I was given hope. When we embark on our daily lives, it is important to remember that the simplest of gestures could actually save someone's life. Everyone has a story, and you don't know what the person next to you may be going through. Perhaps a kind word of encouragement would be just what that person needed. Think of the impact if we all reached out just a little bit more.

In 2002, I faced my second major adversity. I was driving to work and had to scratch one of my eyes. As I closed it, I noticed the other eye was very blurry. I went to an eye doctor and was told I was losing my sight. After a second opinion and an appointment with a specialist, it became apparent that my sight would deteriorate. No one wants to hear that he or she is going blind. I was afraid, confused, and determined. Though I definitely had some "poor me" days.

The loss of my driver's license was devastating; it was my sense of freedom being taken away from me. It didn't take long before easy tasks became increasingly difficult: cooking, doing my makeup, and doing my hair, for example. As my sight deteriorated, I thought my life was over—little did I know it was just beginning.

Once I was able to adjust to the fact that I was losing my sight, I became more open to help from others. One day a worker from the Canadian National Institute for the Blind suggested that I come out to a Paralympic regional track meet. After much hesitation, I decided to go. My lack of track knowledge was apparent as I showed up in basketball shorts, a t-shirt, and sneakers; further, I chose to race the 400m, 800m, and 1500m on the same day, within a matter of hours. Throwing caution to the wind, I ran my races, and to my delight I won them! I was ecstatic. National team members approached me, and my life soon made a drastic change into high-performance sport. High-performance sport was not without its idiosyncrasies. Being visually impaired, I needed to learn to run with a guide. This is a process where I have to engulf all my trust in the guide to keep me on track and in my lane. When I worked well with my guide, the two of us could run like a well-oiled machine. Both the guide and athlete must learn from one another in order to foster growth as a dyad.

A race that comes to mind was my final race of 2010. I entered the race with the goal of breaking the Canadian record for visually impaired females in the 1500m. My guide for the race was Mia St. Aubin. We warmed up and discussed our race plan. We visualized the race and maintained our focus. When the race started we executed our race plan to a tee. We ran each lap as we had planned and visualized, and with a final push from Mia at the end we crossed the finish line, successfully beating the Canadian record. We were elated.

Running without sight has been an adventure and although challenging, very fulfilling. As the Paralympics are parallel to the regular Olympics, we are subject to the same rules; therefore, I must run within the boundaries of my lane. This is a huge challenge when you can't see the ground. There are also challenges practicing on a busy track and trying to keep yourself safe; this is where very good communication with the guide needs to be practiced and refined.

When I thought my life was over and so many doors were closing because of my sight, I came to realize my life was only just beginning and so many doors were about to open for me. Losing my sight introduced me to sport, allowed me to travel the world racing, and most importantly it enabled me to go back to school. I completed my master's degree in human kinetics at the University of Ottawa. Once again I had many challenges as a visually impaired student: the copious amounts of reading seeing lectures on PowerPoint, and keeping pace with my able-bodied classmates. I loved school and did very well at it. Losing my sight put me in pursuit of excellence.

The reason I share this story is that we will all encounter roadblocks and challenges that seem insurmountable; however, it is what you do with these challenges that makes you the person you are. Almost anything is possible if you set your mind to do it and focus on doing it. Everyone lacks something at some point in life: money, education, family, or friends; however, you can't live your life by what you lack but must live your life by what you aspire to be. If you focus on the positives in your life and pursue the goals you want to pursue, you can work toward becoming anything that you want to become. When you are in a dark place or facing major adversity, you never know what may be around the corner. Always remember that through time and patience, a positive can almost always be found.

Choose to fully live your life the way you want to live it by continuing to embrace ongoing positive opportunities!

CHAPTER 24
Positive Transitions

Our lives are full of transitions from the time we are born to the time we die. These transitions include opportunities to discover and pursue our passions or dreams; develop positive, meaningful, and supportive relationships; commit to being the best we can be in our chosen sport and other meaningful performance pursuits; embrace the different parts of our lives; nurture ourselves; and support others in positive and life-enhancing ways. The simple and sometimes not so simple goal is to live our lives fully and joyfully in positive and supportive ways with no regrets. The sooner you learn to fully embrace positive opportunities and navigate in positive ways through the many transitions in the different parts of your life, the happier, more productive, more meaningful, and more fulfilling your life will be.

Focusing Through Transitions

Life is full of transitions, from the beginning of your life to the end of your life and everywhere in between. The better you become at focusing in positive and life-enhancing ways, the happier and more fulfilling your life will be. Every day you make choices and move through a variety of transitions. Some of your choices are positive and some perhaps not so positive. When you wake up every morning, do you focus on thinking about something positive you are going to do, or are you thinking about something negative you have to do? If you are thinking about something negative, the best thing you can do is shift your focus to something positive.

From the time we wake in the morning until the time we go to sleep at night we are usually focused on something—some thought, feeling, experience, hope, regret, memory, wish, dream, or worry—negative or positive. Your thoughts and focus lead your reality, for better or for worse, so my advice to you is to focus on the positive and the positive possibilities!

Transitioning Out of High-Performance Pursuits
Kerrin Lee-Gartner

Kerrin Lee-Gartner

Many high-performance athletes and performers in other meaningful high-performance pursuits experience challenges or difficulties when transitioning out of their high-performance pursuit. I asked Kerrin Lee-Gartner, an Olympic gold medalist athlete with whom I had the pleasure of working over the course of her entire career, if she would update me on her life since winning her Olympic gold medal in downhill skiing at the 1992 Winter Olympic Games in Albertville, France. She sent me the following update in July 2014.

When I reflect back and share moments and lessons learned on my journey, it is clear just how important my belief and mental strength was to my success. As a shy little girl, I always dreamed I would win at the Olympics. It was wished for on every birthday as I blew out the candles and on every falling star. I would shake the Magic 8 Ball until it gave me the answer I was searching for. I was relentless.

As it turns out, the dreaming was the easy part for me. I could dream big, it was the first step, but I had no idea what I could do with my giant imagination.

I was extremely fortunate to work with Terry Orlick. Terry taught me the next step, the methods and importance of mental training and imagery. He gave my imagination focus. He taught me to learn, and he taught me how to apply the lessons learned, which ultimately unlocked my true potential.

My commitment to the sport and to my dream was always automatic for me; it never wavered. But with that said, my confidence was fleeting; one moment I had complete faith in my abilities while the next moment was filled with undeniable doubt.

I learned to counter this negativity and doubt with positive images and positive self-talk. I nurtured the positives in any situation. My imagery, mental readiness, and fully focused connection became precise, accurate, and reliable, and my mind became one of my greatest strengths. My confidence grew as I developed the mental attributes needed to win and to overcome adversity.

I retired from racing in 1994 and started work as a sports commentator and motivational speaker as well as my favorite full-time job of being a mom. Now, more than 20 years later, my confidence is stronger than it has ever been, but it remains somewhat fragile. It wavers at work and at play, as a woman and as a mother. At these moments when my doubts creep in, I am thankful for the "athlete trained" automatic positive refocusing that takes place!

Learning to overcome my fear of failure as a racer has helped me in business and in my daily life. When those doubts and nerves present themselves before a speech or a live broadcast, I feel all my "prerace" positive self-talk taking over. I accept the feelings for what they are and refocus on the task at hand. Whether in a boardroom, on air, or on a tee box, when I know I am prepared and have done my homework, I can trust myself to give my best effort.

As I age, I am still learning. I have learned how empowering self-awareness is, knowing my strengths and nurturing them. At the same time, I am keenly aware of my weaknesses and how they affect me. The importance of being kinder to myself has been a blessing, and when I make a mistake I am more forgiving, but this is most definitely an ongoing battle!

At the age of 40, I finally gave myself a break and realized that it is fine if I am not always confident or strong or don't do a perfect job. This milestone has allowed me to recognize all my little successes instead of letting them go unnoticed

Looking back at my time working with Terry, I am thankful for learning such valuable life lessons. Belief in myself grew because I learned how to focus on the right things; this works in everyday life. Seeing the positives isn't about blind faith or about wearing blinders. It is about owning the skill to see something good in an otherwise negative or stressful situation.

I am happy to still be working with my husband, Max. We both remain passionate about high-performance sports and are sharing our insights for business success and athlete mentorship through our company Gold Mettle.

Our two daughters have been raised with many lessons from the sports world and have been encouraged to dream big, imagine, and believe.

Thank you, Terry, for focusing my imagination, for teaching me the strength of a positive mind, and for building my belief system.

Most importantly, thank you for teaching me to learn.

Positive performances, positive transitions, and ongoing positive living and learning become possible when you find a way to remain positive and fully connected through the many challenges, opportunities, performances, and transitions you experience or have the potential to experience every day of your life. When you choose to fully embrace simple opportunities every day and continue to find, share, and embrace simple joys that live within each of those opportunities every day, your life and the lives of your loved ones become infinitely more joyful.

Take a few minutes to think about the following questions and write down your answers.

✦ What do you love most about your life?

✦ What makes you feel most fully alive?

✦ What do you feel you are missing in your life right now, if anything, that could make your life feel more complete or more joyful?

✦ What is it you are doing or not doing, or feeling or not feeling, that you would like to do or feel more often or more fully?

✦ What are you doing that you don't want to do? Why are you doing what you don't want to do?

✦ What do you wish was in your life right now that you do not have in your life right now?

✦ What can you do or change in your life or your focus right now to *live the life you really want to live*?

The circumstances of your transition out of high-performance sport or any other high-performance pursuit, or out of a relationship, can determine how challenging it is. For example, if your transition out of your sport, performance domain, or relationship is something you want and are looking forward to, it will be easier than transitioning out of a sport, performance domain, or relationship that you do not want to end.

When you are contemplating a transition in any part of your life, it is helpful to think about the positives and negatives—the potential benefits and probable drawbacks—of staying or leaving. Think about your reasons for wanting to transition out of your sport or high-performance domain. Maybe you are tired of the same old routine or feel like you have been doing this your whole life; maybe you would like to try something new or different; or maybe your performance is declining, your body is hurting, and your injuries are increasing. Or maybe you are tired of being on the road all the time or have financial concerns or relationship issues at home. Maybe you are just ready for a change.

One of the primary reasons high-performance athletes and performers in other demanding high-performance pursuits begin to think about transitioning out of their performance domain is that their performance begins to decline. At some point in your life as a high-performance athlete or high-level performer in any demanding pursuit, you have to transition out of something you excelled at to something else. One advantage in making a transition is that it can lead to a new positive challenge, and you might finally have some time to do other things you have not been able to do because of your complete commitment to your high-performance pursuit. Having time to explore other positive opportunities or find other interesting or positive things to do or pursue might be joyful and challenging in ongoing positive and life-enhancing ways.

Many high-performance athletes who leave their sport initially experience a sense of loss of purpose, value, or personal meaning. The athlete might think, *I have been a high-performance athlete and a member of this team for most of my life, so what am I now?* However, with time that initial sense of loss can be turned into a golden opportunity to learn or experience something new or different about yourself or find something new that is challenging in positive and life-enhancing ways.

When you are transitioning out of high-performance sport or other performance domains, it is OK to feel disappointed or even a sense of loss, but I can assure you it isn't the end of the world. It doesn't mean that you are a worthless or less valued person. It has nothing to do with your overall value as a human being. Choose to keep things in perspective and learn from your ongoing experiences (good ones and not-so-good ones) by looking for positive lessons in each of those experiences.

Ask yourself these questions:

+ What have I learned about myself from my sport or performance experiences?

+ What have I learned about my best and less than best performance focus?

+ What did I learn from my coaches, teammates, and the people around me?

+ What did I learn about how to perform my best in important competitions, challenges, or events that could be applied to other learning or performance pursuits?

+ What did I learn in my sport or performance experiences that can help me feel better, connect more fully, or focus in more positive ways in my future performance pursuits or ongoing life challenges?

By reflecting on and applying your best focus to new and exciting challenges, you will move forward quickly in whatever pursuit you choose to fully embrace. When you bring a positive perspective and fully connected focus to any future work or performance pursuit, you will contribute more and gain something of real value from each experience, especially when you continue to draw out and act on the ongoing lessons learned.

Overcoming Loss

Significant losses in sport, other performance domains, and relationships have a way of colliding with your confidence or self-esteem. The vibrations can result in self-doubt or self-criticism, worry, and even guilt. Although these thoughts or feelings can become overwhelming, there is no reason they have to be. Remember that this loss or setback is not you; it is just something you are currently experiencing. You have many great qualities that live within you, which can continue to be fully developed and nurtured. You can always learn something from losses or setbacks and can continue to grow from them. Although you may have lost something, you also have gained something of value from that experience, and you are a stronger, wiser, more resilient person because of it.

To lose is to be human, and we are all human. Every thinking, feeling, living person experiences some kind of loss. No one escapes it. Even the greatest performers fail, but they have developed strategies to learn and benefit from those experiences. They certainly don't like falling short of a goal, so they try to put their loss in perspective and do a careful evaluation to prevent similar occurrences in the future. They may conclude that their particular approach, focus, or game plan didn't work this time or that they didn't focus fully on the task for the duration of their performance. They don't tear themselves apart for long in response to a loss or setback. They simply prepare better or respect their best focus in their next opportunity. When Michael Jordan was in his prime, he stated, "I never think about the mistakes I made in a game for more than 10 minutes." When Tiger Woods was at the top of his game, he commented, "I like to look back at matches I've played. I like to look at what I did right." We can learn a lot from great athletes about looking for good things in less than best performances and about not dwelling on negatives or mistakes.

We tend to be most susceptible to feeling down when we expect to do well and do poorly instead, when we expect to win and lose instead, or when we expect love or acceptance and experience rejection. In some cases, our expectations may have been unrealistic. Sometimes we have not prepared or focused as well as we could have, a condition we can correct. Sometimes we have done everything in our power to make good things happen, but for reasons beyond our control events do not go as we had hoped or planned. It is important to recognize the difference between circumstances that are within our control and those that are beyond it. Dwelling on the negatives or trying to control things that are beyond our control is futile. No matter how much energy you invest in trying to control the past, you cannot change it. Instead, use your limited energy constructively by directing it toward positive ends and future possibilities.

Loss can make you feel miserable, inadequate, or less confident. But it can also challenge you to draw on your strengths; persist through the obstacles;

get to know yourself better; improve your focus and reflect on your priorities; put things in perspective; and reflect on where you are going, why you are going there, and how you will get there. A time of loss can challenge or enhance your perspective and redirect your course in positive ways in sport, other performance domains, and everyday life. As unpleasant or hurtful as loss may be, it can result in greater appreciation for what you have or had and what you can have. A loss may motivate you to learn how to prepare for, avoid, cope with, or focus more fully in situations that may arise in the future. If you can draw anything good out of your loss or put what remains in perspective, loss has a positive side.

Life is a constant process of growth, transition, and adaptation. The better you become at finding the positives, living the simple joys, and focusing through the obstacles, the happier, healthier, and more fulfilled you will be. If you can view difficulties or setbacks as a positive challenge, a test of your inner strength, and an opportunity for personal growth, then you can turn those experiences into advantages. Finding the lessons in loss has an interesting, sometimes magical way of putting you back in control.

Learn to put loss in perspective, whether it is a small loss that feels big or a big loss such as losing a loved one. Do your best to grow from the experience and rejoice in the good things you did, had, or shared with someone and still have living in your positive memories. Find a positive reason to support yourself, to support others, and to move on in positive ways. You can honor the people you lost by remembering the good things they have given you—the positive memories, the things that continue to live within you even after they are gone—and by embracing your own life. Choose to live your life fully and joyfully. Don't just go through the motions. The lessons you take from loss can help you to learn, live, and perform better.

Overcoming Adversity
Bruce Malmberg's Story

Bruce was a high-performance international archer—a longtime member of the national team, seven-time national champion, national record holder, and multiple winner of the Atlantic City Archery Classic. Bruce and I worked together for many years on focusing and becoming relaxed to the point that he could shoot between heartbeats, perfecting shots through imagery, following a specific pre-shot routine that worked consistently, and drawing on every experience as an opportunity to learn something of value about himself and his best performance focus. When he was at the top of his game, his life was instantly turned around by a career-threatening setback. Bruce shares his resilient personal journey through a challenging unexpected event that resulted in a severe injury.

I had arrived home after a training session and had sat down to have some lunch when I heard screaming in the backyard. Our cat was being attacked by a vicious pit bull terrier. As I went to the patio door to see what was happening, my wife opened the door and ran inside, closing the screen door behind her. Suddenly the dog came crashing through the screen and into our house. The dog charged at my wife, who was holding our cat. I jumped between them and pushed the dog to the floor. The dog broke free and came at us again. This time I grabbed the dog and threw it toward the door, where I thought I could get it out of the house. The dog jumped up and charged again, attacking another one of our cats. It had our cat clenched in its jaws and ran out the backdoor. I ran through the door and tackled the dog on the lawn, at which point it turned and attacked me. I can still remember feeling the pain of the pit bull's teeth biting through my hand and its crushing grip. This was followed by a flurry of punching, biting, and wrestling to keep the 80-pound (36-kilogram) pit bull off me and my vital organs.

I yelled at one of my neighbors who was watching to call 911. She just stood there, and I yelled, "Go call now!" That five minutes of unexpected terror on the lawn seemed like an eternity. Everything seemed to move in slow motion, yet it was happening too fast to recall. When it was over, our cat was dead, and both the dog and I were bleeding from everywhere. The pit bull did not stop his relentless attack until my wife ran out of our house with a kitchen knife and stabbed him.

The last thing I remember was handing our lifeless cat to my wife and saying, "Get him to the vet." The next thing I knew I was lying in the yard with the paramedics working on me to stop the bleeding and one of them telling me that I was badly hurt. One hundred and eight stitches and three days in the hospital later, my shooting career was over and my life had turned 180 degrees. The deep bites and gashes in my hands, arms, chest, and legs had been heavily bandaged, and I had no use of my hands. I had a great deal of tendon damage in both arms, and for a national archery team champion, that spelled *finished*.

I spent two weeks in a daze and had not even thought about shooting until a good friend of mine asked, "How's this going to affect your shooting?" Wham, what a reality check. The trauma of the event and the ongoing barrage of reporters calling the house had me so focused on the event that I never really thought about the consequences of what had happened. I guess I had assumed that I would always be able to do what I love to do—shoot my bow.

After a week of depression, I literally thought, *If Terry were here he would kick my butt right now.* I made a decision that day that no matter how long it took, I was going to regain the use of my hands.

The first thing I did was to set small achievable goals for myself. The next thing I did was to keep track of them. It was not going to help me to set goals if I did not keep track of them. The physiotherapist said that it would probably take 12 to 18 months to regain full use of my hands, maybe longer. t was then mid-August, and I wanted to make it to indoor provincials and nationals in March.

As I began to shoot again, I actually set a goal to not kill anyone when I went to the shooting range for the first time. I achieved that goal! The entire first month was the most frustrating of all. My hands and arms were healing and the pain was considerable. Before the attack, I used a handheld release to shoot the bow, but that was not possible now. One of my sponsors sent me a release mechanism that I could strap to my arm to release the arrow. I modified it to meet my own needs, and it worked very well. I asked another sponsor to send me a lighter version of equipment and in a short time I was shooting again.

I continued to set and work on achieving my short-term goal. If I was not achieving my short-term goals, I was not trying hard enough. The biggest thing that spurred me on was that a number of my competitors had written me off. They even joked about not having to worry about me anymore. Talk about incentive! After seven months of diligent rehab and training, I shot and won the provincial indoor championships and placed second by 1 point in the national championships. I refused to let the dog attack stop me from doing what I loved.

Now, four years later, I am again using my hands to shoot. Sometimes there is pain, but I think of how far I have come in four years. I think of the four provincial titles, four national titles, and the two Athlete of the Year awards I have won since that dog attack. It shows me that something good can come out of everything. It shows me that what Terry taught me is true—that anything is possible if your mind and your heart are in the right place. In all the time that I was working to get back to top form, I never lost sight of what I saw myself as, and I am now that. I just keep achieving and resetting every day. I am happy in my sport and my life.

Making a Transition

At some points in your life, when things are going well, you might feel a bit like a hero. At other points, when things aren't going well, you may feel more like a zero. This shift in feelings may occur from one second to the next, from one day to the next, or from one week to the next, but the shift is usually most pronounced during major challenges, unexpected setbacks, transitions, or times of uncertainty.

A medalist at the Olympic Games had been convinced that excelling in her sport was the only important thing in her life. Her coach told her that all those people out there (outside the training regimen) "weren't doing anything important." As she said, "Then I stopped competing and became one of them." It took her a long time to regain a positive perspective and confidence in herself as a person.

If you believe that you are important only because of your performance in one area of your life, what remains when you are no longer performing as well or not performing at all in that domain? An all-consuming marriage to sport, work, or a single performance domain to the exclusion of everything leads to imbalance. The breakup of this kind of marriage may be difficult, especially if you leave thinking that you're finished, that you're no longer good enough to be there, and that without the activity you're nothing.

Growing apart from your sport or performance domain doesn't have to produce negative feelings, but it often does. All dedicated performers have a commitment to fulfill a dream of excellence. Preparation, training, and performance regimens become the major focus in life for most high-performance athletes and high-level performers in other domains, particularly during the years of greatest passion and improvement. But distinguishing between "the most important thing" and "the only thing" is important. Both allow you to pursue excellence, but only one allows you to do so without abandoning the rest of your life.

You can pursue high levels of excellence while still embracing simple joys in other parts of your life by choosing to maintain a sense of balance, joyfulness, and harmony in different parts of your life. Joy and balance come from finding passion, beauty, and meaning in the different loves of your life and embracing those loves or simple joys every day or at every opportunity. Ongoing joy and balance become positive realities when you make the best of the time you have and connect fully and joyfully with simple positive experiences. To sustain or restore a feeling of balance in your life, choose to respect the different loves of your life, embrace the simple joys in every pursuit, free yourself to be more playful and more fully connected, enjoy the magic moments in every day and every context, embrace simple positive connections with others, schedule special times for yourself to just relax and embrace moments of silence, and know that you are and will always continue to be worthy, valued, and loved by the special people in your life regardless of what you do or do not do in your performance domain.

One of your first challenges in attaining balanced excellence is to establish priorities for each day, week, month, year, or phase of your life. Then you must focus fully on the priority in which you are engaged, while you are engaged in doing it. Shifting your focus completely from one priority or experience to the next as you move through your day, week, or life is a great asset in all transitions. Each pursuit, opportunity, or adventure that you choose to fully embrace or make a priority in your life can become one of the wonderful adventures from which you will continue to learn, grow, and blossom.

Transitioning Out of High-Performance Sport and Other Performance Pursuits

Virtually all high-performance athletes and high-level performers in other pursuits are destined to experience declines in physical performance and profile in their chosen sport or performance pursuit over time. A certain level of uncertainty usually accompanies a transition out of high-performance sport, which may result in stress, fear, or at least some concern about what lies ahead. The same occurs with other transitions—leaving high school, college, or university and hoping to move into the workplace or moving out of an established home, workplace, or relationship. Ultimately, the challenge is to embrace the many new opportunities, possibilities for personal growth, and unexpected new adventures that transitions can provide.

Dramatic changes can occur for high-performance athletes and other high-level performers in transition. They lose the predictable structure of the day, the clarity of daily goals, the clear direction in which they are headed in both the short term and the long term, and everyday contact with teammates, workmates, and friends, some of whom are like family members. Many athletes initially feel lost upon retirement from high-performance sport and even not-so-high-performance sport. In sport you know the daily, weekly, monthly, and yearly routine. The pattern is predictable and doesn't change much. When you step out of that environment, you have no set routine. No one tells you what to do, when to do it, and how to do it. Nobody plans your day, your workout, your performance schedule, your travel, your hotel, your meals, your life. You have to begin to plan your own day and your own path. This new circumstance offers many advantages when you begin to see it as an opportunity, embrace each day, and open yourself to the unlimited future possibilities of your life.

The initial time of uncertainty between leaving an established routine and creating a new one that has meaning for you is the first challenging part of transition. Finding something to pursue with passion, an activity in which you can find a sense of meaning or make a positive difference, is often the most difficult ongoing challenge of transition. You could choose to pursue a number of things that could be life enhancing for you, for your loved ones, and for others. All noble or uplifting paths are worthy in some way, but choosing your path, a path with heart, is not always easy.

One of the great advantages that you have in transition is being able to apply what you learned and used to excel in your sport (or other chosen performance domain) to the new choices you make and the new directions you take. When one set of physical, mental, or technical skills diminishes, you are not less of a person. You simply channel some of your positive focusing strengths, which can always remain with you, into other meaningful pursuits. What you have learned from your journey thus far in life can help you immensely to contribute and grow for the rest of your life. The ultimate challenge in your life is to continue to live, learn, and grow in positive and life-enhancing ways by drawing on your most positive and best fully connected focus. The focusing skills you learned through your sport or other performance domain will help you excel in other pursuits and find ongoing meaning, balance, and joy in your life. At times this goal may seem elusive, but through time, focus, and persistence, you can make it your new and positive reality.

For some athletes the retirement experience is difficult. Others have a relatively easy transition. One athlete said, "I thought it was easy. I had other hobbies, a career, and a personal life that could easily be expanded and improved." People who have relatively fluid transition experiences seem to have one or more of the following things going for them:

✦ They have been respecting other parts of their life during their competitive years.

✦ They have meaningful options to consider pursuing upon retirement.

✦ They have the complete support of at least one important person upon retirement (a parent, coach, teacher, mentor, brother, sister, close friend, boyfriend, girlfriend, wife, husband, relative, or loved one).

Following are some suggestions from athletes who have been through transitions. Before making the decision to retire, they suggest that you take the following steps:

✦ Find a coach who respects you as a whole person rather than just as a performer. A more personal coaching approach can help you leave your sport feeling more worthwhile after many years of dedicated training.

✦ View your personal development through education, work, family, or friends as an integral part of your overall training program.

✦ Take time to relax and enjoy something outside your sport or performance domain.

✦ Think about what you want from your sport or performance domain and from your life. Get to know yourself well enough to "**do**cide" to do what is best for you.

✦ Change your routine in the off-season. Go to school, take some courses, spend some time in nature, or do something else that you might really enjoy.

✦ Make time for meaningful experiences other than training and performing. Schedule other activities into your overall program (for example, time for you, time with others, time for simple joys, time for seeing something other than competition and training venues, time for educational activities).

- ✦ Focus some of your energy on new areas of interest while still actively competing so that if something interests you, the option is there for continuation or expansion after retirement.

- ✦ Think of transitions as opportunities to enter a new phase of your life, to learn something new, to grow, to develop, to contribute in other areas, and to embrace your life more fully.

The same retired athletes I spoke with suggested taking the following steps after making the retirement decision:

- ✦ Let your family and friends know that you would appreciate having their support. Let them know if there are specific ways they can help you.

- ✦ Consider exploring interesting pursuits, training, adventures, or opportunities in areas in which you already have strengths or an interest.

- ✦ Stay actively involved in sports, fitness, exercise, and other outdoor activities for the sheer joy of participating in them and for health-related benefits. Consider participating in self-paced activities or getting involved in veterans' events. Adjust your goals accordingly.

- ✦ If possible, arrange to share experiences with others who are going through a similar transition. Exchange thoughts and feelings about your experiences, progress, setbacks, and adaptation to a different lifestyle.

- ✦ If the transition situation is getting you down, you might want to discuss your concerns with someone close to you or see a counselor for personal, educational, career, business, or leisure planning. Counselors are available on virtually all university campuses and in most towns and cities.

Finding a New Path

My transition out of competitive sport began with coaching and going back to school. At that time I began doing my master's degree in counseling at the College of William and Mary in Williamsburg, Virginia, and was coaching the university gymnastics team and diving team at the same time to pay for my education. I was also still working out with the gymnastics team and doing an occasional performance. I distinctly remember an incident that made me reflect hard on the issue of transition. A group of gymnasts, acrobats, and circus performers from Europe who were on tour in the United States asked me if I would be willing to perform with them when they were in Williamsburg. I said that I would be happy to do it.

On the day after the performance, I had a meeting with my master's degree supervisor. When I walked into his office, he stood up, shook my hand, and congratulated me. He had been at the performance the previous night and said that he was amazed at what he saw me do. The only other place he had ever seen me was sitting in a classroom or in his office. He went on to say, "If you could ever be as good at counseling people or helping people in this field as you are as a gymnastics performer, that would be truly incredible." I was about 24 years old at the time and never envisioned myself being that good at anything else—probably because I never put that much time or focus into anything else.

After I finished two graduate degrees—one in counseling and another in applied sport and performance psychology—I directed my path to something I thought I would love to do. I wanted to help athletes and other performers become the best they could possibly be in their chosen sport or performance pursuit. I also wanted to help children and youth learn positive and life-enhancing focusing and refocusing skills. That is what I have been fully engaged in doing since that time. The good news is that I still love what I am doing every day, and I am much better at what I do right now than I ever was as an athlete. So if you remain open to opportunities and positive possibilities, you can be at least as good as you were as an athlete or performer and probably better. Choose to find, explore, or do something you really want to do and focus on making your new dreams your positive new reality.

Draw on the positive lessons from your previous experiences in your sport or performance domain and get on with developing other competencies and embracing the rest of your life. Open your own doors. Recognize that as one phase of your life is ending, another phase is just beginning. Consider directing some of your hard-earned knowledge to the benefit of others—for example, by helping, teaching, or coaching others; by nurturing a group of children, youth, or developing performers in positive ways; by giving clinics or workshops; or by writing about your experiences. There are many ways in which you can make a meaningful contribution to others and make a real difference in people's lives. Your profile and experience as an athlete or performer can give you an advantage in opening doors to initiate positive and meaningful contributions to others. My *Positive Living Skills* book (Orlick, 2008) has lots of practical material that you could easily implement to help children and youth enhance their learning, performance, and lives.

Think about the skills you have already developed and the areas you might like to pursue. Then choose to do whatever it takes to move in that positive direction. Your knowledge, your potential to contribute to others, and your understanding of yourself and the needs of others will continue to grow throughout your life, long after your physical or technical performance skills begin to decline. It is never too late to begin something new, to enter a new line of work, to contribute in a different domain, to accomplish new goals, or to do something for the sheer joy of the experience. An 82-year-old woman received her undergraduate degree from the University of Ottawa where I teach. For a variety of reasons she was not able to act on this dream earlier in her life, and when she finally walked across the stage with diploma in hand, she was beaming and crying at the same time. Lesson learned—it is never too late for a new beginning!

Don't let anything get in the way of your personal growth, your positive passions, and the enjoyment of your journey. Remember that you don't have to be highly proficient at everything you do or at all times to contribute to others in meaningful ways or enjoy what you are doing. If you are not exceptionally proficient at some activities, your friends, family members, or colleagues might even like you more. You are human just as they are. You aren't great in everything—yet! But you could be, right?

Hans Selye (1978) wrote the following words in the introduction to his book *The Stress of Life*: "Most of our tensions and frustrations stem from compulsive needs to act the role of someone we are not. . . . 'Resolve to be thyself; and know that he who finds himself, loses his misery'" (p. 1).

Living the Transition

I know from experience that transitions can be challenging for some people. Even those who have had a positive sport or performance experience, are well balanced, and are positive human beings can struggle with transition. The following dialogue highlights the frustration a highly successful athlete can experience in the process of finding a new and meaningful direction. University athletes, national team athletes, and professional athletes who have competed in sport for most of their lives and are living through transition have expressed similar feelings.

> **Athlete:** I am finding it hard to express adequately what is going on at any given moment these days. I decided to put off trying to describe it until I think things have stabilized and I can say, "I feel this . . . or I feel that." The clarity—for better or worse—doesn't seem to be coming though.
>
> **Terry:** Sometimes it is difficult to have clarity within transition because things are not yet clear or stable. You are still in the process of surfacing and deciding on what direction you might want to go with your life. The wind may blow in many different directions before you set a firm course that takes you to a place you really want to go.
>
> **Athlete:** In a nutshell, I'm having a bit of a tough go these days—and have been for quite some time now. The weight of the stress that I feel sometimes in trying to move down a different path or find a new direction, without actually knowing what that is, or even what it might be, could be, or may be, is crushing at times. It is a complex challenge to know and be fully aware that "inner peace" and confidence and happiness and contentment with life have to come from within, and are completely within my control, and yet sometimes I have the sensation that those states are totally out of my reach. I don't really know how else to describe this state of being right now.
>
> **Terry:** Part of the challenge and journey through transition that will ease the crushing sensation of not knowing what your new path is or will be is to slow down, don't rush it. Don't feel obliged to find that new path or accomplish all things right now. Your new path or direction will emerge as you lighten up on the need to know or do it right now. Just enjoy the simple

things outside, inside, alone, and with others and free yourself to do some of the simplest things you love to do. Some good feelings are within reach right now, because you can live them each day. Other meaningful possibilities are not yet within your vision or reach, but they will be. If you try to force them to surface or put pressure on yourself to reach unclear goals right away, that may make them more elusive.

Try easier. Slow down. Breathe. Relax. Be where you are for a little while. There is no rush to the finish line. There is no urgency to know or reach those unknown goals immediately. Do the simple things that lift you every day and trust that the bigger directions will surface. They will come to you when you feel ready. Remain open to possibilities and seize them when they feel right. Let go of feeling obliged to grasp for them or accomplish them today.

Athlete: There are, of course, many great things in my life still and so many things to be thankful for that I also feel quite stupid at times for being down and feeling like I'm not living life to the fullest. How can I be so young, healthy, and accomplished and feel so inadequate and useless?

Terry: We all go through times like this, and it is fine. It is part of living through uncertainty and ongoing transitions of life. It is part of personal growth and self-discovery—growing through the feelings. Sometimes feeling down or feeling that we are not living our lives to the fullest provides the inspiration and insights that eventually guide our future decisions that lead us to better and more positive realities. You are probably feeling the way you are feeling right now because you don't feel you are where you want to be—yet! Remember the *yet*! Finding what you want and doing what you want are just being delayed at this moment. What you want will come if you remain open to positive possibilities.

Athlete: I hope it doesn't sound as if I'm not functioning right now. In fact, I am. I have been doing quite well with the public speaking engagements, and I've taken on a couple of other things that I am really looking forward to doing (some of which we have already discussed). So, I haven't quite retreated to a place of utter despair . . . and I definitely know that staying active physically has a direct impact on my mood and outlook, which was an important discovery.

Terry: This will be true for your whole life, so no matter what else happens, hang on to your physical activity and continue to embrace your special time with nature.

Athlete: I just find that it is harder to stay out of the funk than in it and that this transitory postretirement period has taken much longer than I expected. It is not the training, competing, travel, or even the team that has left a hole so much as knowing there was a purpose to getting up in the morning and that at the end of the day, another step forward (however small or large) had been taken. I had a job and focus and direction and everything came after that. Now, I feel productive if I leave the house and get a couple of trivial things done on the same day—not quite what I had in mind for my life you know. . . . I mean, there were days when I was competing that I couldn't wait to be done and be released from that lifestyle so that I could get on with things and start up one of the thousand ideas or projects that I had in mind.

Terry: The bottom line probably lies in finding something you feel is worthy of your efforts. What were some of those ideas or projects that you had in mind when you were competing? If you can pick one or two of the most interesting things that you might like to do and explore the possibility of pursuing them, then maybe your days will feel more complete or more meaningful. Remember, it is also sometimes nice not to *have to* do anything. Just *choose to* go for a run, spend some time in nature, play, and do one or two things that make you feel good, productive, helpful, or useful in some way. Do happy things with the people you love. And write down any positive activity, idea, or project that you could choose to do that could take on a positive meaning in its own right.

If you are experiencing some of the feelings this athlete spoke about, remember that having those feelings is OK, and you will be OK even if you are feeling some of those things. You are experiencing what many others have experienced. Somehow, they drew on their strengths and found a way through the fog to greater clarity in their lives. Sometimes you have to accept that it takes time to find another meaningful path or absorbing focus. There is no need to make everything happen immediately! Positive new directions often take time to emerge or reveal themselves. An unhurried approach is often the way of meaningful transitions and finding worthy new positive directions in life. Clarity, direction, and focus often come when you stop trying to force things and instead allow possibilities to unfold and grow in their own way naturally. Every path you embark on leads to other paths and opportunities. The process is all about taking little steps—some of those little steps will lead you to clearer insights, better possibilities, and positive new realities.

Each project you embrace that gives you joy or a sense of meaning or purpose will help you move forward. Ultimately, the best place to be is finding a sense of meaningful contribution and feeling a sense of balance in your life. Give what you can give and feel good about it. Continue to embrace the simple joys along your path. This is the best place to be.

You have a great opportunity in front of you to become a better, less stressed, and more balanced person by applying some of the mental skills you have learned and perfected and living some of the strategies presented in this book. You can draw on the focus and positive perspectives you used to excel in your sport or performance domain to become a better performer in anything you choose to pursue. You can use the same skills to become a better person, to embrace each experience, and to continue to live the simple joys every day in your life.

I wish you the best in this transition and the many other transitions that will follow over the course of your life. I know you have the capacity to negotiate this transition successfully and to continue to become a stronger, wiser, and more joyful person. Embrace the steps of your transition and try to find something positive in the uncertainty. Make the best of it. See the transition as a new opportunity, a worthy challenge, a new venue for knowing yourself better, and a wonderful opportunity for ongoing personal growth.

The End and the Beginning of a New and Better Path

Recently I reconnected with Elizabeth Manley, a former Olympic silver medalist in figure skating and current motivational speaker. I worked with Elizabeth many years ago in preparation for the 1988 Winter Olympic Games in Calgary, Alberta, Canada. I asked her if she would reflect back on her memories of what we did together when I was trying to help her perform her best in Calgary. She sent me the following e-mail in October 2014.

Sharing My Journey to Excellence
Elizabeth Manley

I spent many years of my early skating career trying so hard to win and please everyone. As a young teenager, I felt like I was taking the responsibilities of the whole world on my shoulders. I carried the pressures of feeling that I had to compete well and bring home the medals so I wouldn't disappoint people. I carried the guilt of seeing my mom give up so much of her life to keep me in a sport I loved so much. I was consumed with winning and started to lose my passion that brought me into skating in the first place.

A year before my attempt to go to my very first Olympics in Sarajevo in 1984, my body gave out emotionally and physically. I was diagnosed with depression and was having a breakdown. My dreams at that moment felt like they had been ripped away from me, and I felt like there was no help. I lost all my hair and emotionally shut myself down and crawled into a dark place in my heart and my mind.

Then along came Dr. Terry Orlick. Terry wanted to help me understand the thoughts inside me and to help bring out the best person in me, not just the athlete. One session led to five, then to 10, then to countless positive interactions.

He made me realize that I had a voice along with the muscles and that my voice should be heard. He made me realize that holding in feelings and concerns as well as fears didn't make me a weak athlete but an athlete who can learn to deal with these situations in positive ways and explore how they can affect my performance level.

Opening up for many hours with Terry taught me how to become confident and to sustain the passion to not just be a winner on a podium but also to be a person with strength and desire to go after the dreams and goals that I had pursued for so many years—to really go after them.

Four years prior to the 1988 Calgary Olympics, I was at the lowest point of my life and my career. Four years later I was standing on the podium receiving the silver medal at the 1988 Calgary Olympic Games.

I always knew, and my coaches knew, that I had the ability to be the best in the world as far as technique and skating ability, *but* the real competition for me was emotional and mental. I've always said, "If you're at the Olympics you're good enough to be there; the real competition comes down to who can hold it together mentally."

This is what Terry Orlick taught me. He taught me that I was an individual and that I needed to focus on just *me*, not on the circumstances or the individuals around me that I had no control over. If I focused on me, I would perform to the best of my abilities, and if I focused on *me*, I would appreciate and love myself for the person I was and for what I could achieve.

Today, I still carry these lessons learned. I may not be competing in an Olympic competition, but I'm still embracing positive challenges in the different parts of my life and the different parts of my world. The bigger world has so many high expectations and responsibilities that it can make you lose yourself. Terry always taught me, for every 10 steps forward, take 2 steps back to breathe and remember there's a *you*. Continue to believe in yourself and focus on *you*.

Thank you, Terry Orlick, for saving me and for making me the passionate person I am today in everything I strive to do.

My goal in writing this fifth edition of *In Pursuit of Excellence* is to share with you what I have continued to learn from great athletes and performers since writing the fourth edition eight years ago. My goal is also to help you free yourself to believe in yourself, perform your best consistently, reach your potential, enjoy your journey, overcome obstacles, and live your dreams in and out of your performance context. Think about what you are taking out of this book that I have encouraged you to do. Reflect on what touched you in a meaningful way. Continue to act on whatever you feel might benefit you or free you to be the person and performer you have the potential to be. Act on your positive intentions because only action counts in the real-world performance arena. This is what will give you your best chance of living your dreams and embracing your journey.

Your ongoing challenge in sport and life is to *free yourself* to continue to believe in yourself, perform your best, pursue your potential, enjoy your journey, overcome obstacles, act on lessons learned, and live your dreams. What can you suggest, share, or act on that will free you to be the person and performer you have the potential to be?

Remember that what frees you to excel in your sport or performance domain also frees you to excel in the rest of your life. As long as you maintain a positive and fully connected focus in the different parts of your life, you will continue to free yourself to embrace your life fully and live your dreams.

Choose to find and embrace the simple joys and ongoing challenges of your personal journey to excellence today and every day!

APPENDIX

Planning Forms for Positive Performance Enhancement

In Pursuit of Excellence: Initial Questions

1. What competitions, games, races, or performances do you expect to compete in this year?

2. What are some of your best-ever performances or experiences in your sport or performance domain?

3. What are your goals for this year in your sport or performance domain?

4. What is your ultimate goal or dream goal in your sport or performance domain?

5. What is a realistic goal for you to achieve this year in your sport or performance domain?

6. What are the main challenges you are facing right now?

7. What do you think are the main challenges you will face when you are actually out there competing or performing in your sport or performance arena this year?

From T. Orlick, 2015, *In pursuit of excellence*, 5th ed. (Champaign, IL: Human Kinetics).

In Pursuit of Excellence: Performance Questions

1. Describe one of your best-ever performances in your sport or performance domain.

2. Where was your focus going into this competition, performance, game, event, or race (before you actually started performing)?

3. What were you focused on when you were performing your best in this competition, performance, game, event, or race?

4. What do you think will allow you or free you to perform your best when you are out there competing this year?

5. What specific areas do you want to target for improvement this year (mentally, physically, or technically)?

From T. Orlick, 2015, *In pursuit of excellence*, 5th ed. (Champaign IL: Human Kinetics).

In Pursuit of Excellence: Performance Focus Plans

Quality focus leads to quality performance. A positive focus before you perform and a totally connected focus within your performance are the keys to consistent, high-level performance. What do you want to focus on-site just before you perform this year? What do you want to focus on during your performance?

Preperformance Focus Plan

In the following space, outline your preferred on-site preperformance focus plan. What do you want to do, think about, and focus on *before you perform* to prepare yourself for your best possible performance?

Performance Focus Plan

In the following space, outline your preferred on-site performance focus plan. What do you want to focus on *during your performance* to bring out your best possible performance?

From T. Orlick, 2015, *In pursuit of excellence*, 5th ed. (Champaign, IL: Human Kinetics).

In Pursuit of Excellence: Focus Plans for Quality Practice

Quality focus in practice or training leads to quality performance in competitions. A positive and fully connected focus going into each practice or training session is the key to consistent, high-level performance. "**Do**cide" to practice or train with a specific purpose in mind and a high-quality focus to achieve your goals. Every day, ask yourself. *What am I going to do today to move one step closer to my goals?* Before each practice or training session, fully commit yourself to being positive and fully focused so you can continue to get the best out of yourself every day.

In the following space, write down your goals for your next practice or training session. What do you want to accomplish, refine, or improve during your next practice or training session? What are you going to focus on to make that happen?

From T. Orlick, 2015, *In pursuit of excellence*, 5th ed. (Champaign, IL: Human Kinetics).

In Pursuit of Excellence: Focus Plans for Quality Performance

Preperformance Focus Plan

In the following box, outline your preferred preperformance focus plan. What are you going to do before this performance or event begins to get yourself into a positive and fully focused state of mind? What are you going to focus on to get yourself in the most positive and fully connected state of mind so you will have your best possible performance?

Performance Focus Plan

In the following box, outline your preferred on-site focus plan. What are you going to focus on during this performance to make it a great or best possible performance?

From T. Orlick, 2015, *In pursuit of excellence*, 5th ed. (Champaign, IL: Human Kinetics).

In Pursuit of Excellence: Practice Evaluation

Every practice or training session is an opportunity to learn something, refine something, or get better at something. When you draw the positive lessons out of each of your practices or training sessions and act on them, you will continue to learn, grow, and improve both as a performer and as a person.

What were some good things you did in this practice or training session today? What went well?

What were you focused on when things were going well or when you were performing your best?

What could you have done better in this practice or training session? What do you need to focus on to make your skills and your overall performance even better or more consistent?

What lessons can you take from this practice or training session that will help you perform at a higher level more consistently? How will you make sure that you act on these lessons earned in your next practice, training session, or performance?

From T. Orlick, 2015, *In pursuit of excellence*, 5th ed. (Champaign, IL: Human Kinetics).

In Pursuit of Excellence: Performance Evaluation

Every performance is a learning opportunity. When you draw the positive focusing lessons out of each of your performances and act on them, you continue to learn and grow as an athlete, a performer, and a person.

What were some good things you did in this performance? What went well?

Where was your focus when things were going well or when you were performing your best?

What could you have done better in this performance? What needs work or refinement to make your performances even better, more fully connected, or consistently closer to your true potential?

What are the positive focusing lessons you can take from this performance that can help you perform at a higher level more consistently? How will you make sure that you act on these focusing lessons in your next practice or performance?

From T. Orlick, 2015, *In pursuit of excellence*, 5th ed. (Champaign, IL: Human Kinetics).

In Pursuit of Excellence: Build a Confident Focus

You will continue to improve the quality and consistency of your performance if you prepare well, focus in positive ways, believe in your capacity, and focus fully on doing what helps you perform your best consistently. You can become a more confident and focused performer by continuing to look for positive *reasons to believe in yourself.*

Write down your reasons to believe in yourself by answering the following questions. Then read through your list of *why you can* and *how you will* achieve your goals before your practices, training sessions, games and performances. Keep looking for good reasons to believe.

Why I Can Achieve My Goals

In the following space, list anything *positive* you have done, accomplished, experienced, improved on, learned, prepared for, or heard someone say about you that supports your capacity to perform at a very high level in this race, game, performance, event, or competition. Write down your good reasons to believe you can achieve your goals.

This Is Why I Can Achieve My Goals

(continued)

From T. Orlick, 2015, *In pursuit of excellence*, 5th ed. (Champaign, IL: Human Kinetics).

This is How I Will Achieve My Goals

In the following space, write down what you will focus on to have your best possible performance and achieve your goals.

This is what I will focus on during this race, game, or performance to give myself my best chance of having my absolute best race, game, or performance.

In the following space, write down what you will focus on to move forward through potential distractions or challenging times during your race, game, or performance to free yourself to have a great performance and achieve your goals.

This is what I will focus on during this game, race or performance to move forward through potential distractions or tough times to achieve my ultimate goals in this race, game, mission, or performance.

From T. Orlick, 2015, *In pursuit of excellence*, 5th ed. (Champaign, IL: Human Kinetics).

BIBLIOGRAPHY

Armstrong, L. 1998. *It's not about the bike*. New York: Broadway Books.

Arntz, W., B. Chasse, and M. Vicente. 2005. *What the bleep do we know?* Deerfield Beach, FL: Health Communications. www.whatthebleep.com.

Botterill, C., and T. Patrick. 2003. *Perspective: The key to life*. Winnipeg, MB: Lifeskills (available from mcnallyrobinson.com).

Buscaglia, L. 1996. *Love*. Greenwich, CT: Fawcett.

Castaneda, C. 1985. *The teachings of Don Juan: A Yaqui way of knowledge*. New York: Simon & Schuster.

Coelho, P. 1993. *The alchemist*. New York: HarperCollins.

Colgrove, M., H. Bloomfield, and P. McWilliams. 1993. *How to survive the loss of a love*. New York: Bantam.

Ellis, A., and R. A. Harper. 1976. *A new guide to rational living*. North Hollywood, CA: Wilshire.

Frankl, V. E. 1998. *Man's search for meaning*. New York: Simon & Schuster.

Genge, R. 1976. Concentration. *Coaching Association of Canada Bulletin, 12*, 1–8.

Halliwell, W., T. Orlick, K. Ravizza, and B. Botella. 1999, 2003. *Consultant's guide to excellence: For sport and performance enhancement*. www.zoneofexcellence.ca.

Hamill, S. 2005. *Tao Te Ching–Lao Tzu*. Boston: Shambhala.

Hohmann, M., and T. Orlick. 2014. Examining the psychological skills used by elite Canadian military pilots. *Journal of Excellence, 16*, 4–19. www.zoneofexcellence.ca.

Li-Wei, A., M. Qi-Wei, T. Orlick, and L. Zitzelsberger. 1992. The effect of mental imagery training on performance enhancement with 7- to 10-year-old children. *The Sport Psychologist, 6*, 230–241

Mitchelle, S. 1988. *Tao Te Ching–Lao Tzu*. New York: HarperCollins.

Orlick, T. 1986. *Coaches guide to psyching for sport: Mental training for athletes*. Champaign, IL: Human Kinetics.

Orlick, T. 1986. *Psyching for sport: Mental training for athletes*. Champaign, IL: Human Kinetics.

Orlick, T. 1995. *Nice on my feelings: Nurturing the best in children and parents*. Carp, ON: Creative Bound.

Orlick, T. 1998. *Embracing your potential: Steps to self-discovery, balance, and success in sports, work, and life*. Champaign, IL: Human Kinetics.

Orlick. T. 2004. *Feeling great: Teaching children to excel at living*. Carp, ON: Creative Bound.

Orlick, T. 2006. *Cooperative games and sports Joyful activities for everyone*. Champaign, IL: Human Kinetics.

Orlick, T. 2008. *Positive living skills: For children and teens*. Carp, ON: Creative Bound.

Orlick, T. 2008. *Teaching children positive living skills: Teachers and parents guide*. www.zoneofexcellence.ca.

Orlick, T. 2011. *Positive living skills: Joy and focus for everyone*. Renfrew, ON: General Store.

Orlick, T., and J. Partington. 1986. *Psyched: Inner views of winning*. www.zoneofexcellence.ca.

Orlick, T., and J. Partington. 1988. Mental links to excellence. *The Sport Psychologist, 2*, 105–130. www.zoneofexcellence.ca.

Pirsig, R. M. 1984. *Zen and the art of motorcycle maintenance*. New York: Quill.

Ravizza, K., and T. Hanson. 1995. *Heads-up baseball: Playing the game one pitch at a time*. Redondo Beach, CA: Kinesis.

Rotella, B., with B. Cullen. 1995. *Golf is not a game of perfect*. New York: Simon & Schuster.

Russell, B., and T. Branch. 1979. *Second wind*. New York: Ballantine.

Selye, H. 1978. *The stress of life*. New York: McGraw-Hill.

Suzuki, D. T. 1993. *Zen and Japanese culture*. New York: Pantheon.

Suzuki, D. T. 1999. Introduction to *Zen in the art of archery*, by E. Herrigel. New York: Vintage.

ADDITIONAL RESOURCES

CDs by Terry Orlick

All available from www.zoneofexcellence.ca.

CDs for Athletes and Performers (all Zone of Excellence CDs are also available on iTunes)

CD 1 Zone of Excellence—*Relaxation and Stress Control Activities*

CD 2 Zone of Excellence—*Exercises for Strengthening Focus and Performance*

CD 3 Zone of Excellence—*Focusing for Excellence: Practicing in the Zone*

CD 4 Zone of Excellence—*Focusing for Excellence: Performing in the Zone*

CDs for Children (All Positive Living Skills for Children CDs are also available on iTunes)

CD 1 *Spaghetti Toes: Positive Living Skills for Children*

CD 2 *Changing Channels: Positive Living Skills for Children*

CDs for Teens and Adults

CD 3 *Focusing Through Distractions: Positive Living Skills for Tweens, Teens, and Adults*

CD 4 *Relaxation and Joyful Living: Positive Living Skills for Tweens, Teens, and Adults*

Books by Terry Orlick

Athletes in Transition, with Penny Werthner, 1987.

Coaches Training Manual to Psyching for Sport, 1986.

Consultant's Guide to Excellence in Sport and Performance, with Wayne Halliwell, Ken Ravizza, and Bob Rotella, 1999, 2003.

The Cooperative Sports and Games Book, 1978.

Cooperative Games and Sports, 2006.

Cooperative Games: Systematic Analysis and Cooperative Impact with Jane McNally and Tom O'Hara. In *Essential Readings in Sport Psychology*, 2006.

Embracing Your Potential: Steps to Self-Discovery, 1998.

Enhancing Children's Sport and Life Experiences. Chapter in *Children and Youth in Sport*, 2002.

Every Kid Can Win, with Cal Botterill, 1975.

Feeling Great: Teaching Children to Excel at Living, 1998, 2001, 2004.

In Pursuit of Excellence, 1980, 1990, 2000, 2008, 2016.

In Pursuit of Excellence, audio book, 1997.

Mental Training for Coaches and Athletes, edited with John Partington and John Salmela, 1982.

New Beginnings: Transition From High Performance Sport, with Penny Werthner, 1992.

New Paths to Sport Learning, edited with John Salmela and John Partington, 1982.

Nice on My Feelings: Nurturing the Best in Children and Parents, 1995.

Positive Living Skills: Joy and Focus for Everyone, 2011.

Psyched: Inner Views of Winning, with John Partington, 1986.

Psyching for Sport: Mental Training for Athletes, 1986.

The Second Cooperative Sports and Games Book, 1982.

Sharing Views on the Process of Effective Sportpsych Consulting, with John Partington, 1988.

Sport in Perspective, edited with John Partington and John Salmela, 1982.

Teaching Children Positive Living Skills: Teachers and Parents Guide, 2008.

Winning Through Cooperation, 1978.

DVDs

Touching the Void. 2003. www.touchingthevoid.com. A powerful real-world example of how focusing on the little steps makes the impossible become possible.

What the Bleep Do We Know? Science and Spirituality. 2004. www.whatthebleep.com. A thought-provoking presentation on "reality" and the role your mind, mental imagery, and spirit can play in creating new or better realities.

Free Articles (Journal of Excellence)

Many articles relevant to performance excellence and quality living are available for free at www.zoneofexcellence.ca. Click on Free Articles or Journal of Excellence. The following articles are examples of what is available.

"An Analysis of a Children's Relaxation/Stress Control Skills Program in an Alternative Elementary School Setting." Shaunna Taylor and Terry Orlick.

"Coping With Cancer: Lessons From a Pediatric Cancer Patient and His Family." Julie Koudys and Terry Orlick.

"Enhancing the Lives of University Students." Laurence Abbott and Terry Orlick.

"Examining Psychological Skills Used by Elite Military Pilots." Maya Hohmann and Terry Orlick.

"Excellence in Space." Marc Garneau.

"Excellence Through Collaboration." John Partington.

"Excelling in the Olympic Context." Terry Orlick.

"Focusing for Excellence: Lessons From Elite Mountain Bike Racers." Danelle Kabush and Terry Orlick.

"Interview With Chris Hadfield, Canadian Astronaut." Chris Hadfield and Terry Orlick.

"Interview With Curt Tribble, Elite Surgeon." Curt Tribble and Terry Orlick.

"Lessons Learned: In Pursuit of Excellence." Kelly Doell.

"Making a Habit of Happiness." Serena Thatcher.

"Making the Impossible, Possible, Within a Relationship: An Interview With Lisa and Mike." Terry Orlick.

"Mental Strategies of Elite Mount Everest Climbers." Shaunna Burke and Terry Orlick.

"Mental Strategies Used by Professional Actors to Enhance Quality Performance." Tim Murphy and Terry Orlick.

"Nurturing Positive Living Skills for Children: Feeding the Heart and Soul of Humanity." Terry Orlick.

"Patients as Performers." Curt Tribble, Doug Newburg, and Jeff Rouse.

"'Perspective'—Can Make a Difference!" Cal Botterill and Tom Patrick.

"Positive Living Intervention for University Students." Paige Walton and Terry Orlick.

"Success Elements of Elite Performers in High Risk Sport: Big Mountain Free Skiers." John Coleman and Terry Orlick.

"Teaching Positive Living Skills to a Family With Special Needs." Melissa Klingenberg and Terry Orlick.

"Teaching Skills for Stress Control and Positive Thinking to Elementary School Children." Jenelle Gilbert and Terry Orlick.

"The Essence of Excellence: Mental Skills of Top Classical Musicians." Carole Talbot-Honeck and Terry Orlick.

"The Impact of a Positive Living Skills Training Program on Children With Attention-Deficit Hyperactivity Disorder." Kealey Hester and Terry Orlick.

"The Process of Perspective: The Art of Living Well in the World of Elite Sport." Matt Brown, Kathy Cairns, and Cal Botterill.

"The Quest for Gold: Applied Psychological Skills Training in the 1996 Olympic Games." Colleen Hacker.

"Thinking Sound: Reflections on the Application of Mental Training to Opera." Hans Gertz.

INDEX

Note: The italicized *f* following page numbers refers to figures.

A

action steps
    distraction control 101-102
    decide 226-228, 310
    focused connection 210-213
    on-site focus plan 243
    performance improvement 279-280
    persistence 228-232
    personal excellence 3-4
    positive self-direction 310
    purpose 232-234
    team spirit 295-296
adaptable/adaptability
    in focus 319
    positive 318-320
    positive opportunities 316-322
advantages
    personal 114
    of transitions 333, 339
adverse conditions, simulating 133-137
adversity, overcoming of 5, 335-337
Alleston, Kim 150
anger 263, 268
astronauts, simulation and 129-130

B

balance 44, 259-260, 313, 338. *See also*
        overload
barriers to excellence 48-50
Baumann, Alex 114-115
belief, in self 179-181, 305
Belmonte, Juan 149
Bernier, Sylvie
    commitment of 183
    communication with coach 286
    on distraction control 108
    on positive images 120
best focus
    developing and nurturing of 208-214
    respecting of 97-103, 189, 321
Bolt, Usain 151f

Botterill, Cal 294
Boucher, Gaetan 132
Bowman, Scotty 188
Buscaglia, Leo 311

C

Cain, Larry 86
Canadian ice hockey team 218f
Casey, Kellie 150
Castaneda, Carlos 312
challenges
    in balanced excellence 338
    description of 215
    focus and 217
    performance and 215-219
    preparation phases for 219-223
change 104, 324
Chinese simulation training 141-142
choices
    action part of 228
    balance 252
    Beckie Scott on 45
    focus 6-7
    life-enhancing 319
    overview of 5-6
    personal excellence 3-4, 38
    positive self-direction 308-310
Christian, Laura 256-258
Clarke, Bobby 187
coaches
    best 277-278
    communicating with 280-286
    constructive feedback from 276
    errors by 286-289
    excellence reminders for 283f-284f
    failure to listen 289
    feedback from 276, 288
    influence of 279-280
    personal preferences communicated
        to 285-286
    team spirit reminders for 302f

commitment(s)
  Beckie Scott on 44
  Chris McCormack on 190-199
  to dreams 183-184
  goals and 64, 174-176
  guidelines for 188-190
  Kerrin Lee-Gartner on 53
  ongoing, management of 258-259
  in personal excellence 185-188
  personal level of 34, 101, 186-188
  self-assessment of 64, 66f
  sources of 15
  Thomas Grandi on 91
  in wheel of excellence 12f, 15, 24-25, 32f, 238f
communication
  with coaches 280-286
  respectful 284
  for team spirit 295-296, 300
competition venues 125
composure
  commitment and 188
  enhancing of 238-239
  fear and 244-246
  on-site focus plan for 240-244, 242f
  problem avoidance and 239-240
  refocusing plans and 246-248
conceptualization 152
confidence
  Beckie Scott on 45
  building of 166-168
  coaching and 288
  enhancing of 238-239
  focus and 21, 357-358
  Kerrin Lee-Gartner on 55
  losses and 334
  methods of achieving 237-238
  in on-site performance phase 222
  positive perspective and 166-168
  Thomas Grandi on 91
  in wheel of excellence 12f, 20-21, 25-26, 32f, 238f
conflict resolution, for teams 299-304
consistency
  description of 261-262
  focus control for 266-271
  positive perspectives and 266
  setback recovery and 262-266

constructive feedback 276
control. *See also* distraction control; focus control
  docide to take control 218
  goal setting and 172
  in Olympic context 218
  positive perspective and 167
  potential and 10
coping skills 126
Crawford, Chandra 305
criticism 188
Curry, Stephen 245f

D
demands assessment 254-255
distraction control. *See also* refocus
  commitment to 189
  for focused connection 203-206
  in high-level performers 37, 39
  Kerrin Lee-Gartner on 56-57
  in Olympic context 217-219
  overview of 97-98
  plans for 103-107, 105f, 106, 246-248
  positive images for 125-126
  reminders and actions for 100-101
  in simulation training 133-137
  skills in 101
  in wheel of excellence 12f, 21-22, 26, 32f, 238f
distractions
  external 97
  internal 97
  letting go 102
  preparation for 287
  preparing for 217
  source of 98
Djokovic, Novak 19f
docide/dociding
  by Beckie Scott 226
  on control 91, 218
  examples of 226-227
  on focus 34
  on living fully and joyfully 324
  to move forward 320
  on performance 154
  self-direction and 310
  by Silken Laumann 109
  steps involved in 226-228
  by Thomas Grandi 226

docision 4, 104, 227, 238
dream goal 180
dreams
    description of 183-184
    living of 321
    positive 319
    pursuing of 322

E
emotions
    anger 263, 268
    in setbacks 262-266
errors
    by coaches 286-289
    correction of 268
excellence. *See* personal excellence

F
failure 188, 217
fear 78, 244-246
feedback
    clarification of 281
    constructive 276
    positive 288
feelings. *See also* emotions; positive
    images
    focus as 41, 53
    losses and 334
    in overload 251
    as performance reminder 92
feelization 18
finishing strong 196-197
flowing stream 164
focus. *See also* distraction control; refo-
    cus
    adaptable 319
    Beckie Scott on 39-46
    best 97-103, 189, 208-214
    challenges and 217
    as choice 6-7
    confidence and 21, 357-358
    description of 29
    in high-level performers 37-38
    intensity and 76-79
    Kerrin Lee-Gartner on 52-53
    for mental readiness 16
    on negatives 165, 272
    in Olympic context 218-219
    ongoing learning and 23

    in performance 31-36
    in personal excellence 38, 185-186
    personal focus plan 274
    plan for 240-244, 242*f*
    on positive 272
    positive performance imagery for
        sharpening of 118-119
    reminders in 93
    sharpening of 118-119
    strategies for 17-18, 230
    for team spirit 297
    Thomas Grandi on 89-90
    in wheel of excellence 11-13, 12*f*, 24,
        32*f*, 238*f*
focus control
    composure and 248
    for consistency 266-271
    self-assessment of 64, 65*f*
    tips for 230-231
focused connection
    developing 208-213
    distraction control and 203-206
    importance of 201-203
    performance and 206-208
    practicing 213-214
    reconnecting 211-213
focused intensity 78
focus enhancement consultants 279
focus plans
    on-site 240-244, 242*f*
    performance 352-354
    personal 274
    for quality performance 353-354
Fung, Lori 109, 121

G
Genge, R. 206
goals. *See also* mission to excellence
    accomplishing 75, 172-174
    adjusting 178-179
    for best focus 208-210
    Chris McCormack on 199
    commitment and 64, 174-176
    daily 172-174, 188
    focusing on positives as 165
    in high-performance contexts 75
    key 180
    long-term 172
    self-acceptance as 180

goals *(continued)*
    short-term versus long-term 176
    for team spirit 292, 295
    worksheet for 357-358
    writing down 176
Graham, Laurie 109-110
Grandi, Thomas 88-95, 226, 228, 305
Griffith-Joyner, Florence 86

H
Hadfield, Chris
    deciding by 227-228
    on focused connection 205
    on retaining purpose 233-234
    on simulation training 129-130
Heiden, Eric 131-132
Hernandez, Felix 81*f*
high-performance sports, transitioning
    from 339-341
high-stress contexts, performance in 36
Holloway, Sue 86

I
imagery. *See* positive images
imitation 137-138
immune system 259
improvement strategies 70-71
individual differences 299
Indonesian simulation training 138-141
initial questions 350
inspiration, within team 304-306
intensity
    amount of 166-167
    applying 87-95
    focused 78
    relaxation and 73-74
Izzo, Tom 278*f*

J
James, LeBron 37*f*
Jordan, Michael 334
joy 50-52, 338
joyfulness 324

K
Kershaw, Clayton 309*f*
Klawitter, Noella 325-327
Kreek, Adam 29-30

L
Lao-tzu 143, 147-148
Laumann, Silken 108-109
Lee-Gartner, Kerrin 52-60, 330-331
life-enhancing relationships 318
listening 289
Lopetrone, Theresa Jenn 323
losses, overcoming of 334-335

M
Malmberg, Bruce 335-337
Manley, Elizabeth 131, 346-347
Manning, Peyton 207*f*
McCormack, Chris 190-199
mental readiness
    focus needed for 16
    Kerrin Lee-Gartner on 53-54
    positive performance imagery benefits
        for 119
    in wheel of excellence 12*f*, 16-18, 25,
        32*f*, 238*f*
Messi, Lionel 116*f*
Messner, Pat 267-268
mission to excellence
    improvement strategies for 70-71
    self-assessment for 68-70
    steps in 67-68
mood control 272-274. *See also* emotions
Morgan, Alex 229*f*
Morris, Alwyn 181

N
Nadeau, Dan 7-10
National Hockey League 187
negative performance images 118-119
negatives
    dwelling on 5, 274, 288
    focus on 165, 272
    freeing yourself from 274
neuronets 113
neuroscience, positive images and 114

O
Olympic context
    failure in 217
    future challenges and 223-224
    preparation phases for 219-223
oneness 147

ongoing commitments 258-259
ongoing learning
  Beckie Scott on 41
  as choice 10
  Chris McCormack on 197
  from coaching errors 286
  commitment to 189
  focused connection and 202*f*
  Kerrin Lee-Gartner on 57-59
  performance-enhancing focus for 23
  refocus and 212
  Thomas Grandi on 89-91
  transitions and 333
  in wheel of excellence 12*f*, 23, 26, 32*f*, 238*f*
on-site familiarization phase 220-221
on-site focus plans 240-244, 242*f*
on-site performance phase 222, 279
opportunities, positive 316-322
Orser, Brian 121
overload. *See also* stress
  as coaching error 287
  coping with 250-253
  demands assessment 254-255
  description of 249-250
  ongoing commitments and 258-259
  positive time for balance in life 259-260
  preventing 253-260
  signs of 251
  stress management and 255-256
oversimulation 142
overtraining 287

P
pain, commitment and 195-196
Pak, Se Ri 134*f*
Parker, Candace 99*f*
passion. *See* purpose and passion
perfection 161
performance
  best 239-240
  challenges in 215-219
  evaluation of 356
  focused connection and 206-208
  focus in 31-36
  focus plans for 352-354
  in high-stress contexts 36

  mental aspect of 37
  positive images for 112
  preparation phases for contexts of 219-223
  questions about 351
  reminders for 92-93, 95, 154
  rest and 16
  team spirit and 293
  value as person versus 163, 181
performance debriefs 93-95. *See also* ongoing learning
performance imagery. *See* positive images
persistence 4, 228-232
personal advantages 114
personal commitment 34, 101
personal excellence
  as choice 4, 38
  Chris McCormack on 198
  as contest with self 52
  factors that affect 275
  nurturing 36-38
  prerequisites for 189-190
  qualities of 184-186
  quest for 47-48
  reminders for 283*f*-284*f*
  steps to 3
  wheel of excellence and 24-27
personal focus plan 274
personal growth 230-231, 343
personal meaning 51
perspectives. *See* positive perspectives; race perspective
physical activity 50
physiological changes
  in relaxation 82, 87
  as stress response 80
Pirsig, R.M. 311
planning forms 349-358
positive adaptability 318-320
positive images
  best types of 119-120
  for coping 126
  description of 111-113
  developing skills in 123-125
  for focus control 267
  Kerrin Lee-Gartner on 54-55
  for performance 112

positive images *(continued)*
    in wheel of excellence 12*f*, 18-20, 25,
        32*f*, 238*f*
positive opportunities 316-322
positive performance imagery
    mental readiness and 119
    overview of 113-114
    personal advantages created with 114
    sharpening of focus through 118-119
    summary of 127
    technique improvements using 117-118
    video imagery 115-117
positive perspectives
    changing of 162-168
    choosing of 7-10, 159-162
    Chris McCormack on 193-195
    commitment to 189
    consistency and 266
    embracing 158
    importance of 273
    negative perspective versus 157
    reminders for 168-169
    in self-control 266
    for team spirit 292, 295-299
    tips for creating 273
positive possibilities 321
positive self-direction
    choice for 308-310
    description of 307
    path to 311-313
positive thoughts 20
postperformance phase 223
practice 355. *See also* training
preevent preparation phase 219-220
preparation phases, for performance
    contexts 219-223
priorities, for balance 254
problem avoidance 239-240
Purdy, Amy 159*f*
pure connection 145-148
purpose and passion
    joy in 50-52
    in pursuits 14-15, 51
    in relaxation 84
    retaining 4-6, 232-234
pursuits
    high-performance 51, 330-331, 339-
        341
    purpose and passion in 14-15, 51

R
race debriefs. *See* ongoing learning
race perspective 91-92
realistic goal 180
refocus. *See also* distraction control
    Beckie Scott on 42-43
    description of 32
    for focused connection 204
    growth of 22
    Kerrin Lee-Gartner on 56
    in personal excellence 32
    plans for 103-107, 105*f*, 106, 246-248
    practicing of 230
    strategies for 212-213, 230
    stress reactions and 80
    Thomas Grandi on 90
relaxation
    applying 87-95
    best focus and 210
    for focus connection 210
    for focus control 268
    focused 78, 80
    intensity and 74-75
    overload and 251-252
    positive focused action through 274
    practicing 82-84, 85*f*
    purposes of 84
    script for 85*f*
    through exertion 86-87
    understanding 80-82
reminders
    distraction control 100-101
    excellence 283*f*-284*f*
    growth and improvement 230-231
    performance 92-93, 95
    positive perspective 168-169
    problem avoidance 239-240
    team spirit 297-299, 302*f*, 302-304,
        303*f*
    Zen zone 154
Renner, Sara 305
respect 282-285
rest
    commitment to 189
    performance and 16
    stress and 100
retirement 59-60, 340
Rodgers, Aaron 253*f*
Russell, Bill 122

S

Scott, Beckie
  commitment of 183
  dociding 226
  on focus 39-46
  as team inspiration 305
self-acceptance 180
self-assessment
  commitment 66f
  focus control 65f
  improvement strategies and 70-71
  in mission to excellence 68-70
self-care 41
self-confidence. *See* confidence
self-control 266-271
self-directed positive change 104
self-direction. *See* positive self-direction
self-doubt 191, 246. *See also* distraction
    control
self-examination. *See* self-assessment
self-image 180
self-talk 268
self-worth 163
Selye, Hans 343
setback recovery
  consistency and 262-266
  goals and 178
  refocusing in 108-109
simulation training
  benefits of 131-132
  description of 129-130
  excessive 142
  imitation as 137-138
  real-world types of 138-142
  replicating demands in 133-137
Spieth, Jordan 177f
sports
  losses in, overcoming of 334-335
  retirement from 59-60
  transitioning out of. *See* transitions
stepping-up-to-the-challenge phenom-
    enon 305
stress. *See also* overload
  acceptance of 163
  flowing stream approach to 164
  flowing through 163-165
  immune system affected by 259
  management of 244-245, 255-256
  performance and 36

perspective and 160-161
prevention of 164
reactions to 80
reduction of 163-164
rest and 100
Suzuki, Daisetz T. 148-151

T

Tajima, Yagyu 152
team spirit and harmony
  conflict resolution for 299-304, 302f-
    303f
  fostering of 293-295
  goals and 292
  individual differences and 299
  inspiration and 304-306
  positive perspective and 295-299
technique improvements 117-118
10 Focusing Commandments 29-30
training. *See also* simulation training
  Chris McCormack on 190-191
  focus in 34, 78-79, 92
  logbooks for 177
transitions
  advantages of 333, 339
  dramatic changes after 339
  examples of 329
  feelings associated with 345
  focusing through 329-333
  from high-performance sports or pur-
    suits 330-331, 339-341
  living through 343-346
  making of 337-338
  new paths after 341-343, 346-347
  ongoing learning and 333
  performance declines as cause of 332-333
  positives and negatives of 332
  steps to take before 340-341
  suggestions for athletes in 340
  uncertainty associated with 339

V

value as person 163, 181
venues, familiarization with 221
verbalism 152
video performance imagery 115-117
visions 184
visualization. *See* positive images
Vonn, Lindsey 185f

W
wheel of excellence. *See also specific elements*
   commitment in 12*f*, 14-16, 24-25, 32*f*, 238*f*
   confidence in 12*f*, 20-21, 25-26, 32*f*, 238*f*
   distraction control in 12*f*, 21-22, 26, 32*f*, 238*f*
   focus in 11-13, 12*f*, 24, 32*f*, 238*f*
   mental readiness in 12*f*, 16-18, 25, 32*f*, 238*f*
   ongoing learning in 12*f*, 23, 26, 32*f*, 238*f*
   overview of 11, 12*f*, 238*f*

positive images in 12*f*, 18-20, 25, 32*f*, 238*f*
Williams, Serena 48*f*
Wong, Charlene 150
Woods, Tiger 334
worry 162, 203-206. *See also* distraction control

Z
Zen zone
   description of 143-144
   focus reminders for 154
   interpreting of 144-146
   nurturing of 146-148

ABOUT THE AUTHOR

Terry Orlick, PhD, is a professor in the School of Human Kinetics at the University of Ottawa. He obtained his PhD in the psychology of sport and physical activity from the University of Alberta in 1972. He is one of the world's leading authorities on the psychology of excellence and quality living and has worked with some of the world's top performers. His research has focused on enhancing the quality of life and quality of performance with children and high-level performers in a variety of disciplines.

Orlick has worked with thousands of Olympic and professional athletes and coaches; corporate leaders; astronauts; surgeons; top classical musicians; dancers, opera singers, and other performing artists; mission control professionals; and many others engaged in high-stress performance missions.

Former president of the International Society for Mental Training and Excellence, Orlick has authored 30 highly acclaimed books, has published hundreds of articles in a variety of professional journals, and is founder of the *Journal of Excellence*, Positive Living Skills, and the Zone of Excellence (www.zoneofexcellence.ca). He holds distinguished service awards from numerous Olympic and education associations as well as certificates of merit from governments, universities, sport organizations, and schools for distinguished service to the community. He has given lectures on the pursuit of excellence in virtually every corner of the world. Orlick lives with his family at Meech Lake, Quebec.